Elusive Equality

ELUSIVE EQuALITY

The Status of Black Americans in Higher Education

Lorenzo Morris, Senior Fellow

With the Research Assistance of
Steven R. Jones and Schuyler Webb

Institute for the Study of Educational Policy
Howard University

Published for ISEP by
HOWARD UNIVERSITY PRESS
Washington, D.C.
1979

Printed in the United States of America

Library of Congress Cataloging in Publication Data

Morris, Lorenzo, 1946–
  Elusive equality.

  Bibliography: p.
  Includes index.
  1. Afro-Americans—Education (Higher)   I. Title.
LC2781.M674   378.73   79-2579
ISBN 0-88258-080-9

This report was made possible by a grant from the Ford Foundation.

Contents

List of Tables

Appendix Table

List of Figures

Appendix Figure

Foreword

The Institute for the Study of Educational Policy (ISEP) developed with substantial funding from the Ford Foundation out of the need both for a national clearinghouse and for a research center on the issues affecting equal educational opportunities in higher education. As a national clearinghouse, ISEP aims to serve policy makers and interested researchers by keeping abreast of developments in higher education in the public and private sectors. In addition, ISEP assumes responsibility for reporting such information to its constituents.

As a research and policy center, ISEP has three program objectives:

- To prepare a periodic critical assessment of the dynamic status of blacks in higher education.
- To assess the impact of law and social science research on the status of blacks in higher education.
- To use old models creatively and to develop new models and theories of higher education for blacks with implications for elementary and secondary education.

Through its annual reports and monographs, through its seminars and workshops, and through its announcements and public testimony, the Institute for the Study of Educational Policy attempts to fill a vacuum in the organized body of knowledge about higher educational opportunities of blacks and other minorities. In doing so, ISEP attempts to make a significant contribution to the formulation and evaluation of contemporary educational policy.

Elusive Equality: The Status of Black Americans in Higher Education by Dr. Lorenzo Morris, a Senior Fellow at the Institute, is the third in a series of studies on the status of blacks in U.S. higher education. The first study, *Equal Educational Opportunity for Blacks in U.S. Higher Education: An Assessment* (1976) described the status of Blacks in the 1973-74 academic year. The second study, *Equal Educational Opportunity: More Promise Than Progress* (1978), extended those findings to the 1974-75 academic year. This study pertains to the 1975-76 and 1976-77 academic years. Dr. Morris in this study has continued the comprehensive coverage of information on blacks in higher education and has intensified the policy analysis necessary to develop programs and policies which will contribute to equal educational opportunity for blacks. His formidable analysis, the Board hopes, will be of great assistance to decision makers in the public and private sectors concerning higher education.

Finally, Howard University and the Institute gratefully acknowledge the assistance and continued support of the Ford Foundation together with their Program Officer in charge of our grant, Dr. Benjamin Payton, who has been indispensable for all of the work of the Institute, including this study.

Kenneth S. Tollett
Chairman
National Advisory Board
Institute for the Study of
Educational Policy

Introduction

This study investigates the effectiveness of national policy in advancing equal opportunity for black Americans in higher education. Research focusing on the early seventies, including much conducted by the Institute for the Study of Educational Policy, concludes that blacks had made considerable progress toward gaining racial parity with other Americans in higher education. The data on the status of blacks from 1975 through 1977, however, show that progress in all areas of higher education has slowed down, and in areas like professional education, it has come to a standstill.

This study represents a commitment to do as comprehensive a search as the data will permit of factors that affect equal opportunity in higher education. Inequalities in higher education shown themselves at once to be so numerous and dispersed that no summary picture can be very meaningful. As a result, the evidence or the impact of inequality emerges only from a patient sifting through of a considerable amount of descriptive data on enrollment patterns, financial aid, admissions practices, and institutional structures.

The specific effects of various federal programs and regulations can be seen through the data analysis, but the overall effectiveness of national policy cannot be directly measured. In the end, it seems that the impediment to direct measure is also an impediment to equal opportunity. Namely, there is no clear national policy of equal opportunity; there is only a collection of loosely defined programs. Consequently, measuring and promoting progress for blacks has been a little like putting out brush fires: when racial inequalities in one place are dealt with, unseen inequalities emerge in other places.

1

For the next few years, it is probable that no major study of the status of black Americans in higher education will fail to mention the Supreme Court decision in the case of the *Regents of the University of California* vs. *Allan Bakke* (June 1978). The opinion of Justice Powell, speaking for the Court, is widely seen as too ambiguous to permit precise projections of its impact on equal opportunity for blacks in higher education, although its potential impact is enormous. Unlike the 1954 *Brown* decision, the *Bakke* ruling does not say how racial equality is to be measured and pursued. The Court simply says that it should be neither measured nor pursued on the basis of "race" alone unless stipulated by an act of Congress. Educators, the Court advises, may "take race into consideration" in making policy, but they may not use race as the sole criterion for the measurement or remediation of inequality. How equality for blacks should be dealt with is then left open to debate.

Perhaps all that is clear at this time is, first, the Court's recognition that, in one respect, the 1954 decision was correct—equality of educational opportunity is a constitutional right guaranteed to all individuals. Second, unlike the 1954 decision, the *Bakke* decision concludes that this recognition requires the special surveillance of the Court to ensure the rights of white Americans against a presumed overextension of the rights of minorities. Thus, the Court inaugurates the idea of "reverse discrimination" as a legal force to be reckoned with.

One scarcely needs reminding that equality of opportunity is an idea fundamental to American history, predating the Constitution itself. In spite of persistent and widespread inequality hundreds of years later, the idea of equality, and its promise, is nevertheless an essential component to the understanding of American history and politics. This essential component is reflected more in its promise than in its attainment. For black Americans particularly, the denial of equal opportunity has been a dominant issue in every major political thrust. Nowhere has this issue been more evident than in the political and legal efforts of blacks to transform America's highly in-egalitarian educational system into one in which they could participate equally.

The history of black progress in higher education has, until the last decade, been characterized both by the monumental efforts of blacks and by the relentless resistance and indifference of the larger society. Progress in education was so slow before the 1970s that subsequent advances by blacks seem monumental. For example, more black Ph.D.'s in virtually every major field graduated between 1974 and 1977 than had ever graduated in American history.

The record of the last two academic years, 1975–76 and 1976–77, thus contains more impressive figures than those of most recorded years. Yet, these figures, in contrast to those of earlier years do not tell a more impressive success story. There are few major surprises, no unfolding drama of racial progress toward equality shown by the data for these two years. To be sure, one might well be surprised by the lack of progress, and even retrenchment, shown. But then, one has to know a good deal of the larger story of black struggles for equality of educational opportunity to appreciate fully the meaning of the recent setbacks.

The real story concerns how the data correspond to the national mood and the governmental expectations exhibited by *Bakke*. The Court's concession to race-conscious affirmative action programs in higher education reflects the Justices' awareness that blacks have already made some strides through such programs and that greater progress is needed. The elevation of "reverse discrimination" to the protective status of a judicial concern is, in part, an expression of the belief that black progress in higher education has reached the point of threatening the majority. If this viewpoint reflects the national approach to the status of blacks in higher education, the information presented here should have some dramatic value.

Perhaps our most important contribution is not our findings alone, but the place such findings may take within the context of national politics. Our approach to the data is organized to examine the range of issues and policy problems that affect equal educational opportunity. Consequently, the study should facilitate an evaluation of established as well as proposed federal programs that affect blacks and higher education. Moreover, the study is an indirect test of the perceptiveness, if not accuracy, of recent official opinions about the progress of equal opportunity. In the long run, one should find here a basis for judging the soundness of public attitudes toward the need for stronger federal action to promote goals advocated at least since 1954.

It is not too soon to outline some major results of federal policy. Blacks have continued to make progress in most areas of higher education. Unfortunately, the rate of progress has diminished almost to a trickle. In some areas, particularly professional education, progress has all too quickly given way to stagnation. The consequences of current policies can be drawn from a review of the successes and failures of federal programs, and their contributing factors, as brought out by the data presented here. Fortunately, the foreseeable policy options are sufficient to suggest a way out, a solution. There are, of course, no concrete guarantees to be found in this study, nor probably anywhere else, but the consequences of not trying are almost certain and much less attractive.

Higher Education
and Egalitarian Motives

Federal Policy and Higher Education

The *Bakke* case was not the only case before the federal courts in 1978 to have a major impact on the status of blacks in higher education. The *Adams* case is in some ways more critical, because the impact of judicial rulings is already being felt.[1] This suit, filed in 1969 by the NAACP Legal Defense Fund against the U.S. Department of Health, Education, and Welfare (HEW), placed ten southern states under court order to develop plans and timetables for the desegregation of state colleges and universities. The obligation to desegregate was in itself a major break from traditional practices in higher education, but the *Brown* decision had already set the precedent. The significance of the *Adams* rulings was that a branch of the federal government was forced to create meaningful educational policy. Perhaps for the first time in history, responsible federal officials could no longer turn to established practices, state jurisdiction, and, most of all, judicial rulings to determine policy in higher education. The presiding federal judge, John Pratt, has ruled more than once, and without reversals, that HEW had to decide how to bring about desegregation.

HEW's attempts to establish desegregation guidelines generated an inevitable confrontation with traditionally black institutions. If it had not already been growing, the confrontation was certainly there for the making in the form of the unequal treatment and disadvantage that traditionally black colleges had long experienced. Thus, these black institutions, specifically public ones, having always received far less than their share of federal and state allocations, sensed yet another threat to their survival in

HEW's desegregation plans. When black educational associations raised protests, the administration scarcely seemed to recognize the pitfalls and adverse consequences of treading on such ground. This is probably because no administration had ever really trod that ground before. To a large extent, federal decision making in higher education had been led by the courts, or pushed by social pressures resulting from the Civil Rights Movement. Only in the 1970s has the federal government been forced to make clear decisions on equality of opportunity in higher education, rather than simply letting old traditions stand.

The tax-credit issue, which dominated much of federal debate on higher education in 1978, is fundamentally a resurgence of old traditions in conflict with not-so-old traditions. Higher education in this country had been cherished for so long as private enterprise that few people fully recognized how dependent on public funds it had become. The historical expansion of federal financial aid to students and institutions had never been designed to make the system of higher education egalitarian but simply to make it more efficient in the provision of the society's educational needs.[2] On the other hand, equality had always been a strong component of the national belief-system, and at least some public support for federal involvement in higher education had hinged on egalitarian motives. It is therefore reasonable, if not inevitable, that the equalizing effects of federal aid on higher education could be felt, and soon taken for granted, without a clear policy decision ever having been made. In the absence of clear policy it is difficult to recognize an emphasis on tax credits (reimbursement for tuition costs) as anything more than a return to educational opportunity as a function of private wealth. There is no doubt, however, that all current tax-credit proposals favor most those people who have money saved to invest in education—the middle and upper classes.

Federal Aid and the Expansion of Educational Opportunity

The wealthier half of white America continues to dominate participation in higher education, as it has for decades. By the 1970s, however, that dominance was no longer as complete as it had been in the 1960s and before, largely because of federal financial aid. Implied in this wider distribution (not redistribution) is the growth of equality of educational opportunity. Still, the equalizing tendency of federal aid says little or nothing about the concrete aims of federal aid.[3] Progress toward equality of opportunity is as much a function of the unprescribed consequences of federal action as it is a result of legislative intent. Progress to date may be more an accident than a result of a commitment. The question we now face is whether

the achievement of equal opportunity or further progress will require consistent and direct federal commitment. Has the progress of blacks been
slowed and, more recently, threatened because, for the first time, equaliza-
tion rather than simple growth has been recognized as the potential outcome of federal support?

Except for the GI Bill and social security benefits, federal aid to
students in higher education did not exist before the 1960s. These two
sources of aid were incidental supports in that they were designed to aid individuals whose need and merit for federal support was determined by non-
education-related criteria. Direct federal aid to students was widely debated
in the 1950s but not implemented. The National Defense Education Act
(NDEA), enacted in 1958, was a product of national pride and our competition, stimulated by Sputnik, with the USSR. While the immediate benefit of
the program was aid to students in scientific education, its primary goals
were clearly the advancement of American science and the support of national defense. Higher education was comparatively secondary, and the
issue of equality of opportunity was scarcely mentioned. In fact, the earlier
debates over federal aid were stalemated by this issue, as well as by fears of
"big government." Thus, Norman Thomas observes in *Education in National Politics* that opposition to federal aid raised the spectre of the "three
R's: Race, Religion and Reds (or federal control)."[4]

Thomas also finds that since 1963, some federal policy in education has
been "redistributive," meaning oriented toward equality of opportunity.
From the evidence, such a policy intention or purpose does not seem to have
included higher education, except in the case of the 1965 Higher Education
Act (HEA); however, HEA still poses the question of intention versus
results.

Much of federal aid for higher education in the early 1960s was directed
toward the expansion and development of institutions. The Higher Education Facilities Act of 1963 and the Library Services and Construction Act of
1964 are evidence of the government's leading role in higher education. For
years the federal government had indirectly aided institutions through
"research and development" (R & D) grants, but this funding was hardly
amenable to equality of opportunity. In fact, as chapter 6 should show, the
increase in R & D funding to predominantly white institutions has aggravated the comparative disadvantage of black institutions.

Citing Michael Katz, Martin Carnoy argues that government involvement in education generally has sought to stabilize social and racial inequalities. Looking at the approach to public education of nineteenth century
educators, he concludes:

Because they perceived schools as the key agencies for uplifting the quality of city life by stemming diffusion of the poverty, crime and immorality that were thought to accompany urban and industrial development, professionals argued for raising the quality of education by centralizing power over the educational system.[5]

In a sense, the nineteenth century battle was won in that universal education was sought, however little that ideal may be visible in terms of an educated population today. At that time, the concern was with local and state control. In the twentieth century, the parallel concern has been about federal control and/or involvement. The motives for centralization have also expanded beyond local disturbances to include national and international stability. As the legislative background of NDEA shows, the federal government and the public in general sought to strengthen the nation through the expansion of higher education. In the last decade however, black protests have revived the nineteenth century concern about urban tranquility. The expansion of black enrollment in urban colleges and universities in the seventies is but one reflection of such concern at the state and federal government levels.

Still, the development of higher education remains largely under state and private authority. The federal government has not shown a historical inclination toward centralization of educational authority beyond its involvement in selected problem areas. Nevertheless, as a developing trend in higher education, centralization has affected the advancement of equal opportunity in general and the status of blacks in particular. This is because the federal government has provided the primary source of support for blacks and of guidance for state and private institutions. With few exceptions, predominantly white institutions have shown little initiative in going beyond the levels of black participation set by the federal government and facilitated by federal aid.

Even when the federal government takes the lead in higher education, it is still, in a sense, motivated first by the courts and second by its public concerns beyond higher education. Although affirmative action programs have had a positive effect on opportunities in higher education, they have fallen short of their logical adjunct in other areas, particularly employment, where the idea has its only legal foundation, i.e., the 1971 regulation (No. 4) amending Executive Order 11246, issued in 1965. Whether or not the federal government will take a clear and deliberate role in setting educational policy remains uncertain.

An effective equal opportunity policy in higher education means more than generating legislation and programs which are expected to support equal opportunity; it means defining legislation and legitimating programs on those grounds. More important, it means that an outcome is expected and that programs thus conceived are first expected to produce equal opportunity and second evaluated on that criterion.

The Basic Educational Opportunity Grant (BEOG) programs have popularly acquired this image in large part because they have had a positive effect on black enrollment in higher education. BEOG was intended to help all students, white or black, as long as they came from low-income families. But it was not designed to assure any low-income student an opportunity to go to college equal to that of wealthier students. The maximum monetary awards have never been more than half the cost of college attendance up to a ceiling of $1,400, later raised to $1,800. Consequently, low-income students are likely to find it considerably difficult to pay for all college costs.

Beyond the costs themselves is, of course, the problem of access—getting into college—and the problem of distribution—getting into the kind of college the student chooses (sometimes needs). BEOG has no counterpart in social legislation which even begins to deal with these problems. The limits of BEOG legislative intent are demonstrated by the 1972 legislative debate in which Senator Mondale spoke for a more comprehensive position that was subsequently rejected:

> The idea was to guarantee a resource floor for all students to finance postsecondary education. An alternative entitlement approach sponsored by Senator Walter F. Mondale, designed to ensure a greater degree of student choice among types of institutions, was set aside. Under the Mondale proposal, a needy student's eligibility would have been limited not by a flat ceiling but by the actual costs of attending the institution in which he chooses to enroll. A sliding scale of percentages would have determined how much of the student's expenses might be covered by the federal government.[6]

Thus, the legislative intent of federal programs like BEOG may be less impressive than the results in terms of benefits to blacks. Joel Spring, in *The Sorting Machine: National Educational Policy Since 1945*, concludes that federal involvement in education "has not been formulated and executed as a single, coherent plan."[7] Yet he maintains that a coherent national policy has resulted, somewhat by coincidence. He attributes the origin of this coherence, as do several other analysts, to the reaction of the private and quasi-public educational sector against threatened political crises. Thus education has been directed by what some political scientists might call "private powers" "toward the creation of a rationalized and controlled labor market . . . and the control of social conflict arising from racial discrimination and inequalities in the distribution of income."[8]

Political scientist Marguerite Barnett questions whether progress toward equal opportunity for blacks can be sustained by less than a conscious or conscientious policy commitment. Regarding the Great Society programs of the 1960s she observes:

> They [policies] were incremental, non-system-challenging attempts to make minor alterations in what was assumed to be a basically egalitarian society. To the extent these policies succeeded, they helped individuals who, often because of serendipitous circumstances, were in the right place at the right time. They did not alter the life chances of Blacks as a collectivity.[9]

In a limited sense some federal financial aid programs, particularly BEOG, may be exceptions to Barnett's thesis, inasmuch as the low income specifications encompass a meaningful "collectivity." The underlying principle and weakness of incrementalism, however, still characterize higher education programs in general. The programs were designed to move education toward equal opportunity. But as progress toward that goal was made in the 1970s, the programs' effectiveness diminished, in part because they were not specifically designed to achieve equal opportunity. Fortunately, only another incremental policy step seems needed to continue the progress. That step may come through the addition of new programs or the strengthening of established ones. It is, of course, the responsibility of the federal government to make such a commitment. This study will attempt to demonstrate, through an examination of problems and experiences of black students in higher education, the most effective means and options for a policy of equal opportunity.

As a brief outline of how the development of policies normally proceeds, Norman Thomas identifies three sequential stages:

1. *Innovation and formulation*—ideas are generated, demands based on them articulated, and certain demands are accepted and advanced by government officials as specific proposals for action.

2. *Adoption*—policy proposals are formally authorized through legislative enactment and funded through the appropriations process.

3. *Implementation*—administrative action is taken to implement funded programs. This stage involves the determination of organizational arrangements, drafting of guidelines and regulations, and expenditure of

funds. It also involves interpretation of legislation by administrative officials and if necessary, by the courts.[10]

Although federal programs supporting equal opportunity in higher education are described and treated as policies, the first stage of the development process, "innovation and formulation," has been omitted. It is in the first stage that one would normally seek to turn the values and norms of equal opportunity into concrete legislative proposals. Of course, the existing legislation did not spring from thin air. However, the belief that equal opportunity has been legislatively assured seems, in many ways, to have come from no place in particular.

The lack of direction during the formative stages of higher education legislation is further indicated by program-evaluation debates which follow at the congressional level. Consequently, many legislators, particularly Senator Daniel P. Moynihan, could maintain in 1978 that federal grant and loan programs were too inefficient and bureaucratically cumbersome to serve low-income students, and yet fail to propose any improvement in the programs. Instead, Moynihan proposed a tax-credit program, ostensibly to reimburse the "hard-pressed middle-income families" for educational expenses.[11] In opposition, Senator Claiborne Pell, who played a crucial role in the original passage of BEOG, rather inadvertently revealed the lack of direction of the BEOG program when he sought to modify it to include middle-income families. President Carter advanced Pell's objective by suggesting a new "Middle Income College Assistance Act."[12] Pell's plan, in his words, "would expand the existing Basic Educational Opportunity Grant program so that an average family of four with an income of $25,000 would be eligible for an educational-assistance grant of $250."[13] Apparently, given the congressional concern for the financial welfare of the middle class, federal funds in higher education are intended to ease individual financial difficulties and not necessarily to bring about equality of opportunity.

The congressional debates on financial aid illustrate what, according to many political analysts, serves as a substitute for the consideration of goals and values in the innovation and formulation stage: specifically, it is an unarticulated belief in technical or technological feasibility as a guide to policy development. In other words, whatever is technically (e.g., monetarily, educationally, etc.) possible will be done.[14] The consideration of goals and values therefore depends on nongovernmental forces, such as private-interest groups and public protests. The success of proposed legisla-. tion is then limited only by the stronger, direct opposition from similar groups as long as the existing administrative structures and current technological capabilities can accommodate the proposal. Accordingly, aid to middle-income groups is at least as unavoidable as aid to lower-income groups as long as there is organized public support and no organized opposition.

The underlying threat to equal opportunity posed by this perspective is not simply the dispersal of funds to wealthier students. It is the indecisiveness of federal power and policy in higher education. In the face of mounting opposition, what is the future of the federal benefits to black students that were produced by the Civil Rights Movement? These benefits have already begun to dwindle in real terms, as the data will show. Now that the turbulence of the 1960s has faded, will the gains of this brief period fade as well?

A prime example of the technologically centered perspective on educational policy is the current practice of limiting influence in educational decision making to "technically" sophisticated individuals and groups. Increasingly, only those who have bureaucratic, or other institutional professional experience in education have ready access to decision making. In effect those who are responsible for the "how to" aspect in education are increasingly controlling the "why" aspect as well. This reliance on "technocracy" seems to create a problem for equal opportunity at the elementary and secondary school levels as well as at the higher education level. The National Urban League complains in its report, *State of Black America, 1978*, that educational experts have not adequately represented black educational needs:

> As the policy considerations of legislators, board members and educators have become more intricate, education consumers and even newly installed minority legislators have become further removed from a clear understanding and appreciation of the processes and outcomes of reform deliberations. Whether by accident or design, the result has been a general exclusion of nonspecialists and also an insulation of techniques from public scrutiny. The general public is affected by this problem; however, minorities and the poor are most adversely affected.[15]

National Goals and Public Responsibilities

American public education started out with a clear sense of purpose. In the Colony of Massachusetts, the Old Deluder Satan Act of 1647 made clear that schooling must enable the young to ward off the temptations of Satan. In the more than three hundred years since the first public education law was passed, public preoccupation with Satan has apparently diminished, but the basic character of public support for education has not completely changed. An essential concept of the Old Deluder Satan Act is that education serves prevailing social purposes and promotes established values. That much has not changed, even with the additions and expansions of higher education.

What has changed is the process by which legitimate social purposes and values are selected and articulated. Currently, public control of education is decentralized among a host of educational institutions and professional groups. In the legislative process, however, authority has become increasingly centralized at the national level. Higher education is administered, in large part, by individual institutions and professional associations. Although the implementation of public policy is also effectively decentralized among these educational groups, the socially legitimate authority and responsibility to set policy has accrued over time to the federal government.

Thus, a bipolar division of authority in higher education has developed, leaving the federal government and state governments the obligation to direct education, but not the obligation to implement their decisions. Consequently, government tends to provide less than forceful leadership. The result has been persistent ambiguity in the policies and purposes of higher education. If the federal government exercised as much pointed leadership in legislating equality of opportunity as the colonists did in the Old Deluder Satan Act, the status of blacks in higher education would probably be more secure than it is now.

The ambiguity of national policy and issues in higher education may be caused by uncertainty about the legitimacy of any federal involvement. On one hand, the federal government has no constitutional role or authority in higher education. On the other hand, it does have a fundamental obligation to ensure "equal protection of the laws" to all its citizens, and by extension, an obligation to ensure equal educational opportunity. The issue of equal educational opportunity for black Americans heightens the apparent conflict, because the federal government is called on to exercise its constitutional authority in an area not delegated to it by the Constitution.

Constitutional limitations may explain or justify, in part, the lack of federal policy initiatives in higher education. They do not, however, justify the lack of policy direction. Neither the Constitution nor any other legal constraint prohibits the government from developing policy that ensures equal protection in the area of education.

Ultimate responsibility for educational access has, over the years, been carried by state governments. But their success may be misleading. In the past decade, the proportion of students in public colleges and universities has grown about as fast as total college enrollment. Consequently, public responsibility for the provision of higher education is now a fait accompli. Yet, the data also show clearly that without federal involvement, state and private institutions have made very little progress toward equal opportunity. Therefore, the questions of whether and how this responsibility might be assumed more effectively by the federal government become increasingly important.

PROPOSED DEPARTMENT OF EDUCATION

The question of federal involvement in education has resurfaced as a public issue since the 1976 presidential election. In his campaign, President Carter promised to establish a new cabinet-level Department of Education. The new department was advanced as a major component of his overall plan to reorganize the federal bureaucracy and streamline HEW. The department was originally to have incorporated the current education responsibilities of HEW with most of those currently divided among several other departments, such as Labor, Interior, and Agriculture.

When Congress adjourned in October 1978, the proposal had not reached the floor. Since that time, the scope of the proposed department has been scaled down considerably in response to interest-groups that believe centralization would threaten their favorite programs and/or their special influence over those programs. Nevertheless, the explicit purpose of the department, as expressed by the administration, remains unchanged: the more "efficient" delivery of federal services to education. This purpose has been questioned increasingly as new aspects of the proposal have emerged. First, the seemingly arbitrary exclusion of some education programs is thought to reduce efficiency. Second, the proposed budget and staff are thought to be too large to escape the problems of a massive bureaucracy.[16]

The overriding concern of opponents, however, is that the focus on efficiency displaces the more important aspect of reorganization—creating a consistent federal education policy. Strangely enough, some proponents outside the White House often make a similar argument. But, unlike their opponents, they view the development of a clear federal policy as both feasible and desirable. Congressman John Brademas has criticized the efficiency-oriented justification of the proposal as too narrow:

> Reorganization is a fundamentally political act, not political in the partisan sense (although it may be) but political in that every organization—and every reorganization—means a distribution—or redistribution—of power and influence over the substance of policy . . . .

Organization is not just management. It is policy, and in the American democratic system, policy is politics ... .[17]

This interpretation makes apparent substantial arguments for and against reorganization. Support for it depends, in part, on the social importance one attributes to education. Education specialists David Breneman and Noel Epstein maintain that "there has never been a need for an education policy" because "education is an instrument used to achieve a more fundamental federal purpose." They explain:

Instead, there have been national security policies, antipoverty policies, civil rights policies, child welfare policies, veterans' benefits and other policies, all drawing when necessary on educational institutions.[18]

For many people, few concerns are more fundamental to our national interest than education. The goal of equal educational opportunity draws much of its acceptance from that national interest. The promise of a uniform federal education policy would seem to require the creation of a department. A new department, however, like those already in existence, would not ensure a clear policy focus. When one considers its proposed size and diversity, it is easy to imagine the same confusion and contradiction that exist now. Furthermore, it is quite feasible, given the greater focus of public debate on elementary and secondary school issues, that those in higher education could be submerged. Worse yet, the special problems of opportunity could be pushed into the background by the exclusionary issues of formal educational interest-groups, which are likely to have primary influence in the department.

Therefore, a new department is not so important to the future of equal opportunity as a more consistent educational policy, one that permits progress toward equal opportunity, but does not depend primarily on the "incidental" benefits of programs meant to serve other, noneducational purposes.

The magnitude of powers in such a department should not affect a primary commitment to equal opportunity, since that has always been a federal obligation, however well or poorly met. Although a new department might mean, as some suggest, an extension of federal control in higher education, the federal government has the capacity to protect equal opportunity within current constitutional confines. The Old Deluder Satan Act of 1647 exemplifies a tradition of value-based government authority in education as old as the country itself.

Federal involvement in higher education goes back at least to the 1950s, when a college education was still a luxury available only to a privileged few. Today, concern about federal support of equal opportunity is the extent to which the government will require the institutional implementation of a moral commitment. Such a commitment is constitutionally and popularly expressed, but not written into educational programs and practices. Can the voluntary commitments of institutions and professional associations protect and improve the status of blacks in higher education without clear federal guidance?

This question cannot be answered without examining, as is done in the following chapters, what has been accomplished through voluntary commitments to equal opportunity. Substantial progress has been made, but it seems to be more often than not the product of limited, centralized federal power rather than decentralized institutional initiatives.

Modeling Change in Higher Education

In our approach to the problem of institutional change, we use a model of traditional higher education. This model should perhaps consist of many submodels to represent the various types of institutions, but for the sake of clarity we have excluded them. At the same time, considerable attention is paid to differences among types of institutions, particularly differences between public and private institutions, two-year and four-year colleges, and between predominantly black and white institutions. Although institutional differences are important, a good sense of the institutional role in providing equal opportunity for blacks can be developed from a single model. Nontraditional institutions of higher education, specifically black institutions and two-year colleges, are not included in the definition of the model. Obviously, black institutions are an important part of the American tradition of higher education. But their contribution to black educational opportunity is so singular and important that they must be treated separately. In fact, traditionally black institutions provide a useful reference point for the model of traditional American higher education. Two-year institutions are also important in higher education, but they are fairly recent phenomena in terms of the distribution of students. In spite of the large numbers of students they currently enroll, their impact on equal opportunity depends more directly on state legislative authority than on federal or institutional action. Also, blacks are already highly represented in two-year institutions compared to more traditional institutions. The primary problem of educational opportunity raised by two-year institutions involves disadvantages of higher black enrollment in this sector as opposed to enrollment in four-year colleges and universities. It is only at the four-year college and university level that one gets a clear long-term picture of educational progress, or the lack of it, for blacks.

THE TRADITIONAL INSTITUTION MODEL

First, the traditional institutions in which black progress toward equal opportunity can best be measured offer undergraduate and graduate study. For undergraduates, a four-year liberal arts college or university fits the model, and for graduates, a full university that grants several Ph.D's and contains several professional schools, including law and medicine. Second, the college or university has substantial residential facilities and is geared toward full-time attendance. Third, the institution is fundamentally "private," nonsectarian, and predominantly white. "Private" includes any institution that has the major authority to determine its enrollment, curriculum, and matriculation requirements. This concept of "private" is also intended to represent several institutions designated "public," such as the University of California at Berkeley and the University of Wisconsin at Madison, which have restrictive, highly selective admissions policies.

This schematic model is as useful for studying the characteristics it excludes as those it includes. The type of institution that fits the model also exemplifies the historical development of American higher education. Clearly, many institutions started out from sectarian roots; some were initially nonselective for those capable of paying; many universities only recently acquired Ph.D. programs and professional schools. Nevertheless, virtually all institutions which fit the model today had developed, or were well on the way to developing, their present institutional characteristics before the influx of nontraditional students. By 1950, when less than 10 percent of Americans had a college degree, traditional institutions already represented the "mainstream" of higher education. By 1960, when about 12 percent of whites and 4 percent of blacks between twenty-five and thirty-four years old had completed four years of college, traditional institutions produced the majority of college graduates. They now graduate a minority of undergraduates, but still dominate graduate enrollment.

Because of the status they have gained, traditional institutions are the most frequent choice of college applicants. They can be defined as "highly selective" institutions, described in more detail in chapter 3. Their significance here is that although minority participation has increased, these institutions have been among the least responsive in terms of student enrollment as well as faculty employment.

THE TRADITIONAL COLLEGE STUDENT

Our model of the traditional college student is based on a statistical description of the "typical" college student before the 1960s, or, more precisely, before college attendance increased dramatically. Obviously, blacks and other underrepresented minorities are not included in this model. Perhaps less obvious, is the omission of women, older, and part-time students from the model. Students from the latter groups historically have been enrolled in college, but the recent growth in their enrollment proportions makes them more a part of the nontraditional than the traditional student body. In an article on changes in enrollment patterns, Leo Munday describes both types of students:

> While enrollment patterns for different kinds of students may be in a state of flux, one thing is clear. College and university student bodies never again will be made up almost entirely of students who are eighteen to twenty-two years old, white, full-time, from the upper half of their high school classes, *and* from middle- and upper-class socioeconomic backgrounds. These traditional college students are there all right, but they have been joined by other nontraditional students: students who are older, minority, part-time, from the lower half of their high school class, and from lower-strata socioeconomic backgrounds. And if recent history is any predictor of the future, more nontraditional students will be in college in the future. [19]

The data in subsequent chapters support the expectation of continued growth in most nontraditional student enrollments. The primary concern of this report, however, is the status of black students. The data confirm substantial progress of black students until 1975. Beyond that time, confirmation is not possible. The data present a mixed picture which can be interpreted optimistically, but only with the expectation of a renewed federal commitment to equality of opportunity. If there is no such commitment, optimism will fade as the status of blacks in higher education from 1975 to 1977 becomes clear.

CHAPTER 2

Measuring Inequality
in Higher Education

The Data

When social statistics are perceived as "meaningful" in America it is because they relate to values in American society. Conversely, when the conditions of black and white Americans in higher education are compared, no social statistic can be completely neutral unless it is also completely meaningless. The relationship, statistical or not, between values and data in higher education, results from the political importance of race relations in this country and from a national concern with what Gunnar Myrdal calls "the American dilemma." An immediate consequence of this dilemma is that the exploration of racial inequalities is always initiated by the belief that inequalities exist. The reporting or publication of data relating to inequality will usually be guided by interest in the social or political responses to which the data might lead.

This study was initiated in response to evidence of inequality, and it has been guided by the desire to promote equality. We, therefore, make no claim to value neutrality for the overall study. Within the framework of the basic egalitarian values which guide this study, however, the analysis is intended to test all known points of view. At the same time, we have sought to maintain strict standards of objectivity in our research. In large part this is because a strong commitment to equal opportunity requires a broad sampling of data. The range of data analyzed has thus been restricted to those subjects known to contribute to the direction of public policy in higher education, e.g., enrollment and financial need by race. The known perspectives of education specialists, therefore, have clearly helped to determine what subjects are significant for understanding and advancing equal opportunity. In deference to social research standards, however, data on any specific subject within the problem have been widely sampled and given a balanced analytical treatment. Because data on race and education are often rather unreliable and subject to multiple interpretations, every effort is made to ensure reliability and to examine all reasonable interpretations. In other words, the value of equality has determined where we are going but not how to get there.

Ordinarily, a claim to objectivity in social research would be a mundane assertion scarcely worth making. Research on blacks in higher education, however, requires some discussion of standards for objectivity, because such research is both too recent and too controversial to have acquired widely accepted guidelines for measurement. First, there are virtually hundreds of sources of current data on blacks and education which are frequently inconsistent with each other. These sources produce an even larger number of figures on the same subject. The variations in the figures are often not large enough to suggest serious error in terms of general trends, but they are often too large to inspire confidence or demonstrate reliability.[1] Second, many analytical techniques that are used in some secondary data sources but excluded from others lead to and result from quite different interpretations of the primary data. Rarely, however, is there an explanation or justification for the selection of techniques used. As one analyst complains, understanding the problems of blacks in higher education has been thwarted by randomness of research:

> The consensus in all of the surveys or secondary analysis of enrollment data is that enrollment data on minorities are inconsistent and incomplete. Few of these studies have attempted to empirically describe the inconsistencies and none have made any effort to reconcile the substantial differences that often appear at first sight. The majority of these secondary surveys of the data have criticized the primary data collection efforts but have made few contributions to our knowledge of what specifically is wrong with the data and what steps may be taken to assess the type and amount of error in the data from various sources.[2]

Primary data sources such as U.S. Census Bureau reports are relatively free of analytical bias in the treatment of their data, because they are also relatively uninterested in explaining racial or educational data in terms suitable for policy review. It is tempting to say that such data are widely used because they are politically neutral, but frequently they are not. These "intentionally purposeless" data are widely used because they are amenable to a social purpose.

The problem then with many primary sources, the Census Bureau included, is that the data are not equally useful for all research in the same subject area. Specifically, primary sources, especially surveys, cannot adequately explore all phenomena that might be important to policy analysts in higher education. Data collection and survey design tend to be oriented toward problems of the majority group. As a result, data on minorities have been less reliable than data on the general population. Similarly, marginal variations in figures or samples, which are unimportant for most research in higher education, may be critical for studies focusing on blacks. Nevertheless, primary source data on blacks have been proliferating in the last few years, and problems of representativeness and numerical precision are manageable.

In secondary sources, the same assurances are not readily available. Because of the diversity of methods and the impreciseness of secondary source data, our concern for objectivity is especially noteworthy. In policy analysis there is always a temptation to use a variety of "statistical inference" techniques, both in hope of using the data to expand understanding beyond mere description, and in search of the ultimate "causes." It would be interesting to identify the ultimate cause(s) of inequality in higher education, but it is statistically impossible to do that with the data and methods now available. In an age of belief in the magic of technology, where "impossible" never seems applicable, one expects disagreement with the last statement. In the space available, a complete exposition of causation would leave no room to discuss education, per se. The skeptical should simply consider the social values and variables involved in a discussion of existing racial inequalities, and what the statistical identification of the primary "cause" of inequality might look like.

The purpose of this study is, first, to identify and explain (contextually) those inequalities, and second, to facilitate policy initiatives aimed at advancing social equality. In terms of research, this purpose implies the capacity to describe inequality where found, to describe its components, and to suggest what can be done to break up social conditions which keep blacks disadvantaged. Thus, the bulk of policy research goals can be achieved by means of adequate description. We therefore rely on descriptive statistics to approach our goals.

When thinking about social intervention and change, the search for a "key" or a cause often seems to be implied. What is really implied, however, is the recognition of necessary and sufficient causes. Understanding is needed, in this case, of the factors that contribute to racial inequality in higher education and of the kinds of intervention that will affect them. Descriptive statistics can point out such factors. Moreover, most concerned Americans already have a strong sense of many factors involved in racial differences.

What is needed, therefore, is not a button to push, but a willingness to push buttons. The search for a single or hidden cause of inequality should come after efforts to remedy all known causes of inequality have been initiated. If the purpose is to eliminate inequality, it should make no difference what the hierarchy of causes may be, as long as they can be controlled effectively. If education decision makers faced a situation where efforts to remedy racial inequality encountered an intractable problem, policy would have to wait on statistical discoveries. But this is not the case in higher education, as we shall see. It is not a lack of ideas that has impeded black progress; it is, rather, a lack of acceptance of and commitment to remedies already available. Virtually every major national effort to increase black participation in higher education has been followed by progress, and without great sacrifice.

A novel idea in this area would be desirable, because an "easier solution" always is. The problem is simply that such an idea cannot be found through statistical inference, because the solution and the decision where to look for it are matters of social value and commitment.[3] The most effective solutions, particularly to racial issues, are those which policy makers or other influential persons are ready to accept and implement. Policy analysis and the statistical methods employed which look for the easiest solution must then start from the point of view of established policy. Thus, in much secondary literature on blacks and education, inferential statistical techniques have only served to quantify preexisting social biases and policy preferences.

On the other hand, statistical inference may be safely used to expand descriptive data, as well as to raise and explore questions of causation where the value biases are explicit. In this case multiple approaches, and therefore values, should be explored. Even with limited use, one must recognize that primary source data on race and education are in most cases not sufficiently precise or reliable enough to submit to the refinements of statistical inference.

Primary Sources

There are probably hundreds of associations, agencies, and research organizations which regularly collect and circulate original data on students in higher education. Among these, very few showed any interest in separating data by race before about 1972. Since then most data collectors have provided some data which are stratified by race. Still, only a few describe in depth the racial composition of the educational sector observed. Where racial composition is explored, it is rarely done in the same way from one set of data to another. Consequently, it is rarely possible to use or compare multiple sets of data in higher education simultaneously.

A greater constraint of reliance on primary source material is that only two agencies regularly collect extensive data nationwide for all of higher education: the U.S. Census Bureau of the Department of Commerce, and the National Center for Educational Statistics (NCES) of the U.S. Department of Health, Education, and Welfare (HEW). NCES provides the basic enrollment and financial statistics of institutions to the U.S. Office for Civil Rights (OCR) in HEW. OCR in turn verifies and adjusts the data in accordance with its special interest in minorities and women—a special interest mandated for OCR by the 1964 Civil Rights Act.

Both OCR and NCES annually publish reports, as well as make raw data available, on student enrollment. Only OCR, however, reports data on black enrollment annually, and then only since 1974; it reported student data by race for 1972, but not for 1973. NCES produces racial data biennially in its Higher Education General Information Survey (HEGIS). OCR data has, in general, proven more useful than HEGIS data for our study of student enrollment and for degrees conferred by race. Only HEGIS, however, provides aggregate financial aid and institutional data, which are essential at various points in this study. In addition, NCES annually publishes a series of special wide-ranging studies entitled *The Condition of Education*. These studies are invaluable aids to describing the status of blacks in higher education.

Census Bureau data are used differently here from OCR and NCES data on questions of enrollment and race. The Census Bureau conducts a survey; OCR and NCES generate aggregate data based on official, comprehensive institutional reports to HEW. Although the magnitude of the Census sample, in most cases, is large enough to merit complete confidence in the Bureau's findings, the samples of their subpopulations, blacks in higher education particularly, should be treated with some care. Official Census reports exercise care to avoid overinterpretation through calculating and taking into account the margins of survey error. Unfortunately, in some secondary uses of Census data, the margins of error are ignored, with a consequent sacrifice of accuracy.

SURVEY DATA SAMPLING

The second ISEP annual report complains that the Census Bureau "consistently tended to overestimate black enrollment."[4] Compared to OCR and NCES, that still seems to be the case.

Part of the problem in relying on Census Bureau black enrollment data can be seen by looking at "standard error." The standard error is the range in numbers or percentages by which a figure could be nonrepresentative of the real population as a result of an unknown bias or error in the selection of the sample. The smaller the sample in relationship to the total population and the smaller the total population, the greater the range of error.[5]

The proportion of blacks in higher education from 1975 to 1977 is so small that the range of error becomes problematic. For example, OCR and NCES report that black enrollment in all higher education sectors is 9.3 percent, whereas the Census gives a figure just over 1 percent higher. The standard error for percentages between 9 and 10 on populations of this size (total population greater than 10 million) is between 0.5 and 0.6 percent. Consequently, the proportion of blacks could easily be 0.6 percent lower or higher. When one considers that black enrollment did not increase more than 3 percent in each of the preceding three years, this difference becomes important. In fact, Census estimates of black enrollment for 1975 were higher than OCR figures for the subsequent year. If both were accurate, political reactions could be incurred because black enrollment in higher education would have proportionately declined.

Perhaps more important than the possibility of Census sampling error is the Census consistent overestimation of black enrollment. The reasons for the overestimation are not known, but there is at least one probable explanation that exemplifies the social meaning attached to data. Specifically, Census's inquiries about blacks have a special significance for most respondents. The respondents—educational institutions, households, or individuals—are especially inclined to be sensitive to national concern about the level of education among blacks. Those most sensitive to this concern are most inclined to respond (as well as to be available for responses) to Census Bureau inquiries. Thus, in the normal range of error, the biases would consistently move toward overestimation of black enrollment.

This bias potential is parallel to the famous error in the 1948 presidential election polls, when Dewey, not Truman, was predicted the winner. Only after Truman won did social analysts recognize the fault in their survey technique. They used a telephone listing which at that time consisted heavily of the middle and the upper classes. The special interest of the wealthier population in Dewey's election was thus given too much weight.

SURVEY AND SELECTIVE AGGREGATE DATA

The problems with data on education reported by state and private organizations are greater than problems associated with Census data. Although very limited use of such data is made here, some data which are reported with exceptional care provide valuable information not available from other sources. This is particularly true of data from the American Council on Education (ACE), which are used frequently in this study. Both the strength (in terms of accuracy) and the weakness (in terms of utility) of ACE data is their reliance on surveys of freshmen. Although ACE, through its Cooperative Institutional Research Program (CIRP) studies, has follow-up surveys, responses are relatively small and therefore only minimally reliable. Nevertheless, it provides important comparative data on nearly all major socioeconomic and psychological factors in higher education research on students. The reliability of its data for blacks, however, is further compromised by its inadequate sample of black institutions. The sample of black institutions is further distorted by the use of a 50 percent cut-off point for black enrollment, when a much higher percentage of blacks normally characterizes such institutions.

Other associations provide data on special subsets of higher education enrollment, such as professional schools, regional sectors, and kinds of institution. One of the larger associations, in terms of the size of its data base, is the National Association of State Universities and Land Grant Colleges (NASULGC). Although the quality of NASULGC data is at least as good as that of comparable associations, its problems are substantial. The greatest source of difficulty is the changing number and character of institutions surveyed for enrollment from year to year. Although reports of total and black enrollment are issued regularly, comparison of annual changes in enrollment is compromised. But NASULGC, like many agencies that provide enrollment data, has an obligation to report figures for its members, however inconvenient or statistically disruptive that might be.

There is no sound basis on which to determine how adequately subnational data represent various populations. For example, NASULGC data are overwhelmingly from public institutions, but they also include some private and exclude many public institutions, i.e., state colleges. A similar problem, but one that can be compensated for because the samples' representativeness can be assessed, affects data on law school enrollment from the education division of the American Bar Association (ABA). The ABA reports enrollment by race and ethnicity covering several years. However extensive data of this kind may be, they are not reported in terms suitable for comparison. Frequently, the reports do not say how many non-minorities are enrolled at the same time, nor do they provide percentages or other tools of comparison. Consequently, the interpretative value of the data is reduced, because they must be mixed with data from other sources, which will not be perfectly comparable.

Overall, no one primary data source provides the range of data, of whatever quality, necessary to assess the status of blacks in higher education. As a result, a great deal of effort must be devoted to matching data that were not developed to be matched. In fact, data reporting from primary collectors is generally a fulfillment of non-research-related obligations, and occasionally data appear to be collected with little concern for their utility.

Secondary Sources

Utility, particularly social, is a major concern implied in secondary data sources on blacks in higher education. This concern is often impenetrable to the uninitiated reader because the social science language used obscures social values. But then, it is rarely the uninitiated reader who will act effectively in the policy area on the basis of these studies.

The weakness of secondary source material is the primary source material on which it relies. This, however, is a surmountable weakness as long as researchers verify their data, adapt their methods, and moderate their conclusions accordingly. With secondary sources, the methods and conclusions are critical.

As mentioned, descriptive statistics on blacks in higher education generally escape the problems of inferential statistics. The latter are frequently used to deal with this subject and often with great skill and reliability; on the other hand, they are too often overused. The uses of two inferential statistical methods should illustrate this problem.

SOCIOECONOMIC STATUS, RACE, AND CORRELATION ANALYSIS

In correlation analysis the number "one" expresses a perfect correlation between two variables. In the context of correlation analysis, if a researcher could find a "one" by comparing and counterbalancing the effects of race and socioeconomic status (SES) on blacks in higher education, then the conclusion would probably be that either SES or race was unimportant in the problem studied. It is not surprising that no "ones" have been found for SES and race. The finding of a "zero" would mean the inverse—that SES and race are unrelated—and are therefore both important. It is also not surprising that no such "zeros" have been found. What should be surprising is that some researchers in education seem to be looking for "zeros" or "ones."

Statistically, a correlation index of "one" would mean only that SES and race are inextricably tied variables, such that blacks and whites could never be in the same SES group. Similarly, a zero index would mean that race and SES correspond only randomly. Yet, in the context of correlation analysis on higher education and race, rarely is such open-mindedness evident. More often than not, correlation analysis is used to "explain away" racial differences by attributing them to SES or social class differences. Thus the assumption is that to the extent that (a) blacks are poor and (b) the poor have the least education, blacks do not suffer inequality in education as a consequence of racial inequality, but as a result of economic inequality.

The social assumptions of many users of correlation analysis in this area become apparent when one considers that SES, or social class, and race are already known to correspond through simple descriptive statistics as well as through common sense observation. In fact, the relationship between the two has been almost universally recognized. The problem with correlation analysis is that researchers often assume that repeated observation of a close SES or economic relationship to race signifies the primary importance of SES differences over racial ones. They are inclined to revitalize a very old notion that class is more important than race by concluding that SES is more consequential than race.

The typical statistical process by which such conclusions are reached is called "controlling for race and/or SES," or "holding race/SES constant." When analysts "hold race constant" in education analyses, SES differences among students are generally shown to correspond to substantial variance in educational attainment. In other words, the analysis theoretically makes race disappear, i.e., turns everyone the same color, so that only SES (usually defined as income, occupation, and family educational background) is verifiable. Conversely, when SES is "held constant" it is assumed to have vanished, and educational attainment varies by racial group differences.

One of the more prominent examples in recent years of this technique is Christopher Jencks' *Inequality*, which attempts to measure the effects of numerous sociological and psychological factors on educational mobility.[6] The study uses a rather complex version of correlation analysis called "path analysis." The logic of path analysis is the same as that of correlation analysis, except that a "path" of correlations is generated in the data through pyramiding direct relationships and excluding indirect ones. The authors thus attempt to separate the "net" effects of social class and race, as well as other factors, one of which is I.Q. They conclude, among other things, that social class factors, particularly family background, have a greater direct effect on educational attainment than race. Accordingly, they make some strong policy recommendations:

These findings have important implications for both educators and reformers. . . .

None of the evidence we have reviewed suggests that school reform can be expected to bring about significant social changes outside the schools. More specifically, the evidence suggests that equalizing educational opportunity would do very little to make adults more equal. . . . Eliminating all economic and academic obstacles to college attendance might somewhat reduce disparities in educational attainment, but the change would not be large.[7]

Path analysis does not resolve the conceptual weakness of correlation analysis for race and SES differences. Empirically, all Jencks has found is that blacks who come from wealthier backgrounds and who have other advantages also have educational advantages. The descriptive data in the next chapters will show this, among other things, at a glance. Theoretically, Jencks's conclusion implies that the racial identity of poor blacks can be removed statistically, and should be removed by means of public policy. Although there are philosophical difficulties with this assumption, this critique focuses on its utility for public policy analysis.

There is at present no policy or program at any level of government aimed exclusively at aiding blacks in higher education who do not also suffer non-race-specific disadvantages. Affirmative action programs often do not specify these other disadvantages, but they are assumed to exist, and often the evidence of their existence is quite clear. As chapter 3 shows, one of the major disadvantages that affects the educational access of blacks is low SES, particularly low income.

Is it possible for government to "hold race or SES constant" so that educational policy can target one factor and not the others? The answer theoretically may be "yes" in the sense that only a few blacks, who are otherwise unlike most other blacks and just like most white students, could be aided. Politically, however, it would be impossible to justify a policy that reinforced all income inequalities while it carefully selected the atypical blacks who would benefit from government aid; it is difficult enough to get government aid for blacks in higher education when there is evidence of a host of disadvantages.

The question of "holding race or SES constant" is like asking if ice cream can be made to keep its shape while served boiling hot. It is theoretically possible for modern chemistry to provide a solution, but who would really care? We like our ice cream cold. Similarly, if this society is serious about promoting equal educational opportunity, there should be no problem of separating out the context of black student disadvantage by nonracial factors. Inequality is itself a "gestalt"; it is the product of many factors. Government must be willing to address its policy to the elimination of inequality, whatever its root cause.

Social values penetrate statistical methods. Jencks's conclusion that educational attainment will change only slightly if schooling and educational policy are reformed is premised on past evaluations of schooling and educational policy. The correlates of SES, and race, etc., are, at least temporarily, treated as independent variables which do not interact internally once given a quantitative ranking. The result is the methodological assumption that the initial rankings will always count for the same proportion of educational attainment. They then effectively deny the possibility of fundamental educational reform from the very beginning. For example, they do not, and cannot, separate discrimination from their correlates for race. Consequently, the level of racial discrimination before 1972 is built into their analysis of future policy changes. Since black educational opportunity had only begun to advance before that time, it is no wonder they see little hope for government innovation.

Because of the weakness of correlation analysis and related statistical methods for policy development, we make very little use of them in this study. Limited use, however, is made of secondary material in which such statistical methods (regression analysis included) play a large part. Most important among such secondary materials are the studies based on data from the National Longitudinal Survey (NLS), described in chapter 5. Studies that employ NLS data (Thomas, 1977, 1978; Thomas, et al., 1977; Kolstad, 1977), cited throughout this report, are more circumspect in making inferences from statistics than are Jencks's.

Analysis of NLS data is in part protected from overinterpretation because the original data themselves are not conducive to it. NLS data do not contain I.Q. data of the kind used in Jencks's study. This is a crucial omission for policy studies of educational mobility, because it is essential that *all significant* factors in education be considered in order to assess the full impact and potential of policy. The inclusion of I.Q. data demonstrates the researcher's expectation that such data will explain some differences in educational mobility. When the original I.Q. data is known to be unreliable the reliability of the entire piece of research is mortgaged from the beginning. Still, the research may acquire a schematic balance and comprehensive appearance that make it more marketable, although unreliable, in some policy circles. Jencks could not easily omit the I.Q. correlates, because he believes that native intelligence plays a crucial role in educational mobility. Analysts of NLS data cited here have examined the role of intelligence, whether native or acquired, in educational mobility without being preoccupied with the origins of intelligence. The emphasis on native intelligence in policy analysis is ultimately a search for a disclaimer, a release clause, for educational decision makers.

Our present concern is that such a search can only be legitimate if the data permit good analysis. The limitations of primary data for education analysis are thus greatly magnified when they are ignored in secondary policy analysis. Jencks's path analysis flounders on its primary data source for I.Q. (not that there is any reliable measure of I.Q.). Jencks and his coauthors rely heavily—directly or indirectly—on the findings of Cyril Burt. They also use Arthur Jensen's work, which also makes primary use of Burt's data. Only more recently did Leon Kamin, noted policy and I.Q. analyst, expose Burt's major work as partially, if not wholly, fraudulent.[9] Since the policy import of their method depends on the fit of all pieces of data into sets of correlation paths, the whole falls on this inadequate construct of its parts. Jencks and his coauthors talk about their "best guess" in developing their numerical I.Q. index, but they treat it like fact because there is no number for "maybe."

In sum, primary reliance on inferential statistics presents two major difficulties for policy evaluation. First, there is no justification permissible in the method for reaching conclusions about "causes," but the temptation to do so is apparently very strong. Second, policy recommendations are best made when the entire context of all interconnected social factors has been examined. But quantitative indices are not always possible or reliable for many important social factors. One must, therefore, be careful to avoid, or place little reliance on, unreliable measures. The exercise of such care may require that research energies be consumed in primary data collection and description.

INDIRECT CORRELATES OF RACE AND EDUCATIONAL OPPORTUNITY

The safest use of correlation analysis, as has been pointed out, in studies of blacks in higher education is for description. This is because of the misrepresentation which generally emerges from causal analysis. Here again, the relationships important to education policy may not need such inferential quantification. For example, sex differences in educational attainment are observable directly. Sex differences among blacks, however, are different from those among whites and may benefit from a more formal statistical mapping. Thus, we draw on several secondary sources which give in depth analysis of sex/race variations.

Like the sex variable, region, urbanization, and other factors can be studied usefully by descriptive and inferential techniques. What separates these factors from SES is that there should be no misguided assumption of causation. We know that SES and race are tied, but we do not know statistically how closely. Fortunately, we may not need to know. We also know that race is related to other factors, but most of these are not themselves assumed to be the causes of inequality.

Ultimately, policy relevance has been our strongest criterion for the selection of data and methods. What can be shown or done to guide policy analysis and subsequent reform possibilities is more important than demonstrating what cannot be undone.

Financial and Institutional Data

In the course of this study, we frequently draw on primary and secondary source data on the financial aspects of higher education and on institutional behavior. For the most part, financial data are drawn from primary governmental sources or from sources immediately traceable to government documents. Institutional data are more often from secondary material. Occasionally, we have been able to check conclusions drawn from secondary sources against data collected at ISEP. It has generally been necessary, however, to survey the literature as the basic means of checking conclusions on institutional behavior.

The literature on institutional behavior (see bibliography) gives great weight to the impact of institutions on students generally, and on minorities in particular. Unfortunately, these data are difficult to collect and in short supply. One of the uncontested observations one can make about research efforts to improve the status of blacks in higher education is that both the impediments and contributions of institutions to black advancement are not well known, and are in need of careful examination.

CHAPTER 3

Access to Higher Education

In the first chapter, we were concerned with the gradual transformation of American education from a restrictive system, fully accessible only to a privileged few, to a multifaceted system accessible in varying degrees to virtually everyone. The admission of blacks to the once limited centers of privilege has been identified as the point of greatest friction and resistance in the gradual liberalization of an expanding education system. The preceding overview of public policy and policy analysis in this area leaves little doubt that equal opportunity has been a serious concern of education policy makers since the 1960s. But it also leaves less doubt that equal opportunity has never been their primary concern. As a result, the national commitment to equal opportunity in higher education appears to be uneven and even ephemeral. Considering then the limits of the policy commitment, recent progress toward greater educational opportunity by blacks is impressive. At the same time, the uncertainties of federal commitment indicate a need to examine the progress and failures of recent years so that equal educational opportunity can be placed on a more solid foundation.

This chapter will attempt to detail recent progress toward the goal of greater educational access for blacks. This discussion, however, may leave us even farther than previous studies from having a sense of when racially equal educational opportunity may be achieved.

When the Institute looked at progress toward equal educational opportunity in 1976, the data extended only to 1974.[1] At that time, black upward mobility within the educational system had been continuous, if still unsatisfactory. By 1978, however, the data had begun to provide a different perspective. In addition, the major steps toward increased black participation in higher education had only begun to be taken after 1968. Analysts, therefore, found themselves faced with the complex task of exploring a new problem area—that of the changing dimensions of black/white educational inequality. On the other hand, existing inequalities having been so overwhelming, and evidence of those inequalities so blatant, it was in a sense a simple matter for analysts to point out some injustices. It was a simple matter to the extent that anaylsts could make contributions without preoccupying themselves with the nuances of definition and conceptualization that surrounded the meaning of equality. Although the first Institute report on blacks in higher education carefully examined the problems of measuring educational equality, that examination was curtailed by the pressing need to tabulate gross inequalities for which few subtleties of definition were required. The second annual report, *Equal Educational Opportunity: More Promise Than Progress*, followed the lead of the first one, chronicling the extent to which racial inequalities in higher education had been reduced in the subsequent year, 1974–75. The second report serves largely to confirm the conclusions of the first, that gradual but significant progress was being made by blacks towards greater educational equality with whites.

Both reports, however, presage an increasing need for a refinement in our concepts of equality at the level of public policy. They warn against what may be called the *"Plessy* v. *Ferguson* effect", that is, the politically motivated ease of asserting the presence of equal opportunity in the absence of meaningful standards for equality. In an effort to give precision to the definition of educational equality, those reports subdivide the problem of educational opportunity into the concepts of "access, distribution, and persistence." The first report explains:

> Access means that black students have the opportunity to enroll in undergraduate, graduate, or professional schools. Distribution refers to choice, the opportunity for black students to enter different types of institutions and fields of study. And persistence refers to the opportunity to remain in college and complete their training in a timely fashion. In order to have equal educational opportunity, a black student must not just have the opportunity to enroll in college, but a choice of institution and programs, and a chance to complete the training once begun. [2]

In measuring equality of access, distribution, and persistence, earlier studies have relied on black/white populations ratios, either in the school age population or in the population of available high school graduates. With public policy considerations in mind, the first report maintains:

An immediate access goal for equal educational opportunity for blacks is parity with the undergraduate availability pool. That is the proportion of blacks within the availability pool should equal their proportion of the total undergraduate enrollment. As a long-range access goal, however, parity with the age group, regardless of high school completion, is desired. [3]

If there is any single definition or set of definitions which applies to policy-oriented research on equality in American higher education, it would certainly take into account the relative proportions of underrepresented student groups to the numbers of the groups available, in terms of age and educational background, for participation in higher education. Government policies and programs, whether at the federal, state, or local level, rarely define equality of educational opportunity, except in terms of the concrete barrier to it, i.e., discrimination. Operationally, however, one always finds, since the Civil Rights period, some image of "proportional representation" in "equal opportunity" legislation. Some of the most controversial legislative and judicial acts in the past few years have concerned numerical goals in higher education. The *Bakke* case, for example, is widely considered to have resulted from the University of California at Davis's extreme reliance on numerical goals or "quotas" in affirmative action. In this chapter, we are only concerned with goals to the extent that they are an outgrowth of quantitative analysis—analysis which perceives racial equality primarily in terms of numerical proportions. To that end, many affirmative action programs in institutions of higher education have set goals for minority enrollment which claim to equalize minority student percentages with minority percentages in the national or some other "relevant" population.

We will, for the most part, follow the established precedents for the measurement of equality in this discussion. Looking beyond the dimension of *proportional representation* of blacks in higher education, however, will be useful in broadening our analysis. More specifically, our concern for equality of opportunity will require a continued awareness of the unresolved conceptual problems surrounding the problem, which the proportional approach frequently tends to confound.

A primary illustration of (and a somewhat theoretical digression from) the conceptual problem of measuring equal access emerges from operationalizing student access "to college" in relationship to "high school productivity" or age-group size. This analytically-defined access places the college in a dependent position toward equal educational mobility, such that institutions are held responsible for the pursuit of equality only to the extent that "all other things in the educational process are equal." While this method may well reflect a necessary condition for effective public policy—a condition restricting change to marginal steps—it is not the only logical method.

As an alternative, one might well define college access in terms of the broader functions and purposes of colleges themselves. While that might still imply an age-group specificity, it is much more likely to rest on the production of a trained, "culturally-developed," or otherwise highly educated professional and labor supply. Equal access is tied to equal outcomes, and equal opportunity should be judged by the probability of arriving at equal outcomes. Implicit in this alternative is the judgment of racial inequalities at the racial group level rather than at the individual level. The logic behind the judgment is, first, that government policy in education is a response to societal needs, second, that the individual capacity to benefit from higher education cannot be equitably determined by achievement at any age under inegalitarian social or educational (pre-college) constraints. In this case, we would most likely measure equal educational opportunity by weighing several sets of availability pools, defined by age or educational background, against the expected college productivity and/or labor demands. It should be evident that this type of approach would present problems of a social planning nature with which American government has been traditionally hesitant to deal. Nevertheless, when we have explored the more traditional approach to access in more detail, it should become evident that the more traditional approach places a burden of responsibility on individuals for whom American society may have provided unequal opportunitites from the outset.

Parameters of Racial Parity

Returning to the conventional approach to equal access, a brief comparison of the data applicable to various measures of availability helps show the extent to which goals for racial equality of opportunity may vary with the data prescribed. It is important to caution that many studies of educational equality use contradictory parameters to judge access. The most frequent contradiction occurs when one defines availability according to age or high school credentials and then inconsistently relies on the 11 percent figure which represents the 1976 black portion of the population (U.S. Census). [4] As a result of an historically high black birth rate, that 11 percent, or 24.5 million black people, is considerably outdistanced by the black proportion of the high school and college age populations.

There was an estimated fertility rate of 1.76 for all American women in 1976. Black women in the normal years of parent age, 18–44, had 2.05 children, as compared with 1.59 children for white women, in 1976.[5] Drawing on estimates of the U.S. Census Bureau, the black fertility rate during the years in which the 1976 college age population was born is about 160.1 per thousand as against 115.1 per thousand white women (see Table 3-1).

By 1975, more than half, 51 percent, of blacks were between the ages of four and twenty-five, compared with 42 percent of the total population. Almost double the number of blacks were over four and under the age of twenty-five in comparison with those of Western European origin in the same age range, 51 to 26 percent, respectively (see Figures 3-1 and 3-2).

Accordingly, by 1977 the number of college age blacks, "18–24 years old, had increased at almost twice the rate of whites in that age group." Including an increase in the older black population, "the overall effect is that the black population grew by 11 percent compared to 4.8 percent for whites" between July 1976 and July 1977.[6]

Of this increase, however, the black percentage of the nonfreshman college age population, 19–25 years old, remains about the same as that of the larger population.[7] Consequently, we would be at racial parity of access for blacks if blacks had constituted 11 percent of the college population before 1976, but that did not happen. To the extent that we aimed at reaching 11 percent in 1978, in subsequent years we will still not reach age-group parity because the black proportion will be considerably greater.

The black proportion of the total American college age population, those 18–24 years old, is significantly higher than that of the total popula-

Table 3-1   **FERTILITY RATES OF WOMEN AGES 15 TO 44 (PER THOUSAND)**
July 1, 1955–59

Year	Total	White	Non-White
1955	118.0	113.2	155.1
1956	120.8	115.6	161.0
1957	122.7	117.4	163.4
1958	120.1	114.8	161.2
1959	120.2	114.6	163.0
Mean	120.4	115.1	160.1

Source: U.S. Bureau of the Census, *Vital Statistics of the United States*, Vol. 1 (Washington, D.C.: U.S. Government Printing Office, 1961).

Figure 3-1   ETHNIC COMPOSITION OF THE U.S. POPULATION FOUR
              YEARS OLD AND OVER
              July 1975

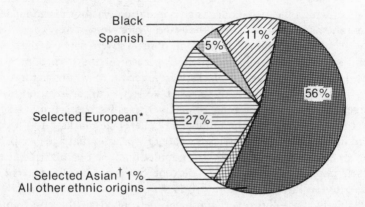

Source: National Center for Education Statistics, The Condition of Education, 1977, Vol. 3, Part 1, (Washington, D.C.: U.S. Government Printing Office, 1977), p. 8.

*German, Italian, English-Scottish, Welsh, Irish, French, Polish, Russian, Greek, Portuguese.

†Chinese, Japanese, Filipino, Korean.

tion. For the period under examination, 1975 to 1977, blacks constituted 12.58 percent of the college population according to "standard" census figures. Along with the lower median age of blacks, one can detect a continued increase in the proportion of blacks in this age group, from 12.46 percent in 1975 to 12.73 percent in 1977 (see Table 3-2).

If one keeps in mind the persistent problem of census error, inclined toward undercounting blacks in the general population, the percentage of blacks in this, as well as other, age groups should be assumed to be significantly higher. In the Census Bureau's own "adjusted" estimates of the population an effort is made to counterbalance the problem. [8] Yet, because the "standard" population estimates are more extensive and more widely used, the problem persists, carrying with it a false sense of security about black enrollment where black students are overcounted. For example, blacks constitute, according to "adjusted" figures, 13.5 percent of Americans 18 to 24 years old. But according to the standard figures, there are about one percent fewer, 12.5. In real terms, that amounts to about a quarter of a million overlooked people (see Table 3-2).

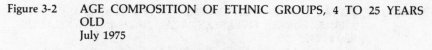

Figure 3-2   AGE COMPOSITION OF ETHNIC GROUPS, 4 TO 25 YEARS
OLD
July 1975

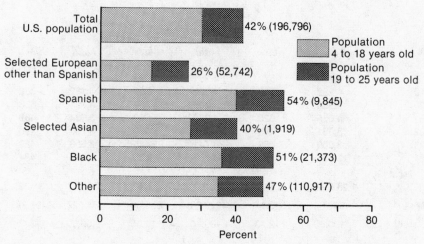

Source: National Center for Education Statistics, *The Condition of Education, 1977,* Vol. 3, Part 1, (Washington, D.C.: U.S. Government Printing Office, 1977), p. 8.

Figure 3-3 gives a rough indication of the extent to which the black proportion of the college age population will be increasing.

A brief, but significant, aside, to which we will return later, can be drawn from Figure 3-3. The variance in male and female populations, and within them, the variance in male and female age-group populations, in contrast to the variance in black males and females in college may call for a sex specific measure of equal opportunity for blacks (see Appendix, Table A3-2).

The best measure of population distribution with which to judge the progress of black higher educational enrollment is one which singles out the age of freshman classes, "normally" 17 to 19 years old. Unfortunately, such precise distribution figures of the population by age and race are not available for the years under study. If they were available, we would still be confronted with considerable uncertainty about the age distribution of freshmen. Yet, the freshman class enrollments of 1975 and 1976, in the light of growth in the modal age group for blacks, should provide a good basis of comparison with the enrollments of earlier years.

However age cohorts may be calibrated or composed in terms of college enrollment, there still remains an almost insurmountable risk of using

Table 3-2   TOTAL POPULATION OF THE UNITED STATES INCLUDING
ARMED FORCES OVERSEAS, AGES 18–24 (IN THOUSANDS)
July 1, 1975–77

Age	1977 Total	1977 Black	1976 Total	1976 Black	1975 Total	1975 Black
18	4,240	573	4,251	559	4,243	559
19	4,288	556	4,282	556	4,132	532
20	4,353	573	4,204	551	4,154	536
21	4,075	523	4,030	509	3,954	489
22	3,961	499	3,890	480	3,796	458
23	3,830	466	3,741	445	3,650	429
24	3,855	451	3,765	435	3,674	434
Total all ages	28,602	3,641	28,163	3,535	27,603	3,439
Mean [1]	4086.00	520.14	4023.29	505.00	3943.29	491.29
Percent	100.00	12.73	100.00	12.55	100.00	12.46

Source: U.S. Bureau of the Census, *Current Population Reports*, Series P-25, No. 721, "Estimates of the Population of the U.S. by Age, Sex, and Race" (Washington, D.C.: U.S. Government Printing Office, 1978), Table 1.

[1] Mean of all three years: Total = 4017.53; Black = 505.49
Percentage of all three years: Total = 100.00; Black = 12.58

biased parameters where racial distribution is concerned. The need to identify an average or normal college age group is tied to a persistent methodological difficulty. The age range of students in college has been different for blacks and whites at least since 1973.

As *Equal Educational Opportunity: An Assessment* points out, black students tend to be older and tend to take longer to finish their advanced education than white students.[9] And, the average age for all college students has been going up substantially since 1973, but the rate of change has apparently not been even across all social groups. Consequently, we can expect that the normal ages of white and black students will be different, but the patterns of change in student ages has been such that it is difficult to say with certainty how far apart they will be.

One important explanation of this age/race disparity may well be indicated by changing patterns of enrollment by age and sex. Aside from the more substantive explanation of age-disparity, which emerges from a range of socioeconomic difficulties that delay the normal cycle of blacks in higher education, we hypothesize a pattern of change in higher education

Figure 3-3 **DISTRIBUTION OF THE WHITE AND BLACK POPULATION**
July 1, 1977

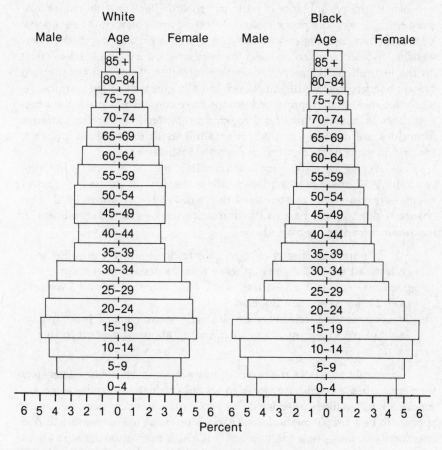

Source: U.S. Bureau of the Census, Current Population Reports, Series P-25, No. 721, "Estimates of the Population of the U.S. by Age, Sex and Race, 1970–1977" (Washington, D.C.: U.S. Government Printing Office), p. 1.

characteristic of all traditionally underrepresented groups. While the data show that women have made greater progress than other underrepresented groups towards equitable participation in educational institutions, their pattern of progress parallels that of the other major groups, Hispanics and blacks, in most areas. Consequently, when we find that the pattern of female enrollment or changes in enrollment diverge from the traditional (male) pattern, there is good reason to expect the black pattern to be closer to that of the pattern of women.

Behind this resemblance in patterns probably lies something more than mere coincidence. The processes of integrating and liberalizing educational institutions are not dependent only on external pressures and the "new students" who attempt to open up the institutions; they are also dependent on the institutions themselves. Whether intentionally or not, institutions present barriers to new students which initially give way at the margins. As a consequence, underrepresented groups have consistently made their biggest dents in higher education through untraditional enrollment patterns. Minorities are more likely than other students to be marginal students, enrolled in marginal programs, in marginal institutions.

The average age of both male and female students has gone up in recent years. By 1977, more than a third of college students, 36 percent, were over twenty-five years old, as compared to twenty-eight percent in 1972. This change is due in great part to the dramatic increases in the enrollment of female students (see Figure 3-4).

> The number of women aged 25 or older who were enrolled in college last fall (1977) was up more than 23 percent over the previous year. In the past five years, the number of enrolled women over 24 has more than doubled.
>
> For men the trend was less dramatic, enrollment of those over 25 was up 2.9 percent in one year and up about 34 percent in five years. [10]

If one seeks to reduce the biases of using age-cohorts as the parameters for parity, then a comparison of high school graduates, keeping some age specification, is a likely approach. Such an approach is deceptive, because it appears to be a simple methodological decision made to compensate for the uncertainty of age-group analysis, yet it is also a normative decision about the criterion of equal opportunity. It is a decision to consider relevant only those who have transcended the *normal standard* for college admission for inclusion in the provision of equal access to higher education. The approach ignores the possibility that those without high school diplomas may be victims of unequal opportunity for college access.

More important, the approach is grounded in the conviction that secondary school conditions, as far as public policy is concerned, are irrelevant to postsecondary school opportunities. While the distinction is quite logical in most situations, it is not clearly so for educational policy. To the extent that opportunity is racially unequal in secondary school, policy decisions for higher education will be more, rather than less, difficult to

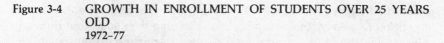

Figure 3-4   GROWTH IN ENROLLMENT OF STUDENTS OVER 25 YEARS OLD
1972–77

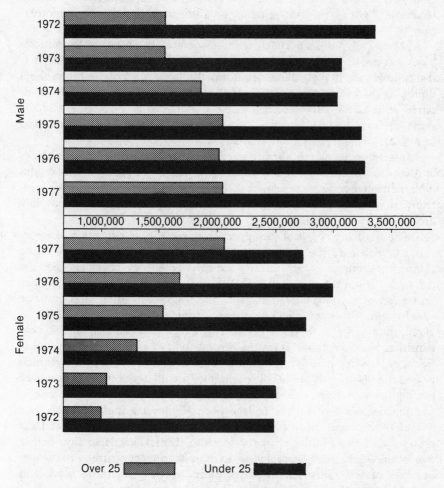

Source: *The Chronicle of Higher Education*, XVI, 7 (April 10, 1978), p. 2. Based on U.S. Census Bureau Data.

evaluate using this parameter. In particular, as the proportion of blacks to whites completing secondary school changes, the assessment of racial equality for college would change. It follows (psychologically) that as racial parity is approached in terms of this parameter, public efforts to increase black enrollment will decline. When this happens, the integrity of the

41

educational policy will hinge on the assumption that high school students are not motivated by the possibility of continuing their education through college. That assumption, as should be seen in this discussion, is hardly tenable in light of the best evidence on student performance and motivation. [11]

Statistically, this approach relieves some of the pressure to improve black access to higher education. Because black high school attrition is disporportionately high, there are distinctly fewer blacks with high school diplomas than their percentage of the age group would indicate. As compared with 12.55 percent of those 18–24 years old in 1976, blacks of the same age range constitute only 11.63 percent of those having completed four years of high school in that year.

Interestingly enough, the gap in educational attainment between blacks and whites under 25 years old apparently widens before both blacks and whites finish secondary school. Table 3-3 shows that blacks in their mid-teens are as far behind whites in terms of median years of schooling as they are in their early twenties.

The normative basis of the approach to equality of educational opportunity which uses the number of high school diploma recipients as the primary parameter is most clearly exposed when one considers that the principle behind the approach is that the structure of college education has no treatable or controllable effects on the rest of education, and that one should take all existing inequalities resulting from secondary school as given. In this case, then, one would excuse a host of social inequalities, now considered unacceptable, from the responsibility of postsecondary educational policy. In particular, inequalities of socioeconomic status and ethnicity and those of region and local community are all developed by the end of the high school years. [12] These inequalities, like those of race, continue in varying degrees through the college years. Following this approach, one would restrict pressure for change, and hold the gaps in equity at their established levels, rather than try to close them. That is to say, higher education would not be expected to do more than react neutrally to the inequalities of secondary school preparation, which characterize black and white college applicants differently.

A further extension of this approach would restrict measures of equality to the "types" and quality of high school education received by potential college students. In this case, equal access would be achieved when students with the same grades from the same "kind" of schools with the same test scores had equal chances of getting into college. Except for irregularities in college admission policies and standard "exceptions," like those made for athletes and children of alumni, American higher education is fairly close to

Table 3-3   **14 TO 24 YEAR-OLDS HAVING COMPLETED 4 YEARS OF HIGH SCHOOL (IN THOUSANDS) 1976**

Age	All Races	White	Black
14–17	203	171	31
18–19	4,156	3,693	412
20–24	8,228	7,092	1,029
Total 14–24	12,587	10,956	1,472
Percent 14–24	100.00	87.04	11.69
Total 18–24	12,384	10,785	1,441
Percent 18–24	100.00	87.08	11.63
Median Number of Years of Schooling By Race, 1976			
14–17	9.3	9.4	9.1
18–19	12.3	12.3	11.9
20–24	12.8	12.8	12.5

Source: Analysis of data from U.S. Bureau of the Census, *Current Population Reports*, Series P-20, No. 314, "Educational Attainment in the U.S.: March 1977" (Washington, D.C.: U.S. Government Printing Office, 1977), Table 1.

this kind of equity. In other words, higher education students experience very little discrimination in gaining access to the extent that they are socioeconomically similar, e.g., urban, northern, upper middle class. It follows, therefore, that blacks who are otherwise like the "conventional" white students encounter considerably less discrimination than blacks who suffer the prevalent socioeconomic disadvantages of their group. At this point, it should be clear that if we restrict our parameters for equality enough we will easily reach a point where nothing will have to be done (at least if social and minority dissatisfaction can be ignored). Public policy in higher education would then simply maintain the status-quo.

Of course, we need not carry the approach of limiting the parameters of racial parity in education to the extent just outlined. But, the question of where, or at what point, parity is reached will remain. The choice as to where to place the measure of parity is obviously not determined by measurement. It is a value-based decision. The values prescribe first the commitment to equality of opportunity and, by the same token, prescribe the extent to which equal opportunity will be less extensive than equality at the input and output phases of education. In this case, equality of opportunity for age-groups in education seems to be as far as most Americans can go, because they fear that a broader policy of equal opportunity will become an obligation to equality of outcomes. Further, there is a value-based decision about the role and responsibility of higher education in promoting equality of opportunity. It is a decision to restrict our performance expectations of educational institutions to the standards for education which they themselves prescribe. Higher education is, accordingly, to be judged only in terms of its *independent* and *deliberate* contribution to equality or inequality. With regard to black access, an "independent" institutional effect excludes student disadvantage occurring prior to, or external to, college eligibility. Consequently, disadvantaged students have an inferior chance to gain a college education, but are considered to have an equal opportunity even though the college does nothing to compensate for the disadvantage. "Deliberate" means that educational opportunity in college will be evaluated as equitable as long as the institution engages in educational practices—intellectual, pedagogical, etc.—that institutions consider legitimate, whatever deleterious or debilitating effect those practices may have on blacks or minorities. In other words, equal educational opportunity, once it is restricted to a set of educational credentials, is intended only to eliminate direct racial bias and not to change higher education in any substantive way.

The demarcation between substantive educational practices and those of racial bias, however, is much easier to name than to explain or apply. For this reason, the direct approach to removing inequality of opportunity is only rarely evident in the determination of federal policy. Such an approach would first require the identification of all race-related barriers to higher education. Second, it would involve the clear separation of those barriers from defensible, if not necessary, academic practices. Third, and perhaps most important, it would involve apprehension about the policy-outcomes, as well as the capacity for repeated readjustment, in part because a new black constituency would be counterbalanced by a disrupted educational community. Invariably, the most direct approach to educational equality expands government control of, and involvement in, educational institutions to a point that would inevitably be considered threatening to institutional freedom and standards.

Institutional Standards and Barriers to Access

In *Equal Educational Opportunity: An Assessment* (ISEP), barriers to educational opportunity for blacks are discussed at length. Unfortunately, those same barriers are still prevalent four years later although they are somewhat less rigid. The apparent growth in the number of blacks in higher education gives evidence primarily of the effectiveness of those outside the institutions—black students and parents, the federal government, and individual educational policymakers—in overcoming institutional resistance. Still, this growth rarely reflects a transformation of institutional practices themselves. Perhaps the sociopolitical movement toward more equal opportunity for blacks since the 1960s was never designed to transform the institutions or to revamp their educational practices, but only intended to change the institutions' outcomes, i.e., racial composition of the student bodies. Such a limited intention may have been the best and most effective way to make progress toward greater racial equality. Yet, there remains a very real question as to whether those limited ambitions are either realistic or achievable. Educational institutions, like most organizations, will more readily expand in response to pressure than undertake structural reform. The question bears on the general assumption that outcomes can be changed without changing their origin and, in particular, the assumption that institutional practices, educational or otherwise, have always been neutral. In other words, there may be an erroneous assumption in policy for higher education that institutions have not assimilated into their behavior at basic levels the racially oriented barriers of the society in which they developed. The problem of access for blacks is only the beginning of our exploration of this assumption—an exploration which will be developed throughout the study.

The first annual ISEP report began to draw the distinction between these behavioral "external" and "internal" barriers to black access, and was able to demonstrate fully the need for public action without detailing the internal barriers.

In that study, barriers to equal opportunity for blacks are classified in terms of "categorical" (racial discrimination), "educational" (institutional policies and practices), and "psychosocial" (negative student attitudes). Abramowitz explains in the study that categorical barriers have waned:

> Categorical barriers arise when two groups are treated differently to the detriment of one group .... In higher education, categorical barriers included such things as quotas that limited college admission and eligibility requirements that limited the availability of financial aid to blacks. Enforcement of Title VI of the Civil Rights Act of 1964 helped to reduce categorical barriers, especially in access. [13]

Referring to sociologist Kenneth Clark's classic "doll-preference" study, Abramowitz defines psychosocial barriers as arising "from negative aspects of the life-styles individuals have adopted voluntarily or through coercion." [14] These barriers are formed through feelings of inferiority

45

generated by racial segregation. "Psychosocial barriers influence distribution among the institutions and fields of study chosen by black students, and persistence in those institutions."[15]

In that study, both the categorical and psychosocial barriers have in common their occurrence outside the institution, and have for a long time been viewed as inconsistent with the institution's primary educational mission. In addition to these barriers, there are others, to which we will turn shortly. For the moment, it is necessary to draw the contrast among all "external" of barriers, categorical and psychosocial, on one hand, and "internal" or "educational" barriers, on the other.

According to *Equal Educational Opportunity: An Assessment:*

> Educational barriers are policies and practices of institutions and
> individuals, that seem neutral, but have an adverse impact on
> blacks .... Educational and categorical barriers differ in that the lat-
> ter are deliberate efforts to discriminate, whereas the racial impact of
> the former may be unintended. Their neutral appearance makes
> educational barriers more difficult to detect and easier to defend
> than categorical barriers .... In addition to admissions tests, college
> costs, financial aid, educational preparation, transfer policies,
> counseling practices, recruitment, extracurricular activities, and stu-
> dent employment all constituted educational barriers for black
> students.[16]

Internal (educational) barriers are perhaps most resilient because their defense is couched in much the same language as that in which the legitimacy and social value of formal education has long been couched. In general, higher education has always been expected to be selective and restrictive—a selectivity based on intellectual capabilities of institutions, employers, and societal functions to absorb the educated. Moreover, it has traditionally been assumed that the "educated"—those who carry the credential and the "creed" (socialization)—should be the ultimate judges of how selectivity and restrictiveness operate, and the judges of who will benefit. It goes almost without saying that these traditions have excluded blacks, and that blacks have not been the beneficiaries of the traditions. It should be added that the same traditions may well have gained a legitimacy based on their exclusiveness with regard to blacks and other minorities. We will have to complete an exploration of traditional biases in later chapters, even though they are directly relevant to the problem of access. This is because the legitimacy of racially biased educational traditions, wherever found, has, as its primary effect, the capacity to give the appearance of objectivity. In particular, blacks would appear to have equal access with whites to higher education except for the legitimate educational, internal requirements of the institution. Max Weber describes a broader aspect of this problem as "bureaucratic rationalism," defined in terms of the regularization, standardization, and objectiveness of administrative behavior. [17]

Applying his analysis to Western education generally, Weber observes a tendency to deny legitimate cultural variation through the "regularization" of educational curricula and the use of "special examinations," both supposedly to serve the ultimate purpose of increasing the market value of educational credentials. "The reason behind it," Weber explains, "is, of course, not a suddenly awakened 'thirst for education' but the desire for restricting the supply for the (economically advantageous) positions and their monopolization by owners of educational certificates." [18] Thus, the tendency is to rationalize the exclusion of students as the result of a bureaucratic mandate.

While higher educational institutions in this country vary widely, the admissions process everywhere has taken on an increasingly bureaucratic form—a singular standard which remains the model, however much actual practice may deviate. It is to these professionally sanctioned standards that demands for improved black access to higher education must be addressed. To address these demands, the trend toward increased bureaucracy in education need not be advocated. Rather, all that should be necessary is to make admissions and other educational standards conform to "reasonable" criteria; this will remove the image that so-called rationalism in higher education is based in reason. In turn, what this means is that educational access should be based on the social responsibility of the institution, and standards restricting black access may simply be the rationalized product of historical racial bias and social inequality.

Prevailing Standards for College Admissions

What makes admission standards critical and questionable for black access is that they are largely irrational and imprecise. A 1973 study commissioned by the American Council on Education (ACE) clearly demonstrates that faculty and administrators' opinions about the applicant and his or her "fit" with the institution play a crucial role. For example, 47 percent of college and university respondents to a national survey describe the process in their institutions as: "highly individualized admissions decisions based on appraisal of the total applicant dossier." [19] Since 1973, there has, no doubt, been some rigidification of the admissions process at most institutions, but evidently no increase in the competitive levels of students on prevailing standards. Aside from two-year colleges, the majority of which have open admissions, only about 10 percent of institutional admissions are automated or concretized to the point of excluding selection for social/institutional purposes. Where such selectivity has operated only "marginally," the marginal differences in standing have been critical, both for simple admissions and for admissions with merit-based financial aid.

William Bowen, President of Princeton University, summarizes general approaches to competitive admissions in a recent article, "Admission and the Relevance of Race" by pointing to "three broad considerations that are involved in choosing among applicants: (1) the basic qualifications of individuals; (2) the composition of the student body; and (3) the potential contributions to society of those applicants possessing the basic qualifications."[20] While institutions vary significantly in the weight they give these broad concerns, the evidence indicates that the vast majority gives a substantial margin to factors other than basic individual qualifications in considering students for admission and financial aid.

A Carnegie Council study on admissions points to a range of criteria, individual as well as "social," which an institution normally considers in admissions. These may be separated into "individual" and "social" as follows:

[Individual]

Prior scholastic grades and rank in class

Test scores—both aptitude and achievement

Special academic interests and abilities—for example, in some branch of science

Special abilities—for example, ability to play in the band or the orchestra, skill in the performing arts, adeptness in competitive sports, talent for peer group leadership

Special interests—for example, in community service

[Individual/Social]

Special identities—for example, by religious or by alumni percentage

Special personal characteristics—for example, proven ability to rise above obstacles including language barriers, poor prior schooling, inadequate home environment, social prejudice, physical handicaps, or, as another example, successful past work experience

[Social]

Contributions to diversity of the student community—for example, by state or nation of origin, by occupations and incomes of parents, by cultural backgrounds

Potential contributions to a profession—for example, by interest in serving in a neglected area or in a neglected specialty

Contributions to a campus tradition—for example, by taking students from a particular locality or ethnic group or stratum of society

Contributions to the political or economic or community needs of the institution—for example, by taking children or friends of a political leader, or a trustee, or a leading donor, or a member of the profession served, or a faculty member. [21]

OPEN ADMISSIONS

What about institutions which do not exercise this level of selectivity, i.e., the minority with open admissions? In these institutions the basic requirement for admission is a high school diploma. They should not be as easily subject to racial bias. One of the problems here is that these institutions are in the minority; they constitute a very small minority of four-year colleges and universities. Restricted access to some institutions, like restricted open housing in some neighborhoods, is not equal opportunity. Consequently, the problem of bias is largely displaced to the realm of all higher education and away from the individual institutions. First, because of size, open admissions schools are not capable of providing students with the same opportunities as those institutions with controlled admissions. One disadvantage of open admissions is an apparent loss of institutional reputation, leading both to a drain of the potentially best applicants and a decline in the marketability of the degree. [22] Moreover, the institutions are faced with demands for student services and pedagogical demands for which they, like most other institutions, have been ill-prepared. In particular, the need for remedial education programs in open admission colleges has greatly expanded, including in some cases almost a third of the student body. The corresponding need for additional financing—$30 million in 1976 at the City University of New York (CUNY) alone—has met increasing opposition from taxpayers. [23] Finally, open admissions programs have been largely experimental, and they have, for a variety of reasons, been curtailed in the past few years. We should recognize that the goal of equal access for blacks is not being met by open admissions programs, nor is it likely to be, given the existing structures. [24]

In a recent study of the effects of open admissions on equal educational opportunity, David Lavin and his co-authors concluded that open admission at the City University of New York has benefited white students more than minorities.[25] In addition, the authors point to a growing criticism of higher education which argues that open admissions inadvertently serves to maintain or to relegate minorities to lower status positions in large college and university systems:

> The transition from selective to open access higher education has been viewed with considerable skepticism by many writers. Critical analysts such as Bowles and Gintis, Karabel, Milner, and Trimberger have concluded that open access higher education is illusory as a means of equalizing educational opportunity. The essential point made by these writers is that access in itself fails to consider the internal differentiation of the higher education system and the differential allocation of social classes and ethnic groups within this system. This differential allocation is seen as having life-long consequences for post college attainment, particularly occupational prestige and income.[26]

SELECTIVE ADMISSIONS AND ACHIEVEMENT TESTS

The criteria that dominate admissions for the individual, beyond the degree or diploma, are basically the secondary school background of the student, standarized test scores, and the applicant's socioeconomic characteristics. The relevance of socioeconomic characteristics has, of course, rarely been salient except in the case of affirmative action, because consideration of these characteristics defies rational justification and their use exposes the institution to moral criticism. The high school background of the individual plays the most salient role, along with test scores (the two are related). High school grades weighted in favor of college preparatory programs, teacher recommendations, behavior records, and reports on motivation and aspiration from varied sources are essential. How heavily these criteria are weighted in college admissions can only be estimated, because institutional procedures are rarely specified or even summarized in terms suitable for independent review. Institutions, public and private, have instead treated admissions reporting as a private, almost artistic domain, tied to their institutional purposes and "personalities."

Nevertheless, institutional claims of meritocratic and rational procedures have grown. Academic credentials have become increasingly important. Increasing reliance is apparently being placed on high school records and tests: the Scholastic Aptitude Test (SAT) and American College Tests (ACT).[27] Along with a dramatic growth in the numbers and proportions of high school graduates applying to college, competition based on these criteria has increased:

With the exception of most two-year institutions and some land-grant universities that still maintain open admissions policies, most major universities and the better liberal arts colleges have become increasingly selective. Twenty-five years ago, a typical state university, like Illinois or North Carolina, admitted about a fourth of its freshman from the bottom half of their high school classes. Today, these institutions admit very few students who did not graduate from the top quarter of their class. [28]

On the other hand, student performance on standardized tests, particularly the SAT, improved during the 1960s and then underwent a slight but consistent decline in the 1970s (see Appendix, Table 3A-9). This decline in scores, however, does not reduce competition. Rather, it is more likely to increase competition by increasing uncertainty, given a greater concentration of scores in a narrow range. In fact, institutions have increasingly become dependent on the most marginal numerical variations in scores to judge between individual applicants.

The average achievement test scores vary considerably among types of institutions. The variance is generally related to their degree of selectivity in Astin's terms. That is, universities and four-year colleges have higher average SAT scores than two-year colleges. Private four-year institutions have higher scores than public ones. The range of scores of institutions in each type is, however, greater than the difference in the average of each type. The standard deviation (SD), shown in Table 3-4, indicates that, in terms of test scores, the average student in the least selective type of college would be within the normal range of students in the most selective type of institution. [29] In other words, the low end of the normal range (SD) at private four-year colleges is 656 (912 $\bar{x}$SAT -256SD $= 656$) which is 24 to 76 points below the average point score at two-year institutions. Assuming a normal distribution of scores, more than a third of the selective institutions have average scores below the average score of the least selective type. Yet, it is on the basis of such relatively small differences that students are frequently denied access to the college of their choice.

The effect of the emphasis on test scores on black access can only be partly determined because sufficient data is not available. More certainly, as long as admissions processes are clothed in secrecy, comprehensive data will never be available. Some assessment of the effects on blacks can be made, however, based on survey data. The findings of most surveys of admissions vary enormously but they generally agree that blacks do less well both on standardized achievement tests and grades. Because, as observed in *Equal Educational Opportunity: An Assessment*, the standardized test in-

Table 3-4   MEANS AND STANDARD DEVIATIONS OF THE SCHOLASTIC
APTITUDE TEST (SAT), SCHOLASTIC APTITUDE TEST—
MATHEMATIC (SAT-M), AND AMERICAN COLLEGE TEST
(ACT)
1974–75

Type of Institution	SAT	x̄ SAT − M	x̄ ACT
Private university			
Average	850	435	19.0
Standard deviation	438	223	9.9
Public university			
Average	835	445	18.6
Standard deviation	330	174	7.5
Private 4-year			
Average	912	469	20.4
Standard deviation	256	129	5.9
Public 4-year			
Average	849	451	18.6
Standard deviation	203	106	5.0
Private 2-year			
Average	680	326	15.0
Standard deviation	356	188	7.9
Public 2-year			
Average	732	383	16.2
Standard deviation	305	164	6.8

Source: Analysis of College Entrance Examination Board and American Council of Education data.

variably contains "cultural biases" against blacks, it is probably more detrimental to access than are high school grades. And grades themselves can easily be the product of bias, where and when blacks suffer discrimination and its effects in public schools. [30]

According to recent studies, the effect of grades on limiting black admissions is considerably smaller than that of testing. "Furthermore," the Carnegie Council reports, "grade-point average (GPA) or rank in class tends to be a more accurate predictor than test scores at the undergraduate level." A crucial flaw, however, in the reliance on tests, and to a lesser extent, grades, resides in the prevailing practices of standardizing predictions on the basis of white student performance. In addition, the Carnegie Council observes:

The classical and accepted model of fairness in selection has been to select those students with the highest predicted performance. . . . Thorndike (1971) demonstrated, however, that while that accepted procedure was fair to individuals, it was not necessarily fair to groups. He showed that under assumptions not out of line with known conditions, the usual selection procedure can result in selecting a smaller proportion of the minority group who could succeed as compared to the proportion of potentially successful majority students that is selected. [31]

What, then, can be done to measure the institutionally internal barriers to black access? It will first be necessary to make admissions practices more verifiable and objective. Initiative in regulating or guiding institutional admissions practices is an educational policy concern at all levels, but only the federal government is capable of verifying the objectivity of these practices on a national level. What must be kept in mind is that greater objectivity is not likely to come from increased use of standardized achievement tests. First, as long as their content remains culturally biased, if only marginally, a decreased use would be more consistent with objectivity. Second, as long as they fail to generate meaningful distinctions among black test-takers, and fail to predict black student performance as well as they do for whites, there will be an implicit racial bias in them. Third, and most important, the degree of accuracy of the tests themselves says nothing about how institutions may use or abuse them. Because admissions practices are rarely reported, and then only informally and in general terms, we can only estimate the role of testing.

Substantial evidence of the probable and potential barrier to college access that achievement tests may constitute for blacks emerges from the strong consensus of studies on this problem. That consensus is first that blacks generally score lower than whites on these tests, and second that their lower scores underestimate their ability to do college work. A clear illustration of the barrier to access thus created is found in a study of disadvantaged minority students, who by means of a special program called "A Better Chance," were able to overcome this barrier. Pointing to the "dangers of underprediction" of black student capabilities, which result from the typical use of SAT scores, the study finds:

> While it is true that minority students obtain lower test scores than their white colleagues at the same institution, there is strong evidence that those scores do not mean minority students are "unqualified" or even "less qualified" for admission to and scholastic success at these colleges. Although there is approximately a

200-point gap between the scores of the minority students studied and other students at sample colleges, their major fields and gradua-tion rates are comparable. And within the group of minority students, the graduation rates do not vary from those with the lowest scores to those with the highest. [32]

Had these students not had the help getting into college they received from the special program, and if there were no "race-concious" admissions process, those with the lower scores would almost certainly have been ex-cluded from the colleges to which they were admitted. The 200-point dif-ferential is almost as large as the total differential between the scores at all major types of colleges and universities, noted earlier. The difference be-tween the average SAT scores at black institutions and those at white in-stitutions is much smaller. Yet, few of these students would have been re-jected from black institutions on the basis of SAT scores, though they would probably have been rejected from white institutions without a special program for minorities.

As for the use of these tests in predicting student behavior, it is parallel to timing one of four runners in a relay race while judging the others by nonquantifiable, irregular criteria, and yet claiming objectivity. In this sense, the apparent exaggeration of institutional claims and expectations based on tests generates a barrier to blacks. A striking example of the way the entire admissions process may be biased is found in the role that other standardized tests may play in student access. Brin, Goslin, Glass and Goldberg in a Russell Sage Foundation study found that high school teachers frequently refer to student I.Q. test scores in making college recom-mendations and in providing counseling on college selection to students. [33] In other words, the effects of I.Q. testing can be felt, but not seen, in admis-sions decisions, a hidden effect that does not have the precision of culturally neutral quantifiable scores. It is therefore all the more likely that achieve-ment tests immeasurably penetrate the admissions process.

A large part of the college admissions question cannot be appropriately discussed under the rubric of student access, because each institution is in-dividual. In terms of access, as generally defined, admissions standards are not restrictive as long as blacks can get into *some* colleges. Open admissions at some four-year colleges and most two-year institutions has helped to solve the problems of blacks getting in somewhere. Of course, the real ques-tion for equality of opportunity is: where are blacks admitted; how are they admitted; with what constraints are they admitted; and what effect do selec-tive admissions have on their educational futures? These are all questions to be explored in chapter 4 where we will examine the irregular distribution of black students among institutions of higher education.

What Equal Access is Not

In brief, equal access to higher education as a whole is such a limited part of equal educational opportunity that it may be achieved under conditions of great inequality. Institutions vary enormously, and consequently, the kinds of educational services they provide to students vary. Two-year and four-year colleges and universities each offer different opportunities and different benefits to students. Traditionally, black institutions have different assets from white ones. "Prestigious" colleges tend to provide greater economic mobility than nonprestigious ones. Some institutions offer majors and programs that others do not. In all, the Carnegie Commission identifies twelve institutional types, some, but not all, of which are distinguished along value-related criteria.

Within institutions, the patterns of access and persistence (retention) for blacks vary enormously. For example, in the mid-seventies, 50 percent of black undergraduates were enrolled in two-year institutions, as compared with just over 40 percent of whites. Also, during the same period, a substantial majority, about 80 percent of blacks in all colleges, were enrolled in predominantly white institutions, while about 40 percent of blacks granted college degrees received them from black institutions. Thus, persistence rates for blacks at white institutions trail behind those at black institutions. Moreover, black enrollment tends to be heavily weighted toward some disciplines, particularly Social science and Education, more than others (see Appendix, Table 3A-5).

As blacks have approached parity with whites in simple access to higher education, a range of differences and inequalities among institutions has become accentuated. While it may be coincidental to the progress of racial integration, it would certainly not be inconsistent with the history of American education for racial inequality to subside at one point only to reemerge resilient elsewhere. (A newly-integrated neighborhood can easily lose property value.) Alexander Astin sees a consciously, if not intentionally, created hierarchy among institutions, which leads him to emphasize the avoidance of simple approaches to access:

> Many legislators and policy makers are content to define "access" simply in terms of the student's being able to enroll somewhere. . . .
>
> Rather, legislators and policy makers should be encouraged to take a more critical look at what has been somewhat euphemistically called "diversity," and to examine the consequences of current admissions policies in terms of such diversity.

To put institutional diversity in a somewhat different light, it is possible to argue that higher education in the United States has evolved into a highly refined institutional status hierarchy. Like most status systems, it comprises a few elite and widely known institutions, a substantial middle class, and a large number of relatively unknown institutions. While most people are familiar with the hierarchical nature of private higher education—with a few prestigious private universities occupying the top positions—it is not always recognized that a similar hierarchy exists within many public systems. Unlike the private hierarchy, which evolved more or less by historical accident, the hierarchies within the public system were developed as part of a conscious plan.[34]

In circumscribing the importance of access as a concept or methodological device, we should keep in mind that it does have continued value. It is capable of measuring some significant changes in the availability of higher education to those who have sought it and needed it for so long. By the same token, it has been useful in studies of the past few years for pointing out, in simple terms, the persistent underrepresentation of blacks in higher education years after the advent of affirmative action programs.

Most important at present, access may be an essential concept in defining, as well as guarding against, retrenchment from progress toward equality of opportunity. Particularly when we look at graduate and professional education, the concept of access will be useful in demonstrating the reversal of the heretofore upward trend in black student enrollment.

Finally, the concept of access can provide the broadest measure of the national impact of federal financial aid programs on college attendance, particularly since the legislative approach has generally not distinguished between types of institutions. That is not to say that the distribution of federal aid to students or institutions has been equal or balanced; because, in fact, it has not been so. The contrast, however, between the formal availability of federal funds to students and institutions and the actual distribution of funds should provide a valuable basis for policy-evaluation; particularly in the light of the federal debate over the extension of tax credits to higher education.

Greater Access for All

One of the often overlooked dimensions of increasing black undergraduate enrollment is the continual increase in the college enrollment of all students, whites included. As we shall see, this may be significant to black educational opportunity and mobility because it concerns the relative value and/or marketability of the baccalaureate degree. Yet, still more telling of public policy influence is that public attention to the comparative evaluation of changes in black and white enrollment figures seems to have been spurred by the very recent declines in white undergraduate proportions. Here again, as in chapter 2, caution and concern for the value implications of data should be exercised, because assessments of the status of blacks have too often been made with the single perspective of highlighting black progress without recognizing blacks' continual disadvantage. For example, *U.S. News and World Report* recently joined the trend of a great many magazines and newspapers by running a story emphasizing black socioeconomic comforts. The story indicated that the greatest progress had been made in the area of higher education. Thus, black enrollment between 1970 and 1977 is described as having increased 111.3 percent, while white enrollment is described as having increased only 30.4.[35] Among other things, what is misleading in the story, as a result of its failure to explain or extend the data, is the implication that blacks have been given, or have received more from, changes in the availability of college education than whites. The deception can be most simply identified by recognizing that blacks are still below most definitions of racial parity, less than 11 percent in 1976-77. In addition, if parity in total enrollment had been achieved, that achievement alone would say very little about equality of educational opportunity, because one must also examine the distribution of students.

Perhaps the most prevalent characteristic of misleading analyses of comparative change in enrollment by race is the reliance on percent change or growth figures tabulated within the racial group, and shown without corresponding absolute numbers. For example, the largest yearly gain for blacks in enrollment was made between 1970 and 1971, up 30.3 percent, while white enrollment went up only 9.1 percent. In contrast, the numbers show that blacks gained 158,000 students over their 1970 total, while whites gained 674,000 over their initial total of 7,413,000.[36] In other words, four times as many of the added number of students were white as were black.

In the latter observation, one is reminded that blacks constitute a minority of the population. At the same time, one needs to remember that that fact still says nothing about the need for change in unequal conditions. It is, first of all, essential that black gains be considerably greater than those of whites if real parity is to be attained. Second, what has not been sufficiently recognized is that it may be more costly and less effective, in terms of public resources, to push for comparable increases in white college enrollment, because whites are evidently a lot closer than blacks to the unquantifiable, but ever-present "saturation point." In this regard, we will turn later to the problem of education's cost and benefits, which indicate that the marginal advantages of investment in higher education for blacks are much higher than those for whites. For the moment, recent declines in total college enrollment may be sufficient to generate greater sensitivity to this point.

OVERALL STUDENT ENROLLMENT

The growth in total college student enrollment over the ten year period from 1966 to 1976 is substantial, if not dramatic, as shown in Table 3-5. There were 11,121,426 college and university students at all levels in 1976, almost twice the number enrolled in 1966. In the sixties, college students constituted a minority of those in their age group, 18-24, with high school diplomas. But by 1976 they were clearly the majority (see Table 3-3). Although the number of males enrolled has gone up more than 50 percent, the number of female students has more than doubled, an increase of 106 percent (Table 3-5).

Enrollment in private institutions made the smallest advance while enrollment in public institutions just about doubled. Similarly, for most distributions of enrollment—including full-time and part-time, predominantly black and white institutions, two-year, four-year and university types—gains in enrollment are evident. But also, as with the public-private distribution, it will be important to recognize that the gains are rarely evenly distributed.

The slight decline of 1.5 percent in total enrollment from 1975 to 1976, though suggestive of the future, scarcely puts a dent in the overall growth rate of the decade. Moreover, expectations of a long-range decline in college attendance have not been supported by preliminary estimates of total 1977 enrollment. According to the NCES, there has been a 3.3 percent increase in enrollment, bringing the 1977 fall enrollment to 11,487,967 students. "This increase was somewhat greater than the 2.5 percent increase projected by NCES in the spring of 1977. This fall's increase restored a 25 year trend of ever increasing enrollments that had been broken with a 1.5 percent decrease in 1976."[37]

The smallest part of the growth has generally come in what we have modeled as the "traditional" student sector of higher education (chapter 1). Schematically, this sector is defined by the young, white, full-time male student in a private or quasi-independent institution. Although this model does not hold at every point, it conforms substantially to the general pattern of change in enrollment.

In some ways, this model also fits the period of declining enrollment, 1975–76. Accordingly, one might logically expect the greatest declines to be in the traditional sector. This, however, is frequently not the case. Declines

Table 3-5   CHANGES IN FALL ENROLLMENT FROM 1966 THROUGH 1976

Year	All Institutions			Publicly Controlled Institutions	Privately Controlled Institutions
	Total	Men	Women		
Enrollment					
Fall 1976	11,121,426	5,860,215	5,261,211	8,712,634	2,408,792
Fall 1975	11,290,719	6,198,623	5,092,096	8,896,021	2,394,698
Fall 1974	10,321,539	5,667,053	4,654,486	8,049,595	2,271,944
Fall 1973	9,694,297	5,414,164	4,280,133	7,478,407	2,215,890
Fall 1972	9,297,787	5,275,902	4,021,885	7,122,875	2,174,912
Fall 1971	9,025,031	5,242,740	3,782,291	6,854,635	2,170,346
Fall 1970	8,649,368	5,076,023	3,573,345	6,476,058	2,173,310
Fall 1969	8,066,233	4,775,622	3,290,611	5,939,513	2,126,720
Fall 1968	7,571,636	4,505,833	3,065,803	5,469,472	2,102,164
Fall 1967	6,963,687	4,158,557	2,805,130	4,850,330	2,113,357
Fall 1966	6,438,477	3,880,557	2,557,920	4,381,086	2,057,391
Percent change					
Fall 1975 to 1976	− 1.5	− 5.5	+ 3.3	− 2.1	+ 0.6
Fall 1974 to 1975	+ 9.4	+ 9.4	+ 9.4	+ 10.5	+ 5.4
Fall 1973 to 1974	+ 6.5	+ 4.7	+ 8.7	+ 7.6	+ 2.5
Fall 1972 to 1973	+ 4.3	+ 2.6	+ 6.4	+ 5.0	+ 1.9
Fall 1971 to 1972	+ 3.0	+ 0.6	+ 6.3	+ 3.9	+ 0.2
Fall 1970 to 1971	+ 4.3	+ 3.3	+ 5.8	+ 5.8	− 0.1
Fall 1969 to 1970	+ 7.2	+ 6.3	+ 8.6	+ 9.0	+ 2.2
Fall 1968 to 1969	+ 6.5	+ 6.0	+ 7.3	+ 8.5	+ 1.2
Fall 1967 to 1968	+ 8.7	+ 8.4	+ 9.3	+ 12.8	− 0.5
Fall 1966 to 1967	+ 8.2	+ 7.2	+ 9.7	+ 10.7	+ 2.7
Total percent change	72.7	51.0	105.7	98.9	17.1

Source: NCES, "Opening Fall Enrollment Final," *Bulletin* (August 1977).

in this sector are smaller on the whole. Where there is variability in this enrollment pattern, it does not appear to be random in relationship to the nontraditional sector. This leads to the recognition that the traditional sector is first a meaningful phenomenon with a characteristic behavior pattern, and second that it can be characterized by its great resistance to change. Effectively then, much of the integration of underrepresented groups into higher education occurs at nontraditional institutions or in marginally institutionalized patterns at the traditional ones. The extreme example of marginal integration would be "more black females in part-time attendance at two-year institutions." Aside from racial distribution, a look at Table 3-6 should indicate the pattern to be explored when we come to distribution.

The General Problem of Financing Higher Education

Like most goods and services in the American marketplace, the costs of higher education can, in a limited sense, be said to hit everyone in the pocketbook. Everyone contributes to higher education through taxes: federal, state, and sometimes local. Every family with a dependent student is likely to have to pay for higher education or, at least, carefully examine the cost involved. Only the very rich, a small minority of Americans, do not face the problem of financing higher education with serious concern. Still, it goes almost without saying that the financial problem hits everyone unequally, depending on their income and the type of higher education they seek.

It is understandable that economic factors play a large role in determining college attendance patterns for a vast majority of Americans. There remain, of course, cultural, social, political, and personal values attached to college attendance, but these have rarely been the focus of government education policy in recent years.[38] While motives for federal government support in higher education may be traced to a range of concerns for the national "interest," the actual focus of support is primarily financial, and largely geared to student aid (although funds frequently go to the institution). Research and development assistance from the federal government has been a comparatively small, but important, second.

Federal financial aid to students corresponds, for the most part, with major changes in enrollment. Along with federal aid, private financial assistance to students has grown rapidly in the past ten or more years. Private grants, however, have often been "no need" or "merit" awards. Federal aid, however, is primarily based on need. In addition, loans to students, both public and private, as well as state and local assistance, have generally corresponded to enrollment changes.

Table 3-6 FALL ENROLLMENT FOR ALL INSTITUTIONS OF HIGHER EDUCATION (IN THOUSANDS)
1975-76

| | 1975 | | | | | | 1976 | | | | | |
| | Public | | Private | | All Institutions | | Public | | Private | | All Institutions | |
Students	Number	Percent	Number	Percent	Number	Percent	Number	Percent	Number	Percent	Number	Percent
Full-time												
Male	2,959	33.3	1,006	42.0	3,965	35.1	2,757	31.6	985	40.9	3,742	33.6
Female	2,220	24.9	737	30.8	2,958	26.2	2,283	26.2	778	32.3	3,061	27.5
All students	5,178	58.2	1,744	72.8	6,923	61.3	5,040	57.9	1,763	73.2	6,803	67.1
Part-time												
Male	1,875	21.0	358	14.9	2,233	19.8	1,776	20.4	342	14.2	2,118	19.0
Female	1,842	20.7	292	12.2	2,134	18.9	1,896	21.8	304	12.6	2,200	19.8
All students	3,717	41.8	650	27.1	4,368	38.7	3,672	42.1	646	26.8	4,318	38.8
Total enrollment	8,896	100.0	2,395	100.0	11,291	100.0	8,712	100.0	2,409	100.0	11,121	100.0

Source: Analysis of NCES data, "Opening Fall Enrollment in Colleges and Universities 1977, Preliminary Estimates," *Bulletin* (December 1977).

The critical points, however, in public policy's role in the relationship between financial aid and student enrollment are found where the correlation breaks down. First, there would appear to be a capacity for the federal government to sustain or increase enrollment by increasing its dollar input. Yet, data from the last few years have begun to cast serious doubt on that idea. The most salient question to be explored, in this regard, concerns the effectiveness of refining federal standards for financial eligibility. Second, there has been a relative decline in private funds available to students, making government contributions at all levels increasingly important to the viability of higher education. Questions about government impact on the whole of higher education, institutions and students alike, need to be explored further. Such an exploration can begin by comparing the explicit purposes of federal financial aid programs, as described by NCES, with the actual outcomes of that aid, to which we will turn next.

An important component of Federal aid to institutions of higher education is financial assistance to students. There are five major U.S. Office of Education (OE) student assistance programs: Basic Educational Opportunity Grants (BEOG); Supplemental Educational Opportunity Grants (SEOG); College Work-Study (CWS); National Direct Student Loans (NDSL); and Guaranteed Student Loans (GSL). The Basic Educational Opportunity Grants programs offer eligible students who are enrolled at least half-time direct grants of up to $1,600 a year (or half the cost of attending the institution of their choice), the awards being made on the basis of financial need.

The Supplemental Educational Opportunity Grants program, as its name suggests, supplements the BEOG program. OE gives funds for this program to participating institutions, which make the awards to students. Students who are attending at least half-time are eligible to receive from $200 to $1,500 per year, or up to one half the amount of the other student aid that must be provided by the institution on a matching basis, up to a maximum grant of $4,000 over four academic years.

The College Work-Study program provides grants to institutions for partial reimbursement of wages of students enrolled at least half-time. Students may work up to twenty hours a week during school and up to forty hours a week during vacations. The participating institution decides who get jobs.

The National Direct Student Loan program provides grants to institutions for making low interest loans to their students. Undergraduates enrolled at least half-time can get as much as $2,500 in low-interest loans over their first 2 years and up to $5,000 total, while graduate and professional students may receive up to a total of $10,000, including loans for their undergraduate education. Repayment of the loan extends over a 10-year period after leaving school.

The Guaranteed Student Loan program is designed to encourage banks and other commercial lending agencies to provide low-interest loans of up to $2,500 a year, up to a maximum of $7,500, for students who are enrolled at least half-time. The Federal Government insures or reinsures the loans (if they were originally insured by State or nonprofit institutions) and pays the interest on the loans while students attend college if their family incomes are below $25,000 annually. The loan repayment period is 10 years after leaving school. [39]

BROAD IMPACT OF FEDERAL STUDENT AID ON HIGHER EDUCATION

Federal dollars spent on student aid increased consistently until the mid-seventies. Its subsequent stagnation corresponds generally with the stagnation in total enrollment (see Figure 3-5).

From Figure 3-5, one also gets a strong impression of the extent to which noneducational social forces may affect federal support to higher education. In particular, the abrupt drop in funds from the G.I. Bill between 1976 and 1977 may well represent the educational costs of peace. The benefits to individuals, however, have been relatively small compared to World War II benefits. Major national military involvement has often preceded an important influx of money into higher education. Thus, with the end of the Vietnam War, the potential for this source of support vanished for the foreseeable future.

Federal aid to students in other categories has apparently not taken up the slack. The only clear increases in the 1974–77 period have been in BEOG and Social Security benefits, and the latter has not been substantial. Moreover, Social Security benefits for education are not easily altered for educational policy. In terms of managing educational policy, Social Security benefits to students constitute an environmental condition of education.

In the remaining federal aid programs, those administered by the Office of Education (OE), there was some growth in the 1974–77 period. The proportion of students receiving these OE grants and loans stabilized at about one-fifth of total enrollment, but the amounts of individual benefits rose significantly. The greatest increase of benefits were in BEOG, which also had by far the largest number of grant recipients. The smallest increase,

Figure 3-5   GROWTH IN FEDERAL STUDENT AID (IN MILLIONS)

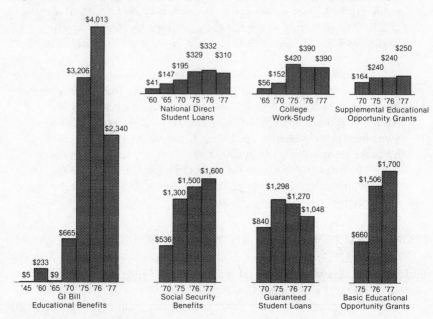

Source: *The Chronicle of Higher Education*, XV, 6, (October 11, 1977), p. 5.

$10 per recipient, was in SEOG, an insignificant increase (see Table 3-7).

Student demands for financial aid have remained stable when measured in terms of family dollar income. An overview of Census Bureau income distribution data shows only a small decline in the family incomes of college students from 1967 to 1976. What the family income data show, whether stable or declining, is that relatively poor students are going to college because growth in inflation has raised incomes in the larger economy. Still, because a constant dollar index is used, it is safe to say that the figures do not disguise a mass influx of the poor into higher education.

Between 1967 and 1976, the percentage of dependent students with annual family incomes under $5,000 (1967 dollars) was up a few percentage points in 1976 from the initial 20 percent. But the proportion of students below that income level had been as large in 1969. The percentage with family incomes above $15,000 was down about 5 percent from 68 percent in 1967. Yet, both movements were counterbalanced overall by a proportional growth of students in the middle-income brackets. This latter group, with incomes below $15,000 and above $5,000, is often deceptively defined as the broad middle class.

An important note of caution here: these estimates may have to be replaced if we concentrate on black students, because the estimates are based on dependent students only. Joseph Froomkin's research, among others', indicates that the data are biased by grossly undercounting lower income students—students who are disproportionately "independent."[40] Nevertheless, the picture of change in income ratios over time may not be seriously affected, because the bias has been evident for some time.

Whatever income ratio data are used, the relative growth in the middle class student population has not been impressive. Depending on the distribution and the definition of data, it may be larger or smaller. This is important in the context of the major federal debate over income tax credits and the expansion of grant support geared to the middle class. Again, we

Figure 3-6 COLLEGE ENROLLMENT RATES OF DEPENDENT FAMILY MEMBERS, 18 TO 24 YEARS OLD, BY FAMILY INCOME October 1967–October 1976

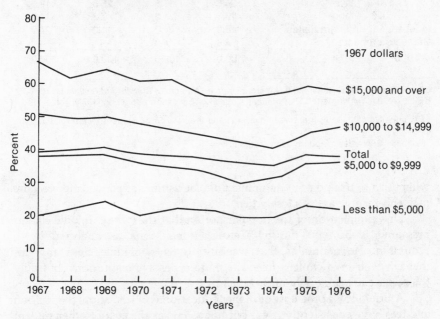

Source: U.S. Bureau of the Census, Current Population Reports, Series P-20, No. 318, "School Enrollment—Social and Economic Characteristics of Students: October 1976" (Washington, D.C.: U.S. Government Printing Office, 1978.)

Table 3-7 FEDERAL STUDENT AID TO HIGHER EDUCATION
1974–75 and 1976–77

Characteristics	Total (unduplicated count)		BEOG	
	1974–75[a]	1976–77[b]	1974–75	1976–77
Number of recipients	1,584,000	1,937,000	543,000	1,411,000
Average award	—	—	$620	$820
Sex				
Women	51.0	53.5	54.5	55.1
Men	49.0	46.5	45.5	44.9
Ethnic group				
Minority	33.6	34.9	40.1	43.0
Nonminority	66.4	65.1	52.0	57.0
Status				
Dependent undergraduates				
Family income				
Less than $7,500	33.3	32.9	53.5	43.5
$7,500–$11,999	24.8	17.8	25.3	19.6
$12,000 or more	19.1	21.2	7.3	11.9
Independent undergraduates	18.0	24.0	14.0	24.9
Graduate students	4.8	4.0	—	—
Total	100.0	100.0	100.0	100.0

Source: Frank Atelsek and Irene Gomberg, *Estimated Number of Student Aid Recipients 1976–77*, HEPR, No. 6, (Washington, D.C.: American Council of Education September 1977), Table 11.

[a] Excludes Guaranteed Student Loan program, and *includes* State Student Incentive Grant program.

[b] Excludes Guaranteed Student Loan program.

will return to this point in the context of black student financial aid, because race and income are so closely tied.

One explanation of the popular notion that the (white) middle class is pressured is brought out by Census Bureau data as analyzed by J. Froomkin. He maintains that wealthy students, middle class and up, through their own choice, go to the more expensive institutions, but only the upper class can easily afford them.

A brief look at the cost of higher education will first show that tuition and fees have consistently risen, but not as fast as the cost of other student expenses. For all kinds of institutions, public and private, two-year, four-year, and university, the annual rate of increase has been less than five per-

	SEOG		CWS		NDSL		GSL	
	1974–75	1976–77	1974–75	1976–77	1974–75	1976–77	1974–75	1976–77
	350,000	432,000	575,000	698,000	749,000	757,000	669,000	695,000
	$540	$550	$560	$670	$690	$750	$1,250	$1,300
	54.1	53.7	54.0	55.0	49.6	49.7	45.0	46.3
	45.9	46.3	46.0	45.0	50.4	50.3	54.2	53.7
	47.8	39.1	32.6	29.3	20.9	25.7	18.0	17.0
	52.3	60.9	67.5	70.7	71.1	74.3	82.0	83.0
	54.3	35.4	38.5	28.1	30.8	21.8	13.5	13.5
	22.4	20.5	25.9	18.4	24.7	17.8	18.2	12.9
	5.3	18.6	17.2	28.0	21.4	31.0	37.3	40.6
	18.1	25.6	14.5	20.5	17.0	21.6	15.6	18.4
	—	—	3.9	5.0	6.1	7.8	15.4	14.6
	100.0	100.0	100.0	100.0	100.0	100.0	100.0	100.0

cent since 1971. An inflation rate that low in the broader economy is a long-lost ideal.

Citing data developed by the Congressional Budget Office, Lois Rice of the College Entrance Examination Board observes

> that family incomes of those with 18–24 year old dependents have been rising faster than college costs in the last decade, so that the percent of family income required to finance higher education has been declining rather than rising. This is not to say that the 1967 college financing burden was just right—there is no "just right" proportion in such matters—but there do appear to be far more obvious culprits for the pinch about which families are now complaining. For

Table 3-8   THE INCREASE IN COLLEGE COSTS SINCE 1971

| | *Resident Students* | | | | | |
	1971–72	1972–73	1973–74	1974–75	1975–76	1976–77
Public institutions						
2-year	*	*	$2,024	$2,153	$2,411	$2,588
Tuition and fees	*	*	251	287	301	389
Room and board	*	*	1,032	1,086	1,213	1,305
Other expenses	*	*	741	780	897	897
4-year	$1,875	$1,985	$2,242	$2,400	$2,679	$2,890
Tuition and fees	439	465	498	541	578	621
Room and board	890	945	1,042	1,116	1,272	1,371
Other expenses	546	575	702	743	829	898
Private institutions						
2-year	$2,484	$2,540	$3,194	$3,617	$3,690	$4,009
Tuition and fees	1,192	1,210	1,389	1,578	1,652	1,740
Room and board	877	910	1,159	1,303	1,239	1,410
Other expenses	415	420	646	736	799	859
4-year	$3,171	$3,280	$3,693	$4,039	$4,391	$4,663
Tuition and fees	1,652	1,725	1,942	2,080	2,240	2,329
Room and board	1,007	1,035	1,159	1,207	1,302	1,429
Other expenses	512	520	592	752	849	905
Proprietary institutions	*	*	*	$3,817	$3,822	$4,271
Tuition and fees	*	*	*	1,651	1,627	1,808
Room and board	*	*	*	1,387	1,363	1,507
Other expenses	*	*	*	779	832	956

Source: The Chronicle of Higher Education, XVI, 7 (April 10, 1978), p. 15. Based on College Scholarship Service data.

*Insufficient data.

example, from 1967 to December 1977 food prices on the average rose 96 percent, medical care 124 percent, household services (less rent) 121 percent, fuel oil 188 percent, and all items 86 percent—with college costs up about 72 percent. [41]

The majority of all dependent students with yearly family incomes below $20,000, according to Froomkin's SIE data, received just over half their financial support for college from government in 1976–77. Above that income level, parental support is the dominant factor. [42]

Adequate data on the distribution of college costs and how Americans pay for them are only now beginning to emerge. Consequently, this discussion proceeds cautiously. Any review, however, of the historical development of American education would reinforce recent data that indicate a

Commuter Students

1977–78	1978–79	1971–72	1972–73	1973–74	1974–75	1975–76	1976–77	1977–78	1978–79
$2,707	$2,666	$1,526	$1,635	$1,665	$1,922	$2,058	$2,223	$2,314	$2,426
389	408	185	200	251	287	301	387	389	408
1,375	1,320	566	615	681	778	791	813	864	897
944	938	775	820	733	857	966	1,023	1,061	1,121
$3,005	$3,054	$1,659	$1,760	$1,775	$2,085	$2,266	$2,448	$2,486	$2,604
621	651	439	465	498	541	578	621	621	651
1,450	1,436	494	545	625	704	716	793	780	817
934	967	726	750	652	890	972	1,034	1,085	1,136
$4,113	$4,264	$1,993	$2,090	$2,583	$3,287	$3,421	$3,595	$3,680	$3,922
1,812	1,930	1,192	1,210	1,389	1,578	1,652	1,740	1,812	1,930
1,422	1,461	382	395	647	917	850	902	874	966
879	873	419	485	547	792	919	953	994	1,026
$4,905	$5,110	$2,599	$2,745	$3,162	$3,683	$3,950	$4,141	$4,331	$4,577
2,476	2,647	1,652	1,725	1,942	2,080	2,240	2,329	2,476	2,647
1,483	1,536	469	525	721	796	778	840	842	890
946	927	478	495	499	807	932	972	1,013	1,040
$4,395	$4,580	*	*	*	$3,414	$3,382	$3,726	$3,914	$4,151
1,895	2,038	*	*	*	1,651	1,627	1,808	1,895	2,038
1,568	1,579	*	*	*	946	863	899	963	1,015
932	963	*	*	*	817	892	1,019	1,056	1,098

direct correlation between family income and college expenditures. While the Froomkin data shown in Table 3-9 are not conclusive, they are credible first because they are consistent with other sources of information, and second because they are based primarily on the Survey of Income and Education (SIE), the most comprehensive survey on the subject.

A plurality of the low-income students, 36 percent, are enrolled in institutions costing $2,000 or less a year, while a plurality of those in the wealthiest category, 38 percent, are enrolled in the most expensive institutions. What is perhaps most striking, here, is the distribution of students who are middle class, but distinctly less than affluent. Students with family incomes between $12,000 and $15,000 are about as likely to attend the most expensive institutions as they are to attend the least expensive ones. If the public college enrollment were discounted, the bias of income and college

Table 3-9   PERCENTAGE DISTRIBUTION OF COSTS FOR FULL-TIME
DEPENDENT STUDENTS BY PARENTAL INCOMES*
1976–77

	Costs				
Income	Less Than $2,200	$2,201– $3,300	$3,301– $4,400	$4,400 and Over	Total
$0–$7,500	36	30	21	13	100.0
$7,501–$12,000	35	27	20	18	100.0
$12,001–$15,000	27	27	20	26	100.0
$15,001–$25,000	25	26	21	28	100.0
$25,000 and over	15	25	22	38	100.0
Average	28	27	21	24	100.0

Source: Joseph Froomkin, Prepared Testimony before Committee on Ways and Means, U.S.
House of Representatives, "Middle Income Relief" (February 17, 1978). Based on 1973 CPS and
1976 SIE data.
*Costs and incomes inflated to 1976/77.

costs would be much greater, and the middle would be more heavily
weighted toward expensive institutions.

PATTERNS OF ENROLLMENT AND FINANCIAL AID

Characteristics of participation in higher education for the general student population indicate that access has grown substantially, so much so
that growth should not to be expected to continue at anywhere near its past
rate. At the same time, the opportunity to acquire an advanced education
has apparently not been equal at all, even without regard to race. The structure of higher education, both institutionally and socioeconomically, tends
to create an unequal distribution of students, based on many nonintellectual
characteristics—a distribution which, in turn, creates a gap between equal
access to college and real equality of educational opportunity. Internal
characteristics or structural biases of higher education are summarized by
the concepts of individual performance, institutional purpose, and social
responsibility.

These structural biases, it shall be argued, are exacerbated when race
becomes a factor. For blacks, then, who already suffer discrimination external to the institution, progress toward equality of access is made only with
great difficulty. Moreover, the progress made is being mortgaged to an unequal distribution, which serves to obscure a real denial of equal educational
opportunity.

Access to Higher Education for Black Undergraduates

Although equal access to higher education constitutes only the threshold of the problem of equal educational opportunity for blacks, it has still not been achieved, although progress has been made. If one relies on what we consider an artifically restrictive definition, however—matching inequalities of college enrollment with inequalities in high school gradua-tion—then parity can be foreseen in the near future. If, on the other hand, a concern for equality is to be paramount, then educational policy cannot segment social/institutional responsibility to create sterile pockets of "pari-ty" as if individuals could pursue educational mobility from the start—from high school—without being influenced by awareness of higher education. The end of a path in education, as elsewhere, may determine the readiness with which one takes the beginning and intermediate steps on that path.

A point made earlier bears reiteration here. An awareness of educa-tional opportunity all along the path to a terminal degree conditions up-ward mobility and student effort at a very early age. The recent data drawn from the National Longitudinal Survey (NLS), the major data source of its kind, indicate that teenagers' orientations toward college while in high school have a stronger affect on their rates of graduation and access to col-lege than previously supposed. This is especially important for blacks and others who have experienced discrimination, because assurance of real op-portunities in their educational future is essential to overcome a justifiably nurtured skepticism about the existence of equal opportunity.

COLLEGE EXPECTATIONS AND HIGH SCHOOL COMPLETION

Specifically, high school students who expect to go to college or plan early for that possibility must select an appropriate college preparatory cur-riculum. For those so young, the decision is usually made or suggested by adults in the school, in the community, and at home. Significant factors in the failure of black high school students to prepare themselves adequately for college, in terms of academic programs, are inadequate guidance and counseling:

> According to data from the National Longitudinal Study, 33% of the black high school seniors in 1972 thought that they were enrolled in an academic or college preparatory program (compared with 49% of the white students). Yet, in that same sample of high school seniors, the school administrators reported that only 27% of the black students were in academic or college preparatory programs (49% of the white students were identified as being in such pro-grams). These data suggest that 6% of the black students may have

71

believed they were enrolled in a curriculum that would provide them with adequate preparation to enroll in college, when in fact they were not. [43]

For black teenagers, much more than for white teenagers, the "significant others" are outside the educational community, because blacks are substantially underrepresented in positions of educational leadership.

Robert Crain and Rita Mahard's study based on NLS data finds that a major disadvantage for black students in desegregated high schools emerges from the discouragement they experience at the hands of white teachers. Their college expectations are apparently low before they are put to the test. Crain and Mahard conclude:

> In our attempt to explain the low attendance and survival rates of Southern blacks from white high schools, two interrelated factors emerge offering an unpleasant but convincing explanation. .... It would appear that race of teachers, not of students is a significant part of the college attendance and survival problem in the South. What is it exactly that teachers do that has such an impact on Southern black college outcomes?
>
> First ... teachers in predominantly white schools grade their black students relative to white student performance .... When the absence of black teachers discourages black students from further education, the picture becomes bleak indeed. We hypothesize that those black students who do manage to get into college despite poor grades and lack of encouragement may not be going to the kinds of colleges where survival is likely. [44]

A student's expectations are determined by current and past environment, including family, school and peer group influence, socioeconomic status, and personal characteristics. [45] These environmental factors mediate the high school student's awareness of college opportunities. The student learns from parents, friends, and teachers whether or not it is realistic to expect to go to college. At the same time, unless there are real and attractive college opportunities, the environmental encouragement to stay in school, high school and/or college, will be weak and ineffective. Accordingly, there is a strong correspondence between student plans to attend college and the educational background of their parents (see Appendix, Figure 3A-2).

A more significant aspect of the impact of the expectation of college on high school performance is the difference between high school graduates and high school seniors in their college expectations. Taking only those high school graduates, ages 18–24, who are *not* attending college, blacks are proportionately more likely than whites to be "interested in attending college."

Yet, among high school seniors, blacks are less likely than whites to *plan* to attend college, according to NCES. Moreover, recent black high school graduates show a stronger interest in college than black high school seniors even though they do not actually go to college. Apparently, black high school graduates can be distinguished from those blacks who have not graduated by the stronger college-orientation of the graduates. Apparently, college expectations also play a positive, though imprecise, role in the rate of black high school graduation. [46]

RACIAL PARITY AMONG HIGH SCHOOL GRADUATES

Even assuming the restricted definition of parity, one should not feel comfortable that the proportional growth in black college enrollment is significantly due to a passing coincidence of external factors. First, the abrupt 1976 decline in white enrollment, and second, the long term but ephemeral expansion of the general and educational economies have, in opposite ways, contributed to this proportional increase. Relying for the moment on the census data for 1974 (which are not precise enough for other use), the black proportion of the total college population went up only one tenth of one percent in the two years under study, from 9.2 percent in 1974 to 9.3 percent in 1976. That is, by far, the least impressive increase in nearly a decade.

In Figure 3-7, two important aspects of black progress toward parity of access are evident. First, blacks have lost substantial ground in equalizing college attendance rates with high school graduation rates. That these losses have occurred when the black proportion of the population was fairly stable is important to note. The recent rate of growth, which is likely to hold for at least the next decade, will place a comparatively greater demand on higher education for black access. Second, the extension of the lines that chart the years 1972 to 1976, shows that most of the advance was made before 1974.

Because the data up to 1974 are from the Census Bureau, and, after that year, are based on the Office of Civil Rights (OCR) reports, we can not assume that the intervals are precise. [47] The trend in the data, however, is unmistakable. The rate of growth in black college enrollment has never been as small as in the years under study except in those prior to 1967, and between 1972 and 1973, when enrollment actually dropped. On the average, in the decade since 1966 the yearly rate of growth in black enrollment has been 4.7 percent, almost five times as large as in the past two years combined.

As far as the need for public effort to support greater college access for blacks is concerned, we are apparently a long way away from the point of

Figure 3-7   BLACK PROPORTION OF TOTAL POPULATION, ALL
COLLEGE STUDENTS AND ALL HIGH SCHOOL
GRADUATES, 14-34 YEARS OLD
Fall 1964-76

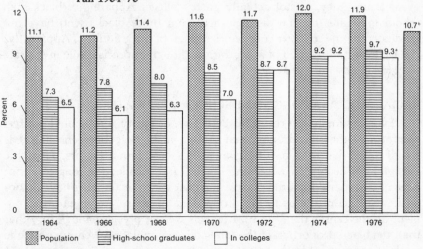

Source: Reanalysis of data from U.S. Bureau of the Census, *School Enrollment—Social and
Economic Characteristics of Students, October 1975*, Table 2. Data published in ISEP, *Equal
Educational Opportunity: More Promise Than Progress*, p. 13.

[a] This figure is derived from DHEW, Office for Civil Rights, *Opening Fall Enrollment, 1976*.

[b] This figure is derived from data from the U.S. Bureau of the Census, Series P-20, No. 319, *School
Enrollment—Social and Economic Characteristics of Students: October 1976*.

saturation. The number of blacks in the American population who have
completed four years of college is still relatively small. The remaining
vacuum, created by so many years of discrimination, is enormous. For example, the percent of blacks with four years of college is only 4.4 percent, as
compared to 8.8 percent in the general population over 24 years old. That
figure for blacks is only slightly less than half the comparable figure for
whites, 9.1 percent (see Table 3-10).

If the gap between the need for an adult, black, college-educated
population and the historical black output of higher education is to be
filled, then progress in that direction only really began after 1974, when
black college enrollment passed 9.1 percent of the student population.
Turning to the data on enrollment in 1976-77, the last year for which data is
available, what we see at first glance is considerably more comforting than
what emerges on close inspection.

For aggregate data on black enrollment in higher education, we draw
primarily from sources of the U.S. Office for Civil Rights. While we also use

Table 3-10   PERCENTAGE OF POPULATION 25 YEARS OLD AND
OLDER HAVING COMPLETED 4 YEARS OF COLLEGE
1976

Race/Gender	Total Population (in Thousands)	Population Having Completed 4 Years of College (in Thousands)	Percent of Population Having Completed 4 Years of College
Total population	118,848	10,401	8.75
Male	55,902	5,728	10.25
Female	62,946	4,672	7.42
White	105,603	9,591	9.08
Male	49,951	5,368	10.75
Female	55,651	4,223	7.59
Black	11,375	501	4.40
Male	5,048	198	3.92
Female	6,327	303	4.79

Source: Analysis of data from U.S. Bureau of the Census, Current Population Reports, Series P-20, No. 314, "Educational Attainment in the U.S.: March 1977 and 1976" (Washington, D.C.: U.S. Government Printing Office, 1977).

and compare multiple sources of data, we consider the OCR tabulations something of the standard because only OCR has a legal federal responsibility to tabulate college attendance "accurately" by race. Like all other research in this area, however, OCR's methods of organizing the data are subject to variable and uncertain standards of coding. Moreover, in dealing with a college population as small as the black one, seemingly minor statistical discrepancies may easily create substantial distortions of college attendance. Unfortunately, such discrepancies are not uncommon in data on minority education. In the case of OCR, perhaps the greatest source of discrepancy in data comes from reports by individual institutions to the Office. Given the institutional obligations under the Civil Rights Act of 1964 and under federal affirmative action orders, there may be a consistent tendency for institutions to overrepresent slightly their minority enrollment figures. Yet, considering that there are about 3000 institutions of higher education, it is probably neither possible nor desirable to insist on precise variation. Still, in rare instances, we have adjusted the figures in subsectors of the black population based on additional verification. [48] In addition, we have found that interpreting minority enrollment from OCR figures is not as straightforward a matter as it might initially seem.

According to the data, there were 11,079,370 students in all institutions of higher education in 1976. This total, it may be recalled, is about forty thousand less than the one reported earlier, which is drawn from the HEGIS reports of the National Center for Educational Statistics (NCES). Although OCR data come from the NCES compilations, they undergo additional verification before being released by OCR. In whichever direction the difference of totals may be explained, it is not critical for such a large population. Similarly large discrepancies for black enrollment would be significant.[49]

For blacks we find a total enrollment of 1,034,455, or 9.33 percent of the total student population, in higher education. Of this number, 866,315 are undergraduates, or 10.2 percent of all undergraduates are black (see Table 3-11). Excluding the "unclassified" students from the total, black undergraduates constitute 91.9 percent of the total black enrollment in higher education. By contrast, all undergraduates constitute a much smaller percent, 86.5 percent of the total student populations (Table 3-11). This imbalance will be important in understanding where the most severe problem of black access lies, at the graduate and professional level. In this chapter, we should look more closely at undergraduate enrollment.

If going to college means much for equal opportunity beyond college, then blacks should be able to expect the rewards of equal or greater college access to be comparable to the rewards traditionally acquired through a college education. This means, first of all, that access will be followed, for the most part, by four or five years of study as an undergraduate, and then by the granting of a baccalaureate degree. Second, it should mean that the courses of study and the degree granted will conform to reasonable choices for professional/intellectual development and economic participation. Ultimately, it should mean equal opportunity in professional and economic life.

In the educational process, real equal opportunity may be pursued through many patterns of enrollment, and not necessarily the traditional pattern to which we have referred. There have been, for example, tremendous increases in the numbers of two-year college students, in the numbers of older students, and in the numbers of part-time undergraduates in the past few years. All these changes in enrollment and other patterns apply to all racial and ethnic groups. Students may all reasonably expect to profit from their nontraditional approaches to higher education. The changes may not apply "equally", however, to racially/ethnically different students. To the extent that the patterns of access are unequal, the benefits are also likely to be unequal.

The best evidence of whether the traditional goals of educational access are being effectively shared by blacks is, first, the extent to which black pat-

Table 3-11 FULL AND PART-TIME ENROLLMENT IN INSTITUTIONS OF HIGHER EDUCATION Fall 1976

Enrollment Status	Black			Total Minority			White			Total	
	Number	Percent of Black Enrolled	Percent of Total Population	Number	Percent of Minority Enrolled	Percent of Total Population	Number	Percent of White Enrolled	Percent of Total Population	Number	Percent of Total Population Enrolled
Undergraduate											
Full-time	605,116	69.84	10.19	1,010,765	67.73	17.02	4,820,716	69.95	81.21	5,935,902	69.72
Part-time	261,199	30.25	10.13	481,577	32.37	18.68	2,070,377	30.05	80.32	2,577,408	30.27
Graduate											
Full-time	22,058	33.75	5.13	41,565	37.00	9.66	340,926	37.51	79.31	429,839	39.61
Part-time	43,287	66.24	6.60	70,587	63.00	10.77	565,933	62.30	86.36	655,292	60.39
Professional											
Full-time	10,029	89.69	4.52	20,533	90.50	9.27	198,071	90.00	89.44	221,453	90.00
Part-time	1,152	10.30	4.73	2,136	9.50	8.77	21,988	10.00	90.34	24,337	10.00
Total undergraduate, graduate, and professional											
Full-time	637,203	67.58		1,072,854	65.93		5,359,713	66.84		6,587,194	66.91
Part-time	305,638	32.42		554,300	34.06		2,658,298	33.15		3,257,037	33.02
Total	942,841	100.00	9.57	1,627,154	100.00	16.52	8,018,011	100.00	81.44	9,844,231	100.00
Total undergraduate	866,315	91.88		1,492,342	91.71		6,891,093	85.94		8,513,310	11.02
Total graduate	65,345	6.93		112,152	6.89		908,859	11.33		1,085,131	2.59
Total professional	11,181	1.18	7.12	22,669	1.39	13.30	220,059	2.74	85.03	245,790	11.15
Unclassified	91,614	8.85	9.33	164,384	9.17	16.17	1,050,317	11.58	81.84	1,235,139	
Total	1,034,455			1,791,547			9,068,328			11,079,370	

Source: Analysis of data from U.S. Department of Health, Education and Welfare, Office for Civil Rights, *Opening Fall Enrollment,* 1976.

Note: Percentages may not total 100% because of rounding.

terns of enrollment conform to those of Americans who have enjoyed the success that comes of meeting those goals. This measure implies that traditional enrollment can be a useful standard against which to measure enrollment patterns of blacks. Yet, traditions in education, as elsewhere, change; they adapt to different situations and become more or less efficacious under changed socioeconomic conditions. We therefore should be open to the possibility that irregularities in black enrollment, vis-à-vis most college students, may emerge from the most efficacious, adaptive response to their living conditions.

We now turn to a brief exploration of different modes of access among college undergraduates. Although most of our questions about enrollment status will be dealt with in terms of distribution, some of them are also appropriate to the discussion of access, because access to college has never been open ended. Certain prescriptions about the kind of access, internal and external to the particular institution, are necessary from the start, the day one registers or is admitted to college.

COMMITMENTS ON REGISTRATION DAY

Probably one of the first decisions to be made, generally by students and family, after one decides to commit oneself to a college education, concerns the amount of time, money, and other resources involved. In addition to the all-important financial resources problem, which seems to play a part in student decisions from first to last, one must decide how intensively one's time and energy will be committed to higher education. An important distinction along this line, for which data are available, is the distribution of full-time and part-time student enrollment.

A slightly higher percentage of blacks were full-time undergraduates, 10.19 percent, than were part-time undergraduates, 10.13 percent in 1976-77 (see Table 3-11). This distribution is similar to the one for white students, 81.21 and 80.32 percent respectively, but it is dissimilar to the general minority undergraduate pattern of 17-plus percent full-time and 18-plus percent part-time. If a normal or modal pattern can be assumed, then one might conclude that black undergraduates are in the middle, with white students as the standard, and all minorities as the abnormal distribution. Again, looking at the distribution across race, one finds a similar pattern (Table 3-11). Black undergraduates are only slightly more likely than white undergraduates to be part-time, and they are slightly less likely than all minorities to be part-time. Insofar as full-time/part-time distribution is an independent element, black undergraduates are apparently closer to the majority standard in higher education than all minority undergraduates.

Full- or part-time attendance status, however, is not an independent element. Among other things, attendance status is determined by the particular institution. In this case, it is relevant first that traditionally black institutions are disproportionately full-time, and second that two-year institutions are disproportionately part-time.

Blacks base their decision to attend a traditionally black institution (TBI), on many factors. As will be explored in chapter 6, the expectation of full immersion into college life seems to be a major factor in the choice of such institutions. Full-time attendance and residency are characteristics of the greater assimilation of black students on traditionally black campuses. About 20 percent of all black undergraduates were enrolled in TBI's in 1976. Unfortunately, precise attendance-status figures are not presently available, but it is reasonable to assume that only a few percentage points are taken up by part-time attendance.

On the other hand, blacks, more than whites, were enrolled in two-year institutions, 50 to 43 percent respectively. The distribution of the other major minority group, Hispanics, in two-year institutions was 59 percent. Because these institutions are more heavily attended part-time, the minority distribution can be partly explained.

Nevertheless, the two-year college weighting of black and other minority enrollment should be subject to the same test of comparability. Namely, two-year enrollment may be an explanation, but not an excuse, for long-run inequality in higher education. The "access" aspect of that problem is sufficiently described by the fact that such institutions generally carry with them a lower chance of educational/professional and economic mobility than four-year colleges and universities. There is, therefore, in the imbalance of minorities toward them, a strong indication of restricted educational opportunity. The bulk of this problem can only be described in the context of the transfer of the inequality problem away from the threshold of access to what happens within the system of higher education, i.e., distribution.

Another choice to be made before one registers in college is the choice between public and private institutions. It rarely appears as a concrete choice, largely because applicants tend to think in terms of a specific institution. Still, the public vs. private difference can, and often does, play a role. In large part, the substantial difference in cost often leads applicants to opt for the savings of a public institution. In addition, accessibility, both in terms of number of campuses and in terms of student facilities, can attract applicants to public institutions. Moreover, ease of access, as suggested by open enrollment, has been a source of the public sector's enrollment gains over the private sector.

In introducing our traditional model of higher education, we included private institutions primarily because they are more characteristic of "preferred" higher education. This, of course, does not mean that public institutions are not also among the most prestigious, because they frequently are. What is meant is that public institutions as a group conform much less to the traditional model than private ones—in terms of the private institution's relative inaccessibility on a range of criteria for access.

Focusing on the access aspect of public and private distribution, it is evident that black students have been disproportionately enrolled in the public sector of higher education. Since the beginning of the decade, black students have constituted between 19 and 20 percent of those enrolled in private institutions, while for all students generally enrollment is between 23 and 21 percent in such institutions. Admittedly, it is a fairly small difference, and moreover, one that seems to be moving, though quite slowly, toward greater balance (see Table 3-12). Here again, the role of black institutions is a crucial one. Traditionally black private institutions accounted for about (or a little over) 60,000 of the 202,000 blacks enrolled in private institutions in 1976–77. They contained a third, 32.7 percent, of blacks in private institutions, while traditionally black public institutions accounted for less than a fifth, 17.4 percent, of black students in the public sector. If blacks are to achieve equal access to private institutions other than predominantly black ones, much greater emphasis will have to be placed on expanding access to private institutions than to public ones.

Moreover, the model of the black institutions serves as some indication that the relative underrepresentation of blacks in private and four-year institutions is not simply a function of choice. First, the rates of change in TBI enrollment since 1973 have been positive, and substantially so, only for the private four-year institutions. Between 1976 and 1977, their enrollment was up 20 percent, while the enrollment of all other TBI's, public and two-year, declined (see Table 3-12). Second, while advising caution in interpretation because of the limited number of two-year TBI's, the data may also indicate a continued preference on the part of black undergraduates for four-year institutions. The numbers in two-year institutions, public and private, are down (see Table 3-13).

FINANCING ACCESS TO HIGHER EDUCATION

The fastest growing source of funds for institutions of higher education is government: federal, state, local. This fact is easily visible in the records of public institutions, but only with closer scrutiny is it evident in the records of private ones. The latter have had their greatest increases in funds from student tuition and fees (see Appendix, Table 3A-6), but the sources of

Table 3-12 RATES OF CHANGE IN ENROLLMENT IN INSTITUTIONS OF HIGHER EDUCATION
1970–71, 1974–75 and 1976–77*

Type of Institution	Number (in Thousands)	1970–71 Percent	Percent Change	Number (in Thousands)	1974–75 Percent	Percent Change	Number (in Thousands)	1976–77 Percent	Total Percent Change 1970–1976
Black									
Public	422	88.84	+ 56.16	659	80.96	+ 26.40	833	80.56	97.39
Private	100	19.16	+ 55.00	155	19.04	+ 30.32	202	19.54	102.00
All races									
Public	5,699	76.88	+ 21.16	6,905	78.23	+ 26.17	8,712	76.64	52.87
Private	1,714	23.12	+ 12.12	1,922	21.77	+ 25.29	2,408	21.73	40.49

Source: Analysis of data from Scientific Manpower Commission and the U.S. Office for Civil Rights.

*Figures are approximate because the sources of data for the years 1970–74 are from the Manpower Commission, while those for subsequent years are drawn from the U.S. Office for Civil Rights.

Table 3-13 ANNUAL PERCENTAGE CHANGE IN TOTAL ENROLLMENT FOR 102 TRADITION-
ALLY BLACK INSTITUTIONS
1968–77

Type of Institution	1968	1969	1970	1971	1972	1973	1974	1975	1976	1977
Public										
4-year	5.7	5.9	5.3	6.9	2.1	2.8	0.9	13.3	-0.6	-7.3
2-year	-7.5	26.1	10.2	3.1	9.4	5.6	15.0	9.7	11.7	-6.0
Total	5.4	6.4	5.4	6.8	2.4	2.9	1.3	13.2	-0.3	-7.2
Private										
4-year	3.0	-0.3	0.7	3.4	0.6	-0.8	4.2	7.6	2.4	20.4
2-year	4.0	-3.7	4.1	3.1	-6.1	-8.1	-1.7	-8.7	-0.1	-9.0
Total	2.6	-0.4	0.9	3.4	0.2	-1.2	-3.9	7.0	2.4	18.8
Grand total	4.5	4.3	4.1	5.8	1.8	1.8	2.0	11.5	0.4	-0.6

Source: Institute for Services to Education, Washington, D.C., Report, (1978).

Note: Does not include graduate and professional schools.

students' funds are, increasingly, the federal and state governments. Government funds amount to about half of all institutional resources.

While private institutions account for about one fifth, 21 percent, of all student enrollment in higher education (Appendix, Table 3A-8), they contain more than 27 percent of all student recipients of U.S. Office of Education funds awarded to students in 1976–77. Since black students are comparatively underrepresented in private institutions, they risk being further disadvantaged by the greater inclination of federal funds to these schools (see Table 3-14).

The average amounts of individual grants to private institutions clearly exceed those to public ones. According to an American Council on Education (ACE) study, the average awards in BEOG funds for private institutions were 14 percent higher than those for public institutions in 1976–77. The only instances in which the inverse ratio applies is in College Work-Study grants (CWS), which are smaller in the average amount of awards, and much smaller in total federal funds committed.

Of course, the additional costs of attending a private institution account for the bulk of the difference in the amounts of individual awards. But, this "accounting for" is not the same thing as a justification for the difference. In terms of the commitment of public funds, justification of the difference requires equal opportunity for all students. It, therefore, requires that the additional funds to private institutions do not serve to perpetuate racial or other bias. This means that students should have free choice between the two types of institutions, in terms of access, or that financial constraints on equal access should make no socially valued difference. In the latter case, that amounts to saying that one gets nothing from the added funds going to private institutions that is valued in society as a whole. If, in fact, this were the case, then public institutions, like those in France for example, would almost completely efface the private ones.

On the individual level, the lower income students in general, and black students in particular, received a relatively high percentage of federal student funds in 1976–77. Blacks received about 30 percent of all BEOG awards. Here again, blacks in private institutions received a smaller percentage of the funds going to those schools, 22.9 percent, than blacks in public institutions, 31.3 percent.

With the median income of black families at only about 60 percent of that of white families,[50] one should expect a comparatively greater amount of need-based financial aid to go to black students. In addition, when one considers how little disposable income could be available to families earning under $9,000 a year, the black family median income, the need for federal funding for blacks in higher education is evident.

Table 3-14 PERCENT DISTRIBUTION OF STUDENTS RECEIVING AID AND AVERAGE AMOUNT OF ASSISTANCE AWARDED UNDER OFFICE OF EDUCATION ASSISTANCE PROGRAMS 1976–77*

Type of Institution	BEOG Program		SEOG Program		CWS Program		NDSL Program		GSL Program	
	Percent of Students Receiving Aid	Average Award per Student	Percent of Students Receiving Aid	Average Award per Student	Percent of Students Receiving Aid	Average Award per Student	Percent of Students Receiving Aid	Average Award per Student	Percent of Students Receiving Aid	Average Award per Student
Total		$820		$550		$670		$750		$1,380
Control										
Public	79.9	$800	63.3	$510	64.1	$690	61.4	$690	56.0	$1,260
Private	20.1	910	36.7	610	35.9	640	38.6	840	44.0	1,520
Type										
Public 2-year	36.5	740	20.6	440	20.8	680	9.6	580	8.0	1,130
Private 2-year	2.3	950	4.6	500	3.1	620	2.6	640	1.7	1,380
Public 4-year	26.9	830	24.9	530	25.5	670	25.9	670	22.5	1,260
Private 4-year	14.6	910	26.0	620	26.0	600	25.7	780	26.1	1,480
Public university	16.6	870	17.7	580	17.8	750	25.9	760	25.4	1,310
Private university	3.2	880	6.1	660	6.8	820	10.2	1,060	16.2	1,620
Number of recipients	1,411,000		432,000		698,000		757,000		695,000	

Source: F. Atelsek and I. Gomberg, Estimated Number of Student Aid Recipients, 1976–77, HEP Reports, No. 36, American Council of Education (1977).

Note: All tables show weighted national estimates unless specifically stated otherwise. On this and subsequent tables, numbers of recipients are rounded to the nearest thousand. Totals may not add due to rounding and weighting.

*Awards rounded to the nearest ten dollars.

How much more of federal funding should be earmarked for economically disadvantaged students should be calculated on the basis of more than simple income distribution figures. In addition to the family income disadvantages black students face, there are other racial inequalities which translate into greater economic disadvantage. For one, the continually high rate of unemployment for young blacks—over 40 percent for young black males—means that they cannot expect additional income to support their education while in school. Second, their need to compensate for the many disadvantages of precollege education means that part-time work carries greater educational costs in terms of lost time. Third, the fact that blacks do not generally benefit as much from merit-based financial aid as others—and this ranges between 20 and 25 percent of all aid—means they must rely more on federal grants and loans. Moreover, lower family incomes, as well as persistent banking discrimination, mean that black students have relatively limited access to credit.

IDENTIFYING UNMET ECONOMIC NEED

The general economic plight of black Americans has been so widely recognized that its details need not be reiterated. That is to say that the American news media have widely disseminated information on black economic progress since the last decade and before. Unfortunately, information on the slowdown in economic progress experienced by blacks in the past few years has been less widely dispersed. Policymakers, as well as the general public, may need to be reminded of the economic stalemate in which black families have recently found themselves. The 1977 Annual Report of the Carnegie Corporation succinctly summarizes the negative turn in black economic development by looking at a range of economic indicators. For example, it says of income and employment:

> From 1947 to 1975 the ratio of income earned by blacks to that earned by whites narrowed by only 11 points, from 51 to 62 percent. Today the average earnings of black families have receded to only 59 percent that of whites.
> ... In 1958 minority unemployment was 12.6 percent, and it remained over 10 percent until the Vietnam War. Even in the mid-sixties the rate was 7.4 percent while that of whites fell to under 4 percent. Black unemployment since 1975 has fluctuated between 12 and 14 percent. In November 1977 it was 13.8 percent.[51]

When one looks at most current economic indicators of racial inequality, the full picture of real economic disadvantage facing black students is usually left unfinished. There are multiple nonmonetary and/or intangible

Table 3-15   CHARACTERISTICS OF STUDENTS RECEIVING BEOG AID
1976–77

Characteristics	Total Institutions	Public Institutions				Private Institutions			
		Total	2-year	4-year	University	Total	2-year	4-year	University
Number of recipients	1,411,000	1,127,000	514,000	379,000	234,000	283,000	33,000	206,000	44,000
Sex									
Women	55.1	55.8	58.1	55.4	51.3	52.1	61.9	52.2	44.2
Men	44.9	44.2	41.9	44.6	48.7	47.9	38.1	47.8	55.8
Total	100.0	100.0	100.0	100.0	100.0	100.0	100.0	100.0	100.0
Racial/Ethnic Group									
Black (Nonhispanic origin)	29.6	31.3	34.2	31.8	23.8	22.9	17.7	23.4	24.3
Hispanic	10.2	11.4	17.0	6.5	6.5	5.5	2.0	5.6	7.8
Asian or Pacific Islander	2.0	1.9	2.1	1.3	2.6	2.5	1.2	2.3	4.1
Indian or Alaskan Native	1.1	1.3	.9	1.7	1.5	.7	.6	.8	.4
White (Nonhispanic origin)	57.0	54.1	45.9	58.7	65.6	68.4	78.4	67.9	63.4
Total	100.0	100.0	100.0	100.0	100.0	100.0	100.0	100.0	100.0
Enrollment									
Full-time	90.2	88.5	82.9	93.5	93.1	96.6	96.2	97.2	94.0
Part-time	9.8	11.5	17.1	6.5	6.9	3.4	3.8	2.8	6.0
Total	100.0	100.0	100.0	100.0	100.0	100.0	100.0	100.0	100.0
Status									
Dependent undergraduates									
Family income									
Less than $6,000	30.0	30.5	33.5	29.4	25.4	28.4	35.9	27.0	29.5
$6,000–$7,499	13.5	13.2	11.4	15.1	13.9	15.0	15.4	15.0	14.7
$7,500–11,999	19.6	18.3	14.7	20.1	23.6	24.7	25.9	24.7	24.0
$12,000–14,999	8.6	8.0	5.8	9.3	10.9	10.7	8.3	10.8	12.0
$15,000 or more	3.3	2.7	1.4	3.5	4.3	5.7	3.1	5.3	9.3
Independent undergraduates	24.9	27.3	33.1	22.6	21.9	15.5	11.3	17.3	10.5
Graduate students	—	—	—	—	—	—	—	—	—
Total	100.0	100.0	100.0	100.0	100.0	100.0	100.0	100.0	100.0

Source: F. Atelsek and I. Gomberg, *Estimated Numbers of Student Aid Recipients, 1976–77,* HEP Reports, No. 36 (September 1977).

benefits from financial soundness which black families often lack in comparison to white ones. For example, the greater job insecurity that blacks experience limits their capacity to risk the long-term investment often required to finance higher education. Moreover, concrete economic factors in financing education are frequently overlooked in the measurement of racial inequality. For example, economist Marcus Alexis, drawing on other research, shows that in 1971 blacks had only 2 percent of all accumulated wealth in this country. He shows that blacks had only 3.4 percent of all "equity in homes" and yet more than half of all black assets were tied up in home ownership.[52] This becomes particularly significant for educational finance, when one considers first that for most parents of college students, home equity is the largest single asset. Second, this and other assets are substantially underrepresented or omitted in financial-aid reporting.[53]

In terms of assets on which they could draw to finance education, blacks at every income level approached the mid-1970s with much less accumulated wealth than whites. When whites and blacks were grouped into comparable income classes, whites had about three times as much accumulated wealth as blacks in the same class, according to Alexis's analysis of 1971 data (see Appendix, Table 3A-10).

When a family has to sell inessential property, or has to mortgage its home to pay for the college education of a dependent, it is a certainly a burden and a sacrifice. Still, to the extent that an established lifestyle can be maintained, private family expenditure for college is a tolerable sacrifice. When a family must forego current and needed income to pay for education, however, as black families more often do, lifestyles must be sacrificed, and the burden is thus more difficult to tolerate.

Federal programs often underestimate the real needs of the disadvantaged in financing college. In addition to showing a substantial contribution of federal aid programs to equal educational opportunity, a careful look at these programs can also show that the "boot-strap" approach to black progress has never been far from view in the implementation of federal financial aid to higher education.

POLICY IMPLICATIONS

Progress made toward equal access in higher education since the beginning of this decade is quite impressive. Access to higher education for all Americans nearly doubled from the mid-sixties to the mid-seventies, and for blacks, access more than doubled in the same time period. Yet, progress is not the "most important product" of education. Progress toward equal opportunity in higher education does not mean that the educational system has reached the end of its immediate material and creative capacity to accommodate social demands. Current technology may, for example, be inadequate for the development of new, more efficient machines for industry, but the achievement of equal opportunity does not require a new technology.

Progress toward equality of educational opportunity is like progress toward justice; failure to achieve the goals means that injustice and inequality persist. How much a "little injustice" hurts, or how wrong it may be, depends on whether or not the victim of injustice can be compensated. The same could also be true of inequality of opportunity, but the society's rules, to the extent rules exist, for compensating victims of unequal educational opportunity, are at best flimsy. There is no systematic compensation for inequality in education. College affirmative action programs, for example, have only begun to minimize the disadvantages of precollege education. Social injustices are generally understood to be acts of man for which compensation is therefore easily conceived, while educational inequity is treated like an act of God, and is thus assumed to be beyond control.

Social justice is generally seen as a goal in itself, while educational opportunity is more often seen as a preliminary goal or a means to other goals both for the society and for the individual. College education for the individual is primarily a step toward an advanced degree, and/or toward a career that includes professional development and financial security. An individual's financial security in turn affects not only his/her other life opportunities, but also those of his/her dependents. Inequality of educational opportunity is therefore *cumulative*. Marginal disadvantages can, at any moment in the educational process, multiply in a competitive society where marginal advantages count heavily. The educational disadvantage of blacks in the 1940s has evidently weakened the competitive position in schooling of their descendants in the 1970s. Similarly, the persistent racial inequalities of the 1970s will apparently mortgage the educational prospects of blacks into the turn of the century, unless something is done to stop that from happening.

To the extent that higher education is a competitive system, and educational credentials provide a competitive edge, equal opportunity becomes a zero-sum game. The historical inequalities which blacks have suffered are like weights on the track-runner who is otherwise equal to the opponents. The weights have been lightened in the 1970s, but as long as any weight remains, the runner with the extra burden will come in second; and second place is not as well rewarded as first. Consequently, blacks as a group would be further disadvantaged in competitive admissions to advanced education. On the individual level, the college degree frequently represents an all or nothing situation; it is virtually obligatory for graduate and professional school admission, and the most desirable careers require one or more higher educational degrees.

When a career is the goal of advanced education, it is not enough for blacks to be well-educated; they must be as well-educated as others in the job market, because selection can always be based on marginal differences. The way in which educational differences need not, and frequently do not, correspond to job-related capabilities does not prevent them from playing a crucial role in job mobility. American higher education has traditionally responded to inequalities among individuals and among groups by generating hierarchical credentials to label those at the top and by rewarding the "first among unequals." The business community cannot be expected to ignore the labels of superiority—whether symbolic or real, whether appropriate to job demands or not—as long as the labels are legitimated by the same system through which its values were also filtered.

Equal Access and Institutions of Higher Education

Colleges and universities have demonstrated a concern for equal access through the establishment of various programs aimed at helping disadvantaged students. With the probable exception of "open admissions," however, these programs do not substantially affect the structure of inequality among students within institutions. Including open admissions programs, special "help" for disadvantaged students has left the structure of inequality among institutions largely intact. Both within and among institutions, programs for the disadvantaged are oriented toward preserving traditional institutional standards, along with their built-in hierarchies, by bringing disadvantaged students up to the "normal" minimal standard. Effectively then, special admissions programs assume that their students will be at or near the bottom of the class. In any case, such students, and especially those recruited through affirmative action programs, are defined as barely or minimally admissible.

One fairly obvious result of the labeling associated with such admissions programs is that the student may be discouraged after admission from trying to excel, and subsequent academic performance may suffer. Nevertheless, black students admitted to college by almost any means tend to perform as well or better than their ranking at admission would suggest. Accordingly, the rates of retention among black college students is fast approaching that of whites, as will be shown in chapter 5.

A less obvious consequence of current admissions practices involves the way in which they may discourage minorities from ever reaching the threshold of admission. While students are still in high school, and often before high school, their awareness, and that of their parents, of college opportunities clearly influences their progress through high school. First, the choice of an academic program suitable for admission to a competitive college must be made by the first or second year of high school. Second, grades and overall academic performance are influenced by the expectation of college admission. Third, and perhaps most important, the motivation to finish high school is stimulated by the promise of greater opportunities which college admission holds.

Blacks and whites with high school diplomas are rapidly approaching parity in college access. But the proportion of students who never finish high school is substantially higher for blacks than for whites. The reasons for a higher black drop-out rate are many, but certainly a contributing factor is the awareness of constraints on college opportunity. The alternative outlet for the black high school graduate—that of getting a better job than a drop-out—has never been a sufficiently strong, secure incentive. Unemployment among black youth has been high for years, with little regard for the high school diploma; among those with high school diplomas, blacks are two and a half times as likely to be unemployed as whites.

Awareness of college opportunity is to some extent guided by historical limitations on black access, because parents who experienced severe limits are a major source of guidance for the young. Current admissions practices, however, particularly affirmative action, can have a substantial positive or negative impact on student expectations. The development of college affirmative action corresponds to the decline of black high school drop-out rates in recent years. Similarly, the continuation of a high black drop-out rate is probably associated with the weakness and instability of affirmative action programs.

In the years of *DeFunis* and *Bakke*, affirmative action programs appear more fragile than at any other time since their development. Although only a few schools have explicitly curtailed their programs in the past few years, affirmative action is clearly under attack in schools across the country. Black students in high school who are thinking about college can therefore only be discouraged by the apparent threat to their college access.

Even without a calculable decline in such programs, the prevailing institutional approach to affirmative action has fostered a countervailing element of uncertainty among black students. By insisting, for the most part, that minority students admitted under affirmative action do not meet "the admission standard," the institution discredits the few models of success which black high school students may emulate. As long as institutions claim that most students meet superior standards—rather than recognizing that "different" standards are appropriate in different cases—minority students associated with affirmative action programs will be thereby led to doubt their college chances.

Depreciating admissions practices which support the increased access of blacks and other minorities to higher education may discourage black students in two instances. First, their attitude toward and preparation for college may be impaired before they reach the college threshold. Second, after admission to college, their performance and expectations for advanced study may be similarly constrained. Special programs, including affirmative action, have obviously contributed much to the tremendous expansion of college access in the last decade. Given the relative stagnation in growth since 1974, however, continued progress toward equal access may depend on a more positive approach which gives a fair recognition to the educability of minorities. Moreover, for equal access to be sustained once achieved, institutions and involved government agencies must uphold meaningful standards for both admissions and financial aid that reflect a primary commitment to equal educational opportunity.

Equal Access and the Federal Government

The primary approach to equal access in higher education for blacks reflects the established importance of college credentials for the individual in the larger society. An underlying assumption of federal efforts to bring more blacks into the protected enclaves of higher education has been that, with the inclusion of more minorities, institutional stability would be sustained, if not reinforced. In other words, federal programs have sought to expand access only to the point that expansion would not require institutional transformation. There has thus been a latent "hold harmless" provision in equal opportunity programs for higher education in which the government seeks to expand the once very restricted educational privilege without otherwise touching the control and distribution of privilege. In effect, then, federal policy has simply been one of expansion.

The resulting problem is not that simple expansion does not work, because it has worked reasonably well in increasing access for blacks. The problem is rather the values and related expectations on which the simple expansionist approach to higher education is apparently founded. These consist of at least two unwarranted assumptions. First, federal efforts to expand access to higher education are assumed to be taking root in an otherwise stable system. The changes, however, current and potential, which state and private authorities make in the educational system are not realistically considered in the development of federal policy. A clear consequence of not evaluating the internal character of the educational system is that the inequality of distribution within it may be overlooked—this is a problem for discussion in the next chapter.

A more immediate consequence for equality of access is that the federal government, by concentrating only on expansion, is not in a position to evaluate the broader educational and socioeconomic impact of its programs. Meaningful evaluation in terms of equal opportunity is effectively precluded by the failure to tie expanded access to educational criteria beyond simple growth in numbers.

Second, there is a widespread assumption that the progress toward racial parity achieved in the past decade of growth in higher education is somehow guaranteed or protected by those federal programs associated with that progress. This is especially questionable in light of the no-growth future of higher education. As much as any federal program, BEOG addresses the fundamental problem of racial inequality in higher education by providing funds in inverse relationship to ability to pay. For the sake of simplicity, we call this method of financial support "need-based," but on closer inspection it is something less than that. There is, in all the federal Office of Education programs, an implicit exclusion of need as a criterion for federal support to students. This is partly evidenced by the maximum amount of student support—one half of tuition and fees. It is more profoundly evidenced by the fact that the costs of education, escalating institutional costs and the costs beyond family income, are scarcely taken into account. The greater uncertainty of impact made by all Office of Education programs can be further demonstrated by the fact that more federal funds have been provided to college students by the G.I. Bill and Social Security, individually, than by all the Office of Education programs operating prior to 1976. It is especially significant that these former programs, primarily concerned with defense, employment security, and welfare, were more crucial to the recent growth in higher education than programs expressly designed for that purpose.

The stagnation in progress toward racial parity in recent years further serves to bring into question the implicit assumptions of federal programs, although the values of equal opportunity to which they relate have been retained. Perhaps as long as the Civil Rights Movement remains fresh in our national memory, the value of equal opportunity will be strong. But the continued progress in that direction can not be guaranteed on the basis of a national memory. Given an apparent quiescence in the national mood, governmental initiative is more crucial than ever. If a sense of security about the future realization of equal educational opportunity is to be justified, that justification will have to involve currently proposed federal programs.

CHAPTER 4

Distribution:
Inequalities From Within

The problem of access to higher education for blacks is like the problem of employment for blacks. It is better to be employed than not, just as it is better to have access to college than not. Yet, if blacks are to have equal opportunity with others, not just any job is sufficient. A good job means a decent salary and a chance for job mobility. Similarly, access to college education hardly demonstrates equality of opportunity when that access is restricted to the least rewarding educational path. Unlike the employment situation in this country, however, where black unemployment is practically double that of whites, blacks are beginning to attend college in about the same proportion as whites. But beyond simple access, the situation in higher education for blacks is like that of employment; blacks are heavily clustered in the less profitable positions.

Questioning black distribution within institutions of higher education does not always imply social criticism, nor lead to recommendations for action. Equality of opportunity can be reasonably assumed to exist when blacks and whites are equally distributed among institutions and among their various kinds of programs. Such an equal or "uniform" distribution, however, is not necessary to assure equal opportunity. Uniform distribution may not be desirable. Because black students have different backgrounds from whites, and because they usually face different socioeconomic constraints than do whites, they may have different educational needs. All the same, all students are, or should be, in preparation to make a meaningful and rewarding living in the same society. Because economic, professional, and social obligations will be the same or similar for all, some uniformity of educational preparation will invariably be necessary to assure racially equal opportunity. It will, therefore, be important to keep two fundamental concerns in mind throughout this chapter: First, interracial uniformity in distribution is a model against which interracial discontinuities are measured to judge their impact. Second, uniformity, or interracial balance, is not necessarily a goal. Rarely is a heterogeneous social system perfectly equal, but rarely are its inequalities expressions of perfection in the system. In other words, all inequalities are not equal, but any interracial inequality in higher education should be suspect unless and until it is shown not to carry race-related disadvantages.

Variations in Student Distribution

In the realm of undergraduate education, there are a great many choices that students or educators make which distribute students in different ways. This distribution should of course conform to the needs of the individual as well as to the capabilities of the educational system, where possible. Few undergraduates get or need exactly the same education. Consequently, this study need not explore all variations in the distribution of undergraduates. Rather, discussion will be limited to those variations in distribution which are related to race. These variations can be classified into three categories: (1) *systemic* or interinstitutional, (2) *institutional-*attendance, and (3) institutional-*programmatic.*

SYSTEMIC VARIATION

Systemic variations in the distribution of undergraduates are largely those which emerge in the discussion of access. The variations in the distribution of students are an expression of the variations in the kinds of institutions of higher education. Students begin to distribute themselves among institutions when they fill out their applications. Sometimes, but not always, selection is a function of the individual's free and informed educational choice. Yet, more often than not, the individual's action is constrained by some considerations: financial, academic, familial, and social.

Institutions, in turn, distribute applicants during the admissions process. Except for the minority of institutions, those with open admissions, all schools have a pool of applicants from which they choose those they consider most desirable. Frequently, the criteria for the most desirable students emphasize demonstrated intellectual ability. But, a substantial amount of the time, other criteria, ranging from athletic ability to individual influence, become pivotal. In addition to formal admissions, institutions have an important distributive impact on individuals both before and immediately after admissions. Financial aid decisions which usually follow admissions decisions, but are sometimes made simultaneously, increasingly have the effect of real admission or rejection. This is especially true for poor and most minority students, who find the cost of higher education prohibitive. It is still more so the case when these students consider financing four or more years at selective private institutions where total expenses of $7000 a year are commonplace.

By preparing, encouraging, or assisting potential applicants to meet both the admissions standards and the financial demands of the institutions, institutions also affect the distribution of students. In what is commonly called "recruitment," faculty, administrators, and students frequently encourage or discourage applicants. Because potential minority applicants tend to have less information about college than others—i.e., fewer professional contacts or college alumni in their primary social group—this recruitment function takes on a special importance for equal opportunity.

Whatever may be the criteria and methods involved in the whole process of admitting students, the process itself appears to be primarily controlled by the individual institution. Even open admissions public institutions use some discretion, although it is most often in the promulgation of written rules and public laws. For example, there are rules relating to minimum entering grades for various programs, and state and city laws extending or restricting residential and community benefits.

Control over the students institutions admit and support is not completely independent, except in a very formal sense. Informally, all institutions of higher education form a system or a few subsystems in which public and private, two-year and four-year institutions are grouped. It is a system in which the institutions are the primary decision makers and the ultimate authorities over their own practices. No one university or private college is obligated to another. Yet, when in mid-April virtually all of the most competitive private institutions send out their admission and rejection notices, written in practically the same language, relying on the same procedures, it is certainly no simple coincidence. In this case, there is no need to look for a secret organization or plan for concerted action because what is happening is so obvious that it is all too often overlooked.

Individual institutions subjugate themselves to what they see as the highest or the prevailing standards for higher education. Since these standards are largely unwritten, as well as difficult to grasp concretely, they are pursued by means of imitation. Education administrators, like artists in any given period, imitate each other in the determination of their own goals. There is little need for making fundamental policy decisions in a group, though this may occur, because virtually every institution has sought legitimacy from its academic counterparts. Where institutional behavior has changed, it has been, with rare exception, largely a slow and evolutionary process. The process of change when initiated individually is always defined as "experimentation," as was the case with special admissions for minorities. Institutions uniformly resist external pressures to change, and when they concede, their concessions are effectively simultaneous. When they select any student, institutions judge both the student's fit (qualifications) within the prevailing higher educational standards and his/her potential to serve and reinforce those standards.[1]

Much of the uniformity of institutions comes from the exchange of faculty and curriculum materials. This exchange occurs more among four-year colleges and universities than among two-year ones, and it is especially strong within subsets of institutions such as highly selective, Ph.D.-granting institutions. Graduate students are generally placed through the recommendations and influence of their faculty supervisors who have made contacts in other similar institutions. These contacts are likely to have been made when the supervising faculty member was a student, and developed through related research, through mutual interests in publications, and/or sustained through membership in professional associations. Faculty members are highly mobile in comparison with other professionals, and contacts among institutions are frequently sustained through temporary or permanent faculty exchanges.

Over time, the resemblance among institutions in educational standards and their treatment of students has become increasingly strong for subsets of institutions. That resemblance has grown as a result first of public and student political pressures on institutions—pressures to meet new educational demands in a changing sociopolitical environment. During the sixties, university faculty and administrators experienced nontraditional pressures for which a response was inevitable. Their response has apparently been guided by traditional prerogatives. Second, institutional behavior has been guided by a growing sense of identity and community between faculty and administrators, who seem to be drawn together in reaction to the size and complexity which increasingly characterize education. Consequently, their ties, like those of the typical bureaucrat, are often more to the institution than to the teaching profession. Accordingly, Gross and Grambsch describe, on the basis of extensive surveys, the direction that universities have taken away from student-focused planning and toward the extension of their special institutional subgroup characteristics:

> Universities remained in 1971 what they had been in 1964: institutions oriented to research and scholarly production, set up to pro-

vide comfortable homes for professors and administrators, and according students and their needs a distinctly secondary position. But important changes had also taken place. Professors and administrators both felt a stronger congruence between the actual emphasis in their universities and the kind of emphasis they felt proper. Universities had grown more stratified to the point of fragmentation. Private universities—already differing from public universities in 1964—were even more distinctive in goals; highly "productive" universities were increasingly differentiating themselves from less productive universities, and the more prestigious universities were even more distinctive from the others than they had been in 1964. In essence, distinct "leagues" were being carved out, with decreasing competition between them.[2]

Institutional uniformity is likely to be more formally reinforced by the power and authority of educational and professional associations. The impact of the authority of associations is particularly evident in the case of professional schools such as Medicine and Law. The American Medical Association (AMA) and the American Bar Association (ABA) have the government-sanctioned authority to accredit their respective professional schools, as well as the authority to rule on the licensing of practitioners. Ultimately, this authority allows these associations to determine how institutions will treat their students. The educational authority of these associations is formally supplanted by the independent power of school associations in Medicine and Law. In fact, they do not counterbalance each other, but serve to reinforce direct control of educational practices by professional interests. In addition, the Association of American Medical Colleges (AAMC) complements the AMA's authority through its institutionally-granted powers to judge student applicants and to evaluate curriculum. Here it should be noted that, while the AAMC relies on basic standards, it can serve to reinforce "planned" institutional variation because its role and powers may vary with each member institution. Although most professional associations do not have the real authority of the AMA, their roles are close to that of the AAMC, with varying degrees of power. They can not always determine how a school or department will act, but they generally represent and reinforce uniform professional standards for various departments.

The effect of these associations on equality of opportunity in academic life is illustrated by the orientation of their journals. For example, the American Political Science Association has dominated the study of Political Science for at least two decades. Its primary journal, *The American*

Political Science Review, only became interested in the problems of race relations near the end of the Civil Rights Movement. One prominent political scientist points out that between 1906 and 1963 only 13 of 2,611 articles published in the *Review* seemed to be concerned with racial issues.[3] It is safe to say that major professional journals have been more a source of educational stability than of change. As such, they and the associations which produce them have been an integral part of the conservative institutional conscience.

Many analysts of the political character of higher education, Ladd and Lipset among them, state the case more strongly. In *The Divided Academy*, Ladd and Lipset maintain that colleges and universities have a substantially one-sided and conservative character:

> Although a visible cadre [of faculty] has played significant roles in leading and supporting protest movements of both the left and the right at different times in history, most have accepted the status quo. Universities remain primarily educational institutions, which implies that they are part of the social apparatus designed to transmit the existing culture, including the beliefs that help to legitimate the authority system of the society. . . . They are not . . . knowledge creating centers. The school requires the faculty to be primarily involved in the transmission of useful skills and the indoctrination of accepted values. . . . In essence, therefore, the "school" components of higher education are conservative aspects.[4]

The effects of these interinstitutional or systemic forces on black enrollment create stable but marginally flexible barriers to change. Thus, all institutions may easily concede to the recruitment of black and other minority students, but only to the point that their position (image and status) with regard to other institutions is unaffected. Consequently, programs for minorities in selective private institutions are very similar to each other. Programs in public institutions vary largely as a result of the proportion of minorities in the state and local population, rather than as a result of institutional independence. Even here, the institutional hierarchy among public institutions is not only salient nationally, but also replicated within states, e.g., the Berkeley campus in California and the Madison campus in Wisconsin. It is no accident that the proportion of minorities in all state universities is relatively small at their "elite" campuses. That those proportions are not the smallest is not a contradiction of their status concerns vis-a-vis minorities, but rather a confirmation of the need to protect their status with a good public image. This is not to say that institutions are insincere when they accept minorities, because they frequently have good intentions. The problem is that they, particularly their conservative white faculties, tend to believe that minority recruitment beyond a minimal level threatens the quality of the school.[5]

The evidence indicates that most nonminority faculty members behave as though any differences between black and white students which affect instruction create impositions on their time and energy. Accordingly, a study by James Mingle found that white faculty members consciously "interact" less with black students than with other students. Moreover, the study observes: "When faculty believe that black students should meet the same 'standards' as whites, this tends to be translated into an unwillingness to alter traditional teaching styles or support institutional changes."[6] In addition, the finding that young faculty members are often less responsive to the needs of black students than older ones suggests the behavior is not a result of "simple" racial prejudice. Rather, it supports the conclusion that resistance or indifference to black student needs is built into institutional structure and inculcated in graduate students through an unverified belief that educational meritocracy prevails.

Within the public sphere more than within the private one, there is a planned division of higher education between two-year and four-year institutions designed to channel different kinds of students into each. The planning is generally intended to distribute students according to their educational orientations and professional interests. While not always intended, there is, in most public systems, a clear expectation that two-year students will have weaker academic backgrounds. As a consequence, the distribution of black and other minorities toward these institutions can be defended in nonracial terms. Serious question, however, remains as to how good such a defense can be. There are two parts to this question. First, to what extent has unequal racial distribution been consciously built into the system, where it has not been "planned"? Second, to what extent may blacks more than others be disadvantaged by their relative underenrollment in four-year institutions? These questions and others related to the system of higher education should be juxtaposed to other questions on interinstitutional variations.

In the late 1960s and early 1970s, most interested educators were in favor of expanding the number of two-year institutions as well as the size of their enrollments. The expectations were: (1) that they would respond better to the educational and related needs of local communities; (2) that they would expand and diversify access to higher education; and (3) that they would serve to increase and facilitate entry into four-year institutions. The number of two-year institutions expanded rapidly from 600 in 1954 to over 1100 in 1968. Evidence that these schools have satisfied, or are going to satisfy, the first expectation is weak. Evidence for the second is stronger but not particularly satisfying to those concerned with socioeconomic mobility.

In the latter expectation, that of providing greater access to four-year institutions, little has been achieved. The failure to extend access, however, may result more from the resistance of four-year colleges than from the deficiencies of two-year colleges. The majority of black students enrolling in two-year institutions plan to get a bachelor's degree or more, but only a small minority of them ever get that far. As we shall see, this creates a special problem for black students, because they, more than others, are likely to select academic curricula oriented toward continuing their education. Unfortunately, such preparation at a two-year college is statistically unlikely to reach fruition in a baccalaureate degree.

Black/White Institutional Distribution

A special question of distribution is raised by the separation of black and white institutions. In particular, black enrollment in predominately and traditionally black institutions always means racial separation, but it rarely means segregation in the historical and legal sense of the term. By "segregation" we generally refer to a racially oppressive situation in which an oppressed minority is compelled by a majority to submit to isolated and inferior conditions. W. E. B. DuBois, writing in *The Crisis* in the 1930s, consistently articulated the distinction between this concept of segregation, in which inequality is an essential component, and what he called "self-segregation" or separation.[7] Self-segregation in his view is first, voluntary with regard to the minority and second, not malevolent or deprecatory toward others. Third, the self-segregation of blacks is understood to be inwardly directed toward racially specific needs rather than being intentionally exclusive of others.

It is only in this last aspect of "self-segregation" that one can reasonably apply the term to traditionally black institutions (TBI's). For predominantly but not traditionally black institutions (PBI's), the same concept is somewhat less appropriate. To the extent that PBI's are creatures of the state, and not controlled or guided by blacks, they may reflect an oppressive situation for which the label of segregation is appropriate. Of course, public TBI's started out simply as PBI's, most more than a half-century ago. The important characteristic of TBI's is that they represented a qualitatively meaningful option in higher education. Not very many years ago, black institutions started or supported by liberal whites were always the product of concessions to black needs and demands, of which the most striking was the virtual denial of integrated education. PBI's created and largely governed by whites during a time of relative integration, did not always serve the same functions as TBI's. Rather, some PBI's (and not many of them) can have as a primary consequence of their origin the substitution of an inferior version of education in place of greater integration. Still, it should be kept in mind that most black institutions, whatever their "quality," have a much more meaningful and, as yet, irreplaceable primary social role to play.

Consequently, the impact of black institutional enrollment on total enrollment has to be weighed carefully. For the most part, increased numbers of blacks in higher education only demonstrate equal educational opportunity for blacks when they are in integrated institutions. Of course, enrollment figures for black institutions are not the opposite of equal educational opportunity; in fact, they also demonstrate the degree of educational opportunity. What they cannot show *by themselves* is the degree of equality. This is because enrollment in the two kinds of institutions represents two different kinds of social and political phenomena, however similar the educational experiences may be. Enrollment in black institutions intersects with enrollment in other institutions only when there is a free choice between the two for black students. Such freedom must be demonstrated before we can reasonably treat the two sets of enrollment figures indiscriminately.

What that means for the measurement of distribution is first that the number of black institutions should be subtracted from the total enrollment figures to get a real sense of equality of opportunity in some instances. Second, it means in most cases, that it will be necessary to combine the two figures, since we cannot generally measure the extent to which students freely choose to attend black institutions. At the same time, one must especially guard against the assumption that such inclusive figures correspond directly with equality of opportunity. Ultimately, we are back to the important analytical principle that numbers, although we must rely on them, are never sufficient for the assessment of social conditions and policy.

INSTITUTIONAL VARIATION

Institutional or intrainstitutional variations in the distribution of students refers to the multiple educational and career alternatives that are likely to be available to students within any given curriculum. Institutions vary among themselves in the range and peculiarities of their curricular offerings; the present concern, however, is with basic alternatives found in almost every school. This means that a distinction between two- and four-year institutions will have to be made, since two-year institutions have much more limited offerings, as well as special, i.e., vocational, programs not found in four-year schools. For the most part, this discussion focuses on institutions with full four-year programs.

As a rule, colleges and universities allow or encourage students to make a variety of choices, during or after enrollment. Perhaps the first choice to be made by the student is whether he/she will enter a degree or nondegree program. The student may select a nondegree program with the intention of later pursuing a degree, but the prevailing expectation is that freshmen will enroll in degree programs. Although a particular specialty or major often must be chosen simultaneously, the student is usually free to change his/her major later. Under any circumstances, there are basic course requirements which the student must satisfy to be eligible for any degree, as well as specific requirements for the degree tied to each major.

Because extensive data on degree versus nondegree enrollment have not been available, analysts of higher education have paid little attention to the problem of distribution involved. Yet, if black enrollment is found to be more heavily weighted toward nondegree enrollment, there would be substantial indication that a problem exists. The opportunity to attend college is greatly depreciated by an unequal opportunity to pursue a degree. Nondegree enrollment serves best to complement existing careers or previously developed lifestyles. For those who have low employment possibilities and only a high school degree, like most black students, the baccalaureate degree is a critical part of their educational mobility.

Perhaps as important as the acquisition of the degree is the integration of the student into academic life. Beyond the value of extracurricular campus life, which may also be part of integration, the new student needs some informed guidance toward his/her educational/professional goal. This guidance is structured into the degree programs by definition. College counselors are prepared to advise students enrolled in these programs. For the typical student, starting college at age 17 or 18, it should be apparent that the informed planning involved in a degree program is necessary. Moreover, for the older, mature students with little or no previous higher education, such planning is probably useful, if not essential, because they would not know what higher education has to offer, or how best to profit from it.

Associated with degree-program enrollment is the distribution of students by attendance status: full-time and part-time. While part-time attendance may lead to the baccalaureate degree, full-time enrollment is normally associated with undergraduate degree programs. The apparent disadvantage of part-time attendance is that it takes longer to finish a program. This disadvantage may be outweighed, however, by positive values such as the ability to maintain full-time employment while in school. That such employment may only be gainful, as opposed to educational, does not necessarily detract from the process. What does detract from part-time enrollment is the possibility that substantive educational benefits will be sacrificed.

That possibility emerges first from the socialization function of most full-time college education, and second from the bias of curriculum planning toward full-time enrollment. As for socialization, formal education is understood to be an integral part of social and psychological development. The student is socialized by learning social and professional values and norms as well as by adopting professional modes of behavior through consistent contact with those people and perspectives to be imitated. The importance of school socialization is that it cannot be dictated. It is, rather, a process of immersion and assimilation. As such, the ultimate value of all socialization may be questionable, because many things in higher education may not be worthy of emulation. In addition, some analysts argue that "higher education no longer serves 'primarily as a means of preparation for maturity,' but accommodates lifelong educational needs as people perceive them: career advancement, career change, or personal fulfillment."[8]

There are various aspects of socialization in education, some more desirable than others to students. Most notably, older students, who make up a large part of part-time enrollment, are not likely to benefit from the broad model of socialization in terms of acquiring social or basic professional values and norms. Still, the older student may need a more professionally-oriented socialization, which would seem to come most readily from full-time enrollment. Part-time attendance alongside a complementary and educational job, however, would also have advantages. The problem here is that there is little reason to believe that blacks have equal access to such educationally supportive jobs. Rather, unemployment among college-age blacks is persistently worse than lack of education in comparison to whites.

The fact of socialization and its importance in producing the "educated" individual is undeniable.[9] Although difficult to quantify, some elements of socialization are important to professional development, at least as seen by potential employers.[10] Training, like acquiring good study habits, is more likely to be adopted through socialization than to be taught in classes. There is evidence that minorities, particularly Mexican Americans and blacks, rely more heavily than others on the school for this kind of training.[11] We should therefore be suspect of any imbalanced distribution of minorities toward attendance patterns which may not provide for necessary socialization.

Similar concern has been expressed about the differences between residential and nonresidential enrollment. Although the residential pattern fits the traditional image of higher education, there are very good reasons for nonresidential education, reasons which, no doubt, outweigh any disadvantages for many individuals. Most students, for example, can benefit by saving the cost of residency, about $1,000 a year on the average. In addition, many institutions, especially the less costly public ones, lack residential facilities for their students. Older students with dependent families need the nonresidential option. In brief, residency has begun to lose its prominence in higher education largely as a result of the changes in student ages and the urbanization of higher education.

Still, residency has some continued value and, therefore, relevance to equal opportunity. In general, that value would seem to hinge on the greater value of socialization. In particular, the contrast between the private living conditions of the disadvantaged and the typical minority student versus those of other students might well point to an implicit inequality. Those students who, for financial reasons, may not be able to live on campus are also those who are likely to live in homes least conducive to studying. For example, how many students who cannot afford to live on campus have a study, with adequate books and supplies, to work in? We cannot, therefore, exclude the possibility that a racial imbalance toward off-campus living may carry some disadvantage.

In addition to the basic option in types of attendance, more institutions offer "special programs" which define the overall attendance and educational choices available for the students. Most institutions offer a variety of experimental programs, some of which particularly affect minority enrollment. For example, "community studies" and urban related programs tend to bring students into the institution for a short period of time, usually from one semester to two years.

Special programs, geared toward overcoming student disadvantages, have generally included large proportions of minorities. In most cases, there has been no clear distinction between minority student needs and those of the "disadvantaged" or "special" student. From the perspectives of many studies, including a Carnegie Council study of special programs, such an emphasis on minorities is both reasonable and worthwhile. They observe that "it is important to understand that ethnic or racial group membership often reflects a broader deprivation of educational opportunity than low social and economic status implies."[12]

In addition, some affirmative action oriented programs bring minorities into college on a "provisional" or less than "full-status" basis. In such cases, the student is understood to have met the minimum qualifications for an unrestricted student status, but also understood to be in need of special help in order to compete with other students from academically superior backgrounds. Participation in these special remedial programs for designated students is more often expected than required. Sometimes aligned with other supportive services for students, these programs have emphasized counseling and tutoring. Increasingly, separate remedial courses in study skills, expository writing, and mathematics are included.[13]

In general, special programs are beyond the purview of this study because specific programs vary too much across institutions to permit an accurate examination of their effects on black student distribution. Some, such as remedial programs, have apparently helped to increase black enrollment. The available data are insufficient to explain the effects of special programs on other areas.

PROGRAMMATIC VARIATION

Almost as obvious as the irregular distribution of blacks among types of institutions is their irregular distribution among types of curricula or majors within institutions. Blacks, more than whites, in college tend to concentrate in a few undergraduate majors, particularly the humanities and Education. This maldistribution not only predates the development of affirmative action but shows every sign of persisting. Moreover, the imbalance toward Education and away from Science and Technology, is aggravated in graduate schools. Unlike the uneven distribution of blacks among institutions, however, the uneven distribution among programs has a fairly clear connection with economic mobility and therefore a clear relationship with unequal educational and economic opportunity. The extact extent of that relationship, of course, requires further examination.

Before turning to the data on the variations in distribution, some additional indication of where to look for biases with reference to blacks should be helpful. Again we draw on our model of the traditional student in higher education. By this model, the best evidence of stable minority integration in higher education comes from the equal representation of minorities in the more traditional sectors. Although the measure of integration will not be limited to these sectors, we will look to them first. In particular, private, selective, Ph.D.-granting universities or highly selective colleges are viewed as traditional institutions. The middle- and/or upper-class white male attending college full-time in pursuit of a degree while in residence is the traditional model. Again, it should be recalled that the most competitive institutions and the most upwardly mobile student-types are not all included in this model. Its inclusiveness, however, is not important for the present, as long as changes in these areas adequately represent changes in other traditionally restrictive areas.

Little has been said about the variation in majors and kinds of degrees conferred across race; to some extent, there has, until recently, not been sufficient data to allow for much discussion of it. But to a larger extent, variations in this kind of distribution have only in the past few years come to be viewed as a problem, actual or potential. Historically, a college degree alone, of virtually any kind, was sufficient to guarantee employment opportunity and to assure some economic mobility. Education policy makers were not encouraged to concern themselves with seemingly small inequalities among an already advantaged, favored few. Today's college graduates may still tend to be among the top half in the country economically, but their advantages are far from secure. For black Americans, economic security effectively begins with the acquisition of the baccalaureate degree.

It follows from our approach to traditional higher education that in the programs in which traditional students are most highly concentrated, compared to minorities, the rewards tend to be relatively high, or at least equal to those in other major fields. Consequently, to the extent that black students are concentrated in different major fields, questions about parity should be raised. To reiterate, all inequalities of distribution are not equal. But where such inequalities exist, and where there is no direct evidence to the contrary, they are suspect.

More than most other kinds of distribution discussed, variation in the major field distribution of students is likely to leave an indelible mark on their careers and economic mobility. The specialization decisions of undergraduates do not constitute binding career choices because they are frequently changed by postgraduate education or redirected through employment experience. These choices are, nevertheless, restrictive and significant for the life-time opportunities of students. Consequently, the distribution of black students across major fields constitutes one crucial measure of equal opportunity.

Current Variations in Black Undergraduate Distribution

SYSTEMIC VARIATIONS

While inequalities in access to higher education for blacks are clearly diminishing, inequalities in distribution seem not only to persist, but, in some cases, to have been reinforced. This is particularly a problem with systemic variations in distribution inasmuch as improved black access to higher education has been largely depreciated by the stratification of institutions. As more blacks and whites have been admitted to American colleges and universities, an increasing proportion of students have found themselves in institutions which can not provide the rewards, economic and educational, that are traditionally associated with advanced study.

Institutional Selectivity and Black Enrollment

A problem with the assessment of institutional selectivity is that it is generally approached in several ways. Analysts try to measure the amount of competition for admission to a given institution or set of institutions by looking at its standards for admission, the achievements of its students, and the ratio of acceptances to applications. Alternatively, a more indirect measurement is to look for the consequences or logical correlates of institutional selectivity by measuring the reputation of the institution in the academic community and the status of its faculty as well as the professional mobility of its graduates. The most direct measure of selectivity, however—the quality of student input—is fairly meaningless because one is primarily concerned with educational preference or academic status. But the quality of the student input also encompasses noneducational preferences such as costs, location, religion of institution, and race of institution. The alternative to measuring student input, that of looking at the consequences of selectivity, is equally difficult to measure, because factors involving reputation and mobility are practically impossible to quantify.

The only alternative then, to which analysts generally have recourse, is to measure the statistical (and not necessarily logical) correlates of selectivity. More specifically, these are institutional characteristics which function as the components and/or environment of selectivity, but are not directly tied to student input/output differences. For example, educational expenditures obviously contribute to the quality of education; but exactly how they contribute, and how important they are are largely unknowns. Nevertheless, several data-based variables which correlate with selectivity can be used to draw useful distinctions among institutions.

Alexander Astin, using ACE/CIRP data, has identified six basic categories of differences among institutions (with a seventh category, mean per student subsidy, applicable only to public institutions):

Educational and general expenditures
Value of buildings, land, and equipment
Library expenditures
Median faculty salary
Percent freshmen living in resident halls

Effects on chances of persistence
Mean per student subsidy (for public institutions only)[14]

These categories demonstrate first what any American thinking about a "good" school no doubt believes: namely, there is an informal but precisely defined hierarchy of institutions of higher education. Second, and more important, they show that this hierarchy is not simply the result of some impenetrable educational savoir-faire on the part of elite institutions and their students. It is rather a function of clear differences in institutional financial resources and expenditures. According to Astin, "the magnitude of these differences is remarkable: selective universities spend three times more per student than the least selective four-year and two-year colleges."[15] As can be seen in Table 4-1, the dollar amount of differences in the six basic categories among public institutions are consistent and reinforcing.

The student-based content, or rather "input", aspect of institutional selectivity can be seen in the uneven distribution of incoming freshmen grades as one moves along the scale of selectivity. The most selective universities take in more than three times the proportion of entering freshmen with B+ or higher average grades than do two-year colleges, and about twice as many as the less selective four-year colleges.

There is probably a widespread assumption that the differences among institutions as indicated by admissions, public ones included, are socially legitimate because institutions should have special "purposes" and serve specific groups. Accordingly, the assumption goes that the "brighter," academically better prepared students deserve the greater investment of public resources. This assumption might be tenable if it could be shown (a) that differences in academic preparation and high school grades fairly reflect student abilities and (b) that institutions of higher education can best serve all students by means of such separation. Although analysis of the former point is beyond the range of the study, it should be recognized that inequalities in elementary and secondary schools, as well as persistent discrimination, make precollege preparation a particularly unreliable indicator of abilities for black students. The latter point—the pedagogical value of separating students in higher education—is addressed by looking for the most salient factors in that separation. First, there is little or no evidence that pedagogical practice changes substantively as one moves along the scale of selectivity among institutions. Second, and in contrast, there is evidence that the higher one goes up the scale the wealthier the students. Third, and particularly discouraging here, is evidence that the proportion of minorities enrolled declines as one moves up the scale, except at the very top (conspicuous) institutions. Thus Astin's data provide evidence of de facto bias.

Table 4-1   EDUCATIONAL RESOURCES AND BENEFITS OF DIFFERENT TYPES OF PUBLIC INSTITUTIONS

Type of Institution	Dollars per Full-Time Equivalent Student			Weighted[a] Dollars per Full-Time Equivalent Student			Median Faculty Salary[c]
	Educational and General Expenditures[b]	Value of Buildings, Land, and Equipment[b]	Library Expenditures[b]	Educational and General Expenditures[b]	Value of Buildings, Land, and Equipment[b]	Library Expenditures[b]	
2-year colleges	1,533	3,982	71	1,533	3,982	71	13,734
4-year colleges							
Low selectivity	1,534	5,514	83	1,485	5,349	80	13,765
Medium selectivity	1,758	6,467	98	1,703	6,263	96	14,794
High selectivity	2,523	7,875	104	2,351	7,292	96	16,508
Universities							
Low selectivity	3,101	7,710	109	2,570	6,431	93	15,662
Medium selectivity	3,230	8,453	116	2,655	6,991	96	16,846
High selectivity	5,408	12,320	212	4,157	9,495	165	18,286

Source: Alexander Astin, "The Myth of Equal Access in Public Higher Education," Southern Education Foundation (July 1975), Table 3, p. 8.
[a]The greater cost of graduate and professional education has been discounted by weighting each graduate student by a factor of 2.5.
[b]From 1971–72 Higher Education General Information Survey.
[c]From 1973 AAUP survey.

Table 4-2   CHARACTERISTICS OF NEW FRESHMAN ENTERING DIFFERENT TYPES OF PUBLIC INSTITUTIONS Fall 1973

Type of Institution	Percent of Students with High School Averages of B+ or Higher	Percent of Minority Students[1]	Medium Parental Income
2-year colleges	21.3	11.8	$12,195
4-year colleges			
Low selectivity	39.9	18.7	$13,427
Medium selectivity	33.0	6.9	$14,055
High selectivity	58.5	4.8	$15,695
Universities			
Low selectivity	49.9	4.1	$16,590
Medium selectivity	51.1	2.4	$15,510
High selectivity	69.3	5.4	$17,843

Source: Alexander Astin, "The Myth of Equal Access in Public Higher Education," Southern Education Foundation (July 1975), p. 5.

[1] Includes black, Spanish and Native American Indian students.

These data indicate that blacks are more than three times as likely to be found in the lower range of public four-year colleges than in the upper range of public universities. Moreover, unless they make it into the very top echelon of universities, they are eight times as likely to be found at the lowest selectivity level of four-year colleges. The meaning of this finding for the regulation of selectivity in public higher education is, first of all, indirect. The fact that selectivity works against minorities and the poor does not, by itself, mean that there is no good educational reason for maintaining an "elite-mass" distribution among higher educational institutions at public expense. What does follow, however, is that such an inequality is inherently suspect unless and until educational justification can be provided. That justification would first have to come from public authorities who sustain, through public funds, the unequal distribution. Second, sufficient justification would have to include evidence that students relegated to the least selective institutions are being offered as much as students in elite public institutions. In other words, it would have to be maintained that the additional resources possessed by the elite schools do not create any real educational advantage for their students over others. If such an argument could

111

be maintained, which seems unlikely, it would then constitute an indictment of educational policy for the waste of public resources.

Stepping back for a moment, the logic of the preceding observation depends on a completely egalitarian value system for higher education. Specifically, the value implied is that higher education should be equal for all students, whatever their individual or competitive social inequalities. Effectively then, students with "A" and "C" precollege backgrounds should be treated equally (not necessarily the same) once admitted to college.

In contrast to this value position, there is the individualistic value position which could view publicly supported inequalities in higher education as establishing different levels of rewards for students, higher ones for those who have achieved the most in their previous academic experiences.

The application of the data to this latter value is somewhat more limited as long as one is not concerned with the nonacademic, i.e., socioeconomic, factors which may well have contributed to the previous academic achievement of the student. Nevertheless, a primary function of public policy analysis is to determine the best, most productive use of public resources. One should therefore determine what kind of educational system, based on rewards, needs, or equity, would best conform to societal needs for professional and responsible members of the community. An "elite-mass" distribution among institutions must then be justified by showing that students rewarded with an elite education play an essential social role which other students, receiving the same public resource investment, could not fill as well. We will return to this problem later. For the present, it should be kept in mind that responding to differing abilities of college students by providing different or "special" kinds of education is not the same thing as maintaining a hierarchical system where students get more or less of basically the same thing.

Student Socioeconomic Status and Institutional Selectivity

Qualitative variation among private institutions of higher education is more consistent with public expectation because education has traditionally grown as a private enterprise, albeit publicly subsidized. For example, those few institutions which take no government funds retain the legal right to discriminate on the basis of race or sex. Consequently, the unequal distribution of resources, greater than that among public institutions, is understandable. Joseph Froomkin, using the SIE data referred to in chapter 3 (Table 3-9), has shown that the increments in the costs of attendance at all institutions correspond to differences in the family wealth of students enrolled. Since private institutions generally cost considerably more than public ones of equal quality, the largest proportions of the middle and upper class students tend to be found in the more expensive private institutions. For example, Froomkin found that 60 percent of the students from families earning $25,000 a year or more were enrolled in institutions costing more than $3,000 a year. This cost is well above the upper range of the most expensive public institutions in higher education. Private institutions cost on the average four times as much as public ones (see Table 4-3).

Because these socioeconomic differences grow out of the same free enterprise tradition associated with higher education, they may, for the most part, be treated as "value neutral" or socially acceptable inequalities. That is to say, every one's right to extend his/her educational and professional mobility based on ability to pay for it is not contested.

Unfortunately, the same socioeconomic differences which allow for educational advantage based on wealth may also obscure some socially unacceptable, racial inequalities. These inequalities begin to come to light when one looks more closely at how students of different family incomes are distributed among the different selectivity levels of public and private institutions. It becomes evident that the less well-off benefit least from the most selective upper range of public higher education. For racial inequalities, the problem is further emphasized when one recognizes that the "better" private institutions are the least accessible to black students.

First in this regard, the ACE data analyzed by Astin, King, and Richardson show that the family wealth of students increases as one moves up the scale of institutional selectivity from two-year to four-year colleges to universities. In 1976, 45 percent of freshmen came from families earning less than $15,000 a year. Of freshmen enrolled in two-year and four-year colleges, however, 53 and 43 percent respectively came from families in that income range. Yet, only 32 percent of university freshmen came from families below the $15,000 a year income level. This disparity is highlighted by the fact that 80 percent of the freshmen in predominantly black colleges are from families below that income, and more than 50 percent of them are from families earning less than $8,000 a year (see Table 4-4). First, all across the board, as we see from Table 4-4, students in the public and private universities are better off than students in public and private four-year colleges, who, in turn, are wealthier than those in two-year colleges.

From Table 4-4, it is evident that, even where cost is not a significant factor, the student's economic status and institutional selectivity seem to go hand in hand.

Black Enrollment in Public and Private Institutions and Selectivity

Similarly, as one moves up the three-part ladder of institutional selectivity, the proportion of black students enrolled declines once traditionally

Table 4-3 TUITION AND REQUIRED FEES PER FULL-TIME UNDERGRADUATE RESIDENT DEGREE-CREDIT STUDENT IN INSTITUTIONS OF HIGHER EDUCATION 1964-65 to 1975-76

Year and Control	Dollars for Year Listed				1975-76 Dollars			
	All	University	Other 4-Year	2-Year	All	University	Other 4-Year	2-Year
1964-65								
Public	$ 243	$ 298	$ 224	$ 99	$ 431	$ 529	$ 398	$ 176
Nonpublic	1,088	1,297	1,023	702	1,931	2,302	1,816	1,246
1965-66[1]								
Public	257	327	240	109	446	568	417	189
Nonpublic	1,154	1,369	1,086	768	2,005	2,378	1,886	1,334
1966-67								
Public	275	360	259	121	463	607	436	204
Nonpublic	1,233	1,456	1,162	845	2,078	2,453	1,958	1,424
1967-68[1]								
Public	283	366	268	144	461	597	437	234
Nonpublic	1,297	1,534	1,236	893	2,115	2,501	2,016	1,456
1968-69								
Public	295	377	281	170	459	586	437	264
Nonpublic	1,383	1,638	1,335	956	2,151	2,548	2,077	1,487
1969-70[1]								
Public	323	427	306	178	475	627	450	262
Nonpublic	1,533	1,809	1,469	1,034	2,252	2,657	2,158	1,518

1970-71								
Public	352	478	332	186	491	668	463	260
Nonpublic	1,685	1,980	1,603	1,109	2,353	2,766	2,239	1,549
1971-72								
Public	376	526	354	192	507	709	477	259
Nonpublic	1,820	2,133	1,721	1,172	2,453	2,875	2,320	1,580
1972-73[1]								
Public	407	566	455	233	527	733	590	302
Nonpublic	1,898	2,226	1,846	1,221	2,459	2,884	2,392	1,582
1973-74								
Public	438	581	463	274	521	691	551	326
Nonpublic	1,989	2,375	1,925	1,303	2,366	2,825	2,289	1,550
1974-75[1]								
Public	470	597	473	316	503	639	507	338
Nonpublic	2,131	2,534	2,035	1,341	2,282	2,714	2,179	1,436
1975-76[2]								
Public	513	656	526	353	513	656	526	353
Nonpublic	2,333	2,775	2,233	1,455	2,333	2,775	2,233	1,455

Source: NCES, *The Condition of Education, 1977*, Table 3.11, p. 184.

[1] Data for 1965-66, 1967-68, 1969-70, 1972-73 and 1974-75 estimated by applying the Consumer Price Index to constant dollar estimates.

[2] Estimated.

Table 4-4 FAMILY INCOME OF FRESHMEN (IN PERCENTAGES) 1976

Estimated Parental Income	All Institutions	All 2-Year Colleges	All 4-Year Colleges	All Universities	Predominantly Black Colleges	2-Year Colleges		4-Year Colleges				Universities		Predominantly Black Colleges	
						Public	Private	Public	Private Nonsectarian	Protestant	Catholic	Public	Private	Public	Private
less than $3,000	3.9	5.2	3.6	1.9	17.0	5.2	4.8	4.3	2.5	3.1	2.8	1.9	1.9	20.1	10.3
$3,000-$3,999	2.4	3.1	2.3	1.3	10.4	3.0	3.5	2.8	1.5	2.1	2.1	1.3	1.2	11.8	7.2
$4,000-$5,999	4.4	5.5	4.3	2.5	13.3	5.5	6.1	5.0	3.2	3.7	3.7	2.6	2.3	14.6	10.5
$6,000-$7,999	4.8	5.7	4.8	3.1	11.9	5.7	6.3	5.2	4.2	4.5	4.2	3.2	2.9	12.7	10.2
$8,000-$9,999	6.1	7.3	5.7	4.2	9.6	7.2	7.7	6.1	4.5	6.0	5.2	4.3	3.8	9.6	9.4
$10,000-$12,499	11.1	12.8	10.5	8.6	10.7	12.8	13.3	10.6	9.3	11.4	10.6	9.0	7.2	10.1	11.9
$12,500-$14,999	12.2	13.5	11.8	10.3	7.3	13.6	12.9	12.4	10.2	11.9	11.4	10.8	8.4	6.8	8.6
$15,000-$19,999	17.2	17.3	17.1	17.2	7.4	17.4	16.6	17.1	16.6	16.7	18.4	17.9	14.5	6.2	10.2
$20,000-$24,999	13.6	12.4	13.7	15.6	4.6	12.6	11.0	14.2	13.1	12.8	13.8	16.3	13.1	3.7	6.6
$25,000-$29,999	7.5	6.4	7.6	9.6	2.6	6.5	5.5	7.7	7.8	7.2	7.5	9.7	9.1	1.8	4.3
$30,000-$34,999	5.5	4.1	5.8	7.7	1.7	4.1	4.1	5.6	6.4	5.6	5.8	7.7	7.8	1.0	3.4
$35,000-$39,999	3.3	2.2	3.7	4.9	1.1	2.2	2.5	3.2	4.8	3.9	3.4	4.8	5.3	0.6	2.1
$40,000-$49,999	3.1	1.8	3.5	4.8	1.2	1.8	2.2	2.6	5.3	3.9	3.9	4.4	6.5	0.4	2.9
$50,000 or more	4.9	2.6	5.7	8.3	1.2	2.5	3.5	3.3	10.5	7.0	7.1	6.2	16.0	0.6	2.5
Percentages of parental incomes below $15,000	44.7	53.1	43.0	31.9	80.2	53.0	55.6	48.4	35.4	42.7	40.0	53.1	27.7	85.7	68.1

Source: Alexander Astin, Margo King, and Gerald Richardson, The American Freshman: National Norms for Fall 1976 (Los Angeles: CIRP/ACLU, 1977).

and predominantly black institutions are discounted. In predominantly white institutions, 44.4 percent of all blacks enrolled are in two-year colleges, 36.7 percent are in four-year colleges, and 19 percent are in universities. The picture is somewhat altered by the inclusion of black institutions, because these are overwhelmingly four-year colleges (see Table 4-5).

This disparity in enrollment is equally large in public and private institutions, but it is quite different in black institutions. In the latter most black students are in four-year colleges, 61.3 percent. Although only 4 percent of all black students are enrolled in black universities, the majority, 2.4 of 4 percent, are in private universities.

In contrast, the overwhelming majority of black students at each level of nonblack institutions is found in public ones. In the case of four-year colleges and universities, the ratio of black enrollment in public versus private institutions is more than 2 to 1. In two-year colleges, the ratio of 29 to 1 public versus private is somewhat distorted by the small number of private two-year colleges. The ratios of students in public versus private two-year colleges are about the same for black and white students; 13 percent are in private two-year colleges (see Figure 4-1).

In comparing the public and private sectors, the four-year colleges and universities contain the significant differences, especially because two-year colleges are overwhelmingly public, about 7 to 3.

Federal Aid, Public/Private Enrollment, and Black Distribution

Federal policy in higher education plays a pivotal role in the distribution of funds to public and private institutions. In the preceding chapter, it is observed that private institutions receive a larger proportion of federal funds for students than their enrollments alone would justify. When this observation is brought to bear on the fact that black students are more likely to be located in public institutions, there is at least a *prima facie* case for the criticism of federal financial aid policies.

In four-year colleges, where blacks are about as underrepresented in the private sector as they are in the private sector of universities, the proportional weight of financial aid is clearly toward the private sector (see Figure 4-2).

In terms of the role of federal financial aid policy, the most obvious "explanation" for the imbalance toward private institutions is that these institutions cost more. What must still be remembered is that there is a difference between a good explanation or excuse and a good reason, meaning socially responsible public policy. The fact that private institutions cost more is only a sufficient reason for giving them proportionately more public

Table 4-5 PERCENTAGE DISTRIBUTION OF BLACK STUDENT ENROLLMENT IN HIGHER EDUCATION
Fall 1976

Type of Institution	All Black Students in Higher Education	Blacks in Traditionally Black Institutions	Blacks in other than Traditionally Black Institutions	Blacks in Predominantly Black Institutions	Blacks in Traditionally Black Institutions and Predominantly Black Institutions	Blacks in other than Traditionally and Predominantly Black Institutions
All institutions	100.0	100.0	100.0	100.0	100.0	100.0
Public	80.5	67.2	83.4	91.2	76.8	82.0
Private	19.5	32.8	16.6	8.8	23.2	18.0
All universities	14.5	6.6	16.2	—	4.0	19.0
Public	10.1	2.7	11.7	—	1.6	13.7
Private	4.4	3.9	4.5	—	2.4	5.2
All 4-year colleges	44.0	88.8	34.3	20.3	61.3	36.7
Public	30.8	61.2	24.2	16.7	43.4	25.5
Private	13.2	27.6	10.1	3.6	18.0	11.2
All 2-year colleges	41.5	4.5	49.5	79.7	34.7	44.4
Public	39.6	3.3	47.4	74.5	31.9	42.8
Private	1.9	1.3	2.1	5.2	2.8	1.5

Source: Committee Staff analysis of Department of Health, Education and Welfare, National Center for Education Statistics data from Fall 1976 HEGIS Survey. Reproduced in National Advisory Committee on Black Higher Education and Black Colleges and Universities, *Higher Education Equity: The Crisis of Appearance Versus Reality, First Annual Report,* 1977 (Washington, D.C., 1978), p. 14.

Note: Percentages may not add to totals due to rounding.

Figure 4-1   ENROLLMENT IN INSTITUTIONS OF HIGHER EDUCATION 1976

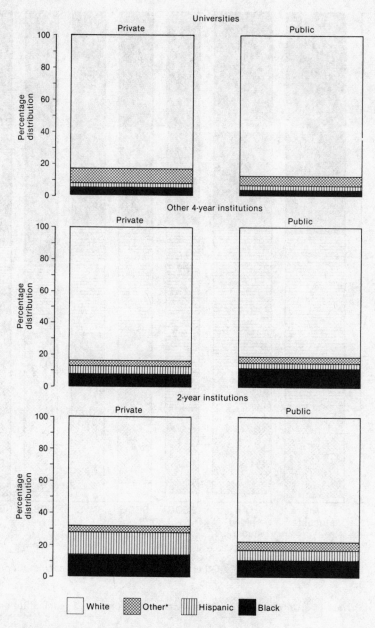

Source: NCES, *The Condition of Education, 1978*, Chart 3.6, p. 119. See also Appendix Table 4A-4.

* Includes American Indian/Alaskan Native, Asian or Pacific Islander, and nonresident alien.

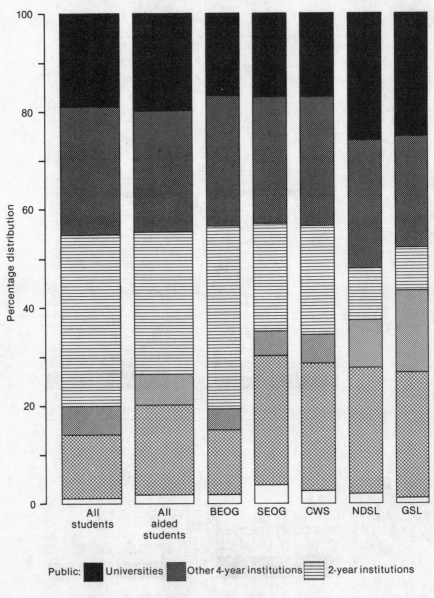

Figure 4-2   INSTITUTIONS ENROLLING STUDENTS RECEIVING U.S. OFFICE OF EDUCATION ASSISTANCE

Percentage distribution

100

80

60

40

20

0

All students   All aided students   BEOG   SEOG   CWS   NDSL   GSL

Public: ■ Universities   ▨ Other 4-year institutions   ▤ 2-year institutions

Private: ▨ Universities   ▨ Other 4-year institutions   □ 2-year institutions

Source: NCES, The Condition of Education, 1978, Chart 5.5, p. 217.

funds *if* they provide more public service than public institutions. We will turn to this point shortly in the context of data on degrees granted.

The explanation also falls short of explaining the maldistribution of students by family income in that the percentage of student recipients of federal aid is also greater at private institutions than at public ones. Cost differences can only be a marginal explanation in this case because student eligibility for federal aid extends only to the $15,000 income level for BEOG and SEOG.

More important, the distribution of federal funds within the private institutions is, by contrast to that in public institutions, disadvantageous for black students. Referring to Table 3-5 (chapter 3), it is apparent that the percentage of that already small number of blacks in private institutions receiving federal basic grants is smaller than the percentage of blacks in public institutions. For BEOG recipients, the ratio is about 23 percent of blacks in private institutions against 30 percent of blacks in public ones.

Of course there is always room for explanation of maldistribution. It might be thought, for example, that blacks in private institutions are relatively better off than blacks in public institutions. It does not seem worthwhile, however, to pursue extensive data on this point, because it clearly is not an appropriate explanation. First, most students in private institutions have higher family incomes than students in public institutions, so that relative to whites, blacks are likely to be as much, or more, economically disadvantaged there. Second, and more important, the public policy dilemma still remains. Namely, federal funds—presumably designed to help equalize educational opportunity in terms of race and income—are made less effective by their maldistribution in the private sector.

Impact of Financial Aid on Distribution

It is important to recognize the extent to which blacks and other minorities depend on federal funds to assist them in paying for higher education. Estimates from the Higher Education Research Institute indicate that black students depend on federal grants two to three times as much as white students. Blacks depend on BEOG and SEOG four to five times as much as white students (see Table 4-6).

The reason for this level of dependence is clearly the lack of private funds among minority students. It is a lack of funds for which they alone apparently can not compensate. As the preceding table suggests, black students are willing to work to support their education when the opportunity is there. Accordingly, black students are disproportionately found in college work-study programs. At the same time, there is evidence that beyond college work-study, blacks do not have the same educationally sup-

Table 4-6 PERCENTAGE OF TOTAL COLLEGE COSTS PAID FROM VARIOUS SOURCES

Race of Student

Source	White	Black	American Indian	Oriental	Mexican American	Puerto Rican	Other	All
BEOG	5.7	30.0	11.8	9.0	22.5	25.4	8.7	8.2
SEOG	0.8	3.8	1.5	1.8	2.3	2.3	1.5	1.1
State scholarship	3.5	4.4	3.8	5.5	5.1	4.3	3.6	3.6
Local, private scholarship	3.6	3.6	4.5	3.7	4.0	3.3	3.1	3.6
Student's GI benefits	0.9	1.7	3.0	1.3	2.1	2.3	1.7	1.0
Parents' GI benefits	0.5	0.6	1.4	0.2	0.9	0.3	0.7	0.5
SS dependents' benefits	1.9	2.2	2.7	1.6	3.8	3.1	2.0	1.9
Total grants	16.9	46.3	28.7	23.1	40.7	41.0	21.3	19.9
Parents or family	46.0	24.6	32.8	45.3	25.2	27.0	40.3	43.8
Spouse	0.4	0.4	1.2	0.3	0.7	1.6	0.5	0.5
Total family assistance	46.4	25.0	34.0	45.6	25.9	28.6	40.8	44.3
Total grants and family assistance	63.3	71.3	62.7	68.7	66.6	69.6	62.1	64.2
College Work Study	1.6	5.3	2.6	2.0	3.3	5.7	2.3	2.0
Federal Guaranteed Student Loan	2.7	3.0	1.9	1.3	1.3	2.0	2.8	2.7
National Direct Student Loan	1.8	3.5	1.4	1.8	1.9	1.6	1.8	1.9
Other loans	1.6	1.4	1.7	1.0	1.0	1.6	1.3	1.6
Full-time work	2.1	2.1	3.4	1.1	4.1	2.0	3.6	2.2
Part-time work	14.0	6.9	12.8	12.5	13.3	9.4	13.6	13.4
Savings	10.5	4.1	9.8	8.4	6.1	5.6	9.5	9.9
Other financing	1.8	1.9	3.4	2.7	1.9	2.0	2.7	1.9
Student net cost	36.1	28.2	37.0	30.8	32.9	29.9	37.6	35.6
Grand total	99.4	99.5	99.7	99.5	99.5	99.5	99.7	99.8

Source: Larry Leslie, "Higher Education Opportunity: A Decade of Progress," ERIC Higher Education Research Report, No. 3 (1977), Table 14, p. 35.

Note: Totals do not equal 100.0 percent due to rounding.

portive job opportunities as white students. As freshmen, both are likely to work full-time to support their education, but blacks are only half as likely to work part-time as whites. When one considers that the part-time employment is more suitable for college life, the question of racial inequality in youth employment comes up. One can hardly expect that black students would have a fair chance at getting an educationally convenient part-time job when black youth unemployment is about three times that of white youth.

Accordingly, black students earn proportionately less of their college expenditures while enrolled in sessions than any other group, including other minorities. In contrast, black parents contribute more to their children's college expenditures as a percentage of family income than other parents. These are particularly striking imbalances when one considers how small the private financial resources of black students and their families are (see Figure 4-3).

The other major sources of student financing, parental contribution and student savings, should not be seen as substitutes for federal commitment. Not only do black families have relatively small resources, they are making a greater proportional commitment of those small resources to the education of their young than wealthier families (see Figure 4-3). According to data drawn from the Census Bureau and the Internal Revenue Service, families earning less than $12,000 a year give as high a percentage of their income to their dependent students as families earning more than $25,000 a year (see Appendix, Table A4-3). This comes to about 10 percent, which, of course, produces quite different dollar amounts at different income levels. The expenditure of ten percent of disposable income at the poverty line is as critical for the family, probably more critical, than an equal expenditure at high income levels. In other words, the real choices as to whether and how most black young people will go to college rest with the government.

Impact of Financial Aid Distribution on Two-Year Colleges

Because the vast majority of two-year colleges (nonproprietary) are public and very low cost, the direct impact of federal financial aid on black student distribution is substantially less than its impact in other institutions. The major systemic difference in impact on black distribution between two-year and other low-cost institutions hinges on admissions criteria and other nonfinancial considerations. Still, when medium and high cost institutions are included, the financial constraints of a private education are not without significant consequences for black student distribution between two- and four-year institutions. These consequences are similar in form to the finan-

Figure 4-3   DISTRIBUTION OF STUDENT EXPENDITURES FOR
POSTSECONDARY EDUCATION
1976

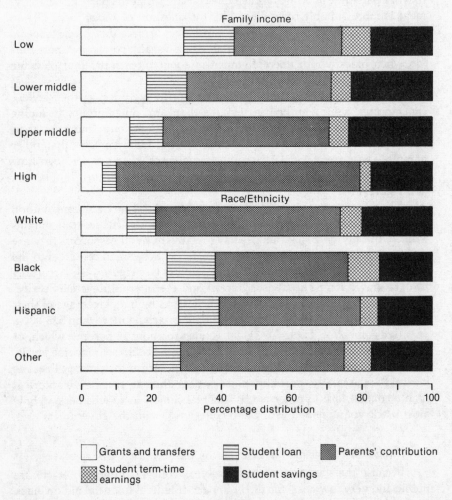

Source: NCES, The Condition of Education, 1978, Chart 5.12, p. 231.

cial consequences on distribution of the public/private four-year alternative, but the impact is probably greater.

There are also financial considerations involved in choosing between a two- and four-year public education. For example, the cost of college residency alone can be prohibitive for the average black student relying on his family's income. Other constraints, however, on black student choice between two- and four-year colleges are so great that available data are largely inadequate to isolate the financial consequences. To illustrate, the difference in tuition and fees between a public university and a public two-year college was $400 a year in 1975–76 (i.e., just under $200 at two-year colleges, and just under $600 at universities). In contrast, tuition and fees at a private two-year institution were more than $1,000 more than at a public one; at a private university they were more than eleven times higher (see Appendix, Figure A4-1).

The primary result of the distribution of federal funds is that two-year college students bear the greatest financial burden. The percentage of students in two-year institutions receiving federal funds is significantly smaller than their percentage of higher education enrollment. For example, in 1972–73, 23 percent of public two-year college freshmen received U.S. Office of Education aid versus 28 percent of all freshmen enrolled in private two-year colleges; yet 97 percent of two-year college enrollment is public.

At the same time, the financial needs of two-year college freshmen were greater than the needs of freshmen in the other public institutions (assuming constant costs). The median family income of freshmen in two-year institutions was about $11,000 a year as against $15,000 for university freshmen in 1972. This family income difference across institutions persisted through 1976. By 1976, two-year college students had mean family incomes of $14,475 a year as compared to $20,090 a year for university freshmen. In all years, four-year college freshmen were in the middle income categories, as Table 4-7 shows.

Special Problems of Unequal Distribution in Two-Year Colleges

In addition to the apparent financially disadvantageous position of two-year college students, they face other current and potential disadvantages in comparison with other students in higher education. Some of these are grounded in the nature and purpose of the institutions themselves, and therefore tend to affect equally all students who choose to enroll in them. For example, the Associate of Arts (A.A.) degree awarded by two-year colleges tends to provide less economic mobility to the degree recipient than a B.A. But, the original intention of the school has virtually never been to equalize the economic consequences of the two types of degrees.

Table 4-7 TOTAL ENROLLMENTS BY FAMILY AND MEDIAN INCOME, AND INSTITUTIONAL TYPE 1972–76

Institutional Type	Total Percentage	$0–3,999	$4,000–$9,999	$10,000–14,999	$15,000–19,999	$20,000–$25,000	More than $25,000	Median Income (in dollars) Current/Constant '78
1972								
2-Year	100.0	11.6	30.2	31.5	12.6	6.3	7.9	11,126/11,126
4-Year	100.0	7.0	22.5	29.4	15.7	9.5	14.9	13,153/13,153
University	100.0	3.4	17.6	29.5	17.0	12.2	20.3	14,908/14,908
1974								
2-Year	100.0	9.1	22.8	31.5	14.3	10.3	12.2	13,031/11,056
4-Year	100.0	6.8	18.8	26.4	15.6	11.9	20.4	14,802/12,559
University	100.0	3.6	14.0	26.2	17.0	14.0	25.2	16,994/14,419
1976								
2-Year	100.0	8.3	18.5	26.3	17.3	12.4	17.1	14,475/10,635
4-Year	100.0	5.9	14.8	22.3	17.1	13.7	26.3	16,025/11,777
University	100.0	3.2	9.8	18.9	17.2	15.6	35.3	20,290/14,911

Source: Analysis of ACE/CIRP unpublished data, (1978).

The only racial impact for which we need to look is in the economic area of "systemic" variations among students. In particular, are black students constrained by economic conditions, financial aid or income, to enroll in these institutions, more than other students, when they could otherwise enroll in a B.A./B.S.-granting institution? It should be evident from the preceding discussion of financial aid and income that there are some race-related constraints intrinsic to the educational system, even when it functions well, because student choice across racial groups is not equally free. The limits of present data, however, will not allow us to give precise numbers to those racial differences.

This first set of problems of racial distribution concerns "normative" institutional differences, i.e., different purposes; a second concerns the behavior or the "behavioral structure" of the institutions. Structural problems include patterns of residence, hours, and length of attendance, for example. The structure of two-year institutions tends to transform the pattern of distribution found throughout higher education into patterns and problems of racial imbalance. In other words, the normative characteristics of two-year institutions are fundamental parts of the systemic variation of higher education, and the structural characteristics are fundamental parts of what has been called "institutional" variation.

In addition, two-year institutions have special characteristics which come under the rubric, "programmatic" variation. In particular, variations in curricular choices and fields of major are important for the distribution of black students. Since problems of racial inequality and institutional variation are similar in all institutions, we will discuss them in the broader context.

Some programmatic variations, however, like major field specialization, also have a systemic character which needs to be addressed separately for two-year institutions. The two-year college degree is not simply a lesser or short-order version of the baccalaureate degree; it is often a different type of degree. While a majority of students, and about three-fourths of black students in two-year colleges, pursue the A.A. degree as a preliminary to further study (see *Equal Educational Opportunity: An Assessment*) only a minority of them ever are able to use it for that purpose. Moreover, much of the curricular programming in these schools is designed for non-B.A./B.S. training. Business and technical science majors in these schools are largely structured to provide terminal A.A. degrees. The course of study in many schools is built around part-time employment, and internships, which are intended to lead to full-time, permanent employment, once the two years, or fewer in some cases, of study are completed. The fact that black students are disproportionately enrolled in these institutions means that there is an additional bias in the racial distribution of students by·major. Nevertheless, it should be that the black/white distribution of majors is more equal in two-year institutions than in others.[16]

Still, black students in two-year colleges tend to be more heavily concentrated than white students in Education, Business, and the Social Sciences. They are most underrepresented in the technical sciences and the "professions" (see Table 4-8). Unfortunately for black students, it is in these latter fields—technical sciences as well as some professions such as pharmacy—that the two-year college degree seems to get its highest rate of return on the job market.

INSTITUTIONAL VARIATION

In terms of observed racial variation in the distribution of students, there are few data to indicate substantial racial bias. The possibility of racial bias remains, however, because there are insufficient data to determine

Table 4-8   MAJOR-FIELD DISTRIBUTION OF STUDENTS IN
2-YEAR COLLEGES (IN PERCENTAGES)
1974

Major Field	Male		Female		Male and Female	
	White	Black	White	Black	White	Black
Education	2.8	5.3	5.6	6.3	4.0	5.8
Business	23.4	25.3	27.1	30.9	25.0	27.9
Social Science	2.2	3.4	2.5	2.9	2.3	3.2
Natural Science	4.9	1.4	2.8	1.3	4.0	1.3
Technical Science	25.4	23.5	2.4	2.1	15.6	13.5
Professions	1.4	1.1	1.7	1.8	1.6	1.4
Social Work and Public Health	9.3	8.8	26.0	23.0	16.5	15.5
Architecture	.6	.3	.2	.1	.4	.2
Agriculture	1.8	.3	.4	.1	1.2	.2
Computer Science	2.4	3.5	1.9	3.2	2.2	3.4
Other	25.7	27.1	29.3	28.4	27.3	27.7
Total (100% =)	(503)	(65)	(375)	(57)	(879)	(122)
Undecided	26.4	23.4	26.5	21.2	26.5	22.4

Source: Gail Thomas, "Equality of Representation of Race and Sex Groups in Higher Education: Institutional and Program Enrollment Statuses," Center for Social Organization of Schools, Johns Hopkins University, Baltimore, Maryland, Report No. 263 (October 1978).

otherwise. Potentially, maldistribution of black students toward nondegree credit enrollment could contradict the appearance of racial equity that racially balanced enrollment figures would imply. To a lesser extent, but in the same vein, a biased distribution of blacks toward part-time enrollment could counterbalance the apparent equality of student headcounts or full-time equivalents (FTE's). In addition, other patterns of attendance, such as resident/nonresident status, which we have discussed, may threaten the quality of education distributed to black students within the institutions.

The limitations of data do not leave us without grounds for suspicion, because there are enough data to suggest that black students, once enrolled in a given institution, do not enjoy the "traditional" mode of college life. Since about half of black undergraduates are enrolled in two-year colleges, it is suggestive of bias that these schools have the highest proportion of nondegree enrollment. Since blacks are disproportionately enrolled in public institutions, it is significant that these institutions have the largest proportion of part-time students, 35 percent in public institutions compared to 27 percent in private ones in 1976 (see Table 3-6).

In addition to the concern generated by the quantitative data, numerous news reports, essays, and other current evaluations indicate that college life in formally integrated schools remains informally segregated. A sequence of reports published in *The Washington Post* makes a rather widely reached conclusion:

> There is pride and prejudice—sometimes indistinguishable from one another. They show themselves in what whites call "tradition" —usually meaning all-white fraternities, sororities and campus clubs—and they frequently show up in what blacks call "black solidarity"—usually meaning black student coalitions, associations and unions, black yearbooks, black newspapers, "black studies" and sometimes "black homecomings."
>
> There are "special education programs" for minority students. Many blacks say these programs hurt as much as they help, getting them into the university on the one hand and stigmatizing them as "inferior" on the other. It is difficult, if not impossible, they say, to enter interracial social relationships from a position of weakness.[17]

Public policy may not be able to deal directly with the causes for this kind of racial separation. There are, no doubt, factors involved which analysts and planners of public educational policy are ill-prepared to address. Yet, racial separation on campuses dominated by white faculty is always symptomatic of black student disadvantage. As was observed earlier, white faculty members tend to communicate more freely with white

129

than with black students. By the same token, blacks students who are fully integrated into college life are more likely than blacks who are not to be able to bridge this unfair barrier.

Nevertheless, there are educationally-valid reasons for variation in institutional-attendance status which should not be ignored. Thus, racial separation on campuses may be a consequence of necessary cohesion and self-help on the part of the black students. Similarly, it should be kept in mind that the other variations, to which we now turn, also have more than one side.

Resident/Nonresident Status

Residency during undergraduate study and especially during the freshman year is a characteristic of the traditional mode of higher education. It has the advantage, as noted earlier, of allowing the student to assimilate into college life. It should facilitate concentration on study as well as encourage broad socialization into the academic milieu. On the other hand, the nontraditional student frequently does not have the money to pay residence fees, and must therefore resign himself or herself to a commuter-education. Consequently, the proportion of black students enrolled in nonresident institutions is relatively high. Those institutions which generally have the highest proportion of black students (excluding traditionally black institutions) tend to have the smallest amount of residential space. For example, two-year colleges allocated only 8.5 percent of their space for residential facilities in 1970 as compared to four-year colleges and universities, which allocated about a third of their space to residential facilities (see Appendix, Figure A4-4). In addition, data from the American Council on Education demonstrate a clear correspondence between residency of freshmen and institutional selectivity (see Appendix, Table A-4-5).

One illustration of the distributive difference thus created is found in the urban/rural ratio of college students. According to census reports, 10.1 percent of the white metropolitan young between three and thirty-four years old were enrolled in college as compared to 6.5 percent of the corresponding nonmetropolitan young—a ratio of about 5 to 3. For blacks, 8.1 percent of the metropolitan young were in college as against 4.3 percent of the nonmetropolitan young—a ratio of about 2 to 1.[18] In whatever region they may originate, more black than white college students attend urban schools.

That this overall difference in patterns of residential study between whites and blacks is a function of factors other than free choice is indicated by surveys of student preference. A 1976 study of preferences by Leo Munday for American College Testing Educational and Programs Services (ACT) found that blacks as much as "traditional" students want to attend college away from home. While a higher proportion of blacks than whites expect to go to college out-of-state, blacks who expect to study out-of-state apparently give in more frequently to financial constraints which obligate them to stay at home.

Part-Time/Full-Time

Like nonresident enrollment, part-time enrollment is a nontraditional mode of study. In general, it is more characteristic of the nontraditional student: "more of the first-time part-time students are women than men, whereas more full-time first-time students are men." The figures show the greatest part-time student growth in public two-year institutions and public universities; private four-year institutions other than universities show a rate of part-time student growth less than that of full-time enrollment.[19] Thus, to the extent that black students are disproportionately located in public and two-year institutions, their attendance pattern is disproportionately part-time. Moreover, because a larger proportion of black students are female than male, one would expect a larger overall proportion of part-time students among blacks.

Referring to Table 3-11, however, the data do not provide significant support for this expectation. The black/white ratio of full- and part-time students seems to be quite balanced once these other factors are held constant. One explanation for this apparently fortunate circumstance is that black students, relying heavily on financial aid, need to be enrolled full-time in order to benefit fully from that aid. Another explanation is that the unemployment rate among black youth is so high that blacks students have less reason to disperse their study time. At any rate, neither the data available nor the probable explanations of present data are sufficient to warrant confidence on this point. As such, we will explore this aspect of distribution in more depth in the next chapter.

Degree/Nondegree

Data on the distribution of degree/nondegree credit enrollment by race are also in short supply. Fortunately, the impact of the distribution can be measured *indirectly* in areas where there are more data available. First, the differences between degrees awarded in black institutions as compared to other institutions are evidence of a degree credit problem (which also includes attrition). We will examine this relationship in terms of black institutions more closely in the next chapter. Second, the rate of graduation at the B.A. level is another indirect indication of a problem. In 1975–76 black undergraduates, while accounting for about 9 percent of all undergraduate enrollment, received only about 6 percent of the B.A. degrees. Almost half of these were awarded by black institutions.

Table 4-9   PREFERENCES IN CHOICE OF COLLEGE FOR NONTRADITIONAL AND TRADITIONAL COLLEGE-BOUND STUDENTS (IN PERCENTAGES)

Preferences	Part-Time Students	Evening Students	Below $7,500 Income	Non-English Speaking in Home	Black Students	Chicanos	Older Students	ACT Composite ≤ 11	Commuter (live at home)	Non-Traditional Students Combined	Traditional Students Combined
Distance from college											
Less than 10 miles	28	25	18	23	18	25	44	21	42	23	5
10–25 miles	25	23	17	23	13	21	30	17	35	19	4
26–100 miles	16	17	25	13	26	18	13	23	10	20	26
More than 100 miles	15	21	29	29	32	29	9	29	4	26	51
No college chosen	15	14	12	12	11	7	3	11	9	12	15
Will attend college											
In-state	80	79	76	70	67	76	76	65	89	79	79
Out-of-state	20	21	24	30	33	24	24	35	11	21	21
Maximum tuition											
$500	25	22	18	18	16	23	41	22	20	16	6
$1,000	22	22	23	19	20	24	24	18	27	23	18
$1,500	12	14	15	9	15	11	4	14	14	14	17
$2,000	9	7	11	11	11	5	5	8	9	10	13
$2,500	4	5	6	5	7	6	2	5	5	7	10
$3,000	1	4	3	6	4	2	0	2	3	3	6
$3,500	1	1	1	3	2	0	0	1	1	1	3
$4,000	0	1	1	2	1	1	0	1	1	1	2
No preference	27	25	21	27	23	30	25	29	22	25	25

Source: Leo Munday, "College Access for Nontraditional Students," Journal of Higher Education, XLVII, 6 (November/December 1976), pp. 686–687.

More directly, nondegree credit enrollment strays from the traditional mode of higher education. It is more prevalent at nontraditional (e.g., two-year) and lower-cost institutions. Still, it can serve an important educational function. Along with part-time enrollment, it is especially important for the retraining of professionals and the initiation of older students into higher education. It poses a special problem for blacks students, however, because nondegree credit has less value for them in the job market than for white students. In some sense, employers are more concerned with the credentials than with the skills of former students.

> For instance, in describing the importance of education for blacks, Jaffe, Adams, and Meyers (1968) noted that a black who fails to obtain a college education is less likely than a white who does not obtain a college education to be a white collar worker or enter a professional or technical job. The authors also note that unlike a white who may have other mobility options, either a black "makes it" or he fails because he has no intervening options.[20]

PROGRAMMATIC VARIATIONS

The racial distribution of students in higher education by major field of study may be described as a problem of maldistribution. The problem may be illustrated by the fact that about a quarter of baccalaureate degrees granted to blacks in 1976 were in Education. The bias toward Education, observed several years ago in ISEP's *Equal Educational Opportunity: An Assessment,* is not, unfortunately, compensated for by a smaller but solidly strong group of black students in other major fields, because these other students, if they do graduate work, are rather likely to be drawn into Education. Of master's degrees granted blacks, 61 percent are in Education, and 55 percent of Ph.D. degrees among blacks are in Education. For those non-Education majors who are fortunate enough to get through graduate school, their undergraduate backgrounds are apparently not sufficient to retain them in their major fields (see Table 4-10 and chapter 5).

This distribution bias finds little or no solace in the marketplace. The areas of heaviest black concentration, it must be reiterated, are among the least financially rewarding. Bachelor's degrees in Education provided their 1975 recipients with an average income of $8,100 a year in 1976; just $200 dollars up from the lowest average (in biological sciences) of the fields surveyed (see Appendix, Table A4-4).

The story of this distribution, of course, begins at least four years before degrees are granted. In fact, it begins at least as far back as secondary school for the student. At first glance, it might not appear to be so because

Table 4-10   PERCENTAGE DISTRIBUTION OF DEGREES AWARDED
1976

	Baccalaureates		Master's		Doctorates	
Major Field	All Students	Black Students	All Students	Black Students	All Students	Black Students
Total	100.0	100.0	100.0	100.0	100.0	100.0
Agriculture	2.1	0.4	1.1	0.4	2.7	1.5
Architecture	1.0	0.4	1.0	1.0	0.2	0.4
Biological Sciences	5.9	3.9	2.1	1.1	10.0	4.3
Business and Management	15.5	16.1	13.6	7.6	2.8	1.4
Education	16.9	24.0	41.4	61.1	23.0	55.2
Engineering	4.9	2.3	5.1	1.1	8.3	1.6
Health Professions	5.8	4.6	4.0	3.1	1.7	1.3
Mathematics	1.7	1.4	1.2	0.6	2.5	0.7
Physical Sciences	2.3	1.1	1.7	0.7	10.1	3.4
Psychology	5.4	5.4	2.5	2.0	7.6	5.4
Public Affairs	3.6	5.6	5.5	7.9	0.9	2.4
Social Sciences	13.7	18.6	5.1	4.3	12.2	9.6
All others	21.2	16.2	15.7	9.1	18.0	12.8

Source: Preliminary data on fall 1976 enrollment from HEW, National Center for Education Statistics. Reproduced in National Advisory Committee on Black Higher Education and Black College and Universities. *Higher Education Equity: The Crisis of Appearance Versus Reality, First Annual Report, 1977* (Washington, D.C., 1978), Chart 8, p. 24.

black students do not differ very much from white students in their preferences for specialization while in high school. Still, racial inequality at that level, no doubt, serves to bias their eventual choices of majors. The maldistribution of students in college, however, is crucially influenced, if not determined, by the racially unequal experiences of students in higher education itself.

All students, blacks included, expect a variety of benefits from higher education. Among the two most constant expectations are to "learn more about things of interest" and to be "able to get a better job"[21] (see Appendix, Figure A4-3). Both of these preferences, and especially the latter one, have a clear relationship to the choice of major. One would expect, therefore, some response of black students to job opportunities in the choice of major while in college.

There is substantial evidence that students are preconditioned to some extent by their socioeconomic backgrounds and by parental preferences in their choice of major.[22] Given the lack of technical expertise in the black

Figure 4-4 AVERAGE SALARY AND UNDEREMPLOYMENT OF RECIPIENTS OF BACHELOR'S DEGREES 1976

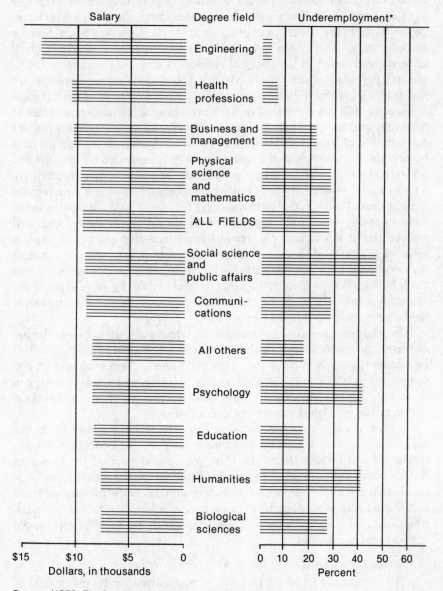

Source: NCES, *The Condition of Education, 1978*, Chart 3.19, p. 145.

* A college graduate working full-time is classified as underemployed if he or she is in a job that is not professional, technical, managerial, or administrative and, when asked, has stated that his or her job did not require a college degree.

community, black students probably miss an important incentive to choose a major in the physical sciences. On the other hand, the college-level training of blacks in the wider community, in any area, including Social Science and Education, is so low as to be inadequate to explain the degree of black underrepresentation in the physical sciences. Using 1974 data from OCR, the only period for which racially-stratified published data are available, we find that 6.9 percent of black undergraduates were enrolled in the technical sciences in 1974, as compared to 11.5 percent of white undergraduates in four-year institutions. There is a similar ratio for all institutions, 8.9 percent compared to 12.4 percent. Looking at Table 4-11, which breaks up the data by sex, one explanation of the racial disparity is suggested by the different sex ratios across race. A larger proportion of black undergraduates are female, slightly more than half. For white undergraduates, the ratio is more than reversed, with males outnumbering females 3 to 2. Because women have generally been underrepresented in the technical fields, and well represented in Education, one could hypothesize that sex would explain some of the racial difference. The sex explanation, however, like that of socioeconomic background, falls short. The disparity among males in these fields by race is even greater than that among females by race. Thus, if the sex ratio across race were the same, one could not assume that the major field distribution would also be the same.

In addition, the racial distribution of Education majors by sex further confirms the independence of the race factor. The ratio of black to white Education majors is about 4 to 3. Among women, there is almost no difference (20 to 19 percent) in the percentage of whites and blacks majoring in Education. Among men, on the other hand, there is a virtual 2 to 1 ratio in the percentages of blacks to whites in Education.

Unfortunately, the OCR data for 1976, the primary source for major field analysis, do not contain a separate category for Education. Nevertheless, it can be seen from the categories presented that the biases of distribution persist. Thus, our analysis (Table 4-12) of raw data from OCR shows that the black proportion of undergraduates in the physical sciences and Engineering, about 5 percent in each case, is less than half of the black proportion in the "all others" category, which includes mostly social sciences and humanities.

Institutional Sources of Bias in Program Distribution

A substantial part of the problem of maldistribution by major field of study is, no doubt, the socioeconomic and high school background conditions which incline black students toward or away from some major fields. Yet, it is not necessarily feasible or desirable for educational policy reform to concentrate on these often imprecise environmental background causes.

Table 4-11 **MAJOR FIELD DISTRIBUTION OF UNDERGRADUATES AT 4-YEAR COLLEGES AND UNIVERSITIES (IN PERCENTAGES) 1974**

Major Field	White		Black		Total	
	Male	Female	Male	Female	Male	Female
Education	7.9	16.2	23.5	26.3	14.8	21.5
Business	20.6	22.4	7.5	14.0	14.7	18.0
Social Science	14.8	19.7	13.6	17.6	14.3	18.6
Natural Science	7.6	4.9	5.1	4.4	6.5	4.6
Technical Science	17.8	11.3	3.7	3.0	11.5	6.9
Professions	.9	.6	6.0	4.7	3.2	2.8
Social Work and Public Health	1.0	1.9	3.0	4.1	1.9	3.1
Architecture	1.7	.8	.5	.2	1.2	.4
Agriculture	3.9	1.2	1.3	.3	2.7	.7
Computer Science	.8	1.0	.4	.7	.6	.8
Other	23.1	20.0	35.6	24.8	28.7	22.5
Total (100% =)	(1,692)	(132)	(1,358)	(149)	(3,050)	(282)
Undecided	16.9	19.7	17.4	19.1	17.1	19.4
	Total Undergraduate Enrollment [1]					
Education	6.7	12.6	19.6	20.8	12.4	16.8
Business	21.2	23.4	11.8	18.7	17.0	21.0
Social Science	11.9	14.4	11.2	13.5	11.6	14.0
Natural Science	7.0	3.7	4.6	3.5	5.9	3.6
Technical Science	19.5	15.4	3.4	2.7	12.4	8.9
Professions	1.0	.8	5.1	3.9	2.8	2.4
Social Work and Public Health	2.9	4.2	8.0	9.4	5.1	6.8
Architecture	1.5	.6	.4	.2	1.0	.4
Agriculture	3.4	.9	1.1	.3	2.4	.6
Computer Science	1.2	1.8	.7	1.4	1.0	1.6
Other	23.7	22.3	34.2	25.8	28.4	24.1
Total (100% =)	(2,196)	(198)	(1,734)	(206)	(3,930)	(404)
Undecided	19.3	20.9	19.5	19.7	19.4	20.3

Source: Gail Thomas, "Equality of Representation of Race and Sex Groups in Higher Education: Institutional and Program Enrollment Status," Center for Social Organization of Schools, Baltimore, Maryland (June 1978). See also Gail Thomas, "Race and Sex Group Equity: Institutional and Major-Field Enrollment Statuses," *American Educational Research Journal* (Forthcoming, Fall 1979).

[1] Includes two-year institutions.

Table 4-12   FULL-TIME ENROLLMENT IN INSTITUTIONS OF HIGHER EDUCATION
Fall 1976

Major Field	Black		Minority		White		Total
	Number	Percent	Number	Percent	Number	Percent	
Agriculture and Natural Resources	2,292	1.89	6,915	5.71	112,370	92.86	121,010
Architecture and Environmental Design	1,983	4.09	5,564	11.49	40,964	84.65	48,391
Biological Sciences	16,929	7.24	32,826	14.04	196,731	84.18	233,696
Business and Management	84,922	11.08	130,513	17.04	620,251	81.99	765,828
Engineering	15,677	5.06	35,830	11.57	251,617	81.30	309,457
Physical Science	4,916	4.71	9,548	9.15	91,626	87.81	104,355
All others	473,397	10.87	789,569	18.14	3,507,157	80.57	4,353,185

Source: U.S. Department of Health, Education and Welfare, Office for Civil Rights, unpublished data, 1977.

Beyond backgrounds, there are perceptible institutional biases in higher education which aggravate, or reinforce, the racially different tendencies toward major field distribution.

For all institutions, one source of bias in the black major field distribution is the unequal distribution of blacks among institutional types. Because black students are more heavily concentrated in two-year colleges than in other institutions, their options for physical science majors, beyond technical-vocational ones, are clearly restricted. And the relative exclusion of black students from the more expensive selective institutions may serve to limit or bias their enrollment towards the more common specializations such as Education, since new specializations are expensive to establish.

Third, and in line with the last observation, enrollment in black institutions has the effect of limiting the physical science options of black students. While most black institutions have solid, established physical science programs, their size and range of suboptions rarely correspond to those of major white institutions. Invariably, this limitation can be explained in terms of the inadequate and unequal funding of black institutions when compared to the funding of white four-year colleges and universities. The amount of federal research support received by all 105 black institutions together has never equaled that given individual, highly selective institutions known for their physical sciences programs.

In 1976 and continuing through 1977, substantial testimony was given by black physical scientists' organizations and individual black faculty before the Senate and House advocating increased federal support in these areas. The policy recommendations of these advocates focused on research and graduate student funding through the National Science Foundation, with the argument that such a funding commitment would "stimulate minority students at all levels."[23] In the initial testimony one gets a glimmer of the amounts of money needed:

> The program that is envisioned would cost a minimum of about $36 million a year divided among six minority institutions. It has been my experience that it takes about $200,000 per year per faculty member to run a first-rate research program. Thus, in the six institutions 30 faculty members in three departments could be funded at this level. The funding would be continued for a 10 year period. . . . The $36 million cost of this program is small compared to the total figure of $453 million in government funds that the top six U.S. universities received in FY 1973.[24]

Following these proceedings a year later, one sees some of the difficulty, if not resistance, in the federal government's support of black institutions through research funds. Black faculty requests had, under pressure, dwindled from $36 million a year for six institutions to $7 million a year for two "resource centers."[25]

Since traditionally black institutions only account for about 20 percent of black enrollment in higher education, the major locus of program distribution bias must rest with white institutions. Here, the special constraints on black students range from the "prerequisites" for admission into certain courses to faculty and administrative attitudes and behavior. The former, course prerequisites, may be unfair to disadvantaged students where adequate academic preparatory courses and/or remedial programs are not available in the institutions themselves. This problem, however, is hard to penetrate through broad policy planning because of the armor, sometimes unjustified, of academic standards.

Faculty attitudes and behavior at white institutions toward black students have been shielded from public scrutiny by the same armor, but often to the greater detriment of black students. Accordingly, there is a strong correlation between white faculty attitudes on a range of nonintellectual issues and black student program distribution.

E. C. Ladd and S. M. Lipset, who have surveyed faculty attitudes for several years, have demonstrated a clear distribution of faculty ideologies by academic discipline. Separating faculty by "liberal, moderate, and conservative" attitudes, they find that social scientists and humanities faculty members are the most "liberal," 58 percent in the liberal category. In contrast, engineering faculty members are found to be among the most "conservative," 29 percent in the liberal category and 48 percent in the conservative

Table 4-13   PROFESSORS' IDEOLOGY BY ACADEMIC DISCIPLINE

Academic Discipline	Ideology			
	Liberal	Moderate	Conservative	None of These
Social Service	58%	18%	18%	6%
Humanities	58%	22%	16%	4%
Natural Science	41%	20%	5%	5%
Law, Medicine	29%	19%	47%	3%
Business,				
Engineering	29%	20%	48%	3%
Agriculture	13%	22%	60%	5%

Source: Everett C. Ladd and Seymour Martin Lipset, "The Ladd-Lipset Survey," Chronicle of Higher Education (January 16, 1978), p. 9.

one. Given that the attitudes toward both black students and affirmative action are highly conditioned by these attitudes, and that black students themselves are more liberal than other students, it is not surprising that blacks gravitate toward the social sciences and humanities.

Moreover, it is understandable that in some of the subfields of the social sciences, such as quantitative political science and sociology, black students would be underrepresented if Ladd and Lipset's interpretation of their data is accurate:

> Social scientists and humanists, more directly concerned with human endeavors than natural scientists, seemingly are more sympathetic with liberal social reforms than those in fields less oriented to such matters.
>
> At the conservative side of the spectrum are the faculty in professional schools, whose ties to the outside world link them to the concerns and interests of established institutions, and who are less theoretically oriented.[26]

The Mingle study, mentioned earlier, helps to concretize the ways in which broad political and especially "professional" faculty attitudes may manifest themselves in negative behavior toward black students. Mingle

Table 4-14   DEPARTMENTAL SUPPORTIVENESS OF BLACK STUDENTS

Discipline	Mean	Minimum	Maximum	Standard Deviation
Humanities				
History	5.28	5.10	5.05	.15
English	5.04	4.53	5.82	.50
Social Sciences				
Economics	4.84	4.40	5.33	.33
Political Science	4.81	4.33	5.50	.48
Psychology	4.52	3.67	5.58	.68
Sociology	4.38	3.67	5.20	.59
Natural Sciences				
Math	4.40	3.33	5.33	.76
Biology	4.06	3.73	4.40	.27
Chemistry	3.77	2.86	5.00	.78

Source: James Mingle, "Faculty and Departmental Response to Increased Black Student Enrollment," Journal Of Higher Education, 49, 3 (1978), Table 1, p. 206.

Note: Index Range = 2 to 8.

looks at a variety of white faculty attitudes toward affirmative action and black students generally, and comes up with the departmental ranking shown in Table 4-14. The rank order of departments clearly corresponds to major field distribution biases of black students. Those departments most "supportive" of black students tend to enroll more of them.

These data also provide evidence of the roles and importance of black institutions as well as those of black programs in all institutions. According to the study, faculty members who recognized a need for gearing education to the students served were also those who supported black students. White faculty members who emphasized "universalism" and "professional neutrality" usually meant by that emphasis that black students should come to college with the same characteristics as white students.

> An active supporter held particularistic values about the application of admissions and performance criteria, viewed the long-term impact of blacks on higher education in positive terms, preferred a separate institutional structure for black programs, and held liberal (or activist) views about the role of colleges in solving problems of racial injustice...

> When faculty believe that black students should meet the same "standards" as whites this tends to be translated into an unwillingness to alter traditional teaching styles or support institutional changes.[27]

Racial bias in higher education is, therefore, a persistent problem. It has simply retreated behind more elusive barriers.

POLICY IMPLICATIONS

If the capacity of black Americans to get into some college, but no college in particular, were enough to satisfy the present concern for equal educational opportunity, then we should be reasonably satisfied with the progress made in higher education since 1974. If one were also unconcerned about the conditions or limitations under which black students may be enrolled in college, then another blemish on recent progress would be removed. Because equal educational opportunity involves the non-discriminatory distribution of students among and within institutions, however, the apparent value of expanded access to higher education for blacks is compromised. Moreover, any prospects for approaching a racially equal distribution of enrollment in higher education in the next few years are diminished by the continuing maldistribution of black students over the last few years.

Recognizing Problems

In policy analysis the first problem in dealing with inequalities of distribution is to recognize them and to acknowledge their current and potential importance. It is only in the last five or so years that analysts in significant numbers have concerned themselves with social inequality among students in colleges and universities. For the most part, the literature on higher education has treated inequality among students as if most inequality was a socially acceptable outgrowth of individual differences. That is to say, inequalities have been encapsulated within the concept of individualism. Accordingly, analysts have first sought to measure differences of individual intellect or personal prowess in their attempts to explain the uneven distribution of students. Second, they have turned to analyses of social and economic inequalities in the student's background, treating these inequalities as if their impact on educational opportunity was beyond the control of educational policy. Consequently, as long as the inequities of distribution were explained in terms of individual intellect or in terms of overwhelming and intractable social and economic inequalities, inequalities of distribution were rarely seen as injustices of higher education, and still less frequently seen as racial injustices.

A big step in advancing public policy on equal educational opportunity is then to recognize that race-related educational inequities often grow out of other types of inequalities. The first part of this step is the recognition that individual and socioeconomic inequalities have historically been tolerated in higher education under the erroneous assumption that other, racially unjust biases were not buried beneath them or obscured by them. In other words, there is more to racial inequality in higher education than simple prejudice and discrimination.

The second part is the recognition that analysis and evaluation of inequalities in higher education have not often been neutral. Evaluators have, for various reasons, precluded a uniform assessment of racial inequality in distribution by focusing their search on more traditional explanations of differences in educational achievement.

The third and most important part of this step is to direct education policy specifically toward the reduction of racial inequities in the distribution of students. Financial aid programs should be designed to take into account the full costs of enrollment for four years or longer in private and public institutions. In this regard, federal aid to students has been progressive in its impact on distribution. But the persistence of racial maldistribution in higher education demonstrates a need for a more comprehensive approach to educational finance. At the same time, the detrimental effects on blacks of state and private institutional practices in selective admissions need to be evaluated for their consistency or inconsistency with policies of equitable distribution.

With regard to both financial aid and institutional variation, the range of problems in the racial distribution of students needs to be more clearly specified. In particular, interinstitutional versus intrainstitutional variations in distribution may need to be treated separately in the development of education policy. Similarly, programmatic variations (specialization options) may need to be separated from overall institutional distribution in refining efforts to reduce racial bias in distribution.

Clarifying the Federal Role in Higher Education

Past and current social inequities in distribution have been largely shielded from federal attempts to redress them. In part, this results from fear of overextending the hand of government. Nevertheless, governmental influence in higher education has grown and continues as an indirect result of unmet public needs. The role that both federal and state governments play, often with different intentions, in determining the access and distribution of students in higher education, can be more precisely directed toward equal opportunity without an extension of governmental authority. The federal role in expanding access for blacks can also serve as a basis for a more consistent federal role in securing equal opportunity for students beyond the threshold of college.

SYSTEMIC INEQUALITIES IN DISTRIBUTION

To ensure an equitable distribution of students, the federal government must recognize and deal with higher education as a system. Students, faculty, professional associations, and virtually all the elements of college and university structures are linked together with similar elements from one institution to another by direct interaction or by indirect impact. The behavior of individuals in any one institution is likely to be fundamentally affected by the behavior of those in other institutions. Faculty research and teaching are guided by national norms. Students' access to college and choices while in college are heavily influenced by the special community to which students belong. The interconnections are often subdivided by institutional type, two-year and four-year, for example, but the connections remain widespread and important. Neither private groups nor state educational authorities seem to be in a position to deal efficiently with such national concerns. Only the federal government is capable of effectively guiding a nationwide system.

In order to provide effective guidance toward the provision of equal opportunity for blacks, the federal government (HEW, including OCR) must reconsider its own role in sustaining or supporting interinstitutional inequalities. These systemic inequalities involve the following areas:

I. The negative relationship between institutional selectivity and black enrollment:
    A. Variations in institutional resources;
    B. Variations in institutional obligations;
       1. to nation, state, and community
       2. to special groups and students
    C. Variations in admissions and financial aid practices.
II. Distribution of public education funds for restrictive groups:
    A. Assessment of all, including indirect institutional support;
    B. Assessment of "real" institutional costs per student and potential student;
    C. Assessment of dollar contribution to institutional selectivity with a concern for societal benefit;
    D. Assessment of institutional responsiveness to current and potential student need in terms of dollar contribution.
III. Evaluation of financial aid/institutional cost-relationship in terms of:

     A. Student/family savings contributions;
     B. Student earnings;
     C. Nonstudent services, particularly research productivity.
  IV. Evaluation of unintended impact of federal financial aid on the distribution of students by type of institution:
     A. Two-year versus four-year college and university attendance;
     B. Predominantly black attendance at predominantly black versus predominantly white institutions.

Since the racial biases which may stem from unequal distribution occur as much inside the individual institution as across institutions, government must have the capacity to assure, validate, or question practices within each institution. This capacity requires first that the federal government maintain consistent surveys and evaluations of a range of institutional practices. Such a task is already implicit in the legislated responsibility of OCR to collect data on minority enrollment in all institutions of higher education. Yet, as has been shown, simple enrollment data are insufficient to measure equality of opportunity. If such data were accurate and consistent, which they often fail to be, they still would not provide a useful picture of institutionally internal distribution. Second, enrollment data must be refined and coupled with a range of socioeconomic and financial aid data in order to get a clear description of racial inequities. Third, no meaningful explanation of racial inequality is possible unless regular institutional behavior (including rules and decision making) is carefully described and evaluated.

Consequently, an essential responsibility of the federal component of effective equal educational opportunity policy is the careful analysis of systemic variations in student distribution inside institutions. HEW should, as has just been suggested, be prepared to say whether or not black students are getting into the same kind of institutions as the majority. The concern now is that the federal government also prepare itself to say whether or not blacks have equal experiences in the years they spend in these institutions. This is important because, in large part, it is the college experience itself which determines the accessibility of opportunity to follow.

While all the variations of the institutional experiences have not been discussed in this chapter, the ones discussed represent the general problem area. Some variations may not now be critical to equal opportunity, but for the most part, one should only reach such a conclusion after making an assessment of the educational and developmental effects of the variations involved. Therefore, an evaluation system should be set up to examine the following institutional variations in distribution:

I. Black student integration in campus life:
   A. Access to, frequency, and openness of contact with faculty and administrators;
   B. Rapport with larger student body and involvement in student activities.
II. Teacher ethnocentrism (openness to black students):
   A. Relative frequency of contact initiated by faculty with students;
   B. Number and institutional status of black faculty and related personnel.
III. Variations in attendance status and conditions:
   A. Residency;
   B. Full-time/part-time attendance;
   C. Degree/nondegree credit.

The major intrainstitutional variation in student distribution, programmatic variation, occurs in the area of major field specialization. The choice of major is so critical to the quality of educational opportunity that it needs to be treated separately. The kind of program a student enrolls in influences not only the immediate personal and developmental value of college, but also the marketability of the college degree. For these reasons, it is essential that those concerned with racial inequality should carefully scrutinize racial imbalance in major field distribution, as well as distribution in subfields and special programs.

The need for closer scrutiny of this problem area has been evident since the first major quantitative study of blacks in higher education appeared several years ago. When the first studies appeared, it was evident that blacks were disproportionately concentrated in a few major fields, and overwhelmingly in Education. It has since become clear, if it was not before, that black students have been ill-prepared, as a result of their maldistribution, to respond to the strongest job market demand. There is thus a demonstrable societal and national value in a more equitable racial distribution, but government has not responded.

This maldistribution is probably caused by many institutional and socioeconomic pressures on black students, but is apparently much less complex. A concerted effort by those who make education policy, including institution, state, and federal officials, could no doubt positively highlight for black students the choices of specialization in which blacks are underrepresented.

Financial incentives in the form of aid to students and black institutions for the physical sciences and other underrepresented areas could be very effective. It would certainly not be the first time the federal government has intervened in higher education to encourage specialization in the physical sciences. It did so after "Sputnik" but with little or no direct benefit to blacks. The time has long since come for blacks to share more directly in those benefits.

To some extent, the maldistribution of blacks across major fields is the consequence of their maldistribution among institutions (systemic bias) and bias within institutions. Efforts to achieve a more equitable distribution across major fields might therefore be most effective by first addressing these sources of bias. Here again, a careful assessment of systemic pressures on black students is needed to determine what leads them to some institutions where their options for specialization are more limited than in others. Second, an assessment of internal college and university practices should be focused on the departmental and faculty pressures and encouragement which black students experience differently depending on the major field and subfield. To make an adequate assessment many variables in the higher education process should be observed. Of those we have discussed, the following variables and relationships seem to be crucial:

I. Departmental differences in faculty attitudes towards:
   A. Teaching as a primary obligation and the social responsibility of educators;
   B. Affirmative action and disadvantaged students;
   C. Professionalism versus cultural variation and multiple standards.
II. Tendency to major in a limited number of fields, particularly Education, as a function of institutional type most frequently attended by blacks, comparing:
   A. Well endowed or highly selective institutions versus poorly endowed or nonselective institutions;
   B. Universities and four-year colleges versus two-year colleges;
   C. "Predominantly" white versus "predominantly" black institutions.
III. Factors leading toward a redistribution of black students including:
   A. Significant numbers and distribution of black faculty by department;
   B. Student support and special programs in underrepresented majors;
   C. Strengthening and expansion of major field options in "predominantly" black institutions.

Although any kind of college education may be better than none at all, limitations on options for specialization, whether formal or *de facto*, effectively move the goal of educational equality one step away. It is therefore incumbent on education policy makers to ensure that the choices of black college students are made under conditions as free from constraint as those of the majority.

CHAPTER 5

Persistence: Learning How to Go on

Importance of Persistence in Equal Opportunity

A remark occasionally made by college counselors is that, except for a self-confident minority, almost half of all new freshmen see themselves as the one mistake the admissions committee made. Of course, virtually all of them are wrong, but they only recognize this after spending some time in the institution and after exposure to college life. By the time they develop more realistic and favorable images of themselves, they will have already undergone an important educational experience. They will have understood what they need to succeed in college and will have perceived a path which they can follow to success: they will have learned the basics of how to educate themselves. In the words of philosopher Ludwig Wittgenstein, the most learned and comprehensive conclusion a student can reach is "now I know how to go on." The key to persistence in higher education may simply be teaching and learning "how to go on."

Although more than a third of blacks of college age had gained access to college by 1974, the gains were late coming. They were only made with considerable difficulty, and, as subsequent fluctuations in enrollment growth suggest, these gains have only been precariously secured. Having made progress at getting into college, blacks have made very little progress at getting into the college of their choice or moving freely among the academic options generally available in higher education. The distribution of black students largely continued to be in 1977 what it was in 1974 and before—resistant to change. Where educational institutions have exhibited concern for equality of access, the preponderant attitude toward the problem of inequality of distribution has remained rather unresponsive, if not intractable. Having faced these two obstacles to higher education with a mixed record of gains and losses, the black undergraduate faces a third major obstacle: to stay in college until a degree is awarded. This need not mean staying four years or longer, but it does mean staying as long as is necessary to achieve racial parity in baccalaureate degrees awarded. For the typical black student, this also means staying longer than should be expected for most students under otherwise similar socioeconomic and academic constraints. Facing these constraints and winning is what we call "persistence."

In the first ISEP annual report on equality of educational opportunity, "persistence is defined as staying in college and earning a degree."[1] Persistence is treated as the positive side of retention; "dropping out" is treated as the negative side. A distinction is drawn between these phenomena and "stopping out." In the second ISEP annual report, "stopping out" is identified as a short-term interruption of an educational program. Students who stop out are generally understood to have educationally external or complementary reasons for leaving school, as opposed to educationally negative reasons. They plan to complete their educations eventually, however indefinite their time frames may be. In this study, the definition of persistence is modified to emphasize continued progress toward the degree initially sought. This means, first, that interruptions which last longer than "normal," e.g., longer than the frequent one-year excursions of undergraduates, will be considered as a problem in persistence. Second, failure to acquire or to move toward the B.A./B.S. by students whose two-year college curriculum and plans are oriented in that direction will also be treated as a problem.

What we are ultimately concerned with in this chapter, however, and what we cannot measure directly is the racial equality of those conditions of higher education that facilitate or impede the acquisition of the degree. If black and white students do not acquire their degrees at the same rate, with the same timeliness, there is an apparent inequality. Since the barriers to access and distribution are greater for blacks than for most students, there is good reason to assume that racial inequality in rates of persistence is more a product of racially unequal institutional conditions than a consequence of the individual deficiencies of black students. In the same vein, the second ISEP report observes:

Persistence is an indirect measure of institutional and student response. Although the tendency may be to credit the student if he graduates and blame the college if he fails, the truth lies somewhere in between. Persistence, as a measure of equal educational opportunity, is the result of the interaction of the minority student with his classmates, instructors, supportive personnel, and with the academic and social environment of the college.[2]

Issues in Persistence

In the first ISEP report, the rate of attrition of black students was found to be higher than that of white students: a degree-earned rate for blacks in college that is 75.3 percent of the rate for whites in two-year colleges and 89.5 percent of the rate for whites in four-year colleges.[3] At that time (1976), only survey data were available for the years under study, pre-1974. In the second study, relatively comprehensive data were available for 1974–75. The findings were striking: black attrition had either become worse, or the survey data had previously underestimated it, or both. For whatever reasons, attrition rates rose for all students, black students included. "Indeed, 57% of all white 1971 freshmen were enrolled in 1974, compared to 41% of all black 1971 freshmen."[4] Yet, even in 1977 when that study was completed, and now as well, persistence was hard to evaluate because it lumped together different educational plans, and because both black and white students were unevenly distributed within and across institutions, e.g., two-year and four-year colleges.

Nevertheless, survey data from a variety of sources, including the American Council of Education and the U.S. Census, confirmed a clear racial disadvantage in persistence (Figure 5-1).

PERSISTENCE AND DEGREES AWARDED

In addition to the conditions of education which support or impede black persistence, the most disturbing characteristic of higher educational patterns of persistence is the racial imbalance in degrees awarded. This imbalance is striking even when limited to a comparison to already racially imbalanced enrollment patterns.

The first ISEP annual report (1976) found that only 2.6 percent of bachelor's degrees granted in 1974, and less before that time, went to black students. This occurred at a time when black enrollment in higher education was more than three times that level, or about 8 percent. Four and five years earlier, when the 1974 graduates would have enrolled in B.A. programs, between 6 and 7 percent of undergraduates were black, and about 6 percent of freshmen were black. For interracial parity in the retention and graduation rates, more than twice as many blacks should have graduated in 1974.

Figure 5-1. PERCENTAGE OF FIRST-YEAR STUDENTS IN FALL 1972 WHO DID NOT RETURN TO COLLEGE IN FALL 1973 AND 1974

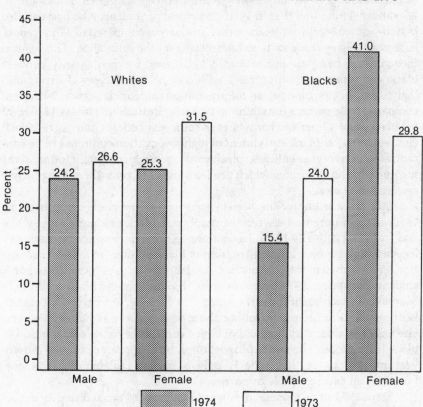

Source: ISEP, *Equal Educational Opportunity*: More Promise Than Progress, 1978, Figure 2-3. Based on U.S. Census, *School Enrollment—Social and Economic Characteristics of Students*: *October 1974*, Table 6, ISEP, *Equal Educational Opportunity for Blacks in U.S. Higher Education*: *An Assessment*, Table 2-40.

The fact of racial inequality in persistence rates before 1975 should need no further demonstration. Yet, that inequality is so extensive that evidence of it, even when limited data are available, compels us to make a few more related observations. These observations concern the systemic variations in the racial distribution of degrees granted up to 1974.

Attention should be called to the lower chances of getting a degree in two-year colleges compared to four-year colleges and universities. This difference is especially important for black students, because they are disproportionately enrolled in two-year colleges. In these colleges, the rate of graduation is habitually lower than in other institutions. For example, Alexander Astin notes that in 1970, 38 percent of students who had enrolled in two-year colleges four years earlier graduated, compared to 47 percent of four-year college students who had enrolled at the same time. This general inequality of two-year institutions is heightened by the disparity between black and white graduation rates within institutional types. Correspondingly, for the same time period the graduation rate for blacks was 29 percent compared to 38 percent for whites in two-year institutions; it was 42 percent for blacks and 47 percent for whites in four-year colleges and universities.[5] Consequently, as black enrollment in higher education continues to be concentrated in two-year colleges, black students are increasingly found in the institutions and programs which are least likely to offer them the concrete rewards they seek.

Still more telling of the persistence problem for black students in the 1970s is the difference between the number of black graduates from white and from traditionally black institutions. Although historically black colleges account for only about 20 percent of black enrollment in higher education, "an estimated one-half of the baccalaureate degrees awarded to black students in spring 1974 were awarded by historically black colleges."[6] Moreover, black institutions awarded less than 3 percent of all degrees. With white institutions controlling about 95 percent of remaining degrees, one has to wonder why they did not even come close to the contribution of black institutions. The larger proportion of black students enrolled in two-year institutions at that time is only a partial explanation; it is not, however, an excuse, whole or partial.

Since 1974 some movement toward reducing the racial disparity in persistence rates has occurred. The real progress, however, is less than that indicated by most standards of evaluation, because the reduction in disparity between black and white student persistence rates corresponds to an increase in white student dropout rates.

Degrees Awarded Since 1974

In the second ISEP report, Elizabeth Abramowitz complains about the absence of systematic national data on the racial distribution of degrees granted. For her analysis she had to rely primarily on limited survey data. Fortunately, there has since been some attempt to rectify this deficiency of information. Raw data on degrees granted by race in 1976 has been acquired from the U.S. Office for Civil Rights and analyzed for this study. Unfortunately, those data still lack important details on the distribution by major field of degrees granted and the associate/baccalaureate degree distinction by race. Except from survey data and hypothetical models, one has the choice of knowing in which institutional categories the degrees are awarded or what major field they are for, but not which major field belongs to which institutional category.

A total of 927,085 baccalaureate degrees were awarded in 1975–76, according to our analysis of OCR data. Preliminary data from OCR published elsewhere, give an inconsequentially larger total count of 929,918. Correspondingly, there are small differences in the totals for minorities.[7] For the most part, we rely on our figures, for reasons explained in chapter 2. Since the numerical differences are not significant, OCR's preliminary data will be used where they provide additional insights.

According to both data sources, blacks were about 6.4 percent or 59,187 of the B.A./B.S. degree recipients in 1975–76. Blacks received 8.4 percent of the 489,075 associate degrees awarded, more than their percentage of B.A./B.S. degrees awarded in the same year (OCR preliminary data). Minorities as a whole received 10.8 percent of all B.A./B.S. degrees awarded.

As small as the 6.4 percentage of black B.A./B.S. degree recipients may be, these graduates make a major contribution in an even smaller population of college-trained black professionals. For example, there were, according to estimates, 10,200 black social scientists with B.A. or higher degrees in the nation's labor force in 1974.[8] The data for 1976 show that 10,990 black college graduates received degrees in Social Science, adding to the current or potential labor force. In other words, the educational impact in the labor market of black social scientists was greater in a single year than it had been for the two or more generations of black social scientists still employed.

Enormous growth has also occurred among white social scientists, but not at the level of growth among blacks. Estimates of white Social Science B.A. graduates in the labor force in 1974 were 172,000, compared to 108,118 in 1976. The rate of change among blacks is thus much more dramatic. Yet, given broader population differences the college output of blacks in this division, as in other disciplines and divisions, over several generations amounts to only a small percentage of the white output in a single year. This recognition does not, of course, bear directly on racial inequality because of population differences. But it does imply a great deal about the potential of institutions to compensate for past educational injustices "with all deliberate speed."

The preceding example indicates the importance of knowing how many college graduates have already been produced in order to judge better how many may be needed. Beyond rates of parity in college, equal educational

Table 5-1 SCIENTISTS AND ENGINEERS HAVING FOUR OR MORE YEARS OF COLLEGE
1974

Field	Total	Race				
		White	Black	American Indian	Asian	Other
Physical scientists	188,000	179,000	3,500	(¹)	4,600	(¹)
Mathematical scientists	60,000	57,000	1,900	(¹)	1,300	700
Computer specialists	125,000	120,000	2,500	(¹)	1,300	(¹)
Environmental scientists	52,000	51,000	(¹)	(¹)	500	(¹)
Engineers	1,072,000	1,035,000	8,500	500	20,200	8,100
Life scientists	194,000	184,000	3,500	(¹)	2,700	3,300
Psychologists	95,000	90,000	1,600	(¹)	2,600	800
Social scientists	187,000	172,000	10,200	500	2,200	2,100
Total	1,973,000	1,886,000	31,700	1,800	36,500	17,000

Source: Scientific Manpower Commission, *Professional Women and Minorities: A Manpower Resource.* Prepared by Betty M. Vetter and Eleanor L. Baber (Washington, D.C.: Scientific Manpower Commission, 1975).

Note: Detail may not add to total because of rounding.

¹Fewer than 500.

opportunity in its fullest significance should be judged in terms of educational aspirations and education-related career expections, as noted in chapter 3. Both of these factors involve the existing professional labor force, since one of the two most prevalent reasons given by students for pursuing an education is the reward of greater employability. The level of identifiable professional opportunities will correlate to the demand for education; thus, black students, more than others, will aspire to higher education, because they can see a greater need through the dearth of college-trained blacks in the labor market.

At first, the reverse might seem to be the case, because there is a need for black role models to encourage and motivate black students. The need for role models primarily represents another tendency, however, which will prevail to the extent that a young person is uncertain of the existence of opportunities and doubtful about their accessibility. The role model perspective is, therefore, likely to be strongest among precollege black students, who have every reason to be insecure about their place in a professional world. In contrast, college students, especially upperclassmen, who have already made something of a place for themselves in the more educated community, will probably be encouraged by the awareness of a market. Consequently, the awareness of an open job market should be correlated positively to persistence in higher education.

In fact, this appears to be the case with black student persistence levels in the seventies. Blacks face a much greater drop in employability than whites if they forego a college education (chapter 3). This is true in any major field, but it is especially so for scientists and engineers.

> Members of minority groups who are scientists and engineers were more likely than their white counterparts to be in the labor force. Thus, about 15 percent of the white scientists and engineers were not in the labor force in 1974, compared to only about 8.5 percent of the minority group members. The higher labor force participation rate for minority group scientists and engineers is somewhat surprising since the proportion of women among minority group scientists and engineers is about twice that for whites and 47 percent of all women scientists and engineers are not in the labor force.[9]

Furthermore, "the sense-of-need" perspective serves to explain the tenacity with which black students, particularly in four-year colleges and universities, pursue the baccalaureate degree under relatively disadvantageous conditions. In fact, college attrition rates of black students have dropped to just above the level of those of white students, whereas the black to white ratio of attrition in high school remains high for blacks (attrition

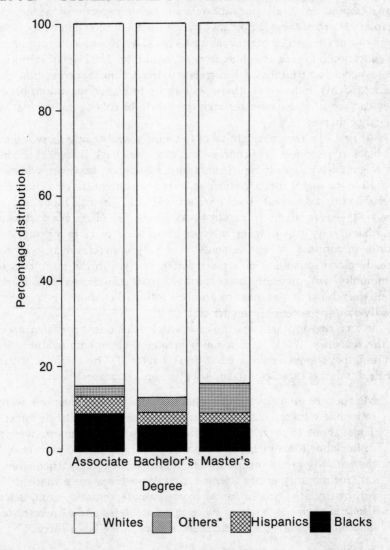

Figure 5-2.   DEGREES EARNED BY RACIAL/ETHNIC GROUP

☐ Whites   ▨ Others*   ▧ Hispanics   ■ Blacks

Source: NCES, The Condition of Education, 1978, Chart 3.17, p. 141.

* Includes American Indians/Alaskan Natives, Asians or Pacific Islanders, and nonresident aliens

differences by race are changed when SES is controlled, chapter 2). Further evidence of this tenacity can be gleaned from the ratio of black to white master's degree recipients compared to the ratio at the B.A./B.S. level. As shown in Figure 5-2, blacks with B.A./B.S. degrees are as likely as whites to get an M.A. degree.[10]

Major-Field Distribution of Degrees Granted and Variations in Persistence

Using 8.7 percent as the proportion of blacks among all college students in 1972 as a yardstick of racial balance in the distribution of undergraduate degrees granted in 1976, there are only three major fields in which the number of black graduates equaled or exceeded the point of balance. Assuming for the moment a four-year interval between entry into college and receipt of a bachelor's degree, the 1976 graduating class of blacks should have been as large as the 8.7 percent black enrollment four years earlier. But black attrition was high. While the exact racial percentage of the 1972 freshman class would be more applicable theoretically, if it were known, the use of that percentage would only raise our minimal standard balance above 8.7 percent, since the proportion of blacks in the freshman class has always been larger than their proportions in subsequent academic years.

An examination of the distribution of degrees granted by major field and race points up a special kind of persistence problem which has not been analyzed in the literature on higher education.

The problem concerns student retention within the planned or preferred major field of study. It is particularly a problem for black students, because they more than others cluster in only a few fields, such as Education, and away from physical sciences as the number of years in school increases. This clustering is statistically evident in the progress of black students from the baccalaureate to the doctoral level, among those who go that far. A similar clustering is observable in the undergraduate years, but statistical evidence of it is still sketchy. We know, however, that blacks drop out of their planned major fields more than whites, because black and white student plans and preferences are much more equally distributed at the beginning of their college enrollment than at the end.

Ideally, if race were not a factor in influencing what students "choose" to specialize in during their college years, and if race were not a factor in the rates of success across major fields, blacks and whites would be distributed in about the same proportions across major fields when they graduate. Since race is a factor in major field specialization, the distribution of degrees granted is not equal. Out of the twenty-three major fields listed in Table

5-2, the only three at or above the point of balance, all in the 9 percent range, are Public Affairs and Services, Library Science, and, of course, Education.[11]

Unequal distributions by major field for blacks are apparently not limited to the scientific or quantitative disciplines. For example, Area Studies is a mere 3.5 percent black. Since African Studies also falls into this category, there is special reason to wonder why few blacks are getting degrees in this major. By contrast, after Foreign Languages, Area Studies has the largest concentration of Hispanics, 5.3 percent. The low representation of blacks in Area Studies is interesting, because with the exception of some divisions such as Chicano Studies, this major field has strong institutional ties, as discussed in chapter 4. That is to say, faculty research has been overwhelmingly focused on long-established political organizations, and has generally been funded by equally long-established organizations. The evidence, cited earlier, that faculty members with such research orientation tend to be more conservative on racial change in academia seems to be confirmed by the underrepresentation of black graduates.

Education, Business and Management, and Social Sciences are by far the three largest areas of specialization for blacks in terms of absolute numbers. Education alone comprises about a quarter of bachelor's degrees awarded to blacks, and together these three areas constitute more than half of all bachelor's degrees awarded to blacks.

RATES OF RETENTION AND ATTRITION

The freshman class of 1972 is perhaps statistically the best-known class in American history. It is the focus of the largest nationwide study of the progress of a single educational group over time (chapter 2). The National Longitudinal Study (NLS) provides important insights into black persistence patterns, although NLS should be used only with reservation where small differences in the absolute numbers of blacks are important. Although NLS was designed to follow, by means of repeated surveys, more than 10,000 high school seniors through the college years and beyond, difficulties with getting responses in follow-up studies have diluted its value substantially. Unfortunately, this seems to be particularly problematic for the analysis of racial differences.

Still, NLS provides a good overall indication of retention and attrition for the class of 1972. Conforming to the long-range growth in higher education, just less than half this class, 44 percent, enrolled in college—less than the majority enrollment of 1976 high school seniors. About 29 percent went to four-year institutions, and 15 percent to two-year institutions.

Two years later, in the fall of 1974, about 8 percent of the entire 1972

Table 5-2　BACHELOR'S DEGREES CONFERRED IN INSTITUTIONS OF HIGHER EDUCATION 1975–76

Major Field	American Indian Hispanic Native	Black Non-Hispanic	Asian or Pacific Islander	Hispanic	Total Minority	White Non-Hispanic	Nonresident Alien	Total
Agriculture and Nature Resources	136 (.70%)	267 (1.37%)	171 (.88%)	218 (1.12%)	792 (4.07%)	18,357 (94.35%)	308 (1.59%)	19,457
Architecture and Environmental Design	35 (.38%)	258 (2.83%)	183 (2.00%)	221 (2.42%)	697 (7.64%)	8,107 (88.89%)	316 (3.46%)	9,120
Area Studies	10 (.33%)	106 (3.51%)	67 (2.22%)	159 (5.26%)	342 (11.31%)	2,646 (87.53%)	35 (1.16%)	3,023
Biological Sciences	143 (.26%)	2,328 (4.25%)	1,218 (2.23%)	1,495 (2.73%)	5,184 (9.47%)	48,613 (88.81%)	941 (1.72%)	54,738
Business and Management	426 (.29%)	9,503 (6.60%)	1,852 (1.29%)	3,973 (2.76%)	15,754 (10.94%)	125,286 (86.98%)	2,991 (2.08%)	144,031
Communications	65 (.30%)	1,275 (5.97%)	182 (.85%)	443 (2.07%)	1,965 (9.20%)	19,167 (89.74%)	226 (1.06%)	21,358
Computer and Information	7 (.13%)	323 (5.97%)	124 (2.22%)	100 (1.79%)	554 (9.92%)	4,811 (86.19%)	217 (3.89%)	5,582
Education	742 (.47%)	14,229 (9.08%)	836 (.53%)	4,447 (2.84%)	20,254 (12.94%)	135,514 (86.57%)	770 (.49%)	156,538
Engineering	150 (.33%)	1,370 (2.99%)	971 (2.12%)	1,226 (2.67%)	3,717 (8.11%)	38,971 (84.98%)	3,171 (6.91%)	45,859
Fine and Applied Arts	155 (.27%)	1,724 (4.09%)	607 (1.44%)	901 (2.14%)	3,387 (8.04%)	38,204 (90.64%)	556 (1.32%)	42,147
Foreign Languages	33 (.21%)	531 (3.44%)	178 (1.15%)	1,277 (8.27%)	2,019 (13.07%)	13,050 (84.52%)	371 (2.40%)	15,440
Health Professions	166 (.31%)	2,742 (5.06%)	865 (1.60%)	1,260 (2.33%)	5,033 (9.30%)	48,465 (89.52%)	640 (1.18%)	54,138
Home Economics	75 (.43%)	1,069 (6.18%)	226 (1.31%)	269 (1.56%)	1,639 (9.48%)	15,467 (89.46%)	184 (1.06%)	17,290
Law	1 (.19%)	27 (5.16%)	1 (.19%)	7 (1.34%)	36 (6.88%)	485 (92.73%)	2 (.38%)	523
Letters	161 (.31%)	2,468 (4.75%)	374 (.72%)	1,489 (2.86%)	4,492 (8.64%)	46,990 (90.39%)	504 (.97%)	51,986
Library Science	4 (.49%)	75 (9.26%)	1 (.12%)	3 (.37%)	83 (10.25%)	725 (89.51%)	2 (.25%)	810
Mathematics	54 (.34%)	800 (5.03%)	314 (1.97%)	338 (2.12%)	1,506 (9.46%)	14,103 (88.60%)	308 (1.94%)	15,917
Physical Sciences	62 (.29%)	647 (3.03%)	312 (1.46%)	377 (1.77%)	1,398 (6.56%)	19,400 (91.00%)	521 (2.44%)	21,319
Psychology	192 (.38%)	3,219 (6.44%)	614 (1.23%)	1,666 (3.33%)	5,641 (11.39%)	43,795 (87.62%)	496 (.99%)	49,982
Public Affairs and Services	180 (.54%)	3,311 (9.93%)	332 (.96%)	1,137 (3.41%)	4,960 (14.88%)	28,133 (84.39%)	244 (.73%)	33,337
Social Sciences	513 (.40%)	10,990 (8.65%)	1,403 (1.10%)	4,135 (3.26%)	17,041 (13.42%)	108,118 (85.14%)	1,831 (1.44%)	126,990
Theology	10 (.19%)	148 (2.80%)	32 (.60%)	65 (1.23%)	255 (4.82%)	4,911 (92.75%)	129 (2.44%)	5,295
Interdisciplinary Studies	178 (.56%)	1,773 (5.54%)	480 (1.44%)	984 (3.07%)	3,395 (10.61%)	28,294 (88.42%)	309 (.97%)	31,998
National total (2,063 institutions)	3,498 (.38%)	59,187 (6.38%)	11,323 (1.22%)	26,220 (2.83%)	100,228 (10.81%)	811,772 (87.56%)	15,085 (1.63%)	927,085

Source: HEW, Office for Civil Rights, fall 1976.

Table 5-3 PERCENTAGE DISTRIBUTION OF BACCALAUREATE
DEGREES AWARDED
1975–76

Major Field	All Students	Black Students
Agriculture	2.1	0.4
Architecture	1.0	0.4
Biological Sciences	5.9	3.9
Business and Management	15.5	16.1
Education	16.9	24.0
Engineering	4.9	2.3
Health Professions	5.8	4.6
Mathematics	1.7	1.4
Physical Sciences	2.3	1.1
Psychology	5.4	5.4
Public Affairs	3.6	5.6
Social Sciences	13.7	18.6
All others	21.2	16.2
Total	100.0	100.0

Source: Preliminary data, fall 1976, from HEW, National Center for Educational Statistics. Reproduced in National Advisory Committee on Black Higher Education and Black Colleges and Universities, *Higher Education Equity: The Crisis of Appearance Versus Reality, First Annual Report, 1977* (Washington, D.C., 1978).

high school class had entered and dropped out of four-year colleges. Another 8 percent of the original class had dropped out of two-year colleges. With less than a third of that high school class enrolled in four-year colleges, the loss of 8 percent gives a 28 percent attrition rate among four-year college students during the first two years. Since only about 15 percent of the class initially enrolled in two-year colleges, the loss of 8 percent of the initial group means a two-year college drop-out rate of 55 percent. Thus, college attrition is very high among what may be called a "privileged minority" of high school graduates.

What is more striking is the institutional imbalance of drop-out rates. Among those enrolled in the most selective type of college (four-year), more than a quarter of the students left and were not replaced. Unfortunate as this drop-out rate may be, it is small compared to the tremendous drop-out rate in two-year colleges. Judging from these longitudinal data, institutional selectivity is associated positively with persistence. Accordingly, as college access for blacks continues to depend more heavily on the less selective two-year colleges—and to a large extent that has already happened—a negative impact on black student retention should be expected.

Table 5-4   COLLEGE ATTENDANCE STATUS OF 1972 HIGH SCHOOL
GRADUATES
1972, 1973, and 1974

| | | Type of Enrollment | | | | |
Graduates	Total	4-Year College	2-Year College	Completion	Dropout	Non-college
All persons, in 1972	100.00	29.38	14.51			56.11
Attended 4-year college in 1972						
Attended in 1973	29.38	23.60	.93		4.85	
Attended in 1974:						
4-year college	21.60	20.13	.26		1.22	
2-year college	.93	.34	.35		.24	
Completion	.08	.00	.08		—	
Dropout	6.77	3.14	.23		3.40	
Attended a 2-year college in 1972						
Attended in 1973	14.51	.90	9.09	.15	4.38	
Attended in 1974:						
4-year college	3.54	.68	2.63	.01	.22	
2-year college	3.40	.05	2.75	.01	.58	
Completion	1.76	.00	1.76	—	—	
Dropout	5.69	.16	1.95	—	3.58	
Noncollege	.13	—	—	.13	—	
Did not attend college in 1972						
Attended in 1973	56.11	2.12	2.41			51.58
Attended in 1974:						
4-year college	2.83	1.41	.14			1.29
2-year college	2.67	.07	1.09			1.51
Completion	.21	.00	.21			—
Dropout	1.61	.64	.97			—
Noncollege	48.78	—	—			48.78

Source: NCES, The Condition of Education, 1977, Table 4.14.

Note: Details may not add to totals because of rounding.

Although the most serious problem of attrition clearly occurs during the first two years of college, attrition continues to be a problem during the last two years. Four years after graduation, only 18 percent of the class of 1972 had earned B.A./B.S. degrees—about 41 percent of those who entered any college in 1972, and 62 percent of those who entered four-year institutions.

Of course, there fairly common delays in the ideal four-year period between acquisition of the high school and college degrees. Within the year after finishing high school, about 5 percent of those students who had not immediately entered college enrolled in college in 1973. During the year of delay after high school graduation, however, the proportion of new college enrollment approached insignificance (less than 2 percent in 1974). This delay period does not, according to the evidence available, directly concern racial equality, since such delays seem to be evenly distributed between blacks and whites. Nevertheless, the probability of there being unrecorded racial differences here is significant because of racial inequities in related areas.

About one-third of the students at four-year colleges and universities report "interruptions" in their studies, most of which last longer than six months. Most of the two-year college students, 63 percent, report such interruptions. Like so many other nontraditional modes of education, interruption or stopping out is more frequent at the kinds of institutions, excluding traditionally black ones, where blacks are more frequently found (see Appendix, Table A5-1).

As noted in earlier ISEP reports, blacks take a much longer time than whites to acquire degrees in higher education. This has been particularly true at the advanced levels, where it takes whites an average of 8.4 years to get a Ph.D. and blacks 13.3 years in the same process (chapter 7).[12] Many of these black students withdraw in the course of their studies (stop out) to earn money needed to continue. In other cases, the process simply takes longer. Whatever its causes, prolongation at advanced levels is relevant to undergraduate studies, though to a lesser extent. Thus, black students are more likely than white students to take more than four years to acquire a bachelor's degree.

The National Center for Education Statistics reports that three years after graduation, only 28 percent of the initial 44 percent of the class of 1972 which had enrolled in college remained in college, and those missing were disproportionately black and Hispanic:

> The majority of students who left college reported doing so for nonacademic reasons. The students who worked full time withdrew at nearly double the rate of those with a part-time job or no job at all. Blacks and Hispanic students withdrew somewhat more frequently than white students, but in four-year institutions these differences disappeared when adjustments were made for socioeconomic background.[13]

Unfortunately, the "adjustments" for socioeconomic background are made purely by statistical control and not by direct social action. Accordingly, blacks and others who suffer from socioeconomic disadvantages as students continue to drop out faster than they otherwise might. Table 5-5 serves both to indicate part of the socioeconomic disadvantage and to illustrate the difficulty of "finding" blacks with large survey instruments inasmuch as there are no blacks in the upper quartile.

What Table 5-5 does not say is that not only do black students have a higher drop-out rate in two-year institutions, they are also disproportionately located in two-year colleges. About a third of the black students in four-year institutions dropped out, compared to the majority of lower SES black students who dropped out of two-year institutions. Even upper-income whites in two-year institutions have a high drop-out rate of 33.9 percent. Although there are no blacks listed in the upper quartile, it is evident from the direction of the data that their withdrawal rate in two-year institutions would also be high.

Those in the upper-income quartile are five times as likely as those in the low-income quartile to have acquired a B.A./B.S. in 1976, even though they are only twice as likely to have enrolled in college. Inequalities of

Table 5-5   PERCENTAGE WITHDRAWN FROM COLLEGE AFTER TWO YEARS (HIGH SCHOOL CLASS OF 1972)

Socioeconomic Background	4-Year Institution	2-Year Institution
Lower quartile		
Black	32.5	51.3
Hispanic	25.2	48.2
White	33.6	44.8
Middle two quartiles		
Black	23.7	45.9
White	27.7	39.5
Upper quartile		
White	17.8	33.9

Source: Andrew Kolstad, "Attrition from College: The Class of 1972 Two and One-Half Years After High School Graduation," National Longitudinal Study of the High School Class of 1972, NCES, Washington, D.C., (1977), Table 7.

Note: The information reported is derived from answers to selected questions from the first and second follow-up surveys for the National Longitudinal Study of the High School Class of 1972 (NLS). The base-year survey (spring 1972), sponsored by the National Center for Education Statistics with support from elements of the Office of Education, used a stratified, two-stage national probability sample consisting of approximately 21,000 high school seniors in 1,200 schools and achieved a response rate of 77 percent. The first follow-up survey was conducted in fall 1973, with a response rate of 92 percent; the second follow-up, in fall 1974, with 89 percent. A third follow-up survey has recently been completed.

socioeconomic status, therefore, are much more severe in their impact on persistence than in their impact on access to higher education. These inequalities, when dispersed among full-time working students versus those working less, and among two-year versus four-year enrollment, cluster together in the comparison of black to white attrition rates—to the disadvantage of black students.

Although there are important variations, low socioeconomic status is associated more with public than with private institutional enrollment, as is black enrollment generally. Attrition rates at public institutions are also higher than at private ones. After two years, the withdrawal rate from four-year colleges for the class of 1972 was 28.5 percent at public colleges and 22.3 percent at private ones. Private universities have a similar advantage over public ones. Among two-year institutions the withdrawal rates in the same years were 39.8 percent for public and 32.2 percent for private institutions.[14]

The problems of low persistence among the lower socioeconomic groups and among students in two-year institutions are part of the larger problem of institutional selectivity and black exclusion from the more selective institutions (chapter 4). Two-year institutions are largely at the low range of selective institutions. Like the four-year institutions which fall into that category, two-year institutions tend to have high attrition rates. In part because selectivity is statistically determined by means of SAT scores and related measures, black institutions fall into the low selectivity category, but, nevertheless, have low attrition rates. With the exception of black institutions, black student attrition rates are aggravated by the underrepresentation of blacks in selective institutions.

Table 5-7 expresses the strong inverse relationship between institutional selectivity and withdrawal after the first year of college for the high school class of 1972. Among students at four-year institutions, those at the most selective ones are only half as likely to have withdrawn as their counterparts at less selective ones.

When the "normal" four years of undergraduate training were over for the 1972 class, according to NLS data (see Table 5-6), about 58 percent of both black and white students had enrolled in college at some time. Of that number, about one-third of the white students and a quarter of the black students had graduated with a B.A./B.S., that is, 19 percent of the initial white high school graduates and 12 percent of the black ones. Thus, there is a 4 to 3 black to white ratio of attrition, holding associate degrees constant. Since blacks evidently have relatively more problems in two-year institutions, the ratio of associate degrees by race would only show a greater black disadvantage.

Table 5-6   EDUCATIONAL ATTAINMENT OF THE HIGH SCHOOL CLASS
OF 1972
1976

Characteristic	Total	Percentage Attaining		
		Bachelor's Degree or Higher	Some College	No Higher Education
Mean	100.0	17.9	39.5	42.5
Ability				
Low	100.0	3.5	27.5	69.0
Middle	100.0	13.1	44.1	42.8
High	100.0	38.6	46.4	15.0
High school educational expectations				
High school or less	100.0	0.9	12.7	86.4
Vocational-technical	100.0	2.1	29.9	68.0
2-year college	100.0	6.8	66.3	26.9
4-year college	100.0	35.4	56.3	8.4
Graduate school	100.0	48.7	45.2	6.1
High school program				
General	100.0	8.9	36.6	54.5
Academic	100.0	34.2	50.2	15.7
Vocational-technical	100.0	3.4	25.7	70.9
Racial/ethnic group				
White	100.0	19.2	39.6	41.2
Black	100.0	12.1	39.9	47.0
Hispanic	100.0	7.3	45.1	47.6
Other	100.0	12.4	36.7	50.8
Gender				
Male	100.0	17.2	43.0	39.8
Female	100.0	18.6	36.4	45.0
Socioeconomic status				
Low	100.0	7.1	29.5	63.4
Middle	100.0	14.7	39.5	45.8
High	100.0	35.2	50.3	14.5

Source: NCES, The Condition of Education, 1978, Table 3.12.

Table 5-7   PERCENTAGE WITHDRAWN FROM COLLEGE AFTER ONE
YEAR (HIGH SCHOOL CLASS OF 1972)

Selectivity	4-Year Institution	2-Year College
Unknown	29.3	30.4
Low	20.4	28.7
Medium	17.9	27.5
High	9.0	—

Source: Andrew Kolstad, "Attrition from College: The Class of 1972 Two and One-Half Years After
High School Graduation," National Longitudinal Study of the High School Class of 1972, NCES,
Washington, D.C. (1977), Table 3.

The level of prolongation of studies among students, and especially
among blacks, means that many students are now returning to college and
graduating later. But the number of returned graduates should not be expected to be large enough to change the 4 to 3 ratio of attrition significantly,
even though blacks may be slightly more likely to return. Given institutional factors and socioeconomic conditions, one expects the 4 to 3 black to
white ratio of inequality of persistence to continue unless some intervention
changes those conditions.

Conditions of Retention and Attrition

Conceptually, the factors that retain black students in college until
graduation are the same as those that serve to retain all other students. Empirically, however, these factors may take on quite different forms, because
students, black or white, cannot and should not completely abandon the
differing social conditions in which they have lived before college. Still, the
causes of attrition are too impenetrable to be resolved here. We can simply
try to determine which of the multiple causes pertain most directly to the
racial inequality in attrition.

A major cause of attrition, according to Alexander Astin's extensive
research, is boredom—boredom with college studies, boredom caused or
maintained by the ineptitude of the institution, its faculty and/or
administrators:

One major clue to the importance of academic factors that lead to
dropping out is contained in the reason students give most frequently for leaving college: boredom with courses. Both men and
women cite this reason more often than poor grades; and it is, in
fact, the single reason given most frequently by men. While

boredom may be a socially acceptable rationalization for leaving college, it also indicates *noninvolvement*. That it is a factor in dropping out is consistent with other evidence which reveals lack of involvement as a critical element in the decision to leave college.[15]

Of course, there are many other credible reasons for dropping out. For example, students with poor grades are especially likely to drop out. In addition to financial difficulties, low grades have been a particularly salient explanation for black student drop outs. If these two explanations are combined with other reported reasons for dropping out, e.g., motivation and other psychosocial factors, they can all be described by the single term "involvement."

Sometimes it appears that the number of theories on why students drop out equals the number of times the topic has been discussed. There is perhaps a slightly different explanation for every dropout, and no one reason is equally important in every case. Other than reasons such as "dissatisfaction," students never give exactly the same one. Only somewhat less vague than dissatisfaction are explanations of boredom, noninvolvement, and nonintegration, but more concrete explanations seem inapplicable to many cases.

Nevertheless, many *correlates* of attrition frequently provide an explanation. These correlates may be said to cause dropping out in that they describe concrete conditions which occur most often when students drop out; i.e., there is an apparent correlation. Most of these correlates are logically involved in the process that leads to student attrition, but even the strongest of them, such as low grades, is not the total cause inasmuch as students are retained even with such problems. The appearance of any of these correlates in an individual case may create a necessary condition for dropping out. The analytical problem here is simply that the necessary condition, the coincidence of attrition correlates, is not the same thing as the sum of its parts. The sum of attrition correlates, where found, would need a name and uniform description which has yet to be identified.

The list below is an overview of the most frequent correlates of attrition that have been salient for black students in recent years.[16] Those correlates that seem to have a logical and/or direct relationship to attrition are listed separately from those that have only an indirect and/or spurious relationship to attrition.

Direct Correlates

Faculty Attitudes
Financial Resources

Grades (low)
Hostile Environment
Marginality
Nonintegration (in college life)
Noninvolvement (academic exclusion)
Sociopsychological Factors
    Motivation
    Identification (institutional)
    Peer Group Socialization
    Stress

Indirect Correlates

Attendance Status (part-time)
High School Academic Background
Institutional Type (two-year)
Nonresidency (a) off-campus (b) commuter
Race of Institution (predominantly white)
Sociopsychological factor
    Family Background
Lack of Financial Aid
Absence of Supportive Services

Boredom may then be a catchword or an emotional expression for factors such as noninvolvement, nonintegration, and marginality. Therefore, boredom, particularly as it relates to noninvolvement, should be worthy of serious consideration in looking at black attrition.

Which students are most likely to be and to feel uninvolved in institutions of higher education? Almost by definition, they are "marginal students," meaning those who are only marginally integrated into the dominant academic structure (chapters 1 and 4). These students are likely to be socioeconomically different from the model college student. They tend to be isolated from the mainstream of campus life. They may be, though not necessarily are, in major fields which are not recognized as "important" in higher education. They may be in institutions with relatively little tradition and uncertain self-images. In sum, these students, by their very presence, are likely to destabilize the traditional sectors of higher education institutions. In return, the students' own security and sense of place in the institution are threatened, if not destabilized, by the institution's tradition-centered and self-centered behavior.

In other words, the uninvolved students are likely to be minorities, females and the poor. In view of the persistent problem of racial prejudice, except in black institutions, these students are very likely to be black. One striking example of the coincidence of these factors is the very high attrition rate among black women, noted earlier.

Black student attrition has been declining over the long-run. Many recent case studies show a fairly even rate of persistence among both blacks and whites.[17] The NSL analysis, cited previously, from NCES, finds that minorities in the same socioeconomic group as whites are no more likely to withdraw than whites are. Apparently, then, something can be done to mitigate the impact of marginality where it is the cause of black attrition.

An important indication of the role of the institutional environment, particularly that part of it which faculty members control, comes from the success of traditionally black institutions in retention (chapter 4). In addition, the special impact of white faculty attitudes and behavior on black student retention, even where no discrimination is assumed, should not need demonstration. Yet, there is some interesting evidence, worth recounting, that is discernable from what may be called "the reverse situation" in black institutions.

White students enrolled in black institutions experience some of the same "withdrawal" symptoms as black students in predominantly white institutions. They express in surveys a feeling of noninvolvement and lower expectations after the freshman year. The withdrawal may, however, vary because of greater support for whites either within the institution itself, or from the larger society.

Moreover, the level of racial prejudice and discrimination in the larger society, if not also in the white institution, would further influence black student persistence. Illustrating the fairly uncommon position of white students at black institutions, a study of persistence from the Institute for Services to Education concludes:

> Students' expectations vary greatly during the freshman year.
> Students tend to evoke more realistic perceptions as a result of their
> college experience. White students tend to experience a greater
> decline in expectations than black students. This decline was not
> consistent across colleges. Black students attending predominantly
> white colleges have similar attitudinal changes after exposure to the
> white college environment.[18]

Obviously, the primary role in reducing black student marginality rests with the institutions. In this regard, the attitudes and behavior of faculty members, who are frequently unreceptive to black students, need rectification. Survey responses of boredom by black students may be a euphemistic expression of their sense of rejection.

Aside from the theoretically private and independent actions of educational authorities, federal, state, and local governments can increase black student involvement in higher education generally. Noninvolvement can be traced to a variety of institutional and noninstitutional forces. The noninstitutional ones—the systemic forces—are most immediately amenable to public policy intervention.

Among these forces, if not at the root of all of them, is lack of financial resources to pay for higher education. Financial aid alone substantially reduces attrition. Whatever the type of institution, students receiving financial aid are much more likely to be retained. Where ability, as determined by standarized tests, makes a difference, the retention of low ability students is more dramatically affected by financial aid than that of high ability students. Similarly, low socioeconomic status students are more likely to be influenced to stay in school by financial aid than are high status students.

The most interesting aspect of the data displayed in Figure 5-3 is the dramatic effect of financial aid on black student retention. Black students receiving financial aid are almost twice as likely as those unaided to be retained, a withdrawal ratio of twelve "aided" to twenty-three "unaided" (see Appendix, Table A5-2). In contrast, white student retention is less dramatically affected by financial aid; a withdrawal ratio of twenty-one "aided" to twenty-nine "unaided."

It is often said that boredom is a luxury of the rich. If that is true, it may still be—as in higher education—a condition imposed on the nonrich, as well as an imposition on black students through the behavior of institutions and the lack of financial support.

THE INSTITUTION AND PERSISTENCE

Those institutions that succeed best at fully educating their students are those that teach their students "how to go on" after graduation. Similarly, those students who manage to stay in school until graduation are those who learn early the "how to" of staying in school. Often this does not mean learning course work, for example, mathematics and social sciences, but rather learning adjustment and socialization.

Many students have to learn relatively little to make the adjustment to college, because the elements of the institution—its faculty, students, and social structure—are similar to the backgrounds from which the new students come. For most black students, however, the structure of college and "going on" is relatively unfamiliar. The special job of the institution in this case is to provide an environment that allows for both transition and

Figure 5-3   FINANCIAL AID STATUS AND COLLEGE WITHDRAWAL RATES

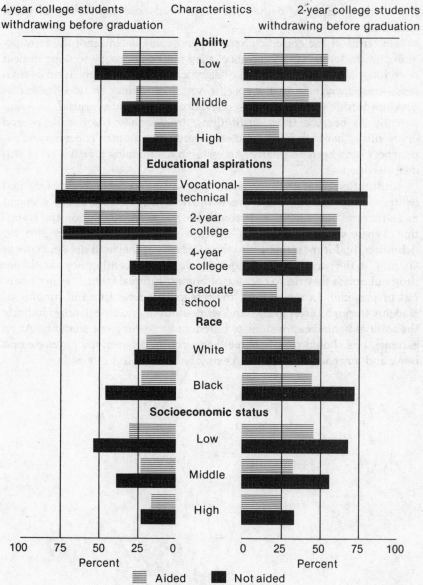

4-year college students
withdrawing before graduation

Characteristics

2-year college students
withdrawing before graduation

Ability

Low

Middle

High

Educational aspirations

Vocational-technical

2-year college

4-year college

Graduate school

Race

White

Black

Socioeconomic status

Low

Middle

High

100   75   50   25   0   0   25   50   75   100
Percent   Percent

▤ Aided   ■ Not aided

Source: NCES, *The Condition of Education, 1978,* Chart 3.14, p. 135.

social relevance. Transition involves the mutual adaptation of the individual and the institution. Relevance involves the sociocultural adaptation of the institution to the continuous needs and experiences of black Americans.

In terms of the episodic character and value-laden sense the term acquired in the late 1960s, "relevance" may not be necessary to raise student retention, although it may be significant. In a more fundamental sense—responsiveness to the specific social conditions in which students develop outside the institution—relevance is apparently crucial. It is apparently so because those institutions, traditionally black colleges and universities, that have been directed toward black student concerns and experiences have been peculiarly successful in maintaining a high level of student persistence.

Institutions that are sufficiently relevant to students, both black and white, to keep them in school create the needed conditions of involvement and structural integration, and provide the means for adaptation and transition. Where students see the college experience as relevant, they also, by definition, find it meaningful. By the same token, they will not find college "boring" in the way dropouts frequently do. Consequently, they should not drop out unless they do so because of noninstitutional factors, either financial or personal. In this regard, the research findings that full funding of students through direct grants and work-study increases retention indicate the realities behind expressions of boredom by low-income students. At an extreme, one should readily agree that a choice between the purchase of a book and a needed meal can make any book seem less interesting.

POLICY IMPLICATIONS

On the surface, few of the conditions that lead to attrition seem readily amenable to federal or state intervention except financial factors, which can be affected through increased governmental financial aid to students. The effectiveness of any financial aid policy in reducing attrition, however, will depend on the institutional environment; and the relevant institutional environment, as described in the previous discussion, comprises factors that are difficult, if not impossible, to control. For all students there is a range of sociopsychological factors tied to persistence that have never been manageable effectively in public policy. The sociopsychological correlates of persistence are generally too vague to guide anyone toward a clearly defined remedy. Rather, practical advice tends to work effectively only on a case-by-case basis with students and potential dropouts.

In addition to the standard sociopsychological factors that influence persistence, black student persistence as a whole seems to be heavily influenced by what may be called "cultural" factors. Inasmuch as culture is a complex of racially localized sociopsychological characteristics, cultural factors may also fall beyond the reach of direct policy management. Unlike general sociopsychological characteristics of dropouts, however, the relevant cultural characteristics of black students can be, and have been, effectively dealt with by traditionally black institutions. Since these institutions provide a model of relative success, they suggest a direction for education policy that can work, whatever the theoretical explanation of racial-cultural variation in persistence may be.

To a similar but lesser extent, the general sociopsychological problems of attrition may be addressed effectively by public policy without a full theoretical analysis of "cause and effect." The data show that problems can be countered indirectly through a more equitable distribution of public financial aid to students. For many students, and especially for minorities, nonmaterial conditions of attrition such as boredom and noninvolvement can be controlled by improving financial stability. The basic sociopsychological maladjustment may well remain, but the student with adequate financial aid is in a much better position to persevere than is the student whose life is complicated by material deprivation.

An outgrowth of nearly all studies of attrition and retention is evidence of a need to study their causes in more detail. In this review that need is also apparent, but a specific need to examine the impact of government spending on the problem should be even more apparent. The federal and state governments have concentrated their evaluation of the direct impact of public funds on students' opportunities, particularly in terms of access, while underestimating the indirect impact of funding on the college environment.

The Primary Policy Option

Although there is a need for research on and evaluation of the full impact of public funds on student persistence, some steps can be taken immediately. We know how to improve black student retention from the information currently available.

First, the federal government already supports greater black student retention whenever it supports traditionally black institutions, because these institutions have a demonstrated capacity to retain black students and to graduate them. But such support is at best fortuitous, because there has been no official recognition of the special achievement of black institutions in this regard. What is needed for a meaningful policy on black student persistence is both a clear recognition of the institutional role in student retention and positive public recognition of the achievements of institutions that retain and graduate black students most successfully.

Second, federal and state financial aid to students at all institutions should be recognized as a crucial vehicle for the implementation of a public policy on persistence. Whatever the individual causes of attrition may be, the level and security of financial support should be treated as contributing factors for the disadvantaged student.

Above all, the federal government needs to develop an explicit policy on persistence, a policy that rewards the success of institutions that produce educated individuals. Students, to a large extent, already have a substantial incentive to graduate in the promise of the career and monetary rewards associated with the advanced degree.

For institutions, the incentives are not so clear. A sound public policy in higher education may need to be concerned with maintaining adequate postgraduate rewards for students. For an effective policy, institutional incentives—probably financial ones—must be generated.

There are many conceivable approaches to structuring such incentives. Based on past federal involvement, they are all likely to entail weighting government dollar contributions to institutions so that greater gains are attached to greater institutional persistence rates. The basic principle of a differential reward structure for persistence has already been expressed in past education legislation—legislation calling for the production of a highly educated and capable labor supply. An essential element in that supply is, of course, student graduation, or output. Unfortunately, federal aid has concentrated only on input under the inadequate assumption that those who enter college to get a degree will go through the system expeditiously and leave with a desirable degree in hand. For nearly half of all college students and expecially for minorities, higher education simply does not work that way. Government, by adding to, or by amending its current financial aid programs, can smooth out and solidify the higher education process in order to bring it closer to the ideal.

CHAPTER 6

A Closer Look
at Black Institutions

For more than a century, Black schools have played a critical role not only in educating black Americans, but fostering social change. From the start, the mission of these schools was inspired by an appreciation of the bond between education and liberty for black Americans. . . . The obstacles facing the new Black schools were many—isolation from white society; inadequate funds, lack of educated black professionals; dire poverty and a legacy of oppression against blacks. But the faith of black citizens in the value of education sustained their pioneering efforts.

> Secretary Joseph A. Califano
> Department of Health, Education
> and Welfare
> August 1, 1978[1]

Data on black participation in traditionally black institutions of higher education should not be treated in quite the same way as data on nonblack institutions. Traditionally black institutions (TBI's) are different from other institutions, not simply because their students are predominantly black, but also because they face different obstacles and serve different purposes. The special obstacles TBI's face are products of the broader obstacles facing blacks as a disadvantaged group. The special purposes of TBI's support blacks in their efforts to remove the conditions of racial inequality through education.

Nonblack educational institutions have only recently, in the past decade or so, become concerned about racial inequality. Yet, despite their sincere concern and support of greater equality, it would be hard to demonstrate that equality of opportunity was one of their primary institutional goals. Historically, nonblack institutions have served many social purposes. Although they have not been opposed to the advancement of equality of educational opportunity, it has been among the least apparent of their purposes, if it has ever been a concern at all.

As individuals, faculty members and administrators have generally been among the most progressive of white Americans on issues of racial equality. As educational professionals, however, they have been concerned primarily with the selection and instruction of the best prepared among the financially capable students applying. Additionally, they have been oriented toward the advancement of scholarly knowledge and the strengthening of their various academic disciplines. The adherence to goals of racial equality has been informally imposed on most institutions by committed individuals within their own ranks (but not institutional representatives), by social pressure, or by legal obligations.

To say that black institutions are primarily concerned with racial equality, whereas white institutions are not, is to state the obvious. On the other hand, there has been a tendency in the analysis of education policy to lose sight of the obvious and to assume instead that the total educational experience of the black student would be the same in whatever institution the student might be. That assumption is often qualified by the added and incorrect assumption that students in these institutions receive an inferior education.

Implicit in the assumption of institutional inferiority, is the belief that there are no educationally justified structural differences between these institutions. The problem of differences in internal structure between black and white institutions and the variable experiences of students in them appears, first of all, as a problem for educational statistics. This is a problem for educational statistics because different types of students and institutions (as well as the interaction between the two) are treated as if they were uniform and interchangeable. It is assumed that numbers and percentages on students in both types of institutions mean the same thing in whatever student situations they emerge. One loses sight of the fact that the pursuit of equality is facilitated by the highest level of intellectual development actually transmitted to the student rather than by a structure in which the intellectual exchange is unequal.

Intuitive awareness of the obvious analytical difference between student and institutional types has been pitted against a statistical rigidity in describing institutions. On the level of federal educational policy, this conflict has been transformed into a political and legal issue. At the core of the policy issue is a question of whether concrete facets of an educational organization, including its enrollment and financing, gain a special meaning through the special character of the institution, involving its special mission and responsibilities. The issue is debated on another, more empirical level, however—a level at which the debate centers on legal approaches to racial segregation. Accordingly, public support of black institutions has been compared and contrasted to public support of historically segregated white institutions. The particular focus around which this issue has developed is the case of *Adams* v. *Califano*.[2] Advocates of black public institutions have sought to insure that black institutions would not be dismembered in the name of desegregation of public institutions. In fact, an association guided by the presidents of all 105 TBI's, The National Association for Equal Opportunity in Higher Education (NAFEO), submitted an *amicus curiae* brief which has substantially influenced court rulings in the case.

Court decisions in the *Adams* case require racial desegregation at the higher educational level, and in light of this requirement, many fear that HEW officials would inappropriately apply criteria for racial balance to black institutions. Advocates of black institutions feel no need to desegregate their institutions because they do not view them as ever having been segregated.

At a fundamental level of the disagreement over the *Adams* case(s) is a conceptual difference concerning TBI's: What are their goals, and what has been the role they fill in society? On one side, they are viewed as being just like all other colleges and universities, except for their histories of unique service to blacks under conditions in which black students and faculty have had no other educational choices. On the advocates' side, the historical conditions are similarly emphasized, but there is a rarely articulated view that TBI's are a product of the choices of black Americans and not simply a byproduct of a no-choice situation. Califano's statement implies that black institutions are an automatic outgrowth of racial inequality. Advocates, however, maintain that black institutions are the willful creations of a people seeking an opportunity for higher education, where that opportunity has been restricted everywhere else. Blacks attend and have attended black institutions under great constraints, but ultimately have made the choice to do so because these institutions offer them what they want and need. Through that free choice, TBI's are understood to have developed a special capacity to serve their communities—a capacity which will constitute an essential part of free choice in the education of blacks for a long time to come.

Secretary Califano has appropriately recognized the historical obstacles to the development of black institutions, including racial isolation and economic deprivation. He has also recognized a major contribution of these institutions to society as "crucibles of protest" against injustice.[3] Regrettably, neither he nor the bulk of his colleagues in the federal government has sufficiently examined the extent to which these historical obstacles continue into the present. Since racial isolation and related economic deprivation continue to be a problem for blacks in general, there continue to be related educational problems as well. Consequently, institutions which work to counter these problems are still needed.

A difficulty so often found in policy analyses of black higher education—and most saliently in the *Adams* case—is the assumption that racial isolation and related experiences "cause" black institutions and, therefore, black institutions "cause" further racial isolation. It is a fallacy of correlation analysis to assume that things occurring together are mutually interdependent. This fallacy remains a factor in education policy, even as its contradictions emerge clearly. Accordingly, black institutions are viewed as the simple residue of a bygone society hostile to the advanced education of blacks, while the education of hundreds of thousands of blacks at these institutions is left as an unexplained anomaly—a few hundred thousand accidents of black American history. Most analysts would agree that racial isolation may have contributed to the development of institutions, but certainly was not the entire cause. Most analysts would agree that black institutions exist in spite of economic deprivation, not because of it. But many fail to carry that agreement to its logical extension. The logical extension of this line of reasoning is the observation that the "cause" of black institutions is the historical and continuing desire of blacks to have them and to have higher education.

Although this observation may seem painfully obvious, it bears reiteration here because it is essential to an understanding of current enrollment patterns in TBI's. The "fallacy of correlation" perspective on TBI's has apparently led to the expectation that these institutions would disappear or fade away in a short period of time from a simple lack of interest on the part of black college applicants. The data for 1976-77 simply do not support that assumption. Although the survival of these institutions may be threatened, the loss of interested and interesting students is the least probable source of threat.

The purpose of this discussion of black institutions is to understand their current enrollment patterns better. It is not, at least for the moment, our intention to advocate special recognition for these institutions. Though their enrollment patterns cannot be understood in the same way as those of most institutions, federal policy officially treats them like most institutions, however differently they may be treated in fact. Specifically, HEW's interpretation of the rulings in the *Adams* cases is to require public black and white institutions in the states with dual systems to justify their academic programs in relationship to each other, as equal components of a single system. Consequently, black institutions have emerged from quasi-official isolation to quasi-official assimilation in the eyes of the federal government.

Still, the federal government is neither the driving force behind the structure of higher education nor, as yet, a creative force in the development of black institutions, although they are not immune to government intervention. The forces lie outside immediate governmental direction. For the present, HEW is only concerned with state action in originally segregated states, and not with the broader system of higher education—one of the two major external forces. This system, with more than 3,000 institutions, has done as much as any segment of society to contribute to the isolation of TBI's. Yet, the system remains largely free of intervention except for legislation associated with equal opportunity and research funding. The second major force, "social" or student choice, is only indirectly influenced by government. Student preference and behavior remain limiting conditions on the effectiveness of public policy. The data presented here can therefore explicate those limits by focusing on the relevant patterns of student behavior. In particular, the data are examined with the purpose of determining just how special and how different from those of most institutions the enrollment patterns of TBI's may be.

Comparison of Traditionally Black and Predominantly Black Institutions

As defined here, the difference between a black and a nonblack institution is easily seen in the racial majority of the student body. This definition, of course, encompasses TBI's, which on the average have more than 91 percent black enrollments. It also includes "predominantly black institutions," known as PBI's. Predominantly black institutions, as a rule, are somewhat less predominantly black than TBI's, but they are so called because their student bodies are majority black, and typically three-fourths black. They lack the special history and traditional commitment to black students characteristic of TBI's. There are other characteristic differences, however, not so easily recognizable between TBI's and PBI's.

First, PBI's are virtually always administered under the authority of nonblack officials. In many cases the presidents and deans of PBI's are black, but they are not likely to be final policy making authorities because

PBI's are, almost without exception, public institutions. They are subject to state education and legislative authority and formally tied to a statewide higher educational system. The known exceptions to this rule are either controlled and directed by a religious group, or provide substantially less than the normal college curriculum. TBI's, on the other hand, are only one-third public.

Second, PBI's came into existence during a period of expanding educational opportunity for blacks in the larger society. Consequently, most of them were more recently established—less than fifty years ago; whereas TBI's tend to have origins in the nineteenth century. Some PBI's are older than many TBI's because the local environment, city or state, was ahead of the nation in integrating public educational facilities. This was especially likely in northern cities with large black populations. At any rate, it is not so much the years of their establishment as the particular racial-political environments that distinguish TBI's from PBI's.

Third, the majority of PBI's provide less than a four-year education—they are usually two-year colleges. The overwhelming majority of TBI's are four-year institutions; only a few are two-year colleges.

Although the overall variations between TBI's and PBI's are not difficult to observe, they are difficult to quantify. TBI's, by their very longevity, have made themselves self-evident. PBI's, on the other hand, are simply defined by the statistical ratio of black to white students. Since black majorities in schools are not always clearly recorded nor necessarily enduring, schools may be added to or subtracted from the list from year to year. More important, PBI's are frequently tied to other state colleges and may be confused with special campus or extension programs of predominantly white institutions. To be appropriately labeled a PBI, the institution should be formally independent of authority from other educational institutions. (Nevertheless, we have developed a list of forty-four PBI's, shown, with a list of all TBI's, in the Appendix.)

Ultimately, what makes a black institution "traditional" has less to do with its longevity than with its independence of orientation and support in environments hostile or indifferent to the higher education of blacks.

Most of the 105 TBI's developed during the period in which racial isolation was the rule. Three TBI's, identified in the list are no longer predominantly black. The transformation is probably an indication of reduced racial isolation, although it may also reflect a loss of educational opportunity for blacks. By the same token, the mere expansion of PBI's is an indication that racial isolation is only moderating; it is far from disappearing.

Longitudinal Enrollment Patterns in Traditionally Black Institutions

In many ways, a comparison of enrollment patterns in black and white institutions shows that the relevant communities of these two institutions are still quite separate and are independently influenced by major changes in the larger society. At a time when overall college enrollment appears to be static, enrollment in TBI's is growing. Currently, their total enrollment is 213,720 students. From 1968 to 1972, when enrollment was growing in most institutions, enrollment in black institutions was static.[4]

Enrollment growth among white institutions in the last few years has been much greater in public that in private ones. Conversely, enrollment has grown much faster in recent years in private TBI's than in public ones. Similarly, while the enrollment percentage in two-year TBI's is declining (although it has never been large), enrollment in non-TBI two-year institutions surpasses the average growth rate.

The most impressive example of the differences in rates of change in higher education enrollment in 1976 is reported by the Institute for Services to Education (ISE). Private, black four-year colleges increased their enrollments by 20 percent, whereas most private four-year colleges only had a 3.7 percent enrollment increase.[5] ISE also describes one of the external social forces that leads to these different institutional experiences in its reports on student availability:

> Discernible demographic trends in the black population seem to set
> the stage for continued growth in total enrollments in the future, . . .
> For example, the net growth rate for blacks from 1960 to 1976 ex-
> ceeds that for the white population and the nation as a whole,
> although the rate for each category has been declining (total popula-
> tion age) steadily. Moreover, cumulative percentage increases in the
> college age cohorts of the black population promise continued ex-
> pansion of the numbers of blacks who will be available for college
> through 1985. . . .[6]

Recent directions of change in enrollment can give misleading indications of current conditions of TBI's and of the distribution of black students among them. For example, TBI's enrolled just under 20 percent of black students in higher education in 1974, but as recently as ten years before, the majority of black students were enrolled in TBI's.[7]

Similarly, the recent growth trend in distribution among TBI's is toward private institutions, although the public ones continue to enroll nearly three-fourths of all students in TBI's, as shown in Table 6-1. Still, the

Table 6-1   OPENING FALL ENROLLMENT AT 105 TRADITIONALLY BLACK
INSTITUTIONS OF HIGHER EDUCATION
1976

Type of Institution	Total Headcount	First-Time Freshmen
4-year		
Public	148,824	31,205
Private	52,973	14,928
Total	201,797	46,133
2-year		
Public	7,277	2,803
Private	2,892	1,475
Total	10,169	4,278
Grand total	211,966	50,411

Source: Institute for Services to Education, "Preliminary Fall 1976 Enrollment in Historically Black Colleges," Research Profile (February 5, 1977), 1, Chart 1.

potential strength of private four-year TBI's can be observed in their pro-portionately larger share of new freshman enrollment in comparison to their smaller percentage of total TBI enrollment.

The positive futures of private TBI's are not easily recognized in the 1976 freshman enrollment data, because TBI's experienced substantial declines in comparison to nonblack institutions. The enrollment percentage in private four-year TBI's, however, declined much less than in public ones, −1.7 percent and −10.4 percent respectively. There was an overall gain in enrollment in all TBI's of 4 percent: four-year public TBI's down −0.8 per-cent, and the private TBI's up 2.6 percent.

The common paths of TBI's separate most clearly when the most recent enrollment data are compared to those of the recent past. ISE data for fall 1976 show the difference of direction between the public and private, but not two-year and four-year institutions. Enrollment data for 1977 show a growth at private four-year institutions (universities included) and a decline in all other TBI's.

This recent trend could be reversed. Some correlates to current enroll-ment patterns in TBI's, however, may have both explanatory and predictive value. In the long range, the condition of TBI's seems to have been most clearly determined by their limited financial resources. The financial cor-relate might thus indicate an advantage for public TBI's, given the relatively large size of state resources. In contrast, the unrealized potential of federal

Table 6-2 ANNUAL PERCENTAGE CHANGES IN TOTAL ENROLLMENT FOR 102 TRADITIONALLY BLACK INSTITUTIONS OF HIGHER EDUCATION 1968–77

Type of Institution	1968	1969	1970	1971	1972	1973	1974	1975	1976	1977
Public										
4-Year	5.7	5.9	5.3	6.9	2.1	2.8	0.9	13.3	−0.6	−7.3
2-Year	−7.5	26.1	10.2	3.1	9.4	5.6	15.0	9.7	11.7	−6.0
Total	5.4	6.4	5.4	6.8	2.4	2.9	1.3	13.2	−0.3	−7.2
Private										
4-Year	3.0	−0.2	0.7	3.4	0.6	−0.8	4.2	7.6	2.4	20.4
2-Year	4.0	−3.7	4.1	3.1	−6.1	−8.1	−1.7	−8.7	−0.1	−9.0
Total	2.6	−0.4	0.9	3.4	0.2	−1.2	−3.9	7.0	2.4	18.8
Grand total	4.5	4.3	4.1	5.8	1.8	1.8	2.0	11.5	0.4	−0.6

Source: Institute for Services to Education, "Preliminary Fall 1976 Enrollment in Historically Black Colleges," *Research Profile* (February 5, 1977).

Note: Does not include graduate and professional schools.

funds for "developing institutions" (Title III program) holds promise for private TBI's. Moreover, the *Adams* cases' regulations hold the threat that state funds to public TBI's may be distributed only with constraints on the level of black student enrollment.

Second, enrollment in private four-year TBI's has always been either moderately stable or growing. The two cases in which enrollment declined show the smallest declines for any TBI in the ten-year period covered in Table 6-2.

Third, and most informative for the two-year/four-year distinction, is the tendency of blacks who go to white institutions to enroll in two-year rather than four-year institutions, in contrast to those who go to black institutions. Since enrollment in two-year TBI's has been declining consistently, one should not expect a reversal there. Rather, it appears that students who choose TBI's are expecting a "four-year" type of education. Consequently, to the extent that two-year colleges continue to grow as the primary option available to blacks in white institutions, TBI's may flourish.

At the same time, the racial environment cannot be overlooked as an important factor. In a recent study of college attendance patterns among blacks, Crain and Mahard bring together these environmental correlates of enrollment in their findings on the college attendance patterns of blacks:

> We found students from black high schools who attended college went mostly to black colleges (by a 6 to 5 ratio) while blacks who graduated from predominantly white schools went mostly to white colleges (by a 7 to 2 ratio). This balances out in terms of total college admission—the attendance rates for all colleges combined is about the same from all-black and predominantly white (high) schools—but nearly half of the white colleges attended by black graduates are junior colleges, ...[8]

The greatest impact of TBI's on general black enrollment occurs among four-year institutions and especially among private ones. Of all black students in four-year institutions in 1976, 35.9 percent were in TBI's and 37.1 percent of TBI students were in private institutions. In contrast, only 11.7 percent are enrolled in two-year colleges.

The largest impact of TBI's on the higher education of blacks is probably made by their high levels of persistence for black students, as noted in earlier chapters, especially in four-year institutions. Accordingly, TBI's, with less than 20 percent of the enrollment in the four years preceding 1975-76, awarded 37 percent of all baccalaureate degrees received by blacks in that year. At the same time, blacks received only 6.5 percent of all baccalaureate degrees.[9]

Table 6-3 DISTRIBUTION OF BLACKS ENROLLED IN COLLEGES AND UNIVERSITIES
Fall 1976

Type of Institution	Total Black Enrollment (All Institutions)		Percent Enrolled in . . .			Percentage of Black Students of All Higher Education Students
	Number	Percent	Traditionally Black Institutions	Predominantly Black Institutions	Other Than Traditionally or Predominantly Black Institutions	
All institutions	1,034,680	100.0	17.8	11.9	70.3	9.3
Public	832,866	100.0	14.8	13.5	71.7	9.6
Private	201,814	100.0	29.9	5.4	64.7	8.4
All universities	150,217	100.0	8.1	—	91.9	5.4
Public	104,908	100.0	4.7	—	95.3	5.0
Private	45,309	100.0	16.0	—	84.0	6.5
All 4-year	455,170	100.0	35.9	5.5	58.6	10.4
Public	318,499	100.0	35.4	6.5	58.1	11.2
Private	136,671	100.0	37.1	3.2	59.7	8.9
All 2-year	429,293	100.0	0.2	22.9	76.9	11.0
Public	409,459	100.0	1.5	22.4	76.1	10.9
Private	19,834	100.0	11.7	32.3	56.0	13.2

Source: Preliminary data on fall 1976 enrollment from HEW, National Center for Education Statistics. Published in National Advisory Committee on Black Higher Education and Black Colleges and Universities, *Higher Education Equity: The Crisis of Appearance Versus Reality, First Annual Report* (Washington, D.C., June 1978), Chart 3, p. 15.

Since most recent data on persistence at TBI's are discussed in some detail in the two previous ISEP annual reports, they need not be repeated here. Still, at least one additional concern brought out by the *Adams* cases can be addressed. Consistent with expectation, Crain and Mahard's study finds a higher rate of persistence at black institutions. It also finds a distinct pattern of college attendance that relates to the "race" of high schools, which should be explored in the context of college retention and graduation. Crain and Mahard observe:

> The two largest studies of school racial composition and black college outcomes show that northern blacks were more likely to attend college from a predominantly white high school (Crain and Weisman, 1972) while southern blacks graduating from predominantly white high schools were less likely to attend college. (NORC, 1973)[10]

For the future of TBI's and the *Adams* cases, the most important aspect of Crain and Mahard's findings is that many predominantly white schools do not serve their black students well, especially the southern ones. They let the explanation of their data rest on the regional factor without looking farther. Regional differences, however, provide only a superficial explanation. A more fundamental explanation seems worthy of consideration.

The difference between black high schools in the South and those in the North is comparable to the difference between TBI's and PBI's. However long the histories of black Northern high schools, they do not generally have the legal and formal traditions of those in the South. The governmental support and recognition, although segregationist in motive, given to black schools as a function of their being predominantly black has probably been greater in the South than in the North.

The advantage in the college mobility of southern black students from black high schools may, therefore, be one of tradition. That is to say that a traditional experience in serving black students provides some payoff, whether at the college or high school level. Traditionally black colleges may continue to be more successful with their students than traditionally white institutions, and lacking the white segregationist aspect of governmental control over black high schools, that service should be consistent with racial equality.

Distribution of Students in Traditionally Black Institutions

The unequal distribution of black students among major fields is often associated with black institutions as well as with nonblack institutions. Frequently, TBI's are regarded as having fostered a greater imbalance of black student specialization toward the more crowded fields such as Education and away from the physical sciences. The statistics showing unequal distribution are generally accurate, but the meaning of the analytical association involved is more often naively considered and occasionally misleading. For example, TBI's do have a higher percentage of Education majors than most institutions, but this concentration may be wholly a function of external factors. Institutionally external factors may be of two types: (1) those carried by the students, and (2) those determined by the larger society.

The student factor consists of the training, preferences, and expectations a student brings to college. The special experiences of black youth prior to college enrollment may precondition their choice of major fields in ways that reflect their early exposure to racial inequality. A black secondary school deficient in Math and the physical sciences and weighted toward the social sciences, in contrast to a white secondary school, is a clear element of precollege inequality. The subsequent preference of black college students to draw on their background strengths, while steering away from their weaker points is understandable in terms of their high school training. It is also understandable in relation to their career expectations. In this regard, there are relatively few black role-models in the physical sciences and Math, while there are more in Education. Thus, black students have historically had more tangible reasons to expect to find jobs in Education than elsewhere. Ultimately, the student factor is traceable to the society's inegalitarian pressures on black students.

What is called the "social factor" consists of those conditions not identifiable in any single set of individuals. The racial inequality that is part of the social factor is most directly measurable through distribution of financial resources among institutions. Federal funds and their allocation among institutions are of interest in this study, and we will return to these subjects shortly.

A comparison of major field distributions, using American College Testing Program survey data, shows a predictably greater concentration of students in Education, Business, and the social sciences at TBI's than at other institutions.

While Table 6-4 points up some unevenness of major field distribution in black institutions, it does not give a full picture. First, white students who constitute approximately 9 percent of all TBI students, are included in TBI figures. Black students, who constitute about the same percentage at white institutions, are included in the figures for all institutions. Consequently, racial differences in distribution are slightly distorted. Second, the com-

Table 6-4   MAJOR FIELD DISTRIBUTION OF STUDENTS AT
TRADITIONALLY BLACK INSTITUTIONS AND ALL
INSTITUTIONS (IN PERCENTAGES)

Major Field	Traditionally Black Institutions	All Institutions
Agriculture	1	1
Business	19	14
Communications	1	2
Education	22	14
Engineering	2	4
Fine/Applied Arts	3	8
Foreign Languages	1	1
Health Professions	5	8
Home Economics	1	1
Humanities	3	11
Mathematics/Physical Sciences	6	8
Social Science	17	14
Trades/Technical	1	2
Other	8	8

Source: American College Testing Program, "Some Characteristics of the Historically Black Colleges." Paper presented to the National Advisory Committee on Black Higher Education and Black Colleges and Universities (Washington, D.C., 1978), pp. 10–11.

parison needs to be "controlled" for institutional type, because 85 percent of TBI's are four-year colleges (fifteen two-year colleges and two full universities, according to NCES categories). Two-year colleges constitute almost half of all institutions of higher education.

Table 6-5, based on 1974 OCR data, provides a more precisely defined comparison of distribution.

The refinements of data in Table 6-5, compared to the data in Table 6-4, show that the distribution of black students by major field in many ways is more unequal than the comparison of all TBI students to other students would show. In addition, one finds that almost 30 percent of black students at TBI's are in Education, as opposed to 22 percent of all TBI students. Similarly, the percentage of TBI students in Business goes up from 4 to 5 percent when only black students are counted. Of course, some of this variance may be an artifact of the difference in sources and reporting techniques, but the overall variance is too consistent to dismiss. The greater concentration of blacks students in Education and Business in proportion to all students is evident.

Table 6-5   MAJOR FIELD DISTRIBUTION OF BLACK STUDENTS IN
TRADITIONALLY BLACK AND TRADITIONALLY
NONBLACK 4-YEAR COLLEGES
1974

| | Institutions | |
Major Field	Traditionally Black	Traditionally Nonblack
Education	29.66	15.84
Business	20.39	16.26
Social Science	18.14	18.94
Natural Science	4.76	4.51
Technical Science	6.10	7.48
Professions[a]	1.68	3.53
Social Work and Public Health	2.39	3.58
Architecture	.23	.60
Agriculture	1.17	.40
Computer Science	.56	1.03
Other[b]	14.93	27.84
Total (100% =)	(116,459)	(165,732)

Source: Gail Thomas, "Equality of Representation of Race and Sex Groups in Higher Education," Center for Social Organization of Schools, Baltimore, Maryland (October 1978), Report No. 263. Table 9.

[a]Professions refer to Nursing, Pharmacy, Pre-Law, Pre-Medicine and similar pre-professional programs offered at the undergraduate level.

[b]"Other" includes majors in Foreign Languages, Home Economics, Library Science, and the precoded category designated in the survey as "others."

The analytical value of looking beyond the TBI's to understand the major field distribution of their students can be gleaned from a careful look at the last table. In particular, social sciences, Social Work, and Public Health each has slightly larger proportions of blacks in non-TBI's than in TBI's. Consequently, at least some element of the black student's attraction to fields other than the physical sciences is related to societal factors and not to the black institution, per se. How much is institutionally external in these, or all cases? More data are needed to provide a concrete answer. What we already know, however, makes the question well worth pursuing.

Returning to the more direct societal factors constraining black institutions, we have indicated that limited financial resources may constrict the development of new major field options at TBI's. In other chapters, particularly chapter 7, the ways in which financial limitations apply to the physical sciences at black institutions are discussed. What seems most pertinent for the present is the extent of these limitations in TBI's relative to other institutions.

Financial Resources of Traditionally Black Institutions

TBI's have relatively few independent financial resources on which to draw. Their endowments are much smaller than those of most white institutions of comparable size, and their alumni are generally able to provide little additional financial support. Consequently, they are heavily dependent on funds from federal and state governments and private foundations. Private TBI's, given their financial needs, also rely heavily on student tuition and fees, but these are on the average five hundred dollars lower than at most institutions.[11]

Colleges and universities generally depend on federal, state, and local governments for about half their revenues, 14 percent of which comes from the federal government. TBI's rely on government sources for 54 to 55 percent of their revenues; 29 percent of TBI revenues are from the federal government. Among private institutions, the reliance of TBI's on federal financial support is even greater; 14 percent of the income of all institutions is federal in origin in contrast to 38 percent of TBI incomes (see Appendix, Table A6-2).

TBI's, as much as black students, suffer from underrepresentation in the allocation of public funds. At the state level, inequities in government funding of black public institutions relative to white ones have seemingly been reduced to a minimum since implementation of the civil rights legislation of the sixties. We cannot be confident that remaining inequities are small, because available data are insufficient. We can, however, be certain that inequities remain, particularly at the federal level. The data confirm not only the existence of inequities in the allocation of federal funds, but also a failure to correct them from year to year.

Analysis of data from the Federal Interagency Committee on Education (FICE) gives evidence of a decline in the proportion of federal education and research funds going to black institutions.

Although Table 6-6 does not, itself, show an inequity in the allocation of federal funds, it does show a decline in funds. The proportion of total federal funds to black institutions (including PBI's) declined 13 percent between 1974 and 1975. Black institutions, however, constitute only about 5 percent of institutions of higher education. Their special difficulties are not apparent until one takes their special needs into consideration.

In the Higher Education Act of 1965, the federal government officially

Table 6-6 FEDERAL OBLIGATIONS TO BLACK INSTITUTIONS AS A PERCENTAGE OF OBLIGATIONS TO ALL INSTITUTIONS
Fiscal Years 1974 and 1975

Agency	Fiscal Year 1974	Fiscal Year 1975
ACTION	10.4	9.7
Agency for International Development	6.5	0
Community Services Administration	45.8	52.2
Department of Agriculture	6.7	5.6
Department of Commerce	0.1	0
Department of Defense	0.4	0.2
Department of Health, Education, and Welfare	6.8	6.0
National Institute of Education	0	0.4
Office of Education	14.8	12.2
Public Health Service	2.5	1.5
Social and Rehabilitation Service	1.6	0
Other HEW	3.6	15.8
Department of Housing and Urban Development	8.4	28.7
Department of the Interior	0	0.1
Department of Justice	2.6	2.4
Department of Labor	2.1	2.9
Department of Transportation	1.2	1.0
Environmental Protection Agency	2.3	1.5
Energy Research and Development Administration	0.2	0.2
National Aeronautics and Space Administration	2.3	2.3
National Endowment for the Arts	8.1	0.9
National Endowment for the Humanities	3.2	1.0
National Science Foundation	1.8	1.1
Nuclear Regulatory Commission	0	0
Total	5.7	4.9

Source: National Advisory Committee on Black Higher Education and Black Colleges and Universities, *First Annual Report: Higher Education Equity* (1978), p. 29. Committee staff analysis of data from the Federal Interagency Committee on Education.

recognized the legitimacy of responding to institutional needs in the allocation of federal funds. Title III of the act authorized a substantial allocation of funds to "developing institutions." The expressed purpose was to support and strengthen institutions which serve large numbers of disadvantaged and poor students. Obviously, TBI's were prime candidates for these grants.

All black institutions got 61 percent of those grants during the first year, 1966. By 1976, however, the proportion given to black institutions dropped to 49 percent (see Appendix, Table A6-1). The drop in their percentage of other funds is significant, but less so than the total amounts of those other funds. A brief reference to the appendix of chapter 3 and Table 6-7 will show that all Title III funds amount to less than the federal research funds given to several individual white universities in a single year. Moreover, Title III has not evolved into a grant program for black institutions. In 1976, white institutions received substantially more funds in absolute dollars and in percentage than did black institutions, although the average grant amounts to black institutions were larger. By 1977 the average size of grants was about one-third of what it had been the year before, in part because the number of institutions receiving funds increased from 23 to 283, while total funds available remained virtually unchanged. The impact of this change had to be felt by black institutions as much, if not more than by white ones, since the proportion of funds going to white institutions increased from just over 50.4 percent to 54.9 percent as the proportion going to black institutions correspondingly declined six points.

In 1975 about $213 million was obligated to all black institutions by various federal agencies. Of this amount, about $201 million was designated for TBI's. Both amounts may appear large in the abstract, but compared to federal funds going to other institutions, they are very small. Three predominantly white universities received more than $250 million in research and development (R & D) funds alone in the same year. Federal government R & D funds to these three universities—the University of Wisconsin at Madison, Massachusetts Institute of Technology, and the University of California at San Diego—provided the bulk of that amount, $183 million. By 1976 the same three white institutions were receiving slightly more in total federal R & D funds than all 105 TBI's combined had received from the federal government for all purposes the year before.[12] Moreover, these three institutions can be grouped with a list of at least fifteen like them which receive only slightly smaller amounts of R & D funds from the federal government (see Appendix to chapter 3).

Not only are the funds on which black institutions can draw limited, federal funds for TBI's show a strong bias away from supporting the major fields where financial support is needed, i.e., the sciences. Of the $213 million obligated to all black institutions, only about $38 million, or less than 18 percent, was awarded for the "academic sciences" (Appendix, Table A6-3). Of the $201 million obligated to TBI's, only slightly more than 18 percent was designated for "academic sciences," as Table 6-8 shows.

To understand fully the uneven distribution of black students across major fields, one must look back to the last century, when black institutions were first developing. The history of this development will show that in generating major fields, black institutions sought to respond to the most

Table 6-7 DISTRIBUTION OF COMBINED BASIC AND ADVANCED PROGRAMS
Fiscal Years 1976 and 1977

	Grantees					Total Funds					Average Grant					
	Number		Percent			Dollar Amounts		Percent			Advanced Program			Basic Program		
Type of Institution	1976	1977	1976	1977	Percent Change	1976	1977	1976	1977	Percent Change	1976	1977	Percent Change	1976	1977	Percent Change
All institutions[1]	237	283	100	100	19.4	110,000,000	110,476,440	100	100	.004	1,705,882	623,656	-63.4	256,157	276,192	7.8
4-year	153	187	64.6	66.1	22.2	83,600,000	83,940,000	76.0	76.0	.004	1,335,757	678,154	-49.2	304,000	326,721	7.5
2-year	84	96	35.4	33.9	14.3	26,400,000	26,536,440	24.0	24.0	.005	1,265,454	497,143	-60.7	170,958	185,536	8.5
Public institutions	114	128	48.1	45.2	12.3	54,652,800	56,586,800	49.7	51.2	3.5	1,774,705	809,290	-54.4	252,400	269,033	6.6
4-year	46	54	19.4	19.1	17.4	30,450,000	34,198,500	27.7	31.0	12.3	2,708,333	1,059,675	-60.9	355,000	382,500	7.7
2-year	68	74	28.7	26.1	8.8	24,202,800	22,388,300	22.0	20.1	-7.5	1,265,454	570,829	-54.9	180,400	196,243	8.8
Private institutions	123	151	51.9	53.4	22.8	55,347,200	52,322,140	50.3	47.1	-5.5	1,637,058	484,408	-70.4	259,596	282,238	8.7
4-year	107	131	45.1	46.3	22.4	53,150,000	48,824,500	48.3	44.2	-8.1	1,637,058	510,919	-68.8	281,333	305,170	8.5
2-year	16	20	6.8	7.1	25.0	2,197,200	3,497,640	2.0	3.2	59.2	—	256,420	—	137,325	147,703	7.6
Predominantly black institutions[2]	68	82	28.7	29.0	20.6	54,580,000	48,270,700	49.6	43.7	-11.6	2,240,769	653,534	-70.8	462,727	540,361	16.8
4-year	58	70	24.5	24.7	20.7	49,305,000	45,470,700	44.8	41.2	-7.8	2,330,000	706,272	-69.7	503,723	601,842	19.5
2-year	10	12	4.2	4.2	20.0	5,255,000	2,800,000	4.8	2.5	-46.7	1,750,000	91,000	-94.8	219,375	280,777	28.0
Predominantly white institutions	169	197	71.3	69.6	16.6	55,420,000	60,638,240	50.4	54.9	9.4	1,374,761	621,459	-54.8	179,391	189,366	5.6
4-year	95	115	40.1	40.6	21.1	34,295,000	37,552,300	31.2	34.0	9.5	1,537,500	663,300	-56.9	190,903	202,261	5.9
2-year	74	82	31.2	29.0	10.8	21,125,000	23,085,940	19.2	20.9	9.3	1,157,777	565,065	-51.2	164,692	171,007	3.8

Source: Reanalysis of data from Advisory Council on Developing Institutions (HEW), *Strengthening Developing Institutions—Title III of Higher Education Education Act of 1965 Annual Report* (March 1977), pp. 52–53 and (March 1978), pp. 39–40.

[1]Data includes grants for Advanced Institutional Development Program for Fiscal Year 1977.

[2]Data does not include one four-year black private institution serving as consortium coordinator in 1976.

Table 6-8 **FEDERAL FUNDS OBLIGATED TO TRADITIONALLY BLACK INSTITUTIONS**
Fiscal Year 1975

Type of Institution	Total, All Activities	Academic Science							Non-Science
		Total Academic Science	Research and Development	Research and Development Plants	Facilities for Instruction in Science and Engineering	Fellowships Traineeships Training Grants	General Support for Science	Other Science	
All black institutions[1]									
Number	213,668	38,285	23,127	0	65	1,217	4,654	9,222	175,383
Percent	100.0	17.92	10.82	.00	.03	.57	2.18	3.98	82.08
Traditionally black institutions									
Number	210,159	36,603	22,301	0	53	1,216	4,558	8,513	165,761
Percent	100.0	18.20	10.61	.00	.02	.58	2.17	4.05	77.92

Source: Federal Interagency Committee on Education, "Federal Agencies and Black Colleges," *FICE Report,* 4, 2 (December 1977), Table 2.

[1] "All Black Institutions" include Traditionally and Predominantly Black Institutions.

pressing occupational needs of the freedmen. In many cases, that involved concentrating on fields where blacks continue to be most heavily represented today. In many other if not most cases, however, the selection of major fields was guided by the availability of rewarding professional opportunities, as well as by a sense of social and civic obligation.

The clearest evidence of deviation from that guidance can be found in the pressures that white philanthropists and creditors placed on black institutions to restrict their major field offerings. Although these white "supporters" facilitated a black institutional response to the most salient needs of black Americans, their expressed intentions were more moderate than the full satisfaction of those needs. When they supported teacher training for blacks, it was not only because blacks needed it, but also because teacher training was considered a politically acceptable focus for black education.[13] There was, therefore, little financial encouragement for black institutions to redirect their focus on teacher training when other specializations grew in importance.

Although the segregationist intentions of the early financial supporters of black institutions have faded from view, the resultant economic biases which limit specialization at these institutions have persisted. Very little has been done to provide federal, state, or private funds to facilitate the expansion of physical science options at TBI's. Recent efforts by black professors to get federal funds for the establishment of "science centers" at TBI's, discussed in chapter 4, received very limited financial support from the National Science Foundation. Had these efforts been fully successful, a greater amount of support would still have been needed to compensate for the long-standing biases of institutional financial support.

POLICY IMPLICATIONS

The condition of education at traditionally black institutions cannot be summarized adequately in a treatment as short as this one. The obstacles TBI's have faced, and continue to face, extend as far into their social environments as the effects of racial inequality on their students. These obstacles are too far-reaching, in their direct and indirect impact on TBI's, to be easily quantified. Nevertheless, the directly observable impediments to the effectiveness of these institutions are sufficiently strong to justify special public support of TBI's.

Similarly, the special services and successes of TBI's are observable in their unique contribution to the education of black Americans, as well as the education of African and Caribbean students. Yet, simple observation cannot readily detect all of their special contributions because these contributions are, in part, submerged in "traditions," and because there has been no racially neutral end-point at which to measure these contributions. What makes a black institution "traditional," in a fundamental sense, is its past and present capacity to build in its students a creative, multifaceted orientation toward equality. Still, as with most traditions, we are a long way from knowing in detail how the special black institutional tradition is manifested on a day-to-day basis. Until these institutions are better understood, education decision makers would be on safer ground supporting them because of their contributions than penalizing them for their traditional differences from the majority of institutions of higher education.

Secretary Califano's statement in support of black institutions might be amended in light of the data. He observes that "isolation from white society" has been an obstacle to TBI's. The data indicate that TBI's are not isolated in any but the most restricted sense of being excluded from opportunities, as they have emerged from quasi-isolation, they have received less than equal treatment. If isolation implies "insulation," it is only one side of the problem. The other side is the exposure of TBI's to competition for students and resources—competition on the basis of educational and financial criteria that exclude from consideration much of the traditional mission of black institutions.

Current federal approaches to developing a policy on traditionally black institutions, commensurate with an expressed commitment to equal opportunity, have wavered between a celebration of the institutions' presumed "emergence from isolation" and a prophecy of their eventual demise, caused by competition with traditionally white institutions.

Policy initiative at the federal level has been impaired by two contradictory views of TBI's. On one hand, TBI's are seen as the byproducts of isolation and the antithesis of racial integration. On the other hand, they are viewed as the institutions most responsible for making progress toward equal educational opportunity and most deserving of reward for the progress made. Whether that reward will come at all, and whether TBI's will be its beneficiaries, will depend on public support, particularly federal. This contingency means, first, that the federal government must explicitly support continuation and development of TBI's if it does not want to contribute to their dissolution. Second, and equally important, federal policy can only be meaningfully supportive of TBI's if it is based on a recognition that these institutions serve a higher purpose than simply providing a second choice for blacks when the presumed first choice, enrollment at traditionally white institutions, proves to be a myth.

Without including the second aspect in the formulation of a federal policy, the first aspect—that of basic support for TBI's—becomes a shallow expression of good intentions. It is shallow because it is compromised by an explicit juridical obligation to "desegregate" all public institutions of higher education, defined primarily in terms of a school's racial composition (*Adams v. Califano*). Lacking an explicit recognition of the nonsegregationist nature of TBI's, federal policy retains a real contradiction. TBI's are still seen as the lamentable residue of segregation whose existence must be tolerated, rather than advocated, until more propitious times. When the times are more propitious for a coherent federal policy, there is little reason to believe that TBI's will not be the victims of that coherence. On the other hand, with the recognition of the second aspect, the special function of TBI's, and a commitment of federal financial support to them, the future role of TBI's in higher education is likely to be as solid and socially valuable for an equitable and coherent federal policy as that of any other kind of institution. Although Secretary Califano has reaffirmed HEW's intention to support black public colleges (while "desegregating" them), such support is likely to be realized only through an explicit recognition that their special mission and function will continue into the future—whether they are integrated or not—and a corresponding commitment of financial support.

That special mission, as has been observed, cannot be defined succinctly until there is a broader consensus on the missions and limits of all other institutions. But the most exceptional aspect of the mission of black public institutions, compared to that of other institutions, is their commitment to educational and social equity. Their specific concern with black students has never permitted them the luxury of indifference to equal opportunity for all.

Although the special functions of TBI's have not been fully described here, some of them should now be evident. Those functions, essential to equal educational opportunity for blacks, which black institutions have traditionally served and continue to serve more effectively than others, involve: (1) educating economically disadvantaged groups; (2) educating black professionals; (3) retaining and graduating black students at all levels; (4) providing a sympathetic, sociopsychologically supportive environment for black students; and (5) setting admission standards which are as sensitive to the potential of black applicants as they are to the limitations of their precollege backgrounds. Perhaps another function, or summary of all the others, is the overall orientation of these institutions toward developing in their students a capacity to deal with racial and nonracial barriers in society—society as it is, rather than as it might be.

Leaving aside the apparent social value of TBI's themselves, these functions are well worth federal support. The largest investments of federal funds to all higher education institutions ignore these functions entirely. Federal R & D funds, on which leading white institutions depend heavily, do not reward them for these essential educational services, but for the production of research. If all institutions received monetary support consistent with the expressed value of these educational services, and based on the effectiveness with which these services are delivered, TBI's would have a more secure future. That is to say, a national commitment to essential education, with or without regard to race, is belied by the imbalanced distribution of federal funds.

In the debate over reauthorization of the 1965 Higher Education Act, the Carter administration has expressed strong reservations about federal support for institutions, as opposed to support for students. As a consequence, funds for developing institutions under Title III of the act have come under careful scrutiny, threatening an important source of federal funds for black institutions, inasmuch as these institutions initially were the primary beneficiaries of the funds. The administration intends to concentrate Title III funds on needy students who "happen" to be disproportionately located in certain institutions, many of which "happen" to be black. Apparently, the administration expects to bring Title III in line with other federal education programs which focus on students, and thereby bring a much-needed coherence and consistency to federal education policy.

The administration has apparently overlooked, however, the inconsistency of trying to impose uniformity in a piecemeal fashion, like telling only one of many runners in a race that he must run on the track. In comparison to "developed" institutions, "developing" institutions, particularly TBI's, have never been on the same track; theirs has had many more obstacles. TBI's have not been free, as most other institutions have been, to serve any students they chose whenever they chose. Their only choice has been to serve the students who need and want them most.

What seems to be guiding or misguiding the reauthorization of Title III is not so much a clear policy reevaluation and redirection as it is a return to the inconsistency of past policies that haunts and constrains new initiatives. Although many would argue that Title III was initially designed to serve black institutions, one of its primary goals was to serve institutions that are committed to equal educational opportunity and that had a substantial history of serving those students for whom opportunity had long been less than equal. The fact that TBI's virtually filled the category of institutions which could be so described may not have needed to be said in 1965. The fact that it was not said left a lingering ambiguity from which the current authorization debate suffers. In the flurry to deemphasize institutional aid, few people seem to remember that Title III never concerned aid to institutions "pure and simple." Rather, it concerned what should have been a national mission, equal opportunity, and the support of those few institutions that had fundamentally committed themselves to that same mission.

Looking at the history of federal aid to students, one can see why such ambiguity may have been unavoidable. Legislation providing for direct aid to students has never acknowledged that disadvantage could be a function of racial inequality, and of the racial discrimination to which traditionally white institutions adhered. Consequently, the legislation said little or nothing about the institutional role in sustaining inequality. To the extent that such legislation is identified with equal opportunity, major ambiguity emerges.

If, in search of greater policy coherence, the ambiguity involved in Title III is removed, then the second ambiguity—that involved in direct aid to students— remains and, as far as equal opportunity for blacks is concerned, policy becomes more inconsistent. If both ambiguities are removed, which would mean denying analytically or factually the relevance of equal opportunity to the two programs, policy becomes coherent, but no commitment to equality remains.

The massive dissemination of public funds to nonblack institutions of higher education indirectly benefits some students, either through the improvement of institutional facilities and faculty or through the availability of research assistantships. As shown in the next chapter, however, the students who benefit most are among those who need it least. Similarly, the fact that the more "developed" institutions are indirectly supported, as institutions, by federal research grants of much larger amounts of money than the amounts awarded to black and "developing" institutions, indicates real value priorities. The fact that one form of institutional support is direct and the other is indirect does not change the resulting fact that equality of opportunity, as far as federal aid to higher educational institutions is concerned, has been of very low priority.

Graduate and Professional Education: Special Problems of Access, Distribution, and Persistence

The problems and prospects for black students in higher education are similar at both the undergraduate and graduate levels, but the magnitude of the problems is much greater at the higher level. Qualitatively, what has been said about the status of blacks in undergraduate education also applies to graduate and professional education. But, in quantitative terms, blacks experience much greater educational disadvantages after the baccalaureate. We have previously concentrated on undergraduate education because the bulk of students are at that level, and because the kinds of inequalities to be expected at the advanced level can be fully sampled from data on the undergraduate experience. Still, the depth of racial inequality at both levels can only be fully assessed by viewing each of them separately.

Historically, the progress of blacks in gaining access to higher education at both levels has been substantial, though insufficient. At the advanced level, however, access is not merely insufficient, it is surprisingly deficient. The critical problems of black access to undergraduate education have been reduced, while those of distribution have persisted almost unchecked. In graduate and professional education, on the other hand, the problems of access and distribution have been equally resistant to change. There is now evidence that the initially positive institutional response to the need for increased opportunity for blacks at the advanced levels has been supplanted by indifference and indecision. Moreover, public pressure for the expansion of educational opportunity has become almost as imperceptible as the institutional response. Although federal and state authorities continue to support positive institutional action, they provide little inspiration and less encouragement for institutions to show initiative. The limited progress made in the early seventies has now effectively given way to stagnation. In medical and law schools, particularly, educational opportunity for blacks is, at best, in a "holding pattern."

Higher education, as has been noted, provides an important credential for employment and career development. The difference in income and job security between blacks with a bachelor's degree and those with less education is substantially greater than the corresponding difference among whites. For those pursuing graduate and professional education, however, problems of income and job security take second place to the more fundamental problem of admission to a profession. The credentials that professional schools, and to a lesser extent graduate schools, award, such as M.D., LLD, Ph.D., serve as permits to work as well as strong assurance of employment. When denied admission to these schools, applicants are effectively denied permission to practice those professions for which the schools are the gatekeepers.

In the Supreme Court case of the *Regents of the University of California* vs. *Allan Bakke* (98 S. Ct. 2733 1978), the University of California at Davis Medical School defended its special admissions program for minorities in part on the grounds that there is a particular need for minority physicians which those students admitted under the special program could be expected to fill. The Supreme Court majority did not rule out the medical school's argument, but rather demanded evidence that such students would indeed fulfill the medical school's expectations at a level commensurate with the numbers so admitted. Thus, the question of society's need for professionals is as important as ever in analyzing inequality in education.

How may such questions be answered? What constitutes racial inequality in the professions, and how are the black community's needs for professionals defined? This primary question may be approached in three ways. First, inequality may be defined in terms of numbers or ratios of blacks to whites in any given profession with regard to the general population. Second, the profession only requires racial balance if there is evidence that nonblack professionals will not serve the black population. Third, professionals, black or white, are only needed to the extent that the job market can absorb them. Obviously, the three alternative approaches must be weighed in terms of social value and other subjective criteria. Consequently, all of these alternatives will be considered in the selection and examination of data. Under any prominent definition of inequality, the evidence of black disadvantage is clear. We will try to balance our references to professional needs to encompass all three. Because the third alternative is apparently the most restrictive in its definition of inequality, we will also concentrate on those professions where, in the more restrictive, market-oriented sense, blacks experience inequality of opportunity.

We can not ignore the great significance of the data on black underrepresentation in the professions. In virtually no profession for which an advanced degree is required do blacks constitute more than 3 percent of the recognized professionals. In some professions that require advanced training, admission (certification) is gained through a closed professional society. The societies are closed in the sense that they alone have the authority to license practitioners in the field and to evaluate their competence. The American Medical Association (AMA) and the American Bar Association (ABA) are prominent examples of such societies. Still, there are other, less prominent societies which, like the AMA and the ABA, directly or indirectly control the availability of advanced training in their professions. An extreme example is the two societies of actuaries, which not only license all actuaries but also directly control and administer nearly all training available through their practictioners in the field. In effect, they determine both professional needs and the adequacy of the educational system designed to meet those needs. Thus, the market-oriented approach to inequaltiy rarely operates for anyone, because the real decisions are made in the private or quasi-public sector. While limiting ourselves for the moment to such an approach, we should keep in mind that the free labor market view represents an artificial, if not mythical, premise of professional and educational mobility. More is really being asked of blacks seeking to penetrate these professions than the simplistic image of free market competition for jobs implies.

The historical inclination in American education policy, as in other public policy areas (chapter 1), has been to delegate important authority to private or near-private groups. Government policy makers are therefore left in the same position as private citizens as far as the assessment of equality of educational opportunity is concerned. Since educators and professionals in the fields that require advanced education exercise decisive control over institutional goals and practices, policy analysis must rely first on the assessment of institutional output to judge performance. Consequently, it is essential to know at what point black underrepresentation should be sufficient grounds on which to question the behavior of higher education practices. Ultimately, such findings should also bring into question those public policies and programs which allow underrepresentation to persist.

Black Professionals in the Economy

The need for black professionals with postsecondary degrees is probably as high now as it has ever been. Limiting the definition of need to the capacity of the American economy to absorb professionals, it is clear that the demands of the market, even with racial discrimination, exceed the supply. This is true in every field, but the demand for Ph.D.'s is especially demonstrable in the sciences.

Out of a total of more than 226,000 employed doctoral scientists and engineers in 1973, only 1,700 were blacks. Since this was the last year in which 1976 Ph.D. graduates, including those with M.A. in hand, were likely to have entered graduate schools, there is little doubt that entering students were aware of the lack of black Ph.D.'s in these areas (see Table 7-1).

In 1973, black's represented less than one-half of 1 percent of the identifiable physical scientists. Including those scientists with doctorates in related areas, Mathematics, Computer and Enviromental Sciences, Engineering, the black proportion employed remained small. The black proportion of working social scientists and psychologists with doctorates was equally small, less than 1 percent. This is particulary striking when one considers the heavy concentration of black undergraduates in the social sciences.

It is not surprising therefore that unemployment among black social scientists with Ph.D.'s has been very low. In 1973 the supply of blacks with

Table 7-1   EMPLOYED MINORITY DOCTORAL SCIENTISTS AND ENGINEERS 1973

Field	Total	Black	American Indian	Asian	Other	No Report
Total	226,750	1,700	100	10,450	300	16,250
Physical scientists	49,100	400	(^{1})	2,350	50	3,400
Mathematical scientists	12,600	100	—	650	(^{1})	1,100
Computer specialists	2,900	50	—	100	(^{1})	250
Environmental scientists	10,550	(^{1})	—	300	—	800
Engineers	36,200	100	(^{1})	3,100	50	2,050
Life scientists	59,350	550	(^{1})	2,600	100	4,000
Psychologists	26,050	200	(^{1})	300	(^{1})	2,250
Social scientists	29,850	300	50	1,100	50	2,400
No report	150	(^{1})	—	(^{1})	—	(^{1})

Source: National Science Foundation, Manpower Characteristics System. Reproduced by National Academy of Sciences, Manpower Commission.

Note: Detail may not add to total because of rounding.

^{1} Less than 50.

Ph.D.'s had scarcely approached the demand of the job market. At a time when the continued presence of racial discrimination in employment was undeniable, reported black unemployment among scientists and engineers with Ph.D.'s was statistically insignificant, as Table 7-2 shows.

Unfortunately, precise employment data on black Ph.D.'s and professionals with postgraduate credentials are not available. It is safe to assume, however, that the unemployment rates in other areas would not be substantially different, except in areas like Medicine, where unemployment is virtually nonexistent.

A rough test of overall employment potential for black Ph.D.'s can be made by looking at faculty positions available. Recently, the availability of faculty positions has declined considerably. Nevertheless, the potential for black faculty employment, given the numbers of black undergraduates, remains relatively high. In addition, those blacks with advanced degrees have not limited themselves to higher education teaching positions. In the past fifteen years, about 60 percent of Ph.D.'s have chosen to pursue a faculty position, but the variations in this percentage from year to year have been significant. Between 1960 and 1964, about 57 percent planned to pursue a

Table 7-2   UNEMPLOYMENT RATES FOR DOCTORAL SCIENTISTS
AND ENGINEERS
1973

Gender and Race	Number	Rate	Standard Error (Percentage)
Total	2,600	1.2	.05
Gender			
Men	1,900	.9	.05
Women	700	3.9	.20
Race			
White	2,200	1.1	.05
Black	([1])	—	—
American Indian	([2])	4.9	5.30
Asian	200	1.7	.30
Other	([2])	3.4	2.30
No report	200	1.3	.20

Source: National Science Foundation, Manpower Characteristics System. Reproduced by National Academy of Science, Manpower Commission.
Note: Detail may not add to total because of rounding.
[1] No cases reported.
[2] Less than 50.

faculty position; by 1969-70 the percentage had risen to 67, and by 1973-74 it had dropped to 58 percent (see Appendix, Table A7-1).[1] In 1970, only 3 percent of college and university faculty positions requiring a Ph.D. were held by blacks (which includes faculty positions at black institutions).[2]

In all fields, the income of blacks with advanced education considerably surpasses that of blacks with only bachelor's degrees. While whites with advanced degrees also earn more than whites having only a bachelor's degree, the difference of income among blacks in those categories is much greater. In fact, among the young professionals, as levels of education go up, blacks come much closer to income parity with whites with the same level of education. As unemployment goes up, those blacks most immediately threatened are the least skilled employees. Consequently, the income differences between the young professionals and nonprofessionals should not decrease as long as the added returns of advanced education hold up. Relying on the preceding table, one can expect to find a near 40 percent gain in the income of black males with postgraduate training, as compared to a 15 percent gain in the income of white males with comparable training.

Table 7-3   EARNINGS OF BLACK AND WHITE WORKERS WITH FOUR AND FIVE OR MORE YEARS OF COLLEGE 1969

	Black			White		
Age Group	5 or More Years	4 Years	Difference	5 or More Years	4 Years	Difference
Men						
Total, 25–64	$11,755	$8,652	$3,103	$16,145	$14,225	$1,920
18–24	6,142	4,767	1,375	5,060	4,777	283
25–34	9,401	8,188	1,213	11,097	10,808	289
35–54	12,984	9,148	3,836	18,687	16,086	2,601
55–64	11,954	8,307	3,647	19,464	16,120	3,344
Women						
Total, 25–64	$ 8,412	$6,545	$1,867	$ 8,144	$ 6,453	$1,691
18–24	4,462	4,250	212	4,432	4,182	290
25–34	2,220	6,219	1,001	6,883	5,940	943
35–54	8,800	6,820	1,980	8,486	6,527	1,959
55–64	8,954	6,667	2,287	9,366	7,594	1,772

Source: Richard B. Freeman, Black Elite, Carnegie Commission on Higher Education (New York: McGraw-Hill, 1976). Based on U.S. Census data.

Estimates of the actual amount of income gains associated with postgraduate education vary, but in all studies clear gains for blacks are reported. Brown and Stent, for example, attribute relatively small income gains to advanced education, but the ratio of black income disadvantage declines as the level of college education goes above four years (see Table 7-4).

More recent data confirm the persistence of a substantial income differential that is attributable to advanced training, as indicated in Table 7-5. The data leave the fifth year or more of higher education as a single category, however, and it is reasonable to assume that the income difference between those with advanced degrees and those with only a bachelor's degree has not been fully measured. Thus, the income differential is probably greater than that shown in Table 7-5. There is about an 11 percent increase in income for the average person with more than four years of college.

No one can count on secure employment based solely on an advanced degree, except perhaps those with medical degrees. On the other hand, blacks without an advanced degree can anticipate greater job insecurity than blacks with one—comparatively greater insecurity than whites. Nevertheless, some long range projections of employment which are based on estimates of the supply of highly trained blacks are not particularly reassuring. Fleming, Gill and Swinton (ISEP) project a fairly high level of unemployment among black Ph.D.'s seeking faculty positions. Even their pessimistic projections, however, postponed any decline in the market for new black faculty until 1982.[3] Graduates should therefore feel reasonably secure that their advanced education will be financially rewarding.

Moreover, the National Science Foundation's projections of the employment potential of doctoral scientists and engineers up to 1985 show reasonable promise. In their static model, they assume that about the same percentage of Ph.D.'s will remain in academics as now. In their "probable utilization" model, they assume that these Ph.D.'s will be employed in related nonacademic areas, expected to provide 30,000 new openings by 1985. While the static model projects very little increase in new employment for Ph.D.'s, the probable model projects a 9 percent increase in overall openings.[4]

Whether blacks will be able to take advantage of available opportunities is, of course, tied to the expansion of educational opportunity. The scarcity of blacks in these professions has been largely a function of their lack of financial resources and the denial of meaningful access to graduate and professional schools. As with undergraduates, educational aspirations have never been primary factors in explaining black access to graduate and

Table 7-4   ANNUAL INCOME OF MALES
1970

| Males | Elementary School | | High School | | College | | | | | |
	1-3 Years	5-7 Years	8 Years	1-3 Years	4 Years	1-2 Years	3 Years	4 Years	5 Years	6 Years
U.S. total	$3,658	$5,000	$6,030	$7,564	$9,042	$10,446	$11,233	$14,229	$13,092	$17,879
Blacks	3,018	4,064	4,669	5,351	6,295	6,992	7,163	8,218	9,338	12,888
Black ratio	.83	.81	.77	.71	.70	.67	.64	.58	.71	.72

Source: Frank Brown and Madelon D. Stent, *Minorities in U.S Institutions of Higher Education* (New York: Praeger, 1977), Table 2.2.

211

Table 7-5   INCOME AND ADVANCED EDUCATION OF U.S. HEADS
OF HOUSEHOLDS, 25 YEARS OLD AND OVER
1976–77

	Employed, Underemployed, and Unemployed Heads			Fulltime Employed Heads		
		1977	*1976*		*1977*	*1976*
	Number (in thou- sands)	*Median Income Dollars*	*Median Income Dollars*	*Number (in thou- sands)*	*Median Income Dollars*	*Median Income Dollars*
Heads						
College education						
4 years	5,173	23,409	22,019	4,102	25,224	23,788
5 years or over	4,389	26,042	24,676	3,342	27,745	26,155
Difference in dollars		2,533	2,657		2,521	2,367
Percentage (income differential from 4th to 5th year in college)		10.82	12.07		9.99	9.95

Source: U.S. Bureau of the Census, *Current Population Reports*, Series P-60, No. 116, "Money, Income and Poverty Status of Families and Persons in the United States: 1977" (Advance Report), (Washington, D.C.: U.S. Government Printing Office, 1978), Table 1.

professional schools. Nor is the deficiency of blacks in professions explainable in terms of availability pools, because the numbers of blacks with baccalaureates have, more than among whites, surpassed the numbers admitted to advanced degree programs.

Socioeconomic Status and Financial Resources of Graduate and Professional Students

The same differences in economic background among graduate students exist among undergraduates, but they are greater. In large part this is because the families of students who pursue advanced education tend to be wealthier than those who terminate their schooling with a bachelor's degree or less. The same tendency can also be found among black students. The range of income variation among blacks, however, cannot be as large as that among whites. Historically, black families in general possessed proportionately much less income and education compared to white families than they do now. Consequently, while there are socioeconomic differences among the parents of today's black students, the range of economic difference among black students is not as great as it is between blacks and whites.

An indirect but reliable measure of the economic differences among students at various levels of education is the educational attainment of their parents. The parents of recent Ph.D. graduates, as a group, were thirty years ahead of the average level of education at the time they finished their schooling.[5] Accordingly, a National Research Council study suggests that it would take thirty years for the average level of education nationwide to reach the level attained in 1920 by parents of current Ph.D.'s (see Figure 7-1).

The socioeconomic advantages of Ph.D. students' families are not very different from those of professional school students' families for whom more precise income data is available. Research on medical school students demonstrates a strong bias toward the wealthy in medical school enrollment. A 1965 study observes that 34 percent of medical students come from the wealthiest 3 percent of American homes.[6] Fein and Weber, in a 1971 longitudinal study of medical students, found that 63 percent of the 1967 students reported annual family incomes of $10,000 or more, while only 34 percent of all families in this country earned as much.[7] As other research shows, this is a rather traditional bias. For 1976–77 this economic bias holds throughout American medical education—a point to which we will return later.

While the average graduate student is capable of working to support himself or herself, the demands of full-time study usually prevent financial independence. This is not a problem for the traditionally large group of graduate students who can rely on family resources, but for students from families with few resources it can be an insuperable problem. Nearly all black students must themselves secure the bulk of the financial resources to pay for their education while in school. This means they must rely primarily on fellowships, loans, or earnings, or all three sources, and too frequently all three. There are special sources of support, including the GI bill, private industry funds, and contributions from spouses, but these accounted for only a small part of student support in 1976-77. Sources of support such as "assistantships" and "traineeships" may be viewed as private fellowships, where equal opportunity is concerned, because they are all distributed in the same way, i.e. as benefits or rewards to students for actual or anticipated achievements.

The largest nonprivate source of graduate student funding at the Ph.D. level is the federal government, through a variety of fellowships and traineeships. The largest source of funds overall for black students in 1973 was "private earnings." The largest private source of funds for blacks was

Figure 7-1   EDUCATIONAL LEVEL OF PARENTS OF U.S. NATIVE
BORN Ph.D's COMPARED TO U.S. GENERAL POPULATION

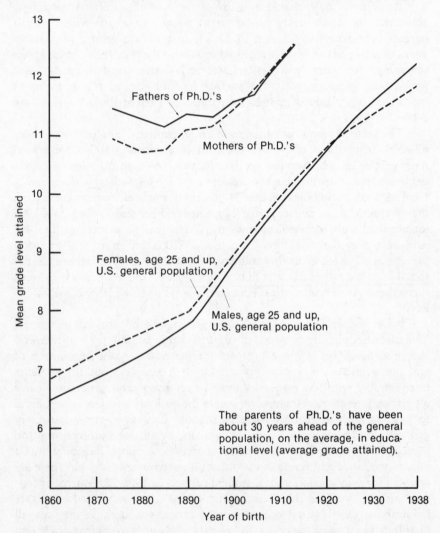

Source: National Research Council, *A Century of Doctorates* (Washington, D.C.: National Academy of Sciences, 1978), Figure 24.

Table 7-6   SOURCES OF FINANCIAL SUPPORT OF DOCTORAL RECIPIENTS
Spring 1973

	U.S. Native Born Only			
	Black		White	
Sources of Financial Support	Number	Percentage of Recipients	Number	Percentage of Recipients
Federal fellowship/traineeships	219	38.3	8,997	45.6
G.I. Bill	93	16.3	2,308	11.7
University fellow	107	18.7	3,616	18.3
Teaching assistantship	178	31.1	9,508	48.2
Research assistantship	94	16.4	6,035	30.6
Private industry funds	53	9.3	1,457	7.4
Institutional funds	82	14.3	1,814	9.2
Private earnings	241	42.1	8,038	40.7
Spouse earnings	83	14.5	4,332	22.0
Family contributions	17	3.0	1,408	7.1
Loans	104	18.2	2,564	13.0
Number answering	552	96.4	19,304	97.8
Total doctoral recipients	572	—	19,731	—

Source: National Board of Graduate Education, National Academy of Science, NRC, Doctoral Records File. Published in ISEP, *Equal Educational Opportunity for Blacks in U.S. Higher Education: An Assessment* (1976), p. 146.

loans. The contributions of any one of these three to the student's educational financing makes the parental contribution look very small, as shown in Table 7-6. The origin of private educational funding, however, is always deceptive, in that students over twenty-one rarely declare themselves as dependent upon their parents. A student's private earnings are, in many cases, where the student's family's financial status is sound, the savings accrued while the student depended on his parents. In fact, the major direction of change since 1973 in financing education has been toward an increase in the proportion of funds coming from parents, as well as private earnings. It is unlikely, however, that black parents or students will be as able as whites to meet further demands on private resources.

With either of these private sources of funding, black students are generally at a disadvantage. Given the very high rate of unemployment among young blacks, black students are likely to have saved much less money to pay for an advanced education. Nevertheless, a somewhat larger proportion of their educational expenses is paid from private earnings than among whites, as Table 7-6 shows. This can be partly explained by the age difference between white and black graduate students. Black students spend twelve years getting a Ph.D., compared to whites, who spend a little over eight years. Thus, within an age range for acquisition of the Ph.D. extending from twenty-nine to forty years of age, blacks tend to be in their late thirties. In large part, the added time seems to have been spent earning money.

The problem of obtaining student loans is more severe for black students at the graduate level than at the undergraduate level. As indicated in chapter 3, undergraduate students can secure loans fairly easily at low interest rates through the Federal Guaranteed Student Loan (GSL) provision. At the graduate level, however, it is not so easy for most black students. First, they frequently have borrowed up to the maximum allowed by GSL to pay for their undergraduate education, and thus are no longer eligible. Black students incur almost twice the debt as white students.

Second, banking policies are not as open to accepting the federal guarantee as the theory of the provision suggests. Although black students are much more in debt, and a higher percentage of them have received loans than whites, blacks are only slightly more likely than whites to rely on bank loans—a 5 percent difference in 1972 (see Table 7-7).

The fourth major source of black student financing during advanced study, after private earnings, direct federal aid, and loans, is assistantships for teaching and research. Although separated in Table 7-6, teaching and research assistantships may be treated together in dealing with institutional practices. Assistantship awards to students are generally distributed in a complementary manner. Eligible students are usually not permitted to receive both types simultaneously unless there is a special institutional or individual reason. Rarely are assistantships awarded on the basis of financial need. Generally, students are selected for these positions based on an individual professor's preference. There is thus an element of merit involved in selection, but only in a remote sense. There is generally no open competition among students for these positions. The faculty member selects the student whose interests and experience fit his/her research or teaching needs and who also can work comfortably with the faculty member. Very often it is a matter of personality preference.

It is therefore noteworthy that teaching assistantships (T.A.'s) are the largest single source of white student support at the advanced levels. Almost half of the white students at advanced levels receive a T.A., compared to less than a third of black students. After direct federal aid, the third largest source of white student graduate support is research assistantships

Table 7-7   DISTRIBUTION OF LOANS AMONG STUDENTS IN
ADVANCED STUDY
1972

Loans	Percentages		Difference (Black-White)
	Black	White	
Amount of loan			
$0.00	33.0	62.0	− 29.0
Up to $2,000	35.0	21.0	14.0
More than $2,000	16.0	10.0	6.0
Amount of indebtedness			
$0.00	20.0	56.0	− 36.0
Up to $2,000	35.0	20.0	15.0
More than $2,000	30.0	19.0	11.0
Source of loans			
Banks	23.0	18.0	5.0
University	20.0	12.0	8.0

Source: Leonard Baird, *Careers and Curricula* (Princeton: Educational Testing Service, 1974), pp. 137–140. Published in ISEP, *Equal Educational Opportunity: An Assessment* (1976), p. 145.

(R.A.'s). About 31 percent of white students benefit from research assistant-ships, almost twice the percentage among black students. Evidently, the selection mechanism and faculty preferences work to the disadvantage of blacks.

Faculty attitudes toward black students, as discussed in chapter 4, may well explain black student underrepresentation in some major fields. While racial prejudice cannot be excluded as a factor, one can explain the apparent bias against black students in other terms. White faculty members, who constitute about 95 percent of all faculty, express in surveys more "uneasiness" with black students than with other students. As a conse-quence, when they select a student with whom they must work closely for several months this racial barrier is likely to have an important and negative impact on the black student's chances.

The other side of this barrier between white faculty members and black graduate students is demonstrated by Leonard Baird's survey results. Graduate students were asked six questions about their relationships with professors. On all questions except one, blacks were consistently less positive about their relationship with professors than white students—an average difference in attitude of about 16 percentage points. In the one ex-ception, black students' responses differ by 17 points from those of whites on the subject "professors exercised a good deal of discipline in class." Black students apparently felt the brunt of discipline.

The more important subject in the survey concerns personal contact and compatibility with professors. On the subject "professors were friendly and accessible," black students dissent most from white students—a difference of 21 points.[8] A slight majority of black students, as opposed to an overwhelming majority of white students, agree with the statement.

Blacks do not seem to have an equal chance to benefit from research and teaching assistantships because of the manner in which they are awarded. This is usually more than a financial loss, because assistantships also serve an important educative and developmental function. In addition, they set the stage for a better rapport between faculty and student, which would benefit the student both academically and professionally, i.e., good faculty recommendations are crucial in the job market.

Because of the deficiency of assistantships awarded and private resources, black students rely most heavily on federal support. Unfortunately, the level of that support has been dwindling in recent years. Since 1971, the proportion of federal funds allocated for graduate and professional school students has declined steadily, from 22.9 percent in 1971 to 16.8 percent in 1976. Estimates for 1977 indicated a continued decline to 13.8 percent. In dollar amounts, ignoring inflation, this means a slight fluctuation from 1.1 billion in 1971 up to 1.5 billion in 1975, and down to 1.3 billion in 1977.

Unfortunately, the data in Table 7-8 do not allow us to determine how much of federal expenditures to graduate and professional schools goes to black students, but there is an indirect indication in the data. One need do little more than recall that between 50 and 60 percent of Ph.D.'s awarded to blacks are in the field of Education. It is noteworthy then that teacher training and educational research expenditures were substantially reduced between 1975 and 1976. Since both these expenditures have a considerable impact on assistantships, through institutional and faculty research funding, an already deficient source of black student support may be weakened. The effect might be to force Education students into other specializations, but it is much more likely to force them out of school altogether, or to make it more difficult for them to study.

Federal expenditures for students at all levels went up until 1976; it declined in 1977 according to estimates. The rate of increase in federal funds between 1971 and 1976 was not sufficient to keep pace with the double financial burden of inflation and the increased numbers of students. Unless federal expenditures can be expanded for higher education, black students, particularly those in graduate and professional schools, may be the first to feel the debilitating effects.

Growth and Distribution of Ph.D. and M.A. Degrees

In the eleven years from 1965 to 1976, the number of Ph.D.'s awarded in this country more than doubled. The number of M.A. degrees awarded almost tripled. In the same period the number of Ph.D. and M.A. degrees awarded to women almost quadrupled. These dramatic growth figures tabulate an overall expansion in higher education from which blacks have also benefited.

Projections up to 1981 of degrees awarded show a relative standstill in the numbers. Since these projections point to a reasonable possibility that the market for people with advanced degrees may reach saturation in the 1980s, relative stability in advanced degrees awarded may be acceptable. The number of blacks holding such degrees, however, continues to be small. The potential advantage which a growth in the proportion of blacks holding such degrees could bring is far from being reached. In fact, long before the goal of equal educational opportunity has been seriously approached, there are signs of retrenchment.

As shown in Table 7-9, while the numbers of master's and doctorate degrees have tripled and doubled, the number of baccalaureate degrees awarded in the same time period has slightly less than doubled. The pyramidal shape of numbers of degrees awarded in higher education is thus losing its steep slope. The middle, and to a lesser extent, the top of the pyramid has been getting wider. In other words, the number who continue their education to advanced levels has been growing faster than the total undergraduate pool.

As might be expected in a developed country where everything has expanded, the numbers and proportions of the population holding advanced degrees have been growing for more than several decades. What may not have been expected is that the proportions of population holding these degrees have scarcely changed in the last two decades. The long-range proportional growth has also been rather slow. The proportion moved from about 1 percent in 1961–1925 to 5 percent in 1966-1975 (see Appendix, Table A7-3).

The slowness of growth is even more remarkable when one considers that the number of Ph.D.-granting institutions have more than quadrupled in the same time period, from 75 in 1925-29, to 307 by 1974. Between 1970 and 1974 (as indicated in Figure 7-2), the increase was about 50 percent.

Table 7-8   FEDERAL EXPENDITURES ON HIGHER EDUCATION
Fiscal Years 1967-77

Type of Support and Level of Institution	Actual									Estimated	
	1967	1968	1969	1970	1971	1972	1973	1974	1975	1976	1977
Type of support					(In Millions)						
Total	$2,069	$2,930	$3,015	$3,633	$4,582	$4,883	$5,801	$5,992	$8,298	$9,901	$9,480
Student support	984	1,455	1,688	2,128	2,997	3,375	4,221	4,391	6,558	8,178	7,886
Institutional support:											
Current operations	208	429	452	659	864	902	1,010	1,083	1,286	1,381	1,308
Facilities—equipment	818	954	761	800	622	487	491	432	375	276	190
Teacher training	}59	76	87	21	156	67	46	45	23	18	34
Educational research		16	27	25	143	52	33	41	56	48	62
				Percentage Distribution							
Total	100.0	100.0	100.0	100.0	100.0	100.0	100.0	100.0	100.0	100.0	100.0
Student support	47.6	49.7	56.0	58.6	65.4	69.1	72.8	73.3	79.0	82.6	83.1
Institutional support:											
Current operations	10.1	14.6	15.0	18.1	18.9	18.5	17.4	18.1	15.5	13.9	13.8
Facilities—equipment	39.5	32.6	25.2	22.0	13.6	10.0	8.5	7.2	4.5	2.8	2.0
Teacher training	}2.9	2.5	2.9	0.6	1.2	1.3	0.8	0.8	0.3	0.2	0.4
Educational research		0.5	0.9	0.7	0.9	1.1	0.6	0.7	0.7	0.5	0.7

Level of institution

(In Millions)

								(²)	(²)	(²)	(²)	$4,883	$5,801	$5,992	$8,298	$9,901	$9,480
Total																	
2-year institution	(²)	(²)		(²)	(²)		(²)	(²)	(²)	(²)	956	1,302	1,572	2,730	3,473	3,274
Other undergraduate	(²)	(²)		(²)	(²)		(²)	(²)	(²)	(²)	2,808	3,220	3,166	4,060	4,766	4,899
Graduate and professional	(²)	(²)		(²)	(²)		(²)	(²)	(²)	(²)	1,119	1,279	1,254	1,508	1,662	1,307

Percentage Distribution

								(²)	(²)	(²)	(²)	100.0	100.0	100.0	100.0	100.0	100.0
Total																	
2-year institution	(²)	(²)		(²)	(²)		(²)	(²)	(²)	(²)	19.6	22.4	26.2	32.9	35.1	34.5
Other undergraduate	(²)	(²)		(²)	(²)		(²)	(²)	(²)	(²)	57.5	55.6	52.8	48.9	48.1	51.7
Graduate and professional	(²)	(²)		(²)	(²)		(²)	(²)	(²)	(²)	22.9	22.0	20.9	18.2	16.8	13.8

Source: NCES, *The Condition of Education, 1978,* Table 5.4, p. 214.

[1] Slight change in definition occurred in 1971.

[2] Consistent data not available.

Table 7-9 ACTUAL AND PROJECTED NUMBER OF DEGREES EARNED ACADEMIC YEARS 1964–80

Academic Year Ending	Bachelor's Degrees			Master's Degrees			Doctorates (Except First-Professional)		
	Total	Male	Female	Total	Male	Female	Total	Male	Female
Actual									
1965	501,248	288,538	212,710	117,152	77,544	39,608	16,467	14,692	1,775
1966	520,248	299,196	221,052	140,548	93,063	47,485	18,237	16,121	2,116
1967	558,075	322,171	235,904	157,707	103,092	54,615	20,617	18,163	2,454
1968	631,923	357,270	274,653	176,749	113,519	63,230	23,089	20,183	2,906
1969	728,167	409,881	318,286	193,756	121,531	72,225	26,188	22,752	3,436
1970	791,510	450,234	341,276	208,291	125,624	82,667	29,866	25,890	3,976
1971	839,730	475,594	364,136	230,509	138,146	92,363	32,107	27,530	4,577
1972	887,273	500,590	386,683	251,633	149,550	102,083	33,363	28,090	5,273
1973	922,362	518,191	404,171	263,371	154,468	108,903	34,777	28,571	6,206
1974	945,776	527,313	418,463	277,033	157,842	119,191	33,816	27,365	6,451
1975	922,933	504,841	418,092	292,450	161,570	130,880	34,083	26,817	7,266
1976	925,746	504,925	420,821	311,771	167,248	144,523	34,064	26,267	7,797
Projected									
1977	980,000	532,000	448,000	322,200	170,900	151,300	35,300	26,800	8,500
1978	963,000	506,000	457,000	334,100	175,000	159,100	36,200	27,200	9,000
1979	996,000	533,000	463,000	346,800	179,800	167,000	37,100	27,600	9,500
1980	1,010,000	541,000	469,000	360,100	184,000	176,100	38,000	28,000	10,000
1981	1,021,000	547,000	474,000	373,200	189,200	184,000	38,900	28,400	10,500

Source: NCES, *The Condition of Education, 1978*, Table 3.16, p. 138.

Figure 7-2 NUMBER OF Ph.D.-GRANTING INSTITUTIONS IN THE UNITED STATES 1920–74

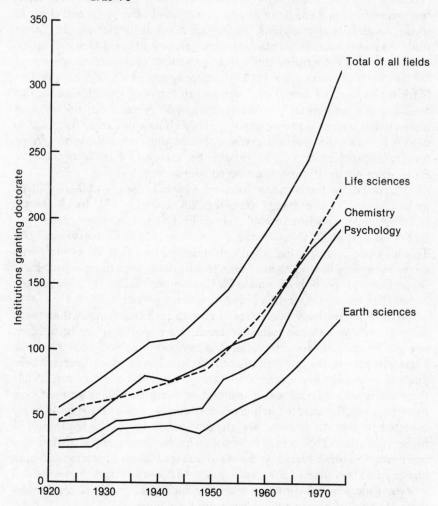

Source: National Research Council, *A Century of Doctorates,* Washington, D.C., (1978), Figure 58, p. 95.

What this relative longitudinal consistency in degrees awarded indicates, is, first of all, a distinct tendency in the system of higher education toward continuing traditional practices and behavior. Where virtually everything else associated with the economy has experienced inflation, educational degrees, until fairly recently, were a stable commodity. What this means for equal educational opportunity is observable in any effort to modify institutional traditions. Higher educational institutions may erect tradition-based barriers to black student access without adequately questioning or even recognizing the inappropriateness of those traditions.

In the four years after 1972, the proportion of Ph.D.'s awarded to black males went up less than 1 percent. In terms of growth figures, this amounts to a substantial increase of close to 50 percent, but the absolute numbers tell a more meaningful story. They show an increase from 427 to 636 Ph.D.'s awarded—an achievement, but hardly a remarkable one. In the four years before 1974, it should be recalled, the percentage of Ph.D.-granting institutions went up equally as fast.

According to the National Research Council, the percentage of black males among Ph.D. recipients went from 2.6 percent in 1973 to 3.4 percent in 1976.[9] The proportion of black female Ph.D.'s has increased faster than that of black male Ph.D.'s—from 3.8 percent in 1973 to 6.8 percent in 1976. This may not be surprising when one considers first that the proportional increases among all women have been much greater than those among men. Second, the proportion of female Ph.D.'s among blacks has always been higher than the corresponding proportion among whites.

This comparatively faster rate of growth for black females than black males is perhaps an understandable result of the way in which institutions concede to pressures for integration. As has been previously observed, the big strides toward the integration of blacks into higher education have been made in places already marginal to established modes of education. While there are other explanations, it seems most likely that black women have been more readily accepted in higher education because of the roles they are expected to play, as women, are already less central to the institution of higher education. That is to say, less of an institutional transformation may be required to bring blacks to the disadvantaged status of white women in higher education than to the traditional status of white men. Nevertheless, women generally constitute a relatively high proportion of the undergraduate pool of blacks available for graduate work.

As shown in Figure 7-3, the Ph.D. (and Ed.D) degree is one in which blacks as a group are most underrepresented. It is noteworthy that, in comparison to their numbers in the highly esteemed professions, Medicine and Law, blacks are still more greatly excluded from the Ph.D. degree. Blacks

Table 7-10   A SURVEY OF NATIVE BORN U.S. CITIZENS WHO
RECEIVED DOCTORATES
Fiscal Years 1973-76

Racial/Ethnic Group	Men				Women			
	1973	1974	1975	1976	1973	1974	1975	1976
White	16,018	17,916	18,030	17,744	3,757	4,562	5,446	5,717
	95.7%[a]	95.1%	94.6%	94.4%	94.4%	92.7%	92.4%	90.8%
Black	427	560	630	636	150	259	339	429
	2.6%	3.0%	3.3%	3.4%	3.8%	5.3%	5.8%	6.8%
American Indian	84	98	112	110	24	23	31	35
	.5%	.7%	.6%	.6%	.6%	.5%	.5%	.6%
Chicano[1]	78	123	147	166	16	25	29	40
	.5%	.7%	.8%	.9%	.4%	.5%	.5%	.6%
Puerto Rican[1]	29	38	48	40	7	17	14	25
	.2%	.2%	.3%	.2%	.2%	.3%	2%	.4%
Asian	99	108	94	99	24	33	36	50
	.6%	.6%	.5%	.5%	.6%	.7%	.6%	.8%
Total reported	16,735	18,843	19,061	18,795	3,978	4,919	5,895	6,296
	100.1%	100.1%	100.1%	100.0%	100.0%	100.0%	100.0%	100.0%
Other and unknown	5,012	1,242	827	801	1,099	263	206	191
Total	21,747	20,085	19,888	19,596	5,077	5,182	6,101	6,487

Source: Dorothy M. Gifford and Joan Synder, Women and Minority Ph.D.'s in the 1970s: A Data Book, National Academy of Sciences (1977), Table I-4, p. 26.
[a] Vertical percentages of total reported (excluding other and unknown).
[1] The group of Spanish-origin is subdivided into the Chicano and Puerto Rican groups when data from this source are used.

received 3.6 percent of all Ph.D.'s in 1976, as compared to 4.7 percent of J.D.'s and 5.2 percent of M.D.'s (see Table 7-20).

The proportion of black Ph.D.'s is more disappointing when the proportion of M.A. degrees awarded to blacks is considered. Blacks received 6.6 percent of M.A. degrees in 1976. As noted earlier, this is about the proportion of B.A./B.S. degrees awarded to blacks. There is no egaliltarian reason why this proportion should drop to little more than half at the Ph.D. level. Black students apparently have the willingness and incentive to continue their education, but confront barriers to their continuation.

The proportion of black men to black women at the master's degree level replicates that at the doctorate level—4.7 percent men and 8.7 percent

Figure 7-3   **RACIAL/ETHNIC DISTRIBUTION OF DEGREES EARNED**
1975-76

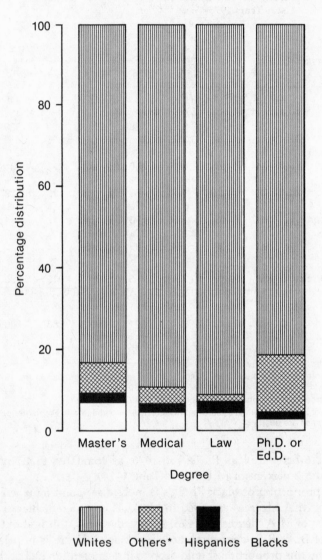

Source: NCES, *The Condition of Education, 1978*, Chart 3.17, p. 141.
*Includes American Indians/Alaskan Natives, Asians or Pacific Islanders, and nonresident aliens.

Table 7-11 HIGHER EDUCATION DEGREES EARNED (AGGREGATE UNITED STATES) 1975–76

Level of Degree	Total		White[1]		Black[1]		Hispanic		American Indian/ Alaskan Native		Asian or Pacific Islander		Nonresident Alien	
	Number	Percentage	Number	Per-centage	Number	Per-centage	Number	Per-centage	Number	Per-centage	Number	Per-centage	Number	Per-centage
Master's														
Total	310,493	100.0	262,851	84.7	20,351	6.6	6,379	2.1	795	0.3	4,037	1.3	16,080	5.2
Male	165,971	100.0	139,539	84.1	7,809	4.7	3,316	2.0	432	0.3	2,499	1.5	12,376	7.5
Female	144,522	100.0	123,312	85.3	12,542	8.7	3,063	2.1	363	0.3	1,538	1.1	3,704	2.6
Ph.D. or Ed.D.														
Total	33,799	100.0	27,435	81.2	1,213	3.6	407	1.2	93	0.3	583	1.7	4,068	12.0
Male	26,016	100.0	20,853	80.2	771	3.0	294	1.1	77	0.3	480	1.8	3,541	13.6
Female	7,783	100.0	6,582	84.6	442	5.7	113	1.5	16	0.2	103	1.3	527	6.8

Source: NCES, *The Condition of Education, 1978*, Chart 3.17, p.140.

Note: Details may not add to totals because of rounding.

[1] Non-Hispanic.

women. It should be noted that a parallel but much smaller female advantage exists among Hispanics. In line with our earlier observation of marginal steps in integration, it would seem to be no accident that the two largest minority groups in this country would experience some parallel forms of integration and resistance in higher education.

It can be seen in Table 7-11 that the general male-female distribution of M.A. degrees is closer to parity than that of Ph.D.'s. White women are not very far below white men in M.A. degrees received, but white women constitute less than a third of white Ph.D. recipients. The high proportion of female M.A. degree recipients among blacks is much less striking than the equally high proportion of black female Ph.D.'s.

Graduate Enrollment: Access and Persistence

Some problems can be effectively removed from public concern by official decree. In the case of equalilty of educational opportunity, an inequality does not create a problem for public policy if evidence of it is not available. This seems to be the case with persistence in graduate schools. The institutionalized means by which the problem is obfuscated is not intentionally deceptive, because it resides in the otherwise useful policy of awarding terminal master's degrees. The problem thus removed from view is that terminal master's degrees often, though not most of the time, represent withdrawal from a Ph.D. program.

The problem of persistence for blacks at the undergraduate level can be encapsulated in the ratio of freshmen enrollment to degrees granted four years later. In 1976, 10.2 percent of undergraduates were black, as compared to 6.4 percent of B.A./B.S. recipients who were black; for associate degrees, the percentage of black recipients was slightly higher, 8.4 percent. In any case, there is a disproportionately low number of blacks graduating. This, of course, does not point specifically to attrition, since the black proportion of the 1976 undergraduate senior class in its freshman year was smaller. Unless the black rate of return/graduation is higher than that of whites, however, there is evidence of attrition, since the full-time freshman class (1972) was 8.7 percent black. Thus, there is a gap of approximately 2.3 percent (8.7 minus 6.4) for blacks between entrance and graduation at the baccalaureate level.

For an analysis of graduate persistence, a comparison of total enrollment and degrees awarded in 1976 is more meaningful, because progress through school is more irregular in terms of time, and because enrollment proportions have not changed as dramatically over time. A factor in the inequality of black and white students in graduate school is the longer amount of time blacks take to acquire their degrees. Levels of persistence among black students are kept from falling by black student perseverance. A large part of interruptions in a regular academic program appear to result from financial or other nonacademic needs. Fleming, Gill and Swinton observe in *The Case For Affirmative Action For Blacks in Higher Education*:

> In 1976, the median age at time of receipt of doctorate was 31.5 years for whites and 36.2 for blacks. Although black and white doctoral students were registered in graduate school for the same number of years—6.0—the time lapse between attainment of the B.A. and of the doctorate was more than 12.5 years for blacks, while only 8.7 for whites. [10]

In most graduate schools there is no clear distinction between master's and doctoral degree program enrollments except in Education. This is not simply a statistical oversight. Most Ph.D.-granting institutions have separate M.A. programs, but student transfer from one to the other is fairly fluid in most fields excluding Education. Students in M.A. programs frequently expect to move up, and frequently do when they have "good" academic records. Students with poor records in Ph.D. programs are frequently forced by their faculty to move "down," and may be awarded an M.A. degree as a "consolation prize."

Still, a comparison of graduate school enrollment with degrees granted can be informative. Blacks constituted about 6 percent of the total graduate school enrollment in 1976–77. This compares to 6.6 percent of master's degrees awarded and 3.6 percent of doctoral degrees awarded to blacks. Again, because of time-sequence changes in enrollment, one can not conclude from these data that there is either a high black retention rate among M.A.'s or a high black attrition rate among Ph.D.'s.

One can conclude, however, first that, for blacks, barriers to the Ph.D. are greater than barriers to the M.A. The numbers of blacks at the Ph.D. level will be much lower than at the M.A. level, because the numbers are much lower for all Americans. In contrast, there is no logical reason why the proportion of black degree recipients should drop at the more advanced level if race were not a factor.

Second, graduates at both levels come, in large part, from the same graduate population, although the first year of Ph.D. enrollment usually predates that of M.A. enrollment by at least three years. What is interesting then is that the proportion of black M.A.'s exceeds the concurrent proportion of black graduate school enrollment, in spite of the fact that the proportion of black degree recipients could not have been as high as the concurrent enrollment when these M.A. graduates started. So, it can be done: the black proportion of degree recipients does not have to drop below the black proportion of entrants. Of course, Ph.D.'s would have started much earlier with an even lower proportion of black graduate enrollment but, by the same token, the proportion of black graduates can be raised.

Above all, what this rather inconclusive comparison of degrees and enrollment suggests is a relatively high rate of "downward" transfer for black Ph.D. students. Given the persistently low rates of black retention in all other sectors of education, it is inconceivable that blacks should have a higher retention rate than whites at the M.A. level. The 6.6 percent black M.A. graduates is probably composed of many intended Ph.D.'s—more so than for nonblacks.

Graduate Major Field Distributions

In no field are blacks represented at a level approaching their proportion of the graduate school age population, 12 percent. Using 12 percent as the point of departure for measuring parity, the proportion of blacks in all areas of specialization at the master's and doctoral levels demonstrates persistent underrepresentation. With the possible exception of Education and "Public Affairs and Services," where blacks received their largest proportion of degrees, black representation does not come close to an equitable level.

In the distribution of master's degrees conferred in 1976, blacks received 9.7 percent of degrees in Education. This constitutes 61 percent of all master's degrees awarded to blacks. Given the small number of all students in the field of Public Affairs and Services, however, blacks managed to reach 9.4 percent of degrees granted, or about two-thirds of the racial parity percentage. In Engineering, blacks received their smallest proportion of master's degrees, only 1.5 percent. While one might expect more degrees to be conferred in areas like Social Science, based on undergraduate concentrations, blacks only received 5.6 percent of those master's degrees.

The distribution of Ph.D.'s awarded follows a similar pattern, but blacks are even more underrepresented on the whole. About 55 percent of the Ph.D.'s awarded blacks were in Education. There are some small surprises in this distribution, however, compared to that of the M.A. Blacks are slightly better represented in Public Affairs and Services, 9.1 percent, than in Education, 8.5 percent. Yet, Public Affairs and Services constitutes only 2.4 percent of black Ph.D.'s, given the relatively small number of students in that major field (see Appendix, Table A7-5).

There is a slight decline in the proportion of black engineers as they move from the M.A. (1.5) to the Ph.D. (.68) level, but the actual number,

Table 7-12 MASTER'S DEGREES CONFERRED IN INSTITUTIONS OF HIGHER EDUCATION 1975–76

Major Field	American Indian Hispanic Native	Black Non-Hispanic	Asian or Pacific Islander	Hispanic	Total Minority	White Non-Hispanic	Non-Resident Alien	Total
Agriculture and Nature Resources	5(.15%)	77(2.32%)	54(1.63%)	38(1.14%)	174(5.24%)	2,589(77.93%)	559(16.83%)	3,322
Architecture and Environmental Design	5(.16%)	195(6.08%)	100(3.12%)	46(1.43%)	346(10.79%)	2,581(78.61%)	340(10.60%)	3,207
Area Studies	2(.11%)	26(2.89%)	39(4.35%)	36(4.01%)	103(11.48%)	727(81.05%)	67(7.47%)	897
Biological Sciences	16(.24%)	215(3.25%)	128(1.94%)	92(1.40%)	451(6.83%)	5,749(87.00%)	408(6.17%)	6,608
Business and Management	71(.16%)	1,549(3.66%)	731(1.73%)	588(1.39%)	2,939(6.95%)	36,216(85.62%)	3,142(7.43%)	42,297
Communications	4(.13%)	170(5.48%)	30(.96%)	34(1.09%)	238(7.67%)	2,693(86.79%)	172(5.54%)	3,103
Computer and Information	7(.27%)	60(2.38%)	66(2.61%)	17(.67%)	150(5.94%)	2,059(81.58%)	315(12.48%)	2,524
Education	390(.30%)	12,440(9.69%)	946(.73%)	2,781(2.17%)	16,557(12.89%)	109,516(85.29%)	2,330(1.81%)	128,403
Engineering	40(.25%)	233(1.46%)	500(3.14%)	235(1.48%)	1,008(6.33%)	11,414(71.72%)	3,492(21.94%)	15,914
Fine and Applied Arts	20(.23%)	277(3.15%)	118(1.34%)	110(1.25%)	525(5.87%)	7,992(90.02%)	273(3.11%)	8,790
Foreign Languages	5(.14%)	119(3.41%)	38(1.09%)	222(6.36%)	384(11.01%)	2,916(83.57%)	189(5.42%)	3,489
Health Professions	48(.38%)	622(4.95%)	215(1.71%)	304(2.42%)	1,189(9.46%)	10,833(86.24%)	540(4.30%)	12,562
Home Economics	1(.01%)	104(4.83%)	42(1.95%)	24(1.11%)	171(7.95%)	1,860(86.43%)	121(5.62%)	2,152
Law	3(.21%)	37(2.57%)	20(1.39%)	25(1.73%)	85(5.89%)	1,073(75.52%)	284(19.69%)	1,442
Letters	23(.20%)	455(4.06%)	108(.96%)	239(2.13%)	825(6.76%)	9,924(88.54%)	460(4.10%)	11,209
Library Science	17(.21%)	426(5.33%)	97(1.21%)	141(1.76%)	681(8.51%)	7,121(89.03%)	196(2.45%)	7,998
Mathematics	8(.21%)	130(3.37%)	94(2.44%)	58(1.51%)	290(7.53%)	3,262(84.68%)	300(7.79%)	3,852
Physical Sciences	9(.17%)	137(2.54%)	141(2.61%)	74(1.37%)	361(6.68%)	4,405(81.53%)	637(11.79%)	5,403
Psychology	14(.18%)	416(5.31%)	89(1.14%)	229(2.93%)	748(9.55%)	6,883(87.92%)	193(2.46%)	7,829
Public Affairs and Services	60(.35%)	1,615(9.42%)	194(1.13%)	664(3.87%)	2,533(14.77%)	14,145(82.47%)	473(2.76%)	17,151
Social Sciences	38(.24%)	883(5.59%)	201(1.27%)	309(1.96%)	1,431(9.06%)	13,071(82.75%)	1,293(8.19%)	15,795
Theology	1(.00%)	55(1.94%)	58(1.76%)	44(1.55%)	150(5.28%)	2,510(88.32%)	182(6.40%)	2,842
Interdisciplinary Studies	8(.21%)	110(2.97%)	36(.97%)	69(1.86%)	223(6.02%)	3,367(90.90%)	114(3.08%)	3,704
National total (2,063 institutions)	795(.26%)	20,351(6.55%)	4,037(1.30%)	6,379(2.05%)	31,562(10.16%)	262,851(84.66%)	16,080(5.18%)	310,493

Source: OCR, Department of Health, Education and Welfare.

231

19 blacks, is too small to be significant. On the other hand, the large decline in the proportion of blacks in Social Science from the M.A. (5.6) to the Ph.D. (2.8) level is significant. Considering the relatively small market value of an M.A. compared to a Ph.D. in Social Science, this drop is especially disappointing. Considering, moreover, the fairly high market value of an M.A. in Engineering compared to a Ph.D. in the same field, the black proportion in Engineering is not particularly comforting.

The distribution of graduate students by major field shows that the racially uneven distribution of the preceding year's degree recipients is being continued. Fortunately, however, the percentage of all black graduate enrollment has risen to 6 percent, from an estimated percentage between 3.5 and 5.2 in 1973-74 (Appendix, Table A7-6). The racial distribution by selected major fields is summarized in Table 7-14, and more detailed data are presented in the appendix (Table A7-4).

Unfortunately, the most current data do not allow us to single out black enrollment in Education and Social Science. The category "All others" in Table 7-14, in which these two majors are classified, however, is also clearly the largest in terms of the black proportion. In fact, it is the only category in which the black percentage, 7.22, is about the same as the percentage of total black graduate enrollment, 6.02.

The fields which we have previously discussed have comparable enrollments. Engineering, for example, is only 1.42 percent. Unless there is a higher attrition rate among whites in Engineering, or unless more whites stop at the M.A., the black proportion of Ph.D. graduates will be even lower in the future than in 1975-76.

Third, the rapid progress of female participation in Engineering demonstrates that progress in opening up Engineering does not have to be so slow. For example, the number of female master's degree recipients more than doubled between 1973 and 1976, while the number of blacks increased only about 50 percent. The fact that the more rapid progress of women is not simply a function of their greater availability is evidenced by the undergraduate proportions. The rate of growth in undergraduate enrollments for women is equally as rapid, though not necessarily suffi-cient, in the same three years, while that for blacks is equally undramatic.

Blacks make up a higher percentage of enrollment in Architecture and Environmental Design than in any other individual fields. This seems sim-ply to result from the smallness of the field. Of the fields with substantial enrollment, Business and Management clearly has the largest black per-centage, 4.12 (see Table 7-14). By any standards, then, maldistribution re-mains a severe problem.

Black enrollment in Engineering is indicative of the overall lack of

Table 7-13 DOCTORAL DEGREES CONFERRED IN INSTITUTIONS OF HIGHER EDUCATION 1975-76

Major Field	American Indian Hispanic Native	Black Non-Hispanic	Asian or Pacific Islander	Hispanic	Total Minority	White Non-Hispanic	Non-Resident Alien	Total
Agriculture and Nature Resources	6(.66%)	18(1.96%)	27(2.95%)	5(.55%)	56(6.11%)	596(65.06%)	264(28.82%)	916
Architecture and Environmental Design	0(.00%)	5(6.10%)	2(2.44%)	0(.00%)	7(8.54%)	58(70.73%)	17(20.73%)	82
Area Studies	1(.57%)	9(5.11%)	3(1.70%)	2(1.14%)	15(8.52%)	151(85.80%)	10(5.68%)	176
Biological Sciences	4(.12%)	52(1.53%)	89(2.62%)	26(.77%)	171(5.04%)	2,861(84.32%)	361(10.64%)	3,393
Business and Management	6(.63%)	17(1.78%)	18(1.88%)	9(.94%)	50(5.24%)	750(78.53%)	155(16.23%)	955
Communications	2(.96%)	8(3.85%)	0(.00%)	5(2.40%)	15(7.21%)	181(87.02%)	12(5.77%)	208
Computer and Information	1(.41%)	0(.00%)	4(1.64%)	1(.41%)	6(2.46%)	192(78.69%)	46(18.85%)	244
Education	35(.45%)	669(8.50%)	61(.78%)	138(1.77%)	903(11.60%)	6,496(83.47%)	384(4.93%)	7,782
Engineering	3(.11%)	19(.68%)	119(4.27%)	17(.61%)	158(5.67%)	1,657(59.41%)	974(34.92%)	2,789
Fine and Applied Arts	1(.16%)	21(3.31%)	6(.95%)	3(.47%)	31(4.89%)	566(89.27%)	37(5.84%)	634
Foreign Languages	3(.35%)	16(2.81%)	8(.93%)	25(2.93%)	44(5.16%)	715(83.82%)	94(11.02%)	853
Health Professions	2(.35%)	5(2.81%)	22(3.86%)	5(.88%)	45(7.89%)	451(79.12%)	74(12.98%)	570
Home Economics	0(.00%)	0(.00%)	3(1.68%)	1(.56%)	9(5.06%)	154(86.52%)	15(8.43%)	178
Law	0(.00%)	0(.00%)	0(.00%)	0(.00%)	0(.00%)	58(76.32%)	18(23.68%)	76
Letters	5(.21%)	63(2.59%)	24(.99%)	24(.99%)	116(4.77%)	2,164(88.94%)	153(6.29%)	2,433
Library Science	1(1.41%)	4(5.63%)	1(1.41%)	1(1.41%)	7(9.86%)	61(85.92%)	3(4.23%)	71
Mathematics	1(.18%)	9(1.06%)	22(2.58%)	12(1.41%)	44(5.16%)	648(75.97%)	161(18.87%)	853
Physical Sciences	8(.23%)	41(1.20%)	88(2.57%)	30(.87%)	167(4.88%)	2,674(78.21%)	578(16.91%)	3,419
Psychology	4(.15%)	66(2.57%)	22(.86%)	39(1.52%)	131(5.11%)	2,341(91.30%)	92(3.59%)	2,564
Public Affairs and Services	2(.63%)	29(9.09%)	5(1.57%)	13(4.07%)	49(15.36%)	242(75.86%)	28(8.97%)	319
Social Sciences	8(.19%)	117(2.84%)	48(1.16%)	43(1.04%)	216(5.24%)	3,382(82.11%)	521(12.65%)	4,119
Theology	0(.00%)	26(2.88%)	9(.99%)	4(.44%)	39(4.32%)	820(90.91%)	43(4.97%)	902
Interdisciplinary Studies	0(.00%)	11(4.18%)	2(.76%)	4(1.52%)	17(6.46%)	218(82.89%)	28(10.65%)	263
National total (2,063 institutions)	93(.23%)	1,213(3.59%)	583(1.72%)	407(1.20%)	2,296(6.79%)	27,435(81.17%)	4,068(12.04%)	33,799

Source: OCR, Department of Health, Education and Welfare.

Table 7-14   TOTAL GRADUATE ENROLLMENT IN SELECTED MAJOR FIELDS
1976–77

Field	Black		Minority		White		Total
	Number	Percentage	Number	Percentage	Number	Percentage	
Agriculture and National Resources	251	1.61	721	4.64	11,806	76.11	15,510
Architecture and Environmental Design	518	5.29	1,038	10.60	7,824	79.92	9,790
Biological Sciences	1,125	2.63	2,938	6.87	36,582	85.57	42,746
Business and Management	6,086	4.12	11,970	8.11	125,765	85.21	147,590
Engineering	824	1.42	4,287	7.40	40,227	69.48	57,889
Law	58	1.66	161	4.61	3,034	87.05	3,485
Physical Science	632	1.80	1,924	5.48	27,967	79.77	35,059
All others	55,851	7.22	89,112	11.52	653,654	84.85	773,062
Total	65,345	6.02	112,151	11.16	908,859	83.75	1,085,131

Source: Analysis of data from OCR, Department of Health, Education and Welfare, Opening Fall Enrollment, 1976.

Table 7-15   ENGINEERING DEGREES CONFERRED
1970–76

Year	Total	Black Number	Black Percentage	Women Number	Women Percentage	Spanish[1]	Oriental	American Indian
				Bachelor's degree				
1976	37,970	777	2.05	1,376	3.62	680	1,074	41
1975	38,210	734	1.92	878	1.30	685	883	44
1974	41,407	756	1.83	744	1.80	640	958	31
1973	43,429	657	1.51	624	1.47	566	684	32
1972	44,190	579	1.31	525	1.19	N/A	N/A	N/A
1971[a]	43,167	407	.94	353	.82	N/A	N/A	N/A
1970[a]	42,966	378	.88	337	.78	N/A	N/A	N/A
				Master's degree				
1976	16,506	154	.93	557	3.37	183	782	14
1975	15,773	141	.90	380	2.41	176	483	3
1974	15,885	158	.99	393	2.47	187	421	4
1973	17,152	104	.61	226	1.31	132	261	5
1972	17,356	78	.45	299	1.72	N/A	N/A	N/A
1971[a]	16,383	47	.29	158	.96	N/A	N/A	N/A
1970[a]	15,548	50	.32	168	1.08	N/A	N/A	N/A
				Doctorate degree				
1976	2,977	10	.34	56	1.88	15	168	N/A
1975	3,138	17	.54	53	1.69	28	141	2
1974	3,362	12	.35	36	1.07	19	106	0
1973	3,587	13	.36	48	1.34	12	55	1
1972	3,774	13	.34	35	.93	N/A	N/A	N/A
1971[a]	3,640	8	.22	25	.69	N/A	N/A	N/A
1970[a]	3,620	1	.03	16	.44	N/A	N/A	N/A

Source: Engineering Manpower Commission, ''Trends in Engineering Degrees Earned by Women and Minority Members'' (New York: Engineers Joint Council, January 1976).
[1] Does not include University of Puerto Rico.
[a] Figures for women and blacks in these years are understated because they do not include estimates for nonreporting schools.

Table 7-16   MAJOR FIELD DISTRIBUTIONS OF BLACK STUDENTS IN TRADITIONALLY BLACK AND TRADITIONALLY NON-BLACK GRADUATE INSTITUTIONS (IN PERCENTAGES) 1974

Major Field	Black Males	Black Females	Total Blacks
Traditionally black institutions			
Education	30.70	45.70	38.97
Business	9.53	5.73	7.43
Social Science	12.24	9.38	10.66
Natural Science	6.12	4.17	5.04
Technical Science	7.45	3.04	5.02
Professions[1]	.21	.13	.17
Social Work and Public Health	1.86	4.64	3.39
Architecture	1.44	.22	.76
Agriculture	2.08	.26	1.08
Computer Science	.05	.04	.05
Other[2]	28.31	26.69	27.42
Total (100% =)	(1,879)	(2,304)	(4,183)
Traditionally nonblack institutions			
Education	26.24	41.55	33.79
Business	12.58	4.48	8.58
Social Science	16.61	11.78	4.22
Natural Science	2.50	1.83	2.17
Technical Science	6.65	1.44	4.08
Professions[1]	1.76	3.07	2.40
Social Work and Public Health	3.58	8.00	5.76
Architecture	2.88	1.41	2.16
Agriculture	1.47	.13	.81
Computer Science	.52	.31	.42
Other[2]	25.20	25.99	25.59
Total (100% =)	(8,599)	(8,371)	(16,970)

Source: Gail Thomas, *Equality of Representation of Race and Sex Group in Higher Education,* Center for Social Organization of Schools, Baltimore, Maryland (June 1978).

[1] Professions refer to Nursing, Pharmacy, Pre-Law, Pre-Medicine, and similar preprofessional programs offered at the undergraduate level.

[2] "Other" includes majors in Foreign Language, Home Economics, Library Science, and the precoded category designated in the survey as "others."

educational opportunity in graduate and professional schools. The percentage figures for black enrollment in Engineering shown in Table 7-15, are slightly different from those based on Office for Civil Rights data (Table 7-16), because of sampling variations in the populations reported, and because the Master of Science (M.S.) professional school degree is included. The changes in the proportions of blacks enrolled in Engineering over the years as shown in Table 7-15, however, are reliable in that the percentages conform to the best available data.

Several relationships in the data seem to be endemic to the status of blacks in advanced education. First, the proportions of blacks at both the M.A. and Ph.D. level are well below racial parity. In Engineering black representation is exceptionally small. Second, as low as these proportions are, blacks are still more underrepresented at the advanced levels than their undergraduate numbers or proportions would lead one to expect. Blacks received 2 percent of the undergraduate Engineering degrees awarded in 1976, but less than 1 percent of master's degrees, and only 0.3 percent of doctoral degrees.* Referring to the years when the 1976 Engineering master's degree recipients should have received their baccalaureate degrees, blacks were still more highly represented at the undergraduate level. Going back one or two years would be appropriate, but one can refer back four years to 1972, taking into account problems of persistence, and the proportion of blacks available from undergraduate school is still higher than the proportion of blacks receiving master's degrees in 1976.

The problem of distribution in the 1976–77 academic year can, to some extent, be penetrated by data from any recent study, inasmuch as the limited data on distribution by field indicate that the distribution of blacks across fields has not changed substantially in at least a decade. Thus, we can gain some insights from the 1974 Office for Civil Rights data on distribution. As shown in Table 7-16, Education and Social Science enrollments are identifiable. Since the figures are reported as percentages within race, and since a few percentage points must be excluded from the graduate pool, those for "professionals," some caution should be exercised in using the table. Nevertheless, distribution among graduate majors is not significantly affected by this slight intrusion into the data.

---

* When focusing primarily on Engineering, the data from the Engineering Manpower Commission (see Table 7-15) are used because they are more precise than the OCR data. However, for more comprehensive analysis, OCR data are used because consistency in measurement is important. At the same time, the differences between the two sets of data are not critical for our purposes.

With this caution in mind one can still see that Education is the dominant major field in black graduate enrollment. Moreover, recalling that 60 percent of black M.A.'s and 55 percent of black Ph.D.'s were in Education in 1976, there is reason to believe that black attrition is exceptionally high in the other fields. Again, the time-sequence factor may be a real problem in reaching such a conclusion about Ph.D.'s, but it should not be so for M.A.'s. Two years is the standard length of time for completing an M.A. degree. Accordingly, the 26 percent increase in the proportion of blacks in Education from enrollment in 1974 to graduation in 1976 must represent a substantial difference in the intradisciplinary graduate school experiences of blacks in Education in nonblack institutions as opposed to other fields. The evidence indicates high black attrition in those other fields where black enrollment is already very low.

It is frequently assumed that a major source of the bias in distribution of blacks across major fields is the traditionally black institution (TBI). The percentage of blacks in Education at TBI's as compared to other institutions, 39 percent to 34 percent, would tend to confirm this assumption. Similarly, the 11 percent in Social Science at TBI's versus 4 percent at non-TBI's would add confirmation.

A closer look at black distribution across other fields, however, raises serious doubts about this assumption. Enrollment in the most underrepresented area, technical sciences, is only slightly lower at TBI's than at other institutions. When TBI's in the South are compared to other southern institutions, there is virtually no difference in technical science enrollment. In the natural sciences the proportion of blacks at TBI's is larger than at all other institutions. Grouping these sciences together the difference of enrollment between TBI's and other institutions amounts to about 4 percent (11 minus 7 percent). Computer Science, with minute black enrollment in both sets of institutions, would appear to confirm that TBI's are a major source of bias in black enrollment distribution. Almost the inverse conclusion however, should be drawn. The key in this case is to recall, as shown in chapter 6, that black institutions have limited computer science facilities, and this limitation is primarily a function of limited financial resources. In fact, the comparatively high proportion of black students in the technical sciences at TBI's is remarkable when one considers that financial limitations also create a special problem in terms of instructional resources.

Of course, the special reasons that institutions may have limited black enrollment in some fields do not change the fact that limitations are thus placed on black enrollment. What is important here, and what provides a lesson, is that in black institutions students seem to have pursued disciplines freely to the extent that institutional resources permitted. Black underrepresentation in selected fields at primarily white institutions cannot be allowed the same excuse. White institutions have the resources to encourage a much more equitable distribution and enrollment of black students.

Professional Schools: Special Problems of Access, Distribution, and Persistence

In the preceding chapters a look at the broad problem of equal opportunity in higher education, focusing on undergraduates, showed that blacks were well below parity with whites. Educational policy, at the federal and institutional levels, was found to be faltering and uneven in the pursuit of equality of educational opportunity. By focusing on graduate education in this chapter, still more evidence of racial inequality has materialized. Educational progress for blacks in graduate school has been shown to be slow, almost to the point of stagnation. In the assessment of educational opportunity for blacks in professional schools, there are no "qualifiers," no mitigating terms needed. The modest progress of the early 1970s has not merely come to a standstill. Access for blacks to professional schools, like Medicine and Law, is apparently regressing.

The discussion of professional education and equality will concentrate on Medicine and Law, first because these are evidently the most competitively pursued and the most traditionally "prestigious" of the professions. Other professions may be equally prestigious and competitive, but the level of competition and the size of the relevant populations are not so easily identifiable as in Medicine and Law. Second, for these two professions, there are considerably more data available from a variety of sources than for others.

ALL AREAS OF PROFESSIONAL EDUCATION

The 1976–77 black enrollment in the professional schools could probably not have been predicted from data on enrollment in the preceding years. The rate of growth up to 1975–76 would probably have led to an overestimation of black percentages for the subsequent year. For those concerned with equal educational opportunity, the facts, as shown in Table 7-17, are perhaps too disappointing to have been calmly anticipated.

Black enrollment in professional schools amounts to only 4.5 percent. Doubling that figure would still leave blacks well below parity. Of the significant professional fields in terms of enrollment size Medicine and "Business and Management" are slightly ahead of the rest, with 5.9 percent and 5.6 percent black enrollment respectively. Law is third, with 4.6 percent

Table 7-17 TOTAL PROFESSIONAL ENROLLMENT IN SELECTED PROFESSIONAL FIELDS
1976–77

Field	Black		Other Minority		White		Total
	Number	Percentage	Number	Percentage	Number	Percentage	
Agriculture and National Resources	0	.00	2	8.69	16	69.56	23
Architecture and Environmental Design	1	4.00	2	8.00	23	92.00	25
Biological Sciences	2	2.94	3	4.41	62	91.17	68
Business and Management	40	5.65	48	6.78	621	87.83	707
Engineering	0	.00	1	1.19	78	92.85	84
Dentistry	822	4.04	2,013	9.90	18,033	88.73	20,322
Medicine	3,454	5.93	6,780	11.65	50,668	87.09	58,178
Veterinary Medicine	125	2.04	258	4.21	5,849	95.47	6,126
Law	5,372	4.60	10,472	8.97	105,594	90.52	116,647
Physical Science	1	6.25	3	18.75	11	68.75	16
All others	1,364	3.12	3,087	7.08	39,098	89.69	43,588
Total	11,181	4.54	22,669	9.22	220,059	89.53	245,790

Source: Analysis of data from OCR, Department of Health, Education, and Welfare, *Opening Fall Enrollment, 1976.*

black enrollment, and second to Medicine among the major professions. Enrollment in Business and Management (this figure excludes master's of Business Administration or M.B.A.) is growing overall, but is still too small to be compared meaningfully with Medicine and Law.

Other professional enrollments, such as those in Engineering and Physical Science, represent specialized degree programs offered at only one or two institutions. In Engineering, for example, there is a specialized master's intended for practicing engineers, but the degree has little, if any, value that cannot be acquired in a regular graduate, "nonprofessional" program.

If there is anything in these data which can make medical school enrollments look good by comparison, from the perspective of equal opportunity supporters, it is the remarkably low level of black enrollment in Veterinary Medicine. Yet, a brief look at changes in black enrollment in medical school from year to year will strain even the positive attitude—a subject to which we will turn shortly.

As shown in Table 3-11 (chapter 3), about 92 percent of all blacks in higher education in 1976 were undergraduates, 7 percent graduates, and, except for the unclassified students, the remaining 1.2 percent of blacks, just over 11,000 students, were enrolled in professional schools.

In 1974–75, there were 9,334 black students in professional schools. During the next two years, the number of blacks went up about 20 percent. In absolute numbers, that is an increase of 1,947 students—not very impressive. And yet, "that's the good news," inasmuch as total enrollment in professional schools has gone up even faster. In meaningful terms, therefore, blacks are losing ground. Their proportion of enrollment in professional schools has actually declined.

Black enrollment has declined proportionately from 5.05 percent in 1974–75 to 4.54 percent in 1976–77. White enrollment has not only gone up, but also appears to account for a larger proportion of all enrollment. On this point, however, the data for white students are not as decisive, because of the large number of "alien" students in the professional category—a classification which is indefinite. In order to circumvent these coding and classification difficulties, Table 7-19 refers only to black and white students in comparing 1974 and 1976 enrollment data.

Since patterns of change in enrollment constitute a major cause for concern, the problem will be examined more closely in the specific discussions of Medicine and Law. Unfortunately, the 1976–77 data are preliminary, and some change in the enrollment configuration might emerge with further analysis. At the same time, it is beyond reasonable expectation that the ad-

Table 7-18   MAJOR FIELD DISTRIBUTION OF BLACK AND WHITE PROFESSIONAL SCHOOL STUDENTS (IN PERCENTAGES) 1974

	Students	
Field	*Black*	*White*
Dentistry	10.0	9.1
Law	41.3	42.2
Medicine	32.6	25.7
Veterinary Medicine	0.2	3.0
Other	15.4	18.6
Undecided	0.4	1.4
Total percentage	100.0	100.0
Total numbers (all = 184,742)	9,334	175,408
Percentage of total	5.05	94.95

Source: OCR, Department of Health, Education, and Welfare, *Opening Fall Enrollment, 1974.* Reanalysis by Gail Thomas, "Equality of Representation of Race and Sex Group in Higher Education," Center for Social Organization of Schools, Baltimore, Maryland (October 1978), Table 3.

Note: See also Appendix, Table A7-3.

Table 7-19   RATES OF GROWTH IN BLACK AND WHITE STUDENT ENROLLMENT IN PROFESSIONAL SCHOOLS 1974 and 1976

	Enrollment		*Change in Enrollment*	
Race	*1974*	*1976*	*Increase in Number*	*Increase in Percentage*
Black/White	184,742	231,240	46,498	25.17
White	175,408	220,059	44,651	25.46
Black	9,334	11,181	1,847	19.79

Source: Reanalysis of data from OCR, Department of Health, Education, and Welfare, *Opening Fall Enrollment, 1974* and 1976 preliminary OCR data, and Gail Thomas, *Equality of Representation of Race and Sex Group in Higher Education,* Center for Social Organization of Schools, Baltimore, Maryland (June 1978.)

ditional data will show a significant improvement in black representation in professional schools.

Since the data on degrees conferred are from earlier years than the data on enrollment, one gets a sense that black students have made greater progress in one year than actually occurred. The apparent progress in degrees conferred prior to 1976 is marred by the clear deficiency in the proportions and numbers of black graduates, even at their highest point.

In 1976, as in 1974, Medicine and Law were first and second respectively in the larger major fields in which blacks pursued degrees. Veterinary Medicine again had the smallest black representation of the larger fields.[11] It should be noted that both the proportions of degrees granted blacks and black enrollment in Medicine and Law are almost identical. This could be a good sign—that black attrition is no higher than average inasmuch as the degrees were granted to students who had enrolled in preceding years. The similarity of proportions at input in 1976–77 with those of output in 1975–76, however, may reflect a real decline in black enrollment, or a greater increase in all enrollment, as indicated in Table 7-20.

Total professional school graduates increased every year from 1965 to 1976–slightly more than doubling in that period. Yet, HEW estimates for 1977 of degrees conferred show a decline from the 1976 level of 62,649 to 61,800 graduates (see Appendix, Table A7-8). If black students were making progress as a group in 1977, the proportion of black enrollment should have been noticeably greater than the proportion of 1976 black graduates. As total numbers are declining, the proportion of black students can only remain the same, or decline when the absolute number of blacks declines. It goes almost without saying that 4 to 5 percent of black participation in the professions is too small a level for absolute numerical reductions to be contemplated, whatever the changes in the total professional student population.

Unfortunately, data on the 1977 graduates by race, which is not yet available, is needed for further comparison of all professions. On the other hand, the subtotals of 1977 enrollment in Medicine and Law will be instructive. Before turning to these fields, a brief comparison of the most recent data on degrees granted in Business or Management can help to preface these concerns.

The proportion of black professional school graduates in Business, M.B.A.'s, has dropped substantially, from 5.1 percent in 1974–75 to 3.7 percent in the next year. Because the data in Table 7-21 are derived from a variety of sources, there is some reason to be skeptical. Reasonable doubt diminishes, however, when one considers the other ratios shown. The proportion of women M.B.A.'s distinctly increased, as did that of women

Table 7-20 FIRST-PROFESSIONAL DEGREES CONFERRED IN INSTITUTIONS OF HIGHER EDUCATION 1975–76

Field	American Indian Hispanic Native		Black Non-Hispanic		Asian or Pacific Islander		Hispanic		Total Minority		White Non-Hispanic		Non-Resident Alien		Total
	Number	Percentage	Number	Percentage	Number	Percentage	Number	Percentage	Number	Percentage	Number	Percentage	Number	Percentage	
Dentistry	10	.18	181	3.30	148	2.70	131	2.39	470	8.58	4,902	89.49	106	1.94	5,478
Medicine	47	.35	708	5.25	227	1.68	304	2.25	1,286	9.54	11,993	88.92	208	1.54	13,487
Optometry	2	.20	14	1.44	43	4.41	9	.92	68	6.97	895	91.79	12	1.23	975
Osteopathic Medicine	3	.37	12	1.47	2	.24	5	.61	22	2.69	794	97.06	2	.24	818
Pharmacy	1	.23	6	1.37	108	24.60	8	1.82	123	28.02	305	69.48	11	2.50	439
Podiatry or Podiatric Medicine	1	.23	3	.70	11	2.57	7	1.64	22	5.14	403	94.16	3	.70	428
Veterinary Medicine	17	1.11	18	1.17	7	.46	7	.46	49	3.19	1,475	96.28	8	.52	1,532
Chiropractic	8	.51	26	1.65	58	3.68	65	4.12	157	9.95	1,318	83.58	102	6.47	1,577
Law, general	75	.23	1,519	4.68	312	.96	858	2.64	2,764	8.51	29,520	90.88	199	.61	32,463
Theology, general	41	.78	206	3.92	46	.88	78	1.49	371	7.06	4,702	89.56	177	3.37	5,250
National totals	205	.33	2,694	4.31	962	1.54	1,472	2.36	5,333	8.53	56,335	90.14	829	1.33	62,497

Source: OCR, Department of Health Education and Welfare (Fall 1976).

Table 7-21   BUSINESS/MANAGEMENT DEGREES CONFERRED TO
BLACKS AND WOMEN
1974-75 and 1975-76

Year	Number	Percentage
	Women MBA's	
1974-75[b]	3,080	9.2
1975-76[a]	4,963	11.7
	Black MBA's	
1974-75[a]	—	5.1 (of 102, 114)
1975-76[c]	1,549	3.7
	Women Ph.D.'s	
1974-75[b]	41	4.2
1975-76[c]	52	5.4
	Black Ph.D.'s	
1974-75[a]	—	2.0 (of 3,017)
1975-76[c]	17	1.8

[a]American Assembly of Colleges and Schools of Business, 1976.
[b]Earned Degrees Conferred 1974-75, NCES, Department of Health, Education and Welfare.
[c]OCR, Department of Health, Education and Welfare, 1977-78.

Ph.D.'s. The Ph.D. might be considered a distraiting force for blacks interested in Business and Management M.B.A.'s, but the factor does not apply here. The proportion of black Ph.D.'s in the field has also dropped precipitously.

MEDICAL SCHOOL: ACCESS AND PERSISTENCE

The overriding problem of equal opportunity for blacks in medical education is one of access rather than persistence. If there is an additional problem of distribution among specialties within medical education (aside from Veterinary Medicine), it is not salient in the data. This is probably because the limitations on getting into medical school for blacks have been so great that questions about specialization have taken a distinct second place to real doubts about accessibility.

Racial inequalities in persistence still remain among medical students. But these differences are relatively small in terms of most areas of higher education. While such inequalities should not be ignored, neither should

245

they be overestimated. This is especially true for an analysis of medical schooling, because one of the most pronounced arguments for limiting admissions is that only a small percentage of applicants are capable of completing the program. Black admissions have been restricted more than that of other students on the grounds that their chances of graduating were low.

Perhaps the most remarkable interpretation of data on black/white differences in retention emerges from the majority opinion of the Supreme Court in the *Bakke* case. The University of California at Davis claimed that its "affirmative action" admission program would, among other things, improve the quality of health care available to blacks and other "disadvantaged" groups. This improvement, it was argued, would be augmented by the admission of minorities to the medical school by means of "preferential classification" for minorities. In his opinion, Justice Powell responds for the Court: "petitioner (U. C. Davis) has not shown that its preferential classification is likely to have any significant effect on the problem."[12]

While Justice Powell could have been referring to several things, including the adequacy of argumentation, he also footnoted his statement with a research article focusing on black attrition.[13]

The article, published in the 1977 *New England Journal of Medicine*, contains only one table on retention/attrition by race, shown here in Table 7-22.

In the article, this table is interpreted as follows:

> As compared to white students, black medical students are less likely to be promoted with their class, and more likely to drop out or to be dismissed. . . . Thus, academic dismissal and the need to repeat first-year studies are the major causes for lower promotion of blacks than whites. Interestingly enough, of the blacks who entered medical schools in 1969, the year many medical schools began to adopt affirmative-action policies, far fewer graduated with their class than blacks who entered medical schools in 1968.[14]

The implications of this conclusion, and more important, its use in the Court, are directed primarily at educational policy, and particularly at the status of blacks in higher education. Accordingly, special admissions programs for blacks are denigrated on the grounds that those admitted through these programs would not survive.

One need only glance at Table 7-22 to see that in fact, blacks are surviving better in the medical than in most sectors of education. Both black and white attrition rates are above 15 percent in virtually every field, while in the last ten years, black attrition in medical school has not gone

Table 7-22   RETENTION AND GRADUATION OF BLACK AND WHITE
              MEDICAL STUDENTS (IN PERCENTAGES)
              1968-72

Entering Year	Blacks Retained	Blacks Graduated	Whites Retained	Whites Graduated
1968	91	90	96	95
1969	89	75	96	91
1970	88	(¹)	97	(¹)
1971	90	(¹)	98	(¹)
1972	93	(¹)	99	(¹)

Source: Boyd Sleeth and Robert Mishell, "Black Underrepresentation in United States Medical Schools," New England Journal of Medicine, 297 (November 1977), p. 1148. Based on data in Davis Johnson and William Sedlacek, "Retention by Sex and Race . . . " Journal of Medical Education, 50, pp. 925-933.

[1] Data not available.

above 11 percent. Moreover, the level of black retention has risen, and has continued to rise, since 1970.

Still more important from a policy perspective, the increase in black retention corresponds to the implementation of affirmative action in medical schools. Affirmative action programs in Medicine were, at best, conceived in 1968; they did not exist then. The first national efforts were begun in 1969, and firm programs took varying lengths of time thereafter to become established. "The late 1970s also saw substantial funding from the Office of Economic Opportunity (OEO) via the AAMC (Association of American Medical Colleges), which helped to finance activities directed at the recruitment, admission, and retention of minority group medical students. Related efforts of the AAMC included (a) the establishment in 1969 of a Medical Minority Applicant Registry (Med-Mar) and (b) the publication that same year of the first edition of Minority Student Opportunities in U.S. Medical Schools"[15]

Another question about the delivery of health care services to blacks and other minorities by black physicians may be implied in Justice Powell's statement. Specifically, are black physicians likely to serve in the needed capacities? The data in Table 7-23 indicate strongly that black medical students are by far the most willing of all students to work in "physician shortage" areas.

Table 7-23 CAREER PREFERENCES OF MEDICAL STUDENTS (IN PERCENTAGES) 1974–75

Demographic and Background Characteristics	Maximum Total N	Major Career Activity in Patient Care	Preference for Primary Care	Mean Number of Years in Residency	Geographic Area of Eventual Location				Environment[1]		
					Large City or Suburb of Large City	Medium or Small City	Small Town or Rural Area	Interest in Physician Shortage Area	Individual or Partnership Practice	Private Group Practice	Hospital or Academic Health Center
All students	7,261	94.1	60.5	3.68	27.0	54.3	18.7	47.9	32.0	36.8	24.0
Gender											
Men	5,993	† 93.7	† 59.6	†† 3.70	† 26.7	† 55.2	† 18.0	45.4	34.0	37.3	22.2
Women	1,237	95.5	65.1	3.55	29.0	48.9	22.1	59.6	22.1	34.1	32.9
Race/Ethnicity											
White/Caucasian	6,447	† 94.2	60.8	†† 3.67	25.3	55.2	† 19.5	45.6	32.2	37.9	23.4
Black/Afro-American	296	93.3	58.1	3.82	43.6	47.3	9.1	78.8	29.8	29.8	27.2
Other underrepresented	106	99.0	68.8	3.51	28.1	51.7	20.2	80.4	39.1	26.1	16.3
Other ethnic groups	412	91.5	54.7	3.75	42.5	45.6	11.9	52.4	28.0	27.4	32.3
Marital status											
Single	4,498	94.4	59.5	†† 3.70	30.4	51.5	† 18.1	50.1	31.8	34.9	26.2
Married, no children	2,113	93.4	61.0	3.66	23.4	57.0	19.5	42.5	31.8	40.3	22.0
Married, one child	412	94.3	67.8	3.60	16.4	62.8	20.8	50.7	34.9	38.2	16.7
Married, two children, plus	238	94.0	61.4	3.56	18.6	63.3	18.1	48.2	32.7	39.2	14.3

		†	†	††	†	†	†				
Size of hometown											
Large city	3,188	93.0	54.1	3.75	47.8	40.8	11.4	44.6	26.9	34.4	30.9
Medium, small sized city	2,698	94.5	61.3	3.69	13.9	71.7	14.5	45.4	32.9	39.1	21.2
Small town or rural area	1,359	95.4	73.2	3.48	7.9	49.8	42.3	60.3	41.3	37.7	14.4
			†	††	†		†				
Parental income											
Less than $5,000	404	93.0	65.4	3.53	26.4	48.9	24.7	65.1	32.8	31.9	26.8
$5,000–9,999	728	94.6	63.7	3.54	25.0	50.5	24.5	53.5	32.8	35.0	22.7
$10,000–19,999	2,352	94.7	64.7	3.60	24.4	55.8	19.8	51.0	33.3	35.7	23.2
$20,000–29,999	1,552	93.9	59.5	3.69	25.1	56.8	18.1	46.6	30.2	38.6	24.2
$30,000–49,999	1,086	93.7	55.7	3.79	31.5	53.3	15.2	41.0	29.0	40.6	24.8
50,000 or more	939	93.6	51.2	3.90	33.8	53.6	12.6	37.4	33.3	36.9	24.5

Source: Association of American Medical Colleges, *Medical Student Indebtedness and Career Plans, 1974–75,* U.S. Department of Health, Education and Welfare, Bureau of Health Manpower (1976), Table 14, p. 28.

Note: "Undecided" responses are excluded in deriving all percentages.

[1] Approximately 7 percent of the respondents indicated preferences for other practice environments. Therefore the percentages do not add to 100.0. The x^2 computed only for the environments given in the table indicates that $p(x^2 > x^2 df) < .05$.

†$p(x^2 > x^2 df) < .05$.

††Using F test, $p < .05$.

Of course, before they can serve any community and before they "sink or swim" in medical school, blacks must be admitted. On this point, pessimism about admissions programs may be apropriate.

The "bad news" could be approached subtly by describing changes in proportions over time, but the facts simply need to be stated. The proportion of blacks enrolled is down 6.3 percent in 1974–75 to 6.1 percent in 1976–77. But that is not the worse part. There were fewer blacks in medical school in 1976–77 than in 1974–75. The absolute numbers are down from 3,555 to 3,517 (see Table 7-24).

Since there is some slight variation in these numbers and those of OCR, an additional check might be worthwhile. A look at the data for first-year medical students confirms the larger pattern. The numbers and proportions of blacks in medical school have declined at the first-year level as well, down by 6 percent. Unfortunately, American Indians have also experienced serious setbacks, as Table 7-25 shows.

Table 7-25 suggests that the black percentage of total enrollment is sustained at its current level by the outgoing classes and will probably decline once they are gone. In any case, at the low level of 6 percent, one might wonder if it can continue to decline, especially since blacks constituted 5 percent of medical school students eight years ago. One percentage point (up to about half the level of racial parity) is hardly substantial progress.

Too much has been said and written about blacks in medical schools to be recited here. Much of the discussion, however, centers on one or two explanations of black access to medical school. First, the number and competence of black applicants have been seriously questioned. Second, their competition in testing performance has been extensively (not intensively) explored. Two brief sets of data may serve to explicate our findings.

Table 7-26 shows first the minority percentage of medical school applicants during the three-year period, ending in 1977. Second, it juxtaposes the percentages of minority applicants accepted over the rejected to the corresponding percentages of all applicants accepted.

The small size of the minority applicant pool, 7.9 percent of all applicants, may be an explanation of low minority enrollment. On the other hand, recalling Table 7-25, the total minority proportion of first-year students was only 0.03 percent higher. The minuteness of this ratio may be obscured by the column which shows that more than four times the percentage of minority than nonminority applicants were admitted. Given the number of medical school applications submitted by individual students, of whom the most competitive are accepted by several schools, it is possible that a much smaller number of the 1,313 minorities accepted in 1976–77 are not multiple acceptances of the most competitive minorities. In other

Table 7-24 TOTAL U.S. MINORITY AND FOREIGN STUDENT ENROLLMENTS 1974-75 to 1976-77

Groups	1974-75			1975-76			1976-77		Total Percentage Change 1974-77
	Number	Percentage[1]	Percentage Change	Number	Percentage[1]	Percentage Change	Number	Percentage[1]	
Selected U.S. minorities									
Black American	3,355	6.26	3.01	3,456	6.19	1.76	3,517	6.09	4.83
American Indian	159	.30	8.18	172	.31	8.14	186	.32	16.98
Mexican American	638	1.19	9.56	699	1.25	11.59	780	1.35	22.26
Puerto Rican-mainland	172	.32	14.53	197	.35	17.77	232	.40	34.88
Subtotal	4,324	8.07	4.63	4,524	8.10	4.22	4,715	8.16	9.04
Other U.S. minorities									
Oriental American	959	1.79	6.57	1,022	1.83	15.17	1,177	2.03	22.73
Cuban American				144	.26	14.58	165	.28	
Other	277	.52	−14.08	238	.43	10.08	262	.45	−5.42
Subtotal	1,236	2.31	13.59	1,404	2.51	14.04	1,604	2.78	29.77
Total U.S. minorities	5,560	10.38	6.62	5,928	10.62	6.60	6,319	10.94	13.65
Foreign students									
Non-U.S. black	287	.5	−13.24	249	.45	−7.63	230	.39	19.86
Other	532	1.0	4.14	554	.99	−7.04	515	.89	−3.20
Total	819	1.5	1.95	803	1.44	−7.22	745	1.29	−9.04

Source: Journal of Medical Education, Vol. 52 (February 1977).

[1] Percentage of total U.S. medical school enrollment.

Table 7-25 FIRST-YEAR MINORITY AND FOREIGN STUDENT ENROLLMENTS IN U.S. MEDICAL SCHOOLS 1974-75 to 1976-77

Groups	1974-75 Number	1974-75 Percentage[1]	1974-75 Percentage Change	1975-76 Number	1975-76 Percentage[1]	1975-76 Percentage Change	1976-77 Number	1976-77 Percentage[1]	Total Percentage Change 1974-77
Selected U.S. minorities									
Black American	1,106	7.49	−6.32	1,036	6.77	.38	1,040	6.66	−5.97
American Indian	71	.48	−15.49	60	.39	−28.33	43	.27	−39.44
Mexican American	227	1.54	−1.32	224	1.46	9.37	245	1.57	7.93
Puerto Rican-mainland	69	.47	.28	71	.46	1.41	72	.46	4.35
Subtotal	1,473	9.98	−5.57	1,391	9.09	.65	1,400	8.97	
Other U.S. minorities									
Oriental American	275	1.86	2.55	282	1.84	23.40	348	2.22	26.55
Cuban American				41	.27	45.24	62	.39	
Other	91	.61	−19.78	73	.48	10.96	81	.52	−10.99
Subtotal	366	2.48	8.20	396	2.59	23.99	491	3.14	34.15
Total U.S. minorities	1,839	12.46	−2.83	1,787	11.68	5.82	1,891	12.11	2.83
Foreign students									
Non-U.S. black	90	.61	−27.78	65	.42	−1.54	64	.41	−28.89
Other	129	.87	25.58	162	1.06	−12.35	142	.91	10.07
Total	219	1.48	12.78	227	1.48	9.25	206	1.32	−5.94

Source: Journal of Medical Education, Vol. 52 (February 1977).

[1] Percentages of first-year medical school enrollment.

Table 7-26   MINORITY APPLICANTS TO U.S. MEDICAL SCHOOLS
1974–75 to 1976–77

First-Year Class	Total Applicants	Minority Applicants		Minority Applicants Accepted		
		Number	Percentage of all Applicants	Number	Percentage of all Applicants	Percentage of Minority Applicants Accepted
1974–75	42,624	3,174	7.4	1,406	9.3	44.3
1975–76	42,303	3,049	7.2	1,308	8.5	42.9
1976–77	42,155	3,323	7.9	1,313	8.3	39.5

Source: T. L. Gordon, "Datagram: Applicants for 1976–77 First Year Medical School Class," *Journal of Medical Education*, Vol. 52, No. 9 (September 1977), Table 3, page 781.

Note: Data include only minorities that are underrepresented in U.S. medical schools (Black American, American Indian, Mexican American, and mainland Puerto Rican).

words, this ratio simply does not show how many minorities or non-minorities were accepted. It simply shows how many times acceptances were issued. The deceptiveness of these data could run in either direction, but it seems likely that a small number of minorities with high test scores would be admitted to many schools. Because the number of whites with high tests scores is large compared to the number of blacks with high tests scores, and because test scores are major admissions criteria, differentiation at the very top may be difficult. "Successful" applicant credentials would thus be more widely dispersed.

The overlap of successful applicants among blacks, however, is not the only explanation of racial differences in rates of acceptance. A more important explanation also derives from the problem of competitiveness and admission standards. It is widely recognized that minority scores on the Medical College Admissions Test (MCAT) are lower than those of white students. Unfortunately, it is not so widely recognized that average test scores of minority students *admitted* are higher than test scores of many white students *admitted*. In addition, MCAT scores have been shown to be particularly inadequate for the prediction of black student performance in medical school.[16] Moreover, numerous studies, including ISEP's annual reports, have demonstrated a clear correlation between income and medical admissions test performance—a correlation strong enough to indicate considerable socioeconomic and racial bias in the test's measurements.

Beyond the problem of measurement bias, there are additional biases in testing and admissions, too often overlooked. Namely, the prevalence of these and related criteria would tend to reduce the number of disadvantaged applicants. Effectively then, black students may be discouraged by medical school practices from pursuing a medical education. Such discouragement could affect students as late as their senior year and as early as their freshman year. Table 7-27 shows the lower income applicants constitute both a small proportion of applicants as well as a disproportionately small percentage of students accepted to medical school.

Among those accepted, there is a 10 percent spread between the lowest income group and the $20,000 to $25,000 income group, but the difference in test scores and grades is only about 5 percent. Thus, lower income groups do less well in admissions than their aggregate performance on admissions tests would lead one to expect.

In sum, equal opportunity for blacks in medical education has not only been limited, a brief period of progress toward improving access for blacks has apparently been reversed.

LAW SCHOOL: ACCESS AND PERSISTENCE

In an uncomplimentary sense, law schools are one or two years ahead of medical schools in retrenchment on access for black students. The increase in black enrollment in law school began to taper off by 1973-74, while the enrollment pattern of medical schools was still on an upward slope. In the same year, law schools anticipated medical school patterns by allowing black first-year student enrollment in law school to declined in both absolute numbers and percentages. When the black enrollment in medical schools was only beginning to taper off, black enrollment in first-year law school dropped for the second year, down a total of 5 percent (Table 7-28).

Medical schools have made up for lost time in the sense that the absolute number of blacks enrolled in that field at all levels has declined. In law school, the absolute numbers had not declined before 1977, although growth had all but disappeared. An ABA survey of enrollment in ABA-approved law schools places black enrollment at 5,503 in 1976-77. At the same time, the survey estimates enrollment for 1977-78 at 5,304. In other words, a decline is shown in absolute numbers, 199 black students.

More important, in terms of equal opportunity, than the absolute numbers of blacks enrolled is the proportional representation of blacks in legal education. As has been indicated, blacks not only continue to be underrepresented at 4.5 percent of 1976-77 enrollment, they gained virtually no ground in the preceding four years. The proportion of blacks in law school increased only one tenth of a percent in those four years, according

Table 7-27 FIRST-YEAR CLASS MEDICAL COLLEGE ADMISSION TEST SCORES, UNDERGRADUATE
GRADE-POINT AVERAGES, AND ACCEPTANCE RATES OF APPLICANTS
1975–76

Parental Income	Applicant Pool		Mean MCAT Scores†				Grade-Point Average	Percentage Accepted
	Total Number	Percentage	VA	QA	GI	Sci		
Less than $5,000	1,652	5.3	501	540	489	514	3.09	33.8
$5,000–9,999	3,156	10.2	523	562	511	543	3.20	36.3
$10,000–11,999	2,981	9.6	535	576	518	559	3.25	38.5
$12,000–14,999	4,059	13.1	539	582	525	566	3.28	38.4
$15,000–19,999	5,024	16.2	546	592	530	578	3.31	41.5
$20,000–24,999	4,640	15.0	553	597	535	585	3.31	43.5
$25,000–49,999	6,063	19.6	560	601	540	588	3.29	46.0
$50,000 or more	2,997	9.7	557	596	538	582	3.25	47.9
No response	412	1.3	562	578	541	568	3.22	36.8
Total‡	30,984	100.0	544	586	528	571	3.27	41.6

Source: Travis L. Gordon and Davis G. Johnson, "Study of U.S. Medical School Applicants, 1975–76," *Journal of Medical Education*, 52, 9 (September 1977), Table 14, p. 727.

Note: Data includes only those applicants to the 1975–76 first-year class who took the MCAT in 1974—approximately 73 percent of the entire pool of 42,303. Incomes reported are for 1973.

†VA = Verbal Ability, QA = Quantitative Ability, GI = General Information, and Sci = Science.

‡The median parental income was $18,400.

Table 7-28   FULL-TIME BLACK ENROLLMENT IN ABA-APPROVED
LAW SCHOOLS
1971–74

Year	Enrollment	Percentage Increase
All black students		
1971–72	3,516	—
1972–73	4,003	13.8
1973–74	4,289	7.1
1974–75	4,334	1.0
—	—	—
1971–74	—	23.2
First-year black students		
1971–72	1,611	—
1972–73	1,712	6.2
1973–74	1,690	− 1.2
1974–75	1,623	− 3.9
—	—	—
1971–74		0.7

Source: Educational Testing Service, 1974 Survey of Minority Group Students in Legal Education. Reproduced in ISEP, Equal Educational Opportunity: More Promise than Progress (1978), Table 2.

to figures collected by the ABA. Between 1974 and 1975, the black percentage actually declined.

In law school, the upperclassmen, third and fourth year students, were less than 4.5 percent black in 1974. The sign of the times is shown by data on first and second year black law students, who represented the same proportion of enrollment, 5 percent.

Longitudinal figures reported by the ABA clearly demonstrate a virtual lack of progress in overall law school black enrollment. The miniscule increase these figures show (see Table 7-30) from 1975 to 1976 disappears when OCR figures for 1976 are substituted, and we generally rely on OCR figures for reasons explained in chapter 2.

In sum, law schools and medical schools, which together dominate professional school enrollment, once showed reasonable promise in expanding educational opportunity for blacks. That promise has not only gone unfulfilled it has evidently been retracted. Moreover, evidence from other professional schools indicates the same loss of commitment to equal educational opportunity. Graduate schools have continued to take small steps in the direction of equal opportunity, but the steps are so small it is hard to be sure that any real progress is being made. In fact, "stagnation" is an accurate description of the status of blacks in graduate education.

Table 7-29   SURVEY OF MINORITY STUDENTS ENROLLED IN
              ABA-APPROVED LAW SCHOOLS
              1969–78

Student Background	Year	1st Year	2nd Year	3rd Year	4th Year	Group Not Stated	Total
Black, not of	1977–78	—	—	—	—	—	5,304
Hispanic origin	1976–77	2,128	1,654	1,488	233	0	5,503
	1975–76	2,045	1,511	1,452	119	0	5,127
	1974–75	1,910	1,587	1,329	145	24	4,995
	1973–74	1,943	1,443	1,207	101	123	4,817
	1972–73	1,907	1,324	1,106	74	12	4,423
	1971–72	1,716	1,147	761	55	65	3,744
	1969–70	1,115	574	395	44	—	2,128
Mexican American	1977–78	—	—	—	—	—	1,412
	1976–77	542	435	446	65	0	1,488
	1975–76	484	421	381	11	0	1,297
	1974–75	559	447	329	17	5	1,357
	1973–74	539	386	271	63	0	1,259
	1972–73	480	337	238	17	0	1,072
	1971–72	403	262	170	11	37	883
	1969–70	245	113	54	0	—	412
Puerto Rican	1977–78	—	—	—	—	—	343
	1976–77	119	94	100	18	0	331
	1975–76	113	121	96	3	0	333
	1974–75	117	87	56	3	0	263
	1973–74	96	47	32	5	0	180
	1972–73	73	40	25	5	0	143
	1971–72	49	25	18	2	0	94
	1969–70	29	14	13	5	—	61
Other Hispanic	1977–78	—	—	—	—	—	792
American	1976–77	255	153	139	9	0	556
	1975–76	217	164	146	16	0	543
	1974–75	182	92	97	11	5	387
	1973–74	94	70	59	4	34	261
	1972–73	96	72	60	3	0	231
	1971–72	74	62	35	3	5	179
	1969–70	35	18	19	3	—	75
Asian or	1977–78	—	—	—	—	—	1,382
Pacific Islander	1976–77	484	439	378	23	0	1,324
	1975–76	436	343	287	33	0	1,099
	1974–75	429	322	288	21	3	1,063
	1973–74	327	297	202	19	5	850
	1972–73	298	218	144	20	1	681
	1971–72	254	142	72	7	5	480

Table 7-29   Continued.

Student Background	Year	1st Year	2nd Year	3rd Year	4th Year	Group Not Stated	Total
American Indian or	1977–78	—	—	—	—	—	363
Alaskan Native	1976–77	133	87	75	6	0	301
	1975–76	118	88	84	5	0	295
	1974–75	110	90	65	0	0	265
	1973–74	109	65	44	3	1	222
	1972–73	79	48	4	42	0	173
	1971–72	71	46	18	2	3	140
	1969–70	44	17	10	1	—	72
Other	1969–70	84	55	44	2	—	185
Group not stated	1977–78	—	—	—	—	—	—
	1976–77	8	5	5	3	0	21
	1975–76	0	0	0	0	9	9
	1974–75	1	1	1	0	0	3
	1973–74	6	5	1	0	0	12
	1972–73	1	2	2	2	0	7
	1971–72	0	23	35	0	0	48
Total minority	1977–78	—	—	—	—	—	9,597
	1976–77	3,669	2,867	2,631	357	0	9,524
	1975–76	3,413	2,648	2,446	187	9	8,703
	1974–75	3,308	2,626	2,165	197	37	8,333
	1973–74	3,114	2,313	1,816	195	163	7,601
	1972–73	2,934	2,041	1,619	123	13	6,730
	1971–72	2,567	1,707	1,099	80	115	5,568
	1969–70	1,552	791	533	57	—	2,933

Source: Educational Testing Service, "1976 Review of Legal Education," Princeton, New Jersey (1976).

Note: 1970–71 figures not available.

Table 7-30   LAW SCHOOL ENROLLMENT 1969-76

Law Students	1969	1970	1971	1972	1973	1974	1975	1976	Percentage Increase in Enrollment From 1969 to 1976	Relative Increase in Enrollment From 1969 to 1976
Total	68,386 (100%)	82,041 (100%)	93,118 (100%)	101,664 (100%)	106,102 (100%)	110,713 (100%)	116,991 (100%)	117,451 (100%)	73%	—
Black	2,128 (3.1%)	(1)	3,744 (4.4%)	4,423 (4.3%)	4,817 (4.5%)	4,995 (4.5%)	5,127 (4.3%)	5,503 (4.6%)	158%	1.5%
Chicano	548 (.6%)	(1)	1,156 (1.2%)	1,446 (1.4%)	1,700 (1.6%)	2,007 (1.8%)	2,173 (1.9%)	2,375 (2.0%)	330%	1.4%
Asian or Pacific Islander	(1)	(1)	480 (.5%)	681 (.6%)	850 (.8%)	1,063 (.96%)	1,099 (.93%)	1,324 (1.1%)	175%	.6%
American Indian or Alaskan	72 (.1%)	(1)	140 (.1%)	173 (.1%)	222 (.2%)	265 (.2%)	295 (.2%)	301 (.2%)	31%	.1%
Female	4,715 (6.8%)	7,031 (8.5%)	8,914 (9.5%)	12,173 (11%)	16,760 (16%)	21,788 (19%)	26,737 (22.9%)	29,982 (25%)	535%	18.2%
Minority	2,933 (4.2%)	(1)	5,568 (5.9%)	6,730 (6.7%)	7,601 (7.2%)	8,333 (7.5%)	8,703 (7.4%)	9,524 (8.1%)	211%	3.9%

Source: Law Schools and Bar Admissions Requirements, American Bar Association (1977); Memorandum QS 7677-9, American Bar Association (1977).
(1) Data not available.

POLICY IMPLICATIONS

Equality of opportunity for students at the threshold of college is a virtue in any society. But it is the pervasiveness of equal opportunity thereafter which tests the society's egalitarianism. An equal chance at the start becomes a demeaning experience for those who encounter barriers later on. Deferred inequality demeans a society's commitment to equality no less than inequality at the start. The hierarchical structures of inequality are barely disturbed by its flirtations with the hopes of aspiring students. Under such conditions, disadvantaged students will eventually come to view equal opportunity as a consumer good with its own built-in obsolescence. Unlike a consumer good, however, an equal opportunity once passed by cannot be pursued later without compensation for the lingering disappointment and disaffection.

Before the disappointments of black students over the resurgence of inequality can be effectively compensated, something must be said about the numerous individuals, educators, and policy makers who seem to believe that while progress toward equal opportunity has slowed, it has not been interrupted. These are the optimistic many who believe that the process of expanding educational opportunity, begun in the late 1960s, was self-perpetuating. Among these optimists, some "liberals" have maintained that progress has been sufficient, and some "conservatives" have argued that progress has been excessive, but virtually no one has shown that the progress made is either permanent or profound. It is primarily through the recent data on graduate and professional education, however, that the ephemeral and shallow aspects of progress in higher education come to our attention. Unfortunately, those in education policy making positions may wait until all progress is erased before they take action. If that happens, at the present rate of regression, the wait will not be long.

To build a solid foundation for equal opportunity in graduate and professional education, one does not have to start over. The limits of post-1960s progress were not the result of ill-conceived changes or programs but of insufficient understanding of the limits and intractability of the institutional structure on which those changes were built. They were preestablished sources of inequality, covered up, but otherwise left intact. Thus, when trying to understand the cycle of growth, stagnation, and decline in black graduate education, we should look beneath the fluctuations to see what was there all along.

The preceding discussion has pointed to several factors involved in the changing rates of black graduate attendance. First, social pressure and black social group needs have inspired a positive, exceptional response and higher expectations on the part of black students. The fact that most black students of the 1970s were products of or influenced by the Civil Rights Movement evidently contributed to the growth in attendance. Similarly, the development of informal affirmative action programs, in response to Civil Rights Movement pressures, contributed to access for blacks. Now, in the latter part of the decade, as the Civil Rights Movement slips into history, the exceptional inspiration it generated has faded and, along with it, the progress of the past years has deteriorated. Left behind is the essential question of whether public policy should be developed to do for the future of equal opportunity what extraordinary social forces did for a brief period of time. In other words, to what extent should black Americans have to depend on the thrust of social movements to secure their status in higher education?

Second, the job market and the need for professionals has created an unusual demand for people with advanced training. At the same time, the long-run growth in the percentage of Americans with basic college training has meant that competition among those without an advanced degree, in a slow-growth job market, has become more acute. Consequently, the financial and social status-related attraction of advanced degrees has acquired added magnetism.

Both these factors, the push of social conditions such as those which sparked the Civil Rights Movement and the pull of socioeconomic reward, are external to the educational system, although higher education is heavily influenced by them. These and related factors, which may be called "extra-systemic," are largely beyond the purview of education policy makers. On the other hand, "systemic" and "institutional" factors, as discussed in chapter 4, refer to those elements in higher education which are the direct and legitimate concern of education policy. These include all variations within and among institutions which government influences. Such variations are, however, often regarded as the legitimate products of the American free enterprise approach to higher education. This in itself is not a problem, because officially public and officially private institutions have both quasi-private and quasi-public elements. The policy problem has rather been in the failure to recognize the extent to which some systemic and institutional variations have been directly sustained by public resources.

The fundamental character of American private and public institutions of higher education has been largely independent of federal direction, but their capacity to respond to the demands of equal opportunity is another matter. Graduate and professional schools, in particular, have an elastic reaction to federal incentives. Their stability, or flexibility, rests on the near permanence of established institutions and the enormous financial and structural barriers against creating new ones. What are politically and socially flexible are the size, quality, and openness of their programs. How many students, in which categories, under what conditions, with which qualifications are admitted and trained? These variables have all shown themselves susceptible to sociopolitical, rather than purely academic, motives. What is more, long term changes in institutional sensitivity to minority problems are clearly responsive to the federal dollar.

Nothing in recent years has shown that sensitivity more forcefully than the *Bakke* case. Yet, the case also brought to the surface an ambivalence about equal opportunity at the national level—an ambivalence which institutions in general seem unable to resolve alone. Their inability to take definite action is ultimately consistent with the need for a national authority to set the standards for a national goal; and equal opportunity is, or should be, a national goal.

The major impediment to federal action appears to be a fear of infringing on the private or reserved rights of institutions. It is frequently assumed that institutions have the independent right to (1) admit whomever thay want, (2) train them in the way they want, and (3) certify them at the level they want, as long as clear academic and professional standards are not violated. While one can debate this interpretation in the case of small private colleges, the behavior of graduate and professional schools removes any serious question. For these schools, if such rights exist at all, they are nevertheless exercised as privileges in the sense that public funds and delegated public authority are an essential part of institutional choice.

At the level of individual admissions, the *Bakke* case has rather inadvertently demonstrated the supremacy of public authority in the decision making process. No part of the process of evaluating applicants can ever again be removed from potential public scrutiny. Unfortunately, there has been no positive direction from the federal government indicating what should and can be done to protect equal opportunity in admissions. Institutions are, therefore, left with only negative signals from the Supreme Court indicating what cannot be done.

At the level of what may be called "preferred" rather than "basic" training, options in graduate school such as research and teaching assistantships are tied to federal funds. Indirectly, therefore, the range of specializations available to students is heavily influenced by those funds. Indirectly also, the kinds of criteria for student admission are also influenced by federal funds. Unfortunately, however, there is no consistent accountability to the public interest, because accountability is limited to closed professional associations, except for the ad hoc intervention by the Courts. Consequently, some federal programs, particularly those for loans and college work-study, have benefited needy low-income students and therefore most black students, but the bulk of federal funds to graduate and professional schools, particularly research grants, have gone to the wealthier students. In part, the perpetuation of this inequity results from internal institutional delegation of authority to faculty and administrators, for whom the promotion of equal opportunity is not a salient responsibility. In large part also, inequity results from inter-institutional inequalities, the effects of which can only be controlled by a national authority.

Professional associations, particularly in Law and Medicine, play a quasi-official role in coordinating advanced education on a nationwide level, but their authority is most often exercised to restrict the availability of professional credentials. Thus, through the institutions, these associations determine the availability of black professionals, and yet they are not fully accountable to the society at large, and much less to blacks, for the social and economic hardships their regulatory powers may cause. Here again, the outcomes are the logical, albeit inequitable, consequences of dispersed and episodic federal efforts to mitigate inequalities in a historically inegalitarian educational system.

Ultimately, educators and policy makers, who may well have expected a large and sustained expansion of opportunity for blacks in graduate and professional schools in the 1970s, will be disappointed with the outcomes. Although there was a promising start, very little has been gained in the past few years. In fact, judging from the proportion of blacks in the first year of professional school, more will have been lost than gained by the end of the decade. The only clear way to avoid the continued disappointment that such a stagnation implies is to make equal opportunity a priority at every step of the decision making process wherever higher education is interwoven with public needs and resources. This means doing more than waiting to see what institutional enrollment figures look like at the end of the year, and pursuing judicial redress when sufficient evidence of civil rights violations can be found. Unfortunately, public officials have scarcely done more than wait for outcomes and attempt to turn the unsatisfactory ones around. It is time for federal officials, particularly in HEW, to take an active role in ensuring the equity of all institutional processes, those processes which have left us so many disappointing outcomes.

CHAPTER 8

Elusive Inequalities

Episodes of Equal Opportunity

While individual instances of equal opportunity may be no more significant of real progress than "dancing in the rain," this study has identified patterns of progress toward equal opportunity in higher education which demonstrate that some profound changes have occurred. The most prominent of these changes is the gradual but consistent progress of blacks toward parity with whites in college enrollment. As discussed in chapter 3, the proportion of black undergraduates in 1976-77 reached 10.2 percent, which is close to the black percentage of the total American population. The proportion of the undergraduate population has continually increased from an estimated 8.7 percent in 1974-75, and from approximately 6.5 percent in 1964-65, to its present level. Thus, the pattern of increased access to college is undeniable and seemingly stable.

Yet, access to college is only a concept, and for blacks a theoretical one. No one goes to "just any college," and because that is all that the concept of access represents, racial parity in that regard does not have much social meaning. Progress toward racial parity in access is stripped of value by the lack of progress toward racial parity in the distribution of college students, as discussed in chapter 4. While black students have, over a decade, been more equitably distributed among types of colleges and universities, that progress has been slow and sporadic. The largest gains have probably been made in the redistribution of black students from predominantly black to predominantly white institutions. The intended social value of this change, however, is eroded by the fact that blacks continue to be heavily underrepresented in those major fields which, in the long run, provide the most remuneration. Moreover, except in the most visible of the prestigious institutions, racial parity for blacks in predominantly white institutions has been effectively confined to those institutions that are low on everyone's list of preference.

Greater access for blacks is still less concretely demonstrable through the data than the fact that blacks have profited from a more general extension of college access to all. In the past decade, higher education underwent a tremendous expansion. The number of institutions, particularly public two-year colleges, almost doubled in anticipation of new students. The number of students, particularly women, more than doubled. Blacks and other minorities headed the list of beneficiaries of this expansion. Consequently, the question of establishing a policy for equalizing opportunity was, to some extent, mitigated by the surge of greater opportunities for all. Equal opportunity for the short-term became something of a social and institutional convenience.

The federal government clearly took the initiative in the expansion of higher education in the 1970s, and it did so with an apparent sense of purpose. The growth of federal Office of Education support for students coincides with the growth in the student population and with the expansion of state support for higher education. Currently spending close to $3 billion for its grant and loan programs, the Office of Education has become a pillar of educational opportunity for all college students. On the average, a quarter of all students' college costs are paid through federal funds. For minorities and low-income whites, the federal contribution is indispensible. There is, therefore, no doubt that federal lawmakers intended black students to benefit from the growth in federal aid. Yet, the distribution of aid and the structure of its implementation give evidence of little more than an attempt to moderate the prevailing level of financially defined inequality in higher education.

With the extension of the Basic Educational Opportunities Grant to include middle-income groups and the proposed removal of all limits on eligibility for the Guaranteed Student Loan Program, federal funds will be more widely distributed in 1980 and after. Not surprisingly, this dispersal of federal support follows the 1977 tapering off of the growth in college enrollment. The intention is no doubt to help the middle-income students to stay in school. Yet, there is relatively little evidence that federal dollars will turn the tide of expected declines in enrollment and current increases in attrition for these students. The efficient use of public funds may thus be sacrificed, although the cause may be a good one. At the same time, there is solid evidence that federal funds have their greatest per dollar impact on the enrollment and retention of black and other minority students. This too is a very good cause.

Although federal programs rarely specify blacks and other minorities as the intended beneficiaries, these students depend on federal funds more than others. The TRIO programs, based on current practices, come closest to being an exception. The special minority image of TRIO programs, however, is grounded in their prelegislative backgrounds. The programs are continued only through the exceptional practices of some institutions, usually those in large urban communities. The structure of an Upward Bound program, for example, is largely determined by the voluntarily participating institutions which, in turn, must bend to the racial/ethnic composition of the local community.

On the other hand, institutions have, as often as not, developed programs explicity focused on minority students. A great deal of media attention has been given to affirmative action programs and to related "liberal" programs such as open admissions. Blacks have apparently taken advantage of the programs to increase their educational opportunities. Yet, in spite of the relatively high visibility of these programs, the actual commitment to black students of resources, monetary or educational, has been marginal compared to federal programs like BEOG.

The greatest strides in increasing black and other minority enrollment in higher education have occurred in institutions where affirmative action for students is either inconspicuous or negligible in its impact. First among these are two-year colleges; second are public four-year colleges and the undergraduate schools of public universities. Yet, the greatest media clamor, judging from the *Bakke* and *DeFunis* court cases, concentrates on postgraduate and professional education and on private, selective institutions. Blacks have also made enrollment gains in these latter schools, but by 1977 progress had come to a standstill. Affirmative action, an infant less than ten years ago, has not yet come to maturation, and its institutional guardians have already stopped preparing for its development.

In many public four-year colleges and in most two-year ones, special minority admissions programs have been obviated by open admissions policies. With the growth of open admissions, simple access to college in the mid-seventies had become a small problem for blacks compared to the persistent problems of having a real choice and of staying in school. Still, even with open admissions, white students have, in many cases, made the largest enrollment gains in the competitive programs at selective campuses of the open admissions institutions.

At the "systemic" level of undergraduate higher education, blacks can feel reasonably secure that their progress is continuous, though slow. At the institutional levels, what we have called "attendance" and "programatic" levels, no such security is justified. At the institutional levels, problems of distribution have scarcely been attenuated in the past few years. Retention for blacks shows signs of approaching parity with that of whites, but in part because of growing white student attrition. At the same time, a more subtle problem of black attrition in the most racially segregated major fields seems to be surfacing from the data. For graduate education, the limits at all levels are almost as severe as they ever were in this decade. A downward cycle in opportunities for blacks seems to have taken a strong hold at the most selective points of higher education.

When the enrollment of blacks in higher education was on an upward slope, the proportion of students enrolling in traditionally black institutions was declining. Many black colleges experienced absolute declines in enrollment in the mid-1970s. The primary exceptions were private four-year colleges and universities, whose enrollments were fairly stable. In a related movement, the proportion, always unimpressive, of federal funds, such as "R & D" grants, going to these institutions, failed to grow like that of other institutions, while financial disadvantages became increasingly evident. By 1977, when the contributions of traditionally white institutions, which were always low in retention of black students, seemed to be stagnating, black institutional enrollment started to grow again. Yet, the continued value of TBI's, using the level of Title III funding and NSF grants they have received as examples, has not been accompanied by a corresponding commitment of public funds.

The implication of this interplay between the enrollments of these two types of institutions is threefold. First, traditionally black institutions have been and continue to be a mainstay of higher educational opportunity for blacks. Second, their status and recognition as institutions are influenced by the apparently episodic response of the majority institutions to black students' needs. Third, and perhaps most important, the capacity of black institutions to accommodate and graduate students may have been heavily influenced by federal funds to institutions, but their continued productivity has been sustained independent of federal support. Looking only at the output of blacks with baccalaureate degrees as a proportion of black enrollment, one could easily conclude that the impact of federal aid on institutions is inversely related to the institution's contribution to equal opportunity.

Unfortunately, institutional practices and those of professional associations, as well as the composition of special educational programs, are not measured on the national scale at which they are likely to operate. Direct contributions to equal opportunity for blacks can not be quantified until there is some greater consensus on the meanings of "equality" and of "opportunity" in higher education. As a consequence, analysts have been content to measure instances of racial parity, and to assume that the greater the number of instances and the greater the consistency of such findings, the greater is the level of progress towards equal opportunity for blacks. While the methodological assumptions may be socially useful, misleading interpretations too often follow. The actual number of instances in which racial parity, or the lack of it, could be measured is infinite. Consequently, the likelihood of finding many instances of progress toward parity in an otherwise unprogressive educational system is very high.

This possibility is heightened by the superficial nature of primary data sources. Beyond basic enrollment and degree data, stratified by race, sex, and economic status with occasional data on major fields, there is very little systematic information available on how students are admitted, on what the conditions of college study are like, or on what happens to specific categories of students in institutions before they graduate or withdraw. As a consequence, the prevailing models along which parity is measured are standardized on the basis of the typical student in the traditional institution. For example, as long as access was consistently improving, many observers were ignoring or failing to see problems of maldistribution, because the typical students in the traditional situation did not confront social barriers of choice in being admitted to college. Unfortunately, the importance to equal opportunity of what goes on inside the not-so-ivy-covered walls still suffers from an analytical blindspot in national data collection.

When analysts have attempted to compensate for the limits of primary data through statistical inference techniques, useful conclusions have often been reached. On the other hand, too often these techniques call for filling in the gaps in data before the techniques can be applied. In such cases, the tendency has been to fill in the gaps by assuming that racially equal opportunity already exists in areas such as achievement and aptitude testing of students, and in economic situations such as racial equality among the lowest income groups.

The result is, first, that institutions will appear to be treating students equally, even though the treatment accorded may be based on a racially-biased parameter. Second, equal opportunity for blacks will be expected to be attained when blacks are at parity with the most disadvantaged of the majority population. Finally, findings of racial inequality are detached from questions about opportunity, and the inequalities are presented in terms of uncontrollable, if not natural, social conditions.

Persistent Inequality

In large part, the analytical tendency to "explain away" the lack of racial parity in the name of uncontrollable environmental factors is an outgrowth of the assumption that higher education is socially and ideologically neutral. For the purpose of lucid description, it is convenient to talk about college attendance in terms of "inputs" and "outputs," and to treat the institutions as isolated systems or individuals which are fundamentally free from outside forces. According to this model, institutions and their supporters, e.g., the federal and state governments, can perhaps contribute to equal opportunity by countering external factors of racial disadvantage, but only in conjunction with independent social changes. Such social changes involve adjusting precollege education to suit established college admission, training students to overcome cultural bias on existing tests, motivating black students to enroll in courses under unsympathetic faculty, and providing financial support based more on the institution's expression of good intentions than on its record of promoting equal opportunity.

The record and social role of professional education provide clear evidence that higher education plays a determining role in equality of opportunity—one that reaches into all areas of social life. The capacity of medical and law schools to determine which people will practice those professions is one of many examples of institutional and societal interaction and interdependence. The private power of institutions to control important social functions beyond internal academic life surfaces in their unique power to select the criteria on which the availability of physicians, lawyers, and managers to serve all Americans will be determined. The defects of the assumption that such decisions are "academic" and not social are illustrated by data showing the decline of black access to professional education since 1976.

Of course, it is unlikely that a single institution can break a pattern common to the bulk of them, although traditionally black institutions have done just that by elevating their social commitment. For most institutions, professional associations, and private and public funders rather systematically determine the character of education available. For this reason, institutions have been viewed as a system, but with the recognition that there are various hierarchical strata within the system. At the same time, elements in the system, in particular the federal government and groups of institutions, have been shown to have the pivotal capacity to improve and sustain opportunities for black Americans in higher education. Unless we recognize the systemic nature of persistent racial inequalities, progress for blacks may never be more than marginal and episodic. Large gains have, of course, been made, but the current data show that without renewed federal and institutional commitment the losses of recent years may well become even greater ones.

A Comment

Those of us who are constantly accused of being too zealous in our pursuit of equal opportunity are often sidetracked by oversimplifications of our positions. Accordingly, criticism is raised that complete equality is not feasible and, as if the problem had ever concerned complete equality, we are exposed to superfluous explanations of the limits of the "real" world. In general, that explanation has two essential components: (a) people, whether individuals or groups, are inherently unequal, and so seeking equal outcomes would mean treating people unequally and/or unfairly; and, (b) the effort to equalize opportunity runs the risk of depriving the historical beneficiaries of equality of their underprotected rights. In higher education, this criticism has been recently revitalized and liberated from its former philosophical covering. The first component has now become a normative vacillation between predestination and laisséz-faire for the genetically unequal, and the second, a preemptive assault on "reverse discriminations" yet unborn.

Whether it is a consequence or a concomitant of negative criticism, progress toward equality of opportunity in higher education for blacks has either substantially slowed down or has been detoured away from the best opportunities. Yet, evidence of inequality has become more difficult to demonstrate. This is not because inequalities are not plentiful enough, but because those of us who identify them are rapidly losing the power to direct the attention of American audiences away from the dazzling symbols of the critics. When blacks make very small gains progress is proclaimed, while the persistent inequalities which characterize higher education scarcely receive mention. Where there is no progress at all, attention to the facts and to the cures is often supplanted by a "bite the bullet" resignation to the intractability of the culturally deprived. Finally, in those isolated incidents of substantial progress, our pleasant surprise is deafened by hasty alarms on behalf of the many for whom equal opportunity has been an uneventful way of life.

As with widespread beliefs, there are grains of truth in the current negative beliefs about equal opportunity. One grain of truth is that some inequalities are and will probably continue to be present in any conceivable social and educational structure. Another is that the attainment of maximum equality of opportunity will have wavelike effects on established social and institutional structures, which have to prepare to accommodate a changing environment. In this study, the analysis has pointed to at least two structural components in the control of systems in higher education where education policy makers will have to do more than agree to accept equal opportunity for blacks; they will have to reform institutional practices to make that goal a realistic possibility.

The first essential component in equalizing educational opportunity is the federal government. Although it is outside the standard concept of systems in higher education, the support and influence that the federal government provides to most of higher education make it an integral part of any change in the system. In order to sustain progress toward equal opportunity, both the legislative and administrative branches must recognize that, authorization aside, the real distribution of federal funds occurs in the independent, private, and quasi-private centers of institutional authority. If equal opportunity for blacks is to be developed and protected, federal guidance will be important at many levels of institutional practice. This means that a clear policy of equal opportunity should be articulated for higher education. The details of such a policy or policies may be difficult to work out, but a primary policy-specific commitment should be possible to make. Unfortunately, the limits and inconsistencies of past federal action suggest that a clear commitment has yet to be made.

The second essential component of progress toward equal opportunity in higher education is the educational and institutional leadership itself. In particular, educators and institutional administrators have a crucial initiative yet to undertake: To create stable structures to support and sustain an institutional commitment to equal opportunity. With the exception of traditionally black institutions, and the possible exception of some affirmative action programs, the dominant approach to expanding opportunities for blacks has been marked as much by its preservation of institutional convenience as by its expressions of commitment. The same institutional hierarchies, the same basic institutional programs, and frequently the same educational professionals who once served in defense of racial segregation are now expected to provide the necessary leadership for desegregation. Their intentions may be good and their attitudes reformed, but the effective capacity to sustain black access at all levels and to provide for more equitable distribution will require creative and forceful initiative. The largely external force of societal factors like the Civil Rights Movement and political-economic factors like the BEOG program, provided the inspiration and the initial steps forward. Institutions can not continue to count on these forces which were only able to bring large numbers of blacks into the marginal areas of higher education. As social movement fades into the past, and the enrollment stimulus of BEOG is diluted by the solvent of "middle income assistance," progress for blacks has stagnated. It is largely up to the institutional and professional leadership to help bring blacks into the center of the higher educational system by reorganizing complaints about the absence of qualified black students into resolutions that qualifications are made, not born. Such resolutions, if effectively carried out, would do a lot to rectify the claimed devaluation of the college credential from which white as well as black students suffer equally.

If we extract the grains of truth in the criticisms of those who say complete equality is not feasible, and turn the criticism around, we can arrive at another more important truth which seems to have escaped attention. Namely, complete inequality is also not feasible. As economic conditions and the demand for skilled labor developed in this country, some incidental, but substantial, changes in racial inequality necessarily followed. After World War II, for example, the number of black males gaining access to higher education through the GI Bill grew substantially. Because the number of blacks who had gained such access earlier was very small, the gains of blacks relative to whites helped to reduce the still enormous disparity. Similarly, as higher education underwent tremendous expansion, particularly at nonselective institutions, the places available to anyone, black or white, helped to reduce the racial disparities of access. Now, as the seventies come to an end and the economy contracts, the tangential benefits blacks experienced earlier are being lost.

There is a lesson to be learned from the inevitable imperfections of inequality. That is, that episodes of equal opportunity, or even its preponderance in selected areas of higher education, do not make the system egalitarian. Unfortunately, many critics have been so impressed by the newly erected monuments to equal opportunity that they have failed to recognize that the foundations are the same as those which for centuries have perpetuated a structure of inequality of opportunity.

Appendix

Table A3-1   SEE PAGES 276–277

Table A3-2   MEDIAN AGE OF THE U.S. POPULATION:
1960 to 1977

Year	Total Population	Race		Sex	
		White	Black	Male	Female
1977	29.4	30.2	24.1	28.2	30.6
1976	29.0	29.8	23.8	27.8	30.2
1975	28.8	29.6	23.5	27.6	30.0
1974	28.6	29.4	23.2	27.4	29.9
1973	28.4	29.2	22.9	27.2	29.7
1972	28.1	28.9	22.7	26.9	29.4
1971	27.9	28.8	22.5	26.6	29.3
1970	27.9	28.8	22.5	26.6	29.3
1969	28.0	28.8	22.3	26.6	29.2
1968	28.0	28.8	22.2	26.7	29.2
1967	27.9	28.8	22.1	26.6	29.2
1966	28.0	28.9	22.1	26.7	29.3
1965	28.1	29.0	22.2	26.9	29.4
1964	28.3	29.2	22.4	27.2	29.5
1963	28.6	29.5	22.6	27.5	29.7
1962	28.9	29.8	22.8	27.8	30.0
1961	29.2	30.0	23.1	28.2	30.1
1960	29.4	30.2	23.4	28.5	30.3

Source: "1960 to 1969," Current Population Reports, Series P-25, No. 519, 1970 to 1977.

Note: Medians are based on data for 5-year age groups. Total population includes Armed Forces overseas.

Table A3-1 POPULATION 4 YEARS OLD AND OVER, BY AGE, ETHNIC ORIGIN/DESCENT, AND LANGUAGE CHARACTERISTICS (IN THOUSANDS)
July 1975

| | Population | | Non-English as Usual or Other Household Language | | | | |
| | | | | Usual Individual Language | | | Household Language not Reported |
Age and Ethnic Origin	Total	English, Only Household Language	Total	English	Non-English	Not Applicable	
Total population 4 years old and over	196,796	167,655	25,344	17,838	6,530	976	3,797
Selected European other than Spanish	52,742	43,730	7,954	6,425	1,238	291	1,058
Spanish	9,845	1,393	8,341	4,171	4,012	158	111
Selected Asian	1,919	475	1,439	828	592	*	*
Black	21,373	20,725	369	310	*	*	279
Other	110,917	101,332	7,241	6,104	673	464	2,344
4 to 5 years old	7,065	6,126	928	613	275	*	*
Selected European	835	710	122	102	*	*	*
Spanish	575	97	478	242	226	*	*
Selected Asian	57	*	*	*	*	*	*
Black	985	966	*	228	*	*	*
Other	4,613	4,344	266	228	*	*	*

6 to 13 years old	29,879	25,664	4,155	3,218	775	162	60
Selected European	4,016	3,276	735	644	55	*	*
Spanish	2,220	283	1,937	1,276	628	*	*
Selected Asian	259	*	210	159	*	*	*
Black	4,135	4,061	58	51	*	*	*
Other	19,249	17,995	1,215	1,088	*	82	*
14 to 18 years old	20,874	17,669	2,584	2,059	432	93	621
Selected European	2,977	2,305	585	520	*	*	87
Spanish	1,185	169	999	655	325	*	*
Selected Asian	176	*	127	98	*	*	*
Black	2,768	2,659	*	*	*	*	64
Other	13,768	12,487	828	742	*	56	453
19 to 25 years old	25,332	21,945	2,970	2,119	691	160	417
Selected European	5,921	5,075	760	641	65	54	86
Spanish	1,316	241	1,063	551	489	*	*
Selected Asian	276	116	160	99	54	*	*
Black	2,926	2,825	59	*	*	*	*
Other	14,983	13,688	928	782	81	65	277
26 to 50 years old	63,338	53,960	8,093	5,288	2,485	320	1,285
Selected European	19,557	16,731	2,481	1,991	377	113	345
Spanish	3,277	463	2,769	1,113	1,600	56	*
Selected Asian	813	207	604	331	266	*	*
Black	6,333	6,099	131	118	*	*	103
Other	33,358	30,460	2,108	1,735	241	132	790

Source: NCES, *The Condition of Education, 1977*, Table 1.03, p. 147.
*Estimates less than $50,000.

Table A3-3   TOTAL ENROLLMENT IN INSTITUTIONS
OF HIGHER EDUCATION (IN THOUSANDS)[1]
1960–85

Year (Fall)	Total Enrollment	4-Year Institutions	2-Year Institutions
1960	3,789	3,171	617
1961	4,047	3,381	666
1962	4,404	3,630	774
1963	4,766	3,922	845
1964	5,280	4,291	989
1965	5,921	4,748	1,173
1966	6,390	5,064	1,326
1967	6,911	5,398	1,513
1968	7,513	5,721	1,792
1969	8,005	6,028	1,977
1970	8,581	6,358	2,223
1971	8,949	6,463	2,486
1972	9,215	6,549	2,666
1973	9,602	6,680	2,922
1974	10,224	6,912	3,312
1975	11,185	7,314	3,871
Projected			
1976	11,693	7,516	4,177
1977	12,146	7,682	4,464
1978	12,572	7,825	4,747
1979	12,928	7,925	5,003
1980	13,214	7,989	5,225
1981	13,477	8,033	5,444
1982	13,629	8,029	5,600
1983	13,643	7,943	5,700
1984	13,524	7,792	5,732
1985	13,360	7,623	5,737

Source: NCES, The Condition of Education, 1977, Table 3.03, p. 177.

Note: Details may not add to totals because of rounding.

[1] Includes degree and non-degree credit enrollments.

Table A3-4 PERCENTAGE DISTRIBUTION OF STUDENT ENROLLMENT IN HIGHER EDUCATION
1969, 1974 and 1976

Family Income (1976 dollars)	Percent Enrolled		
	Peak Year 1969	Low Year 1974	Latest Year 1976
$0–$8,525	24.8	20.3	22.4
$8,526–$17,050	38.8	31.7	36.3
$17,051–$25,575	50.6	41.4	47.5
$25,576 or over	65.2	57.5	58.2
All income groups	41.3	36.2	38.8

Source: Lois Rice, Testimony ... (February 1978), p. 6. Based on data from the U.S. Congressional Budget Office.

Table A3-5 BACHELOR'S DEGREES CONFERRED IN INSTITUTIONS OF HIGHER EDUCATION
1975–76

Major Field	Black Non-Hispanic		Total Minority		White Non-Hispanic		Total
	Number	Percentage	Number	Percentage	Number	Percentage	
Agriculture and nature resources	267	1.37	792	4.07	18,357	94.35	19,457
Architecture and environmental design	258	2.83	697	7.64	8,107	88.89	9,120
Area studies	106	3.51	342	11.31	2,646	87.53	3,023
Biological sciences	2,328	4.25	5,184	9.47	48,613	88.81	54,738
Business and management	9,503	6.60	15,754	10.94	125,286	86.98	144,031
Communications	1,275	5.97	1,965	9.20	19,167	89.74	21,358
Computer and information	323	5.97	554	9.92	4,811	86.19	5,582
Education	14,229	9.08	20,254	12.94	135,514	86.57	156,538
Engineering	1,370	2.99	3,717	8.11	38,971	84.98	45,859
Fine and applied arts	1,724	4.09	3,387	8.04	38,204	90.64	42,147
Foreign languages	531	3.44	2,019	13.07	13,050	84.52	15,440
Health professions	2,742	5.06	5,033	9.30	48,465	89.52	54,138
Home economics	1,069	6.18	1,639	9.48	15,467	89.46	17,290
Law	27	5.16	36	6.88	485	92.73	523
Letters	2,468	4.75	4,492	8.64	46,990	90.39	51,986
Mathematics	800	5.03	1,506	9.46	14,103	88.60	15,917
Physical sciences	647	3.03	1,398	6.56	19,400	91.00	21,319
Psychology	3,219	6.44	5,641	11.39	43,795	87.62	49,982
Public affairs and services	3,311	9.93	4,960	14.88	28,133	84.39	33,337
Social sciences	10,990	8.65	17,041	13.42	108,118	85.14	126,990
Theology	148	2.80	255	4.82	4,911	92.75	5,295
Interdisciplinary studies	1,773	5.54	3,395	10.61	28,294	88.42	31,998
National Total (2,063 Institutions)	59,187	6.38	100,228	10.81	811,772	87.56	927,085

Source: HEW, U.S. Office for Civil Rights, *Opening Fall Enrollment, 1976*.

Table A3-6 COLLEGE AND UNIVERSITY FINANCES

Finances	Fiscal Years			Percent Change	
	1975	1976	1977	'75 to '76	'76 to '77
Private institutions					
Total current funds revenues	$11,733,363,000	$12,935,911,000	$14,262,802,000	+10.3%	+10.3%
From student tuition and fees	4,196,142,000	4,748,958,000	5,244,972,000	+13.2%	+10.4%
(Percent from student tuition and fees)	(+35.8%)	(+36.7%)	(+36.8%)		
Total current funds expenditures	11,617,384,000	12,783,392,000	14,034,375,000	+10.0%	+9.8%
Educational and general expenditures	8,501,810,000	9,378,084,000	10,205,652,000	+10.3%	+8.8%
Scholarships and fellowships	734,084,000	843,856,000	923,952,000	+14.9%	+9.5%
Market value of endowment at end of fiscal year	$11,751,748,000	$12,559,191,000	$13,262,807,000	+6.9%	+5.6%
Public institutions					
Total current funds revenues	$24,201,283,000	$27,022,846,000	$29,569,582,000	+11.7%	+9.4%
From student tuition and fees	3,088,413,000	3,487,867,000	3,776,445,000	+12.9%	+8.3%
(Percent from student tuition and fees)	(+12.8%)	(+12.9%)	(+12.8%)		
Total current funds expenditures	23,683,557,000	26,367,592,000	28,912,216,000	+11.3%	+9.7%
Educational and general expenditures	19,281,116,000	21,460,864,000	23,261,593,000	+11.3%	+8.4%
Scholarships and fellowships	739,617,000	812,910,000	869,532,000	+9.9%	+7.0%
Market value of endowment at end of fiscal year	$ 2,621,354,000	$ 2,939,617,000	$ 3,054,198,000	+12.1%	+3.9%
Universities					
Total current funds revenues	$15,935,399,000	$17,447,011,000	$19,018,374,000	+9.5%	+9.0%
From student tuition and fees	2,822,988,000	3,123,864,000	3,417,139,000	+10.7%	+9.4%
(Percent from student tuition and fees)	(+17.7%)	(+17.9%)	(+18.0%)		
Total current funds expenditures	15,715,593,000	17,138,896,000	18,716,346,000	+9.1%	+9.2%
Educational and general expenditures	11,983,207,000	13,109,772,000	14,105,256,000	+9.4%	+7.6%
Scholarships and fellowships	647,149,000	710,560,000	762,102,000	+9.8%	+7.3%
Market value of endowment at end of fiscal year	$ 8,566,784,000	$ 9,176,278,000	$ 9,756,647,000	+7.1%	+6.3%

4-year institutions

Total current funds revenues	$15,302,468,000	$17,164,808,000	$19,003,108,000	+ 12.2%	+ 10.7%
From student tuition and fees	3,708,123,000	4,197,473,000	4,589,228,000	+ 13.2%	+ 9.3%
(Percent from student tuition and fees)	(+ 24.2%)	(+ 24.5%)	(+ 24.1%)		
Total current funds expenditures	15,078,641,000	16,880,157,000	18,653,201,000	+ 12.0%	+ 10.5%
Educational and general expenditures	11,607,071,000	12,954,220,000	14,168,148,000	+ 11.6%	+ 9.4%
Scholarships and fellowships	691,022,000	786,121,000	864,489,000	+ 13.7%	+ 10.0%
Market value of endowment at end of fiscal year	$ 5,671,629,000	$ 6,171,138,000	$ 6,403,182,000	+ 8.8%	+ 3.8%

2-year institutions

Total current funds revenues	$ 4,696,778,000	$ 5,346,938,000	$ 5,810,902,000	+ 13.8%	+ 8.7%
From student tuition and fees	753,444,000	915,488,000	1,015,050,000	+ 21.5%	+ 10.9%
(Percent from student tuition and fees)	(+ 16.0%)	(+ 17.1%)	(+ 17.5%)		
Total current funds expenditures	4,506,707,000	5,131,931,000	5,577,044,000	+ 13.9%	+ 8.7%
Educational and general expenditures	4,192,649,000	4,774,956,000	5,193,841,000	+ 13.8%	+ 8.8%
Scholarships and fellowships	135,531,000	160,085,000	166,893,000	+ 18.1%	+ 4.3%
Market value of endowment at end of fiscal year	$ 134,690,000	$ 151,394,000	$ 157,176,000	+ 12.4%	+ 3.8%

All institutions

Total current funds revenues	$35,934,645,000	$39,958,757,000	$43,832,384,000	+ 11.2%	+ 9.7%
From student tuition and fees	7,284,554,000	8,236,824,000	9,021,417,000	+ 13.1%	+ 9.5%
(Percent from student tuition and fees)	(+ 20.3%)	(+ 20.6%)	(+ 20.6%)		
Total current funds expenditures	35,300,941,000	39,150,984,000	42,946,591,000	+ 10.9%	+ 9.7%
Educational and general expenditures	27,782,927,000	30,838,948,000	33,467,245,000	+ 11.0%	+ 8.5%
Scholarships and fellowships	1,473,702,000	1,656,766,000	1,793,484,000	+ 12.4%	+ 8.3%
Market value of endowment at end of fiscal year	$14,373,103,000	$15,498,809,000	$16,317,005,000	+ 7.8%	+ 5.3%

Source: The Chronicle of Higher Education, XVI, 12 (May 1, 1978), p. 9.

281

Table A3-7 ESTIMATED EXPENDITURES OF INSTITUTIONS OF HIGHER EDUCATION 1959 to 1976-77*

Source of Funds, by Level and Control

	1959-60	1961-62	1963-64	1965-66	1967-68	1969-70	1971-72	1973-74	1975-76	1976-77
Amount, in Billions of Current Dollars										
Public and nonpublic, total	6.7	8.5	11.3	15.2	19.9	24.7	29.2	34.3	44.8	49.2
Federal	1.0	1.6	2.2	2.9	3.8	4.1	4.6	5.1	7.0	7.4
State	1.6	2.0	2.6	3.5	4.8	6.4	7.8	9.7	13.4	14.9
Local	.2	.2	.3	.4	.6	.9	1.1	1.4	1.8	2.0
All other	3.9	4.7	6.2	8.4	10.7	13.3	15.7	18.1	22.6	24.9
Public, total[1]	3.8	4.7	6.4	8.8	12.3	15.8	19.1	22.9	30.4	33.5
Federal	.5	.8	1.1	1.5	2.1	2.4	2.8	3.2	4.4	4.7
State	1.6	1.9	2.5	3.4	4.7	6.3	7.6	9.4	13.1	14.5
Local	.2	.2	.3	.4	.6	.8	1.0	1.3	1.7	1.9
All other	1.5	1.8	2.5	3.5	4.9	6.3	7.7	9.0	11.2	12.4
Nonpublic, total[1]	2.9	3.8	4.9	6.4	7.6	8.9	10.1	11.4	14.4	15.7
Federal	.5	.8	1.1	1.4	1.7	1.7	1.8	1.7	2.6	2.7
State	(2)	.1	.1	.1	.1	.1	.2	.3	.3	.4
Local	(2)	(2)	(2)	(2)	(2)	.1	.1	.1	.1	.1
All other	2.4	2.9	3.7	4.9	5.8	7.0	8.0	9.1	11.4	12.5
Percentage Distributions										
Public and nonpublic, total	100.0	100.0	100.0	100.0	100.0	100.0	100.0	100.0	100.0	100.0
Federal	14.9	18.8	19.5	19.1	19.1	16.6	15.7	14.9	15.6	15.0
State	23.9	23.5	23.0	23.0	24.1	25.9	26.7	28.3	29.9	30.3
Local	3.0	2.4	2.6	2.6	3.0	3.6	3.8	4.1	4.0	4.1
All other	58.2	55.3	54.9	55.3	53.8	53.9	53.8	52.7	50.5	50.6

Public, total	100.0	100.0	100.0	100.0	100.0	100.0	100.0	100.0	100.0
Federal	14.9	16.0	16.9	17.6	17.3	14.9	14.7	14.1	14.5	14.0
State	41.1	41.2	39.7	38.4	38.2	39.7	39.7	41.1	42.9	43.3
Local	4.6	4.2	4.3	4.1	4.6	5.1	5.4	5.5	5.6	5.8
All other	39.1	38.6	39.1	39.9	39.9	40.3	40.2	39.3	37.0	36.9
Nonpublic, total	100.0	100.0	100.0	100.0	100.0	100.0	100.0	100.0	100.0
Federal	17.0	20.5	23.1	22.1	22.1	18.8	18.3	17.1	17.8	17.0
State	1.5	1.5	1.3	1.5	1.3	1.6	2.0	2.5	2.2	2.3
Local	.2	.2	.2	.1	.3	.7	.5	.6	.7	.8
All other	81.3	77.8	75.4	76.3	76.3	78.9	79.2	79.8	79.3	79.9

Source: NCES, The Condition of Education, 1977, Table 3.08, p. 181.

*Data are for 50 States and the District of Columbia for all years. Details may not add to total because of rounding.

[1]Total expenditures distributed according to the trend of receipts shown in source (appendix B).

[2]Less than $50 million.

Table A3-8   NUMBER AND ENROLLMENT OF INSTITUTIONS OF HIGHER EDUCATION
Fall 1975

Control of Institution	All Institutions		Universities		All other 4-Year Institutions		2-Year Institutions	
	Number	Enrollment	Number	Enrollment	Number	Enrollment	Number	Enrollment
All institutions	3,026	11,184,859	160	2,838,266	1,738	4,376,474	1,128	3,970,119
Public institutions	1,442	8,834,508	95	2,124,221	450	2,873,921	897	3,836,366
Private institutions	1,584	2,350,351	65	714,045	1,288	1,502,553	231	133,753

Source: NCES, The Condition of Education, 1977.

Note: Two-year branches of universities and other four-year institutions and the enrollment in those branches are included in the two-year institutions column.

Table A3-9 MEAN SCORES ON STANDARDIZED EXAMINATIONS 1966-67 to 1975-76

Year	Scholastic Aptitude Test (SAT)[1]		American College Testing Program (ACT)		Graduate Record Exam (GRE)[2]		Law School Admission Test (LSAT)[1]	Medical College Admission Test (MCAT)		Graduate Management Admission Test (GMAT)[1]
	Verbal	Mathematics	English	Mathematics	Verbal	Quantitative		Verbal	Quantitative	
1966-67	467	495	18.5	18.7	519	528	514	524	557	486
1967-68	466	494	18.1	18.3	520	527	516	525	560	485
1968-69	462	491	18.4	19.2	515	524	516	529	568	481
1969-70	460	488	18.1	19.5	503	516	518	517	566	474
1970-71	454	487	17.7	18.7	497	512	519	519	564	466
1971-72	450	482	17.6	18.6	494	508	521	517	557	462
1972-73	443	481	17.8	18.8	497	512	522	513	559	465
1973-74	440	478	17.6	18.1	492	509	527	522	561	463
1974-75	437	473	17.3	17.4	493	508	520	511	568	461
1975-76	429	470	17.2	17.1	492	511	525	523	569	463

Source: NCES, The Condition of Education, 1977, Table 5.04, p. 214.

[1] For all cases attending test administrations during a testing year. Thus, an individual may be counted more than once if he/she was tested more than once in a given year. Furthermore, the cases are aggregated without regard to educational level.

[2] Since 1964-65, the volume of cases attending GRE aptitude test administrations has tripled and the proportion in social sciences has also increased.

Table A3-10   TOTAL NET WEALTH OF WHITE AND BLACK FAMILIES

Income Class	Net Wealth White	Net Wealth Black	Ratio of Black to White Wealth	Wealth-Income Ratio White	Wealth-Income Ratio Black
$0–2,499	$ 10,681	$ 2,148	20.1	7.51	1.61
$2,500–$4,999	13,932	2,239	16.1	3.75	0.62
$5,000–$7,499	13,954	4,240	30.4	2.25	0.69
$7,500–$9,999	16,441	6,021	36.6	1.91	0.70
$10,000–$14,999	24,304	8,694	35.8	2.04	0.74
$15,000–$19,999	43,413	20,533	47.3	2.58	1.22
$20,000 and over	101,009	30,195	29.9	3.37	1.26
All units	20,153	3,779	18.8	2.58	0.81

Source: Marcus Alexis, "Black and White Wealth," ed. M. R. Barnett and J. Hefner, *Public Policy for the Black Community* (New York: Alfred Publishing Co., 1976), Table 6.1, p. 195. Based on Henry S. Terrell, "Wealth Accumulation of Black and White Families: The Empirical Evidence," *Journal of Finance,* 26 (May 1971), Table 1, p. 364.

Figure A3-1   EDUCATIONAL PLANS OF HIGH SCHOOL SENIORS

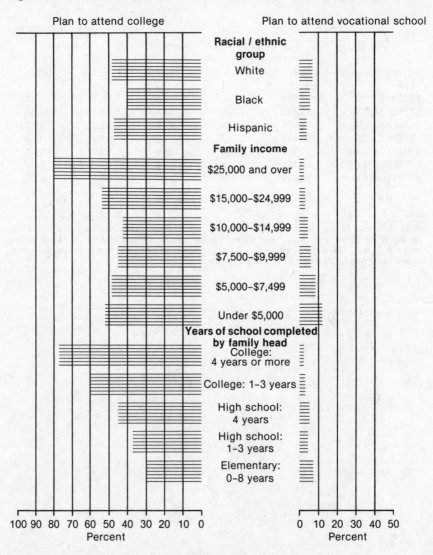

Source: NCES, The Condition of Education, 1978, Chart 3.1, p. 109.

Figure A3-2 HIGH SCHOOL GRADUATES NOT IN SCHOOL, 18 TO 24 YEARS OLD, INTERESTED IN ATTENDING SCHOOL

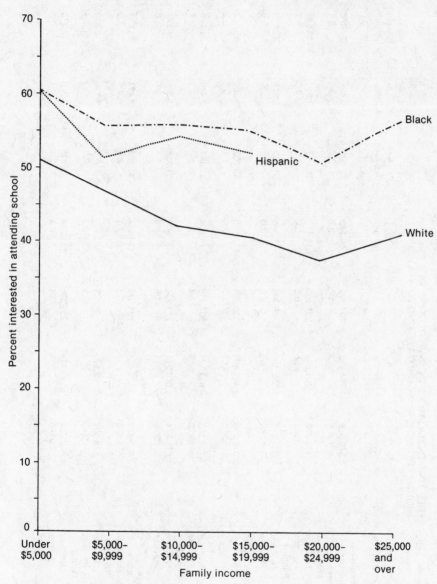

Source: NCES, *The Condition of Education, 1978*, Chart 3.2, p. 111.

Table A4-1 FULL-TIME ENROLLMENT IN INSTITUTIONS OF
HIGHER EDUCATION: AGGREGATE UNITED STATES
Fall 1976

Level of Institution	Total	White[1]	Black[1]	Hispanic	Asian or Pacific Islander	American Indian/ Alaskan Native	Non-resident Alien
University							
Number	2,079,939	1,794,252	107,399	56,115	42,401	9,494	70,278
Percent	100.0	86.3	5.2	2.7	2.0	0.5	3.4
Private:							
Number	480,729	401,856	31,403	10,717	10,511	1,657	24,585
Percent	100.0	83.6	6.5	2.2	2.2	0.3	5.1
Public:							
Number	1,589,210	1,382,396	75,996	45,398	31,890	7,837	45,693
Percent	100.0	87.0	4.8	2.9	2.0	0.5	2.9
Other 4-year							
Number	3,015,236	2,447,698	330,324	113,188	43,202	15,302	65,522
Percent	100.0	81.2	11.0	3.8	1.4	0.5	2.2
Private:							
Number	1,139,262	944,427	107,116	41,584	11,444	3,446	31,245
Percent	100.0	82.9	9.4	3.7	1.0	0.3	2.7
Public:							
Number	1,875,974	1,503,271	223,208	71,604	31,758	11,856	34,277
Percent	100.0	80.1	11.9	3.8	1.7	0.6	1.8
2-year							
Number	1,690,775	1,272,034	221,874	119,444	33,908	18,424	25,091
Percent	100.0	75.2	13.1	7.1	2.0	1.1	1.5
Private:							
Number	118,507	78,920	16,479	18,100	700	1,496	2,812
Percent	100.0	66.6	13.9	15.3	0.6	1.3	2.4
Public:							
Number	1,572,268	1,193,114	205,395	101,344	33,208	16,928	22,279
Percent	100.0	75.9	13.1	6.4	2.1	1.1	

Table A4-2 PERCENTAGE AND FREQUENCY DISTRIBUTIONS OF BLACKS ENROLLED IN COLLEGES AND UNIVERSITIES
Fall 1976

Type of Institution	Total Black Enrollment (All Institutions)		Percent Enrolled in...			Percent Black Students of All Higher Education Students
	Number	Percent	Traditionally Black Institutions	Predominantly Black Institutions	Other than Traditionally Black Institutions/ Predominantly Black Institutions	
All Institutions	1,034,680[a]	100.0	17.8	11.9	70.3	9.3
Public	832,866	100.00	14.8	13.5	71.7	9.6
Private	201,814	100.0	29.9	5.4	64.7	8.4
All Universities	150,217	100.0	8.1	—	91.9	5.4
Public	104,908	100.0	4.7	—	95.3	5.0
Private	45,309	100.0	16.0	—	84.0	6.5
All 4-Year	455,170	100.0	35.9	5.5	58.6	10.4
Public	318,499	100.0	35.4	6.5	58.1	11.2
Private	136,671	100.0	37.1	3.2	59.7	8.9
All 2-Year	429,293	100.0	0.2	22.9	76.9	11.9
Public	409,459	100.0	1.5	22.4	76.1	10.9
Private	19,834	100.0	11.7	32.3	56.0	13.2

Source: Preliminary data on fall 1976 enrollment from HEW, National Center for Education Statistics. Reproduced in National Advisory Committee on Black Education and Black Colleges and Universities, *Higher Education Equity: The Crisis of Appearance Versus Reality, First Annual Report, 1977* (Washington, D.C., 1978), p. 15.

[a]Slight difference between this total and ISEP is not significant.

Table A4-3   FAMILY CONTRIBUTION TO COLLEGE COSTS AS
PERCENTAGE OF AVERAGE INCOME

Income Bracket	Pre-Tax	Post-Tax
$7,500–$12,000	9.2	10.1
$12,000–$15,000	9.8	11.0
$15,000–$20,000	10.6	12.1
$20,000–$25,000	10.6	12.2
$25,000 or more	8.9	10.4

Source: SIE, IRS: Selected income tax by size of adjusted gross income, adjusted for number of postsecondary students in families with different parental incomes: Joseph Froomkin, p. 18, Table 5.

Table A4-4   EMPLOYMENT STATUS OF 1974–75 BACHELOR'S DEGREE
RECIPIENTS
May 1976

Major Degree Field	Bachelor's Degrees Earned		Working Full-time	Average Annual Salary	Percent Under-employed
	Number	Percent			
Total	931,700	100	622,400	$9,400	24
Biological sciences	69,200	7	40,800	7,900	26
Engineering	59,400	6	47,100	13,400	4
Physical sciences and mathematics	38,200	4	18,300	9,900	26
Psychology	52,400	6	32,400	8,500	38
Social sciences and public affairs	147,000	16	85,400	9,100	38
Humanities	99,100	11	52,600	8,000	41
Business and management	157,800	17	131,500	10,500	21
Education	181,700	20	127,600	8,100	16
Health professions	55,600	6	37,700	10,600	4
Communications	19,500	2	14,400	8,900	26
Other	51,800	6	34,700	8,800	17

Source: U.S. Department of Health, Education and Welfare, National Center for Education Statistics, Survey of 1974–75 College Graduates, unpublished tabulations. NCES, *The Condition of Education, 1978*, Table 3.19, p. 144.

Note: Details may not add to totals because of rounding.

Table A4-5   PERCENTAGE OF FRESHMAN STUDENTS LIVING IN RESIDENCE HALLS BY TYPE OF INSTITUTION Fall 1974

Type of Institution	Percentage
2-year colleges	10.3
4-year colleges	
Low selectivity	56.7
Medium selectivity	68.5
High selectivity	89.6
Universities	
Low selectivity	71.8
Medium selectivity	91.7
High selectivity	97.0

Source: Alexander Astin, "The Myth of Equal Access in Public Higher Education," Southern Foundation (July 1975), Table 3, p. 5. Also published in A.W. Astin, M. R. King, J. M. Light, G. T. Richardson, *The American Freshman*: *National Norms for Fall 1974,* Graduate School of Education, UCLA, 1974.

Figure A4-1   TUITION AND FEES FOR HIGHER EDUCATION

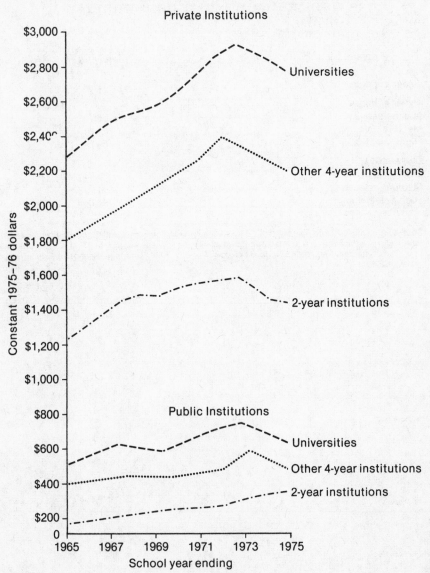

Source: NCES, *The Condition of Education, 1977,* Chart 3.11, p. 60.

Figure A4-2   WEIGHTED NATIONAL NORMS FOR ALL FRESHMEN
SUPPORTED BY PARENTAL INCOME OF $15,000 OR LESS
BY TYPE AND CONTROL OF INSTITUTION
Fall 1976

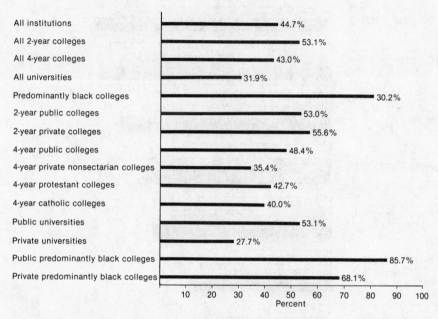

All institutions	44.7%
All 2-year colleges	53.1%
All 4-year colleges	43.0%
All universities	31.9%
Predominantly black colleges	30.2%
2-year public colleges	53.0%
2-year private colleges	55.6%
4-year public colleges	48.4%
4-year private nonsectarian colleges	35.4%
4-year protestant colleges	42.7%
4-year catholic colleges	40.0%
Public universities	53.1%
Private universities	27.7%
Public predominantly black colleges	85.7%
Private predominantly black colleges	68.1%

Percent

Source: Alexander Astin, Margo King and Gerald Richardson, *The American Freshman*: *National Norms for Fall 1976*, (Los Angeles: CIRP/UCLA, 1977).

Figure A4-3   REASONS CITED BY FRESHMEN IN DECIDING TO GO
TO COLLEGE

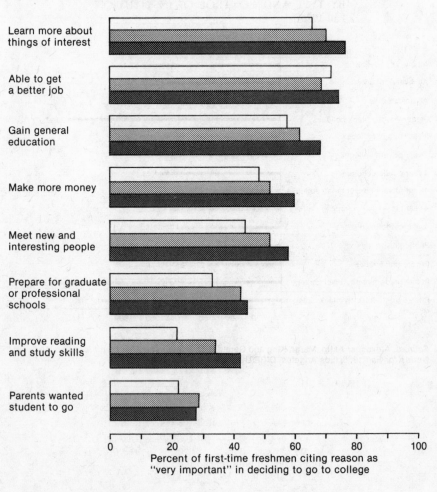

Year: ☐ 1971   ▦ 1976   ■ 1977

Source: *The Condition of Education, 1978*, Chart 3.3

Figure A4-4 **PERCENTAGE DISTRIBUTION OF ASSIGNABLE AREAS IN BUILDINGS OF INSTITUTIONS OF HIGHER EDUCATION**
September 1970

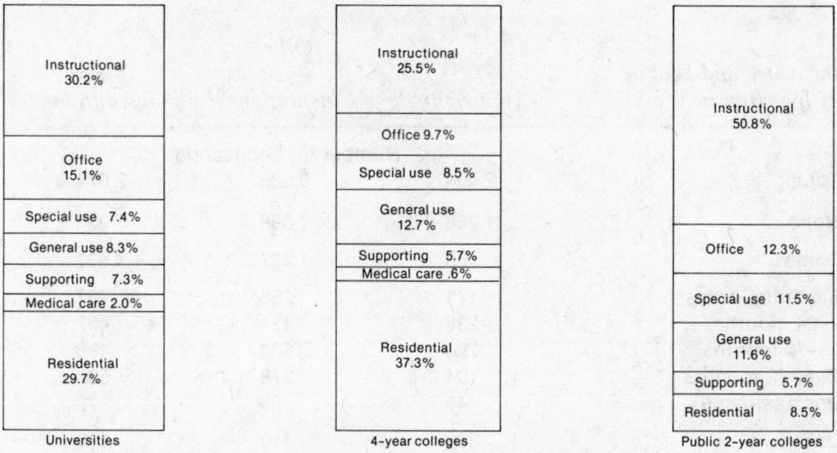

Universities	4-year colleges	Public 2-year colleges
Instructional 30.2%	Instructional 25.5%	Instructional 50.8%
Office 15.1%	Office 9.7%	
Special use 7.4%	Special use 8.5%	Office 12.3%
General use 8.3%	General use 12.7%	
Supporting 7.3%	Supporting 5.7%	Special use 11.5%
Medical care 2.0%	Medical care .6%	General use 11.6%
Residential 29.7%	Residential 37.3%	Supporting 5.7%
		Residential 8.5%

Source: D. Kent Halstead, *Statewide Planning in Higher Education*, (Washington, D.C.: U.S. Government Printing Office, 1974), p. 420.

Table A5-1   INCIDENCE AND LENGTH OF INTERRUPTION OF
              ATTENDANCE AMONG STUDENTS[1] ENROLLED IN
              INSTITUTIONS OF HIGHER EDUCATION
              February 1974

Incidence and Length of Interruption	University	Other 4-year Institutions	2-year Institutions
	Number (in Thousands)		
Total	2,404	3,635	2,874
None	1,288	1,898	926
Some	753	1,327	1,833
6 months or less	171	268	237
7–24 months	238	421	497
25–72 months	200	304	489
Over 72 months	104	278	538
Unclassifiable	40	55	72
Unknown	363	410	116
	Percentage Distribution		
Total	100.0	100.0	100.0
None	53.6	52.2	32.2
Some	31.3	36.5	63.8
6 months or less	7.1	7.4	8.2
7–24 months	9.9	11.6	17.3
25–72 months	8.3	8.4	17.0
Over 72 months	4.3	7.6	18.7
Unclassifiable	1.7	1.5	2.5
Unknown	15.1	11.3	4.0

Source: U.S. Department of Commerce, Bureau of the Census, Current Population Survey (February 1974), and U.S. Department of Health, Education and Welfare, National Center for Education Statistics, Condition of Education, 1978, Table 3.13, p. 132.

Note: Details may not add to totals because of rounding.

[1]Having less than master's degree.

Table A5-2   TOTAL WITHDRAWAL RATE FOR 2-YEAR AND 4-YEAR COLLEGE STUDENTS AND GRADUATION RATE FOR 2-YEAR COLLEGE STUDENTS 1974

| Student Characteristics | Total Withdrawal Rate[1] | | | | Graduation Rate for 2-year College Students | |
| | 4-year College Students | | 2-year College Students | | | |
	Aided	Not Aided	Aided	Not Aided	Aided	Not Aided
Ability						
Low	37.0 (26.5)	53.4 (44.9)	53.1 (40.6)	63.3 (54.8)	11.0	4.1
Middle	26.0 (19.6)	35.1 (27.7)	39.3 (33.7)	47.8 (40.9)	21.3	11.7
High	14.4 (11.1)	21.6 (17.2)	18.6 (15.1)	43.2 (37.7)	31.3	16.2
Race						
White	20.9 (15.6)	29.0 (22.5)	34.0 (25.5)	49.1 (42.4)	25.5	12.2
Black	24.4 (18.4)	46.2 (37.5)	43.5 (33.5)	67.1 (58.0)	11.0	4.1
Educational aspirations						
Vocational-technical school	73.3 (53.0)	79.9 (66.3)	62.8 (48.4)	79.5 (69.9)	13.1	5.1
2-year college	53.8 (45.3)	74.1 (51.8)	60.0 (44.4)	60.4 (51.7)	20.7	10.7
4-year college	25.8 (19.9)	30.9 (25.2)	34.5 (29.3)	41.8 (35.5)	24.2	11.3
Graduate school	14.9 (10.9)	20.2 (15.0)	21.6 (16.0)	36.0 (30.8)	22.7	15.7
Socioeconomic status						
Low	30.8 (22.8)	52.6 (43.0)	46.7 (38.7)	64.3 (56.3)	15.8	6.4
Middle	22.6 (16.7)	37.5 (30.2)	34.5 (29.3)	55.1 (46.6)	25.0	10.4
High	14.4 (10.9)	22.2 (16.4)	25.0 (17.3)	38.6 (33.3)	22.6	13.8

Source: U.S. Department of Health, Education and Welfare, National Center for Education Statistics, National Longitudinal Study of the High School Class of 1972, published in The Condition of Education, 1978, Table 3.14, p. 134.

Note: Data for withdrawal rates of 2-year and 4-year college students includes those attending college in 1972 or 1973, but not in 1974.

[1] Percentage of those in given enrollment and financial aid status who have withdrawn. Data include those who withdrew for academic and nonacademic reasons. Figures in parentheses are nonacademic withdrawal rates; subtracting these figures from the ones preceding them will give academic withdrawal rates.

Table A6-1 FUNDS TO MINORITIES AS PERCENTAGE OF TOTAL
APPROPRIATION
(HEA, TITLE III, BASIC INSTITUTIONAL
DEVELOPMENT PROGRAM)
Fiscal Years 1966–76

Fiscal Year	Predominantly Black Colleges	Spanish-Speaking Programs	Native American Programs	Other	Total
1966	61	3	—	36	100
1967	40	2	1	57	100
1968	47	3	1	49	100
1969	53	3	1	43	100
1970	57	2	1	40	100
1971	59	5	3	33	100
1972	60	5	4	31	100
1973	59	7	6	28	100
1974	57	7	7	29	100
1975	52	8	7	33	100
1976	49	10	8	33	100

Source: Advisory Council on Developing Institutions (HEW), *Strengthening Developing Institutions* (March 1977), p. 36.

Table A6-2 PERCENTAGE OF CURRENT FUNDS TO COLLEGES FROM
PUBLIC SOURCES
Fiscal Year 1975

Institution	Federal	State	Local
Historically black colleges			
Public	21	45	6
Private	38	1	< 1
Total	29	24	< 1
All colleges and universities			
Public	14	44	6
Private	14	2	1
Total	14	31	4

Source: Congressional Research Service, "The Historically Black Colleges: Prospect and Options for Federal Support" (January 17, 1977). Based on data from NCES, HEGIS.

Table A6-3 FEDERAL FUNDS OBLIGATED TO BLACK INSTITUTIONS (DOLLARS IN THOUSANDS)
Fiscal Year 1975

United States Totals	Total, All Activities	Total Academic Science	Research and Development	Research and Development Plants	Facilities for Instruction in Science and Engineering	Fellowships Traineeships Training Grants	General Support for Science	Other Science	Non-Science
All black institutions	$213,668	$38,285	$23,127	$0	$65	$1,217	$4,654	$9,222	$175,383
Public 4-year	93,102	23,415	14,786	0	46	300	2,595	5,688	69,687
Public 2-year	8,428	125	0	0	0	0	0	125	8,303
Private 4-year	110,444	14,575	8,341	0	19	917	2,059	3,239	95,869
Private 2-year	1,694	170	0	0	0	0	0	170	1,524

Source: National Science Foundation. Published in Federal Interagency Committee on Education, *Federal Agencies and Black Colleges, FICE Report,* 4, 2 (December 1977), Table 2.

Table A6-4   UNDERGRADUATE ENROLLMENT IN TRADITIONALLY
AND PREDOMINANTLY BLACK INSTITUTIONS OF
HIGHER EDUCATION
Fall 1976

Traditionally Black Institutions	Federal Interagency Committee on Education Code	Percentage Black
Alabama		
Alabama Agricultural and Mechanical University	1002	81
Alabama Lutheran Academy and College	10554	95
Alabama State University	1005	100
Bishop State Junior College	1030	87
Daniel Payne College	1014	100
Lawson State Community College	1059	99
Lomax-Hannon Junior College	1025	99
Miles College	1028	99
Oakwood College	1033	95
Selma University	1037	100
Stillman College	1044	99
Talladega College	1046	99
Tuskegee Institute	1050	95
Arkansas		
Arkansas Baptist College	1087	83
Philander Smith College	1103	80
Shorter College	1105	95
University of Arkansas at Pine Bluff	1086	86
Delaware		
Delaware State College	1428	68
District of Columbia		
District of Columbia Teachers College	1441	94
Howard University	1448	79
Florida		
Bethune-Cookman College	1467	96
Edward Waters College	1478	99

Notes: Enrollment figures drawn from HEW, OCR undergraduate enrollment data for 1976.
For a more detailed listing of traditionally black institutions, see William H. Turner and John A. Michaels, *Traditionally Black Institutions of Higher Education: Their Identification and Selected Characteristics*, National Center for Education Statistics (Washington, D.C.: U.S. Government Printing Office, 1978).
Atlanta University and Meharry Medical College, traditionally black institutions, are not included in this list because they have only graduate and professional students. They are the only known "TBI's" with no undergraduate population:

Atlanta University	FICE Code: 1551	Percentage Black: 83
Meharry Medical College	FICE Code: 3506	Percentage Black: 80

Table A6-4   Continued.

Traditionally Black Institutions	Federal Interagency Committee on Education Code	Percentage Black
Florida Agricultural and Mechanical University	1480	89
Florida Memorial College	1486	74
Georgia		
Albany State College	1544	97
Clark College	1559	98
Fort Valley State College	1566	90
Interdenominational Theological Center[1]	1568	—
Morehouse College	1582	98
Morris Brown College	1583	97
Paine College	1587	99
Savannah State College	1590	89
Spelman College	1594	98
Kentucky		
Kentucky State College	1968	59
Simmons College[1]	—	100
Louisiana		
Dillard University	2004	98
Grambling State University	2006	98
Southern University Agricultural and Mechanical College, Main Campus	9636	96
Southern University in New Orleans	2026	99
Southern University, Shreveport-Bossier City Campus	4622	100
Xavier University of Louisiana	2032	93
Maryland		
Bowie State College	2062	79
Coppin State College	2068	95
Morgan State University	2083	96
University of Maryland-Eastern Shore	2106	79
Mississippi		
Alcorn State University	2396	99
Coahoma Junior College	2401	94
Jackson State University	2410	95
Mary Holmes College	2412	100

[1]These institutions are not listed with enrollments in the HEW Office for Civil Rights fall enrollment data for 1976.

Table A6-4   Continued.

Traditionally Black Institutions	Federal Interagency Committee on Education Code	Percentage Black
Mississippi Industrial College	2421	100
Mississippi Valley State University	2424	99
Natchez Junior College	2425	100
Prentiss Normal and Industrial Institute	2432	99
Rust College	2433	100
Tougaloo College	2439	98
Utica Junior College	2445	100
North Carolina		
Barber-Scotia College	2909	98
Bennett College	2911	100
Elizabeth City State University	2926	93
Fayetteville State University	2928	95
Johnson C. Smith University	2936	99
Livingstone College	2942	100
North Carolina Agricultural and Technical State University	2905	95
North Carolina Central University	2950	97
Shaw University	2962	93
St. Augustine's College	2968	95
Winston-Salem State University	2986	93
Ohio		
Central State University	3026	92
Wilberforce University	3141	96
Oklahoma		
Langston University	3157	89
Pennsylvania		
Cheyney State College	3317	76
Lincoln University	3290	96
South Carolina		
Allen University	3417	95
Benedict College	3420	99
Claflin College	3424	99
Clinton Junior College	4923	100
Friendship Junior College	3433	81
Morris College	3439	100
South Carolina State College	3446	99
Voorhees College	3455	98

Table A6-4   Continued.

Traditionally Black Institutions	Federal Interagency Committee on Education Code	Percentage Black
Tennessee		
Fisk University	3490	99
Knoxville College	3497	95
Lane College	3499	99
LeMoyne-Owen College	3501	99
Morristown College	3512	98
Tennessee State University	3522	92
Texas		
Bishop College	3548	99
Huston-Tillotson College	3577	70
Jarvis Christian College	3637	98
Paul Quinn College	3602	95
Prairie View Agricultural and Mechanical University	3630	99
Southwestern Christian College	3618	93
Texas College	3638	100
Texas Southern University	3642	87
Wiley College	3669	98
Virginia		
Hampton Institute	3714	97
Norfolk State College	3765	96
St. Paul's College	3739	100
The Virginia College	3762	99
Virginia State College	3764	96
Virginia Union University	3766	95

Traditionally but Not Predominantly Black Institutions	Federal Interagency Committee on Education Code	Percentage Black
Missouri		
Lincoln University	2479	39
West Virginia		
Bluefield State College	3809	16
West Virginia State College	3826	20

Table A6-4   Continued.

Predominantly Black Institutions	Federal Interagency Committee on Education Code	Percentage Black
2-Year Institutions		
California		
Compton Community College	1188	86
Los Angeles Southwest College	7047	92
Nairobi College	9240	96
District of Columbia		
Washington Technical Institute	6957	89
Georgia		
Atlanta Junior College	12165	94
Illinois		
Central YMCA Community College	1644	62
City Colleges of Chicago, Kennedy-King College	1654	97
City Colleges of Chicago, The Loop College	1652	58
City Colleges of Chicago, Malcolm X College	1650	83
City Colleges of Chicago, Olive-Harvey College	9767	95
State Community College	9332	100
Maryland		
Bay College of Maryland	10297	95
Community College of Baltimore	2061	80
Massachusetts		
Roxbury Community College	11930	68
Michigan		
Highland Park Community College	2271	97
Lewis College of Business- Lewis Business College	3968	98
Wayne County Community College	9230	74
Mississippi		
Ministerial Institute and College	9229	99
Missouri		
St. Louis Community College at Forest Park	2471	61
New Jersey		
Essex County College	7107	68
New York		
College for Human Services	9769	71
Collegiate Institute	7807	61

Table A6-4   Continued.

Predominantly Black Institutions	Federal Interagency Committee on Education (FICE) Code	Percentage Black
Interboro Institute	8435	65
Taylor Business Institute	4825	68
North Carolina		
Durham College	4836	94
Roanoke-Chowan Technical Institute	8613	59
Ohio		
Cuyahoga Community College, Metropolitan Campus	7103	60
Payne Theological Seminary	10017	70
Pennsylvania		
Community College of Philadelphia	3249	60
South Carolina		
Beaufort Technical Education Center	9910	52
Trident Technical College, Palmer Campus	3443	67
Tennessee		
Shelby State Community College	10439	72

4-Year Institutions

District of Columbia		
Federal City College	7015	85
Strayer College	1459	64
Trinity College[2]	1460	52
Illinois		
Chicago State University[3]	1694	67
Daniel Hale Williams University	29037	65
Michigan		
Detroit Institute of Technology	2257	60
Shaw College at Detroit	2289	99
Missouri		
Harris Teachers College	2466	72

[2]Excluding part-time enrollment Trinity College is not predominantly black. Full-time black students are 13% of the enrollment.

[3]Enrollment percentages include students enrolled in Master's degree programs, therefore undergraduate figures would be slightly different.

Table A6-4   Continued.

Predominantly Black Institutions	Federal Interagency Committee on Education (FICE) Code	Percentage Black
New York		
City University of New York, Medgar Evers College	10097	83
City University of New York, York College	4759	53
Tennessee		
American Baptist Theological Seminary	10460	84
Virgin Islands		
College of the Virgin Islands	8841	69
Total PBI's = 44		

Table A7-1   EMPLOYER CATEGORIES FOR 1960–74 Ph.D's PLANNING IMMEDIATE EMPLOYMENT

Field of Doctorate	Men						Women						Total					
	1960–1964	1965–1968	1969–1970	1971–1972	1973–1974	Total, 1960–1974	1960–1964	1965–1968	1969–1970	1971–1972	1973–1974	Total, 1960–1974	1960–1964	1965–1968	1969–1970	1971–1972	1973–1974	Total, 1960–1974
Mathematics																		
College/university	68.6	74.5	81.8	81.7	72.7	75.9	78.1	78.7	95.7	84.6	74.9	81.8	69.2	74.7	82.7	81.9	72.9	76.3
Business/industry	14.1	11.1	11.7	8.8	13.4	11.7	5.3	3.0	2.2	5.1	8.4	5.0	13.6	10.6	11.0	8.5	12.8	11.2
U.S. Government	3.4	2.8	2.0	3.8	4.3	3.2		.6		1.9	3.0	1.3	3.2	2.6	1.9	3.7	4.2	3.1
U.S. state/local governments	.3	.1	.3	.2	.2	.2					.5	.1	.3	.1	.3	.2	.3	.2
Non-profit	2.9	1.9	2.1	1.2	1.3	1.8	1.8	1.8		.6	1.5	1.2	2.8	1.9	1.9	1.1	1.3	1.8
Other or unknown	10.8	9.7	2.1	4.4	8.1	7.2	14.9	16.0	2.2	7.7	11.8	10.6	11.0	10.1	2.1	4.6	8.5	7.4
Total employed	100.0	100.0	100.0	100.0	100.0	100.0	100.0	100.0	100.0	100.0	100.0	100.0	100.0	100.0	100.0	100.0	100.0	100.0
Physics																		
College/university	48.3	47.6	43.9	45.5	33.7	45.4	51.2	58.0	70.0	68.6	51.0	59.7	48.4	47.9	44.6	46.2	34.4	45.7
Business/industry	25.1	23.3	31.7	21.6	31.2	25.8	14.0	4.5	6.0	7.8	17.6	9.2	25.0	22.9	31.0	21.1	30.7	25.3
U.S. Government	8.0	10.8	9.7	17.0	16.8	11.4	4.7	4.5	4.0	5.9	5.9	4.9	8.0	10.6	9.6	16.6	16.4	11.3
U.S. state/local governments	.3	.2	1.4	.3	.3	.5							.2	.2	1.4	.3	.3	.4
Non-profit	5.0	3.2	5.0	2.9	2.9	3.9			4.0			.7	4.9	3.1	5.0	2.8	2.8	3.8
Other or unknown	13.2	14.9	8.3	12.8	15.0	13.1	30.2	33.0	16.0	17.6	25.5	25.4	13.5	15.3	8.5	12.9	15.5	13.4
Total employed	100.0	100.0	100.0	100.0	100.0	100.0	100.0	100.0	100.0	100.0	100.0	100.0	100.0	100.0	100.0	100.0	100.0	100.0
Chemistry																		
College/university	22.9	26.0	29.7	35.7	23.9	26.6	39.7	45.4	62.6	61.0	37.0	48.4	23.7	27.2	32.2	37.8	25.2	28.1
Business/industry	58.9	56.5	59.8	45.0	58.7	56.6	27.4	20.9	20.0	19.5	38.2	24.8	57.3	54.2	56.8	42.8	56.6	54.4
U.S. Government	4.0	4.1	3.5	6.2	5.2	4.3	6.4	2.1	4.2	4.5	3.6	4.1	4.1	3.9	3.6	6.1	5.1	4.3
U.S. state/local governments	.3	.4	.8	1.9	1.0	.7			1.1		.6	.3	.3	.3	.8	1.7	1.0	.7
Non-profit	2.3	1.7	2.2	2.0	1.8	2.0	2.3	2.8	2.1	1.9	1.8	2.3	2.3	1.7	2.2	2.0	1.8	2.0
Other or unknown	11.5	11.4	4.0	9.2	9.3	9.7	24.2	28.7	10.0	13.0	18.8	20.2	12.2	12.5	4.5	9.5	10.3	10.4
Total employed	100.0	100.0	100.0	100.0	100.0	100.0	100.0	100.0	100.0	100.0	100.0	100.0	100.0	100.0	100.0	100.0	100.0	100.0
Earth Sciences																		
College/university	38.5	45.8	52.3	51.6	41.8	45.4	50.0	50.0	56.0	73.7	59.0	57.7	38.7	45.9	52.4	52.1	42.7	45.7
Business/industry	23.1	21.7	25.2	21.6	24.2	22.9		3.6	4.0	10.5	20.5	9.8	22.8	21.4	24.5	21.4	24.1	22.6

Table A7-1 Continued.

Field of Doctorate	Men						Women						Total					
	1960–1964	1965–1968	1969–1970	1971–1972	1973–1974	Total, 1960–1974	1960–1964	1965–1968	1969–1970	1971–1972	1973–1974	Total, 1960–1974	1960–1964	1965–1968	1969–1970	1971–1972	1973–1974	Total, 1960–1974
U.S. Government	14.1	13.1	9.4	11.9	14.6	12.8		21.4	16.0	10.5		9.8	14.0	13.2	9.7	11.8	13.9	12.7
U.S. state/local governments	2.4	2.1	3.4	3.6	4.7	3.0			8.0			1.6	2.4	2.1	3.6	3.5	4.4	3.0
Non-profit	3.0	2.0	2.5	1.6	1.7	2.2			8.0		2.6	2.4	3.0	1.9	2.6	1.5	1.8	2.2
Other or unknown	18.8	15.3	7.3	9.7	12.9	13.6	50.0	25.0	8.0	5.3	17.9	18.7	19.1	15.5	7.3	9.6	13.2	13.8
Total employed	100.0	100.0	100.0	100.0	100.0	100.0	100.0	100.0	100.0	100.0	100.0	100.0	100.0	100.0	100.0	100.0	100.0	100.0
Engineering																		
College/university	39.7	34.3	32.6	32.0	25.6	33.2	31.0	24.1	54.2	54.5	53.6	45.7	39.7	34.2	32.7	32.1	26.0	33.3
Business/industry	42.1	43.6	51.0	46.0	54.0	46.8	24.1	37.9	29.2	21.2	24.6	26.6	42.0	43.6	50.9	45.9	53.6	46.7
U.S. Government	3.1	6.1	6.0	10.2	9.3	6.7	6.9	3.4	4.2	9.1	11.6	8.2	3.1	6.1	6.0	10.2	9.3	6.8
U.S. state/local governments	.2	.3	1.1	1.0	.9	.7					1.4	.5	.2	.3	1.1	1.0	1.0	.7
Non-profit	3.5	3.7	3.7	2.6	3.3	3.4		3.4		3.0	1.4	2.2	3.5	3.7	3.7	2.6	3.2	3.4
Other or unknown	11.3	12.0	5.6	8.3	6.9	9.2	34.5	31.0	12.5	12.1	7.2	16.8	11.4	12.1	5.6	8.3	6.9	9.2
Total employed	100.0	100.0	100.0	100.0	100.0	100.0	100.0	100.0	100.0	100.0	100.0	100.0	100.0	100.0	100.0	100.0	100.0	100.0
Employment total																		
College/university	40.1	41.2	42.3	44.3	35.9	40.9	51.1	55.9	73.4	70.9	56.7	61.0	40.4	41.6	43.3	45.3	37.0	41.6
Business/industry	38.8	36.9	42.5	34.4	42.5	38.7	18.9	13.4	12.1	12.3	21.6	15.8	38.3	36.2	41.5	33.7	41.4	37.9
U.S. Government	5.1	6.5	5.6	9.5	9.1	6.9	4.3	3.0	3.5	4.4	4.4	3.9	5.1	6.4	5.6	9.3	8.9	6.8
U.S. state/local governments	.4	.4	1.1	1.1	1.0	.7			.9		.6	.3	.4	.4	1.1	1.0	1.0	.7
Non-profit	3.4	2.8	3.3	2.2	2.5	2.9	1.9	2.0	1.9	1.2	1.5	1.7	3.3	2.8	3.2	2.2	2.5	2.8
Other or unknown	12.2	12.3	5.2	8.4	8.9	9.9	23.7	25.7	8.2	11.1	15.2	17.3	12.5	12.6	5.3	8.5	9.2	10.1
Total employed	100.0	100.0	100.0	100.0	100.0	100.0	100.0	100.0	100.0	100.0	100.0	100.0	100.0	100.0	100.0	100.0	100.0	100.0
Agricultural Sciences																		
College/university	43.5	44.3	59.7	54.5	49.7	49.5	42.3	41.9	61.5	73.9	60.3	58.3	43.5	44.2	59.7	55.0	50.1	49.7
Business/industry	9.5	9.8	14.8	12.6	17.7	12.5	3.8	12.9	15.4	2.2	19.0	10.7	9.4	9.9	14.8	12.3	17.8	12.4
U.S. Government	12.9	12.7	7.7	10.8	8.9	10.9		3.2		6.5	8.6	5.3	12.8	12.5	7.6	10.7	8.9	10.8

U.S. state/local governments	1.7	1.6	4.2	2.1	2.5	2.3		3.2		6.5		2.1	1.7	1.6	4.2	2.0	2.5	2.3
Non-profit	1.0	1.1	1.8	2.3	2.5	1.7							1.0	1.1	1.8	2.4	2.5	1.7
Other or unknown	31.4	30.6	11.8	17.7	18.5	23.1	53.8	38.7	23.1	10.9	12.1	23.5	31.7	30.7	12.0	17.6	18.3	23.1
Total employed	100.0	100.0	100.0	100.0	100.0	100.0	100.0	100.0	100.0	100.0	100.0	100.0	100.0	100.0	100.0	100.0	100.0	100.0
Medical Sciences																		
College/university	47.2	47.5	58.4	60.8	53.8	52.7	50.0	59.0	69.8	64.9	65.6	63.2	47.4	48.7	60.0	61.4	56.5	54.0
Business/industry	19.6	19.4	16.7	15.6	19.4	18.3	7.7	5.7	4.7	4.1	7.0	5.8	18.8	17.9	15.0	14.0	16.6	16.6
U.S. Government	6.3	5.8	7.3	7.0	6.8	6.5	9.6	4.8	3.5	4.1	6.4	5.4	6.6	5.7	6.8	6.6	6.7	6.4
U.S. state/local governments	2.8	3.8	4.9	3.1	6.0	4.0		8.6	4.7	5.2	5.1	5.2	2.6	4.3	4.8	3.4	5.8	4.1
Non-profit	4.4	3.9	3.6	4.8	7.2	4.6	5.8	3.8	8.1	14.4	7.0	7.8	4.5	3.9	4.2	6.1	7.1	5.1
Other or unknown	19.7	19.7	9.2	8.8	6.8	13.9	26.9	18.1	9.3	7.2	8.9	12.5	20.2	19.5	9.2	8.6	7.3	13.7
Total employed	100.0	100.0	100.0	100.0	100.0	100.0	100.0	100.0	100.0	100.0	100.0	100.0	100.0	100.0	100.0	100.0	100.0	100.0
Biosciences																		
College/university	56.0	58.5	70.7	65.6	57.3	60.8	66.1	61.8	77.5	73.9	66.2	68.1	57.2	59.0	71.7	67.1	58.8	61.9
Business/industry	9.8	8.2	10.8	8.9	13.3	9.9	2.7	2.5	3.1	3.7	4.8	3.3	8.9	7.3	9.7	8.0	11.8	8.9
U.S. Government	9.2	9.3	5.5	8.0	8.1	8.3	4.5	4.2	3.1	4.0	3.2	3.9	8.7	8.6	5.1	7.3	7.2	7.6
U.S. state/local governments	2.1	1.7	3.0	3.2	3.6	2.5	1.8	.8	2.9	1.1	2.2	1.6	2.0	1.5	3.0	2.9	3.3	2.4
Non-profit	3.5	3.8	3.4	4.2	4.5	3.8	5.6	6.5	3.8	5.0	4.8	5.3	3.8	4.2	3.4	4.3	4.6	4.1
Other or unknown	19.4	18.5	6.7	10.1	13.3	14.7	19.2	24.1	9.6	12.3	18.7	17.7	19.4	19.3	7.2	10.5	14.2	15.2
Total employed	100.0	100.0	100.0	100.0	100.0	100.0	100.0	100.0	100.0	100.0	100.0	100.0	100.0	100.0	100.0	100.0	100.0	100.0
Life Sciences Total																		
College/university	51.2	53.2	65.7	61.2	54.2	56.3	63.8	60.9	75.5	72.7	65.6	66.9	52.3	54.1	66.7	62.6	55.8	57.5
Business/industry	10.7	9.9	12.8	11.0	15.6	11.6	3.0	3.2	3.9	3.6	6.5	4.0	10.1	9.2	11.8	10.1	14.3	10.8
U.S. Government	10.0	9.9	6.4	8.8	8.2	8.9	4.9	4.2	3.0	4.2	4.4	4.2	9.6	9.2	6.0	8.3	7.7	8.4
U.S. state/local governments	2.0	1.9	3.6	2.8	3.5	2.6	1.6	1.7	3.0	2.7	2.1	2.1	2.0	1.9	3.5	2.7	3.4	2.6
Non-profit	2.8	3.0	2.9	3.6	4.1	3.2	5.4	6.1	4.3	4.9	5.5	5.5	3.1	3.4	3.0	3.9	4.2	3.5
Other or unknown	23.1	22.0	8.7	12.6	14.4	17.3	21.3	23.9	10.2	11.5	16.0	17.3	23.0	22.2	8.8	12.4	14.6	17.3
Total employed	100.0	100.0	100.0	100.0	100.0	100.0	100.0	100.0	100.0	100.0	100.0	100.0	100.0	100.0	100.0	100.0	100.0	100.0
Psychology																		
College/university	46.4	58.0	63.4	56.9	48.7	54.4	47.0	48.0	55.7	54.7	49.4	50.9	46.5	55.8	61.5	56.3	48.9	53.5
Business/industry	7.0	5.0	5.5	3.6	5.1	5.3	1.4	2.0	1.3	2.4	2.5	2.0	6.0	4.4	4.4	3.3	4.3	4.5
U.S. Government	10.0	5.5	3.3	4.7	4.6	5.8	5.7	3.8	2.8	3.5	3.2	3.7	9.2	5.1	3.2	4.4	4.2	5.3
U.S. state/local governments	13.8	12.2	12.0	15.9	14.1	13.6	10.5	11.8	15.3	11.6	14.0	12.8	13.2	12.2	12.8	14.7	14.1	13.4

Table A7-1 Continued.

Field of Doctorate	Men 1960-1964	Men 1965-1968	Men 1969-1970	Men 1971-1972	Men 1973-1974	Men Total, 1960-1974	Women 1960-1964	Women 1965-1968	Women 1969-1970	Women 1971-1972	Women 1973-1974	Women Total, 1960-1974	Total 1960-1964	Total 1965-1968	Total 1969-1970	Total 1971-1972	Total 1973-1974	Total, 1960-1974
Non-profit	9.4	8.2	8.9	9.3	14.0	9.9	11.1	12.2	11.9	11.5	13.5	12.2	9.7	9.0	9.6	9.9	13.9	10.5
Other or unknown	13.4	11.1	6.9	9.7	13.4	11.1	24.3	22.2	13.0	16.3	17.4	18.5	15.5	13.5	8.4	11.4	14.6	12.9
Total employed	100.0	100.0	100.0	100.0	100.0	100.0	100.0	100.0	100.0	100.0	100.0	100.0	100.0	100.0	100.0	100.0	100.0	100.0
Economics and Econometrics																		
College/university	62.1	64.5	77.0	72.0	69.2	68.0	59.3	62.5	72.7	71.0	77.6	69.2	62.0	64.4	76.7	71.9	69.8	68.1
Business/industry	5.9	5.0	5.2	6.0	6.5	5.7	2.3	5.4	5.7	8.1	3.2	5.0	5.8	5.0	5.2	6.2	6.2	5.6
U.S. Government	8.6	7.3	5.3	8.0	8.0	7.5	9.3	8.0	6.8	5.6	8.8	7.7	8.6	7.3	5.4	7.8	8.0	7.5
U.S. state/local governments	.9	.7	1.9	1.2	2.2	1.3	1.2	.9	2.3	.8	.8	.9	1.0	.7	1.9	1.1	2.1	1.3
Non-profit	4.1	3.6	4.7	4.2	3.9	4.0	7.0		6.8	7.3	2.4	4.7	4.3	3.4	4.8	4.5	3.8	4.1
Other or unknown	18.3	18.9	5.9	8.6	10.3	13.5	20.9	23.2	5.7	7.3	7.2	12.5	18.4	19.1	5.9	8.5	10.0	13.4
Total employed	100.0	100.0	100.0	100.0	100.0	100.0	100.0	100.0	100.0	100.0	100.0	100.0	100.0	100.0	100.0	100.0	100.0	100.0
Social Sciences																		
College/university	71.6	78.0	85.9	85.6	78.8	80.2	66.3	77.6	87.1	81.9	80.5	79.7	71.1	77.9	86.0	85.0	79.1	80.2
Business/industry	1.8	1.8	3.2	2.1	2.9	2.4	1.0	1.0	1.9	1.1	1.3	1.3	1.7	1.7	3.0	2.0	2.6	2.2
U.S. Government	5.4	3.0	1.8	2.6	3.1	3.1	2.9	2.2	.7	1.7	2.0	1.9	5.1	2.9	1.7	2.5	2.9	2.9
U.S. state/local governments	2.0	1.7	1.9	1.6	2.9	2.0	3.8	1.0	2.4	3.2	2.3	2.5	2.2	1.6	2.0	1.9	2.8	2.1
Non-profit	3.5	2.9	3.0	2.9	3.5	3.2	5.4	3.2	3.6	4.3	4.1	4.1	3.7	2.9	3.1	3.2	3.6	3.3
Other or unknown	15.7	12.6	4.2	5.1	8.7	9.1	20.5	14.9	4.3	7.8	9.8	10.6	16.2	12.9	4.2	5.5	8.9	9.3
Total employed	100.0	100.0	100.0	100.0	100.0	100.0	100.0	100.0	100.0	100.0	100.0	100.0	100.0	100.0	100.0	100.0	100.0	100.0
Behavioral Science Total																		
College/university	59.0	67.2	75.8	73.1	66.3	68.1	53.4	58.7	67.0	66.6	63.5	62.4	58.3	66.0	74.4	71.9	65.7	67.1
Business/industry	5.0	3.8	4.5	3.4	4.3	4.2	1.4	1.9	1.8	2.3	2.0	1.9	4.5	3.5	4.0	3.2	3.8	3.8
U.S. Government	8.1	5.0	3.1	4.4	4.6	5.1	5.2	3.6	2.4	3.0	3.0	3.3	7.7	4.8	3.0	4.1	4.2	4.8
U.S. state/local governments	2.3	1.9	2.8	3.1	3.6	2.6	4.5	4.2	6.7	5.0	6.2	5.3	2.5	2.1	3.2	3.3	3.9	2.9
Non-profit	3.9	3.4	3.8	3.5	4.6	3.8	6.7	6.5	6.4	6.8	7.1	6.7	4.1	3.6	4.1	3.9	4.9	4.1

Other or unknown	15.6	14.6	6.0	8.9	10.6	11.7	22.6	22.3	9.5	11.9	14.4	16.1	16.0	15.2	6.3	9.2	11.2	12.1
Total employed	100.0	100.0	100.0	100.0	100.0	100.0	100.0	100.0	100.0	100.0	100.0	100.0	100.0	100.0	100.0	100.0	100.0	100.0
Science total																		
College/university	47.4	50.0	56.1	57.0	50.4	51.8	56.0	58.8	70.3	68.7	62.9	63.3	48.0	50.6	57.4	58.2	52.2	52.9
Business/industry	23.8	23.3	26.1	19.7	23.5	23.3	5.3	4.5	4.3	4.1	5.9	4.8	22.5	21.9	24.2	18.1	21.1	21.6
U.S. Government	7.0	6.8	5.1	7.7	7.3	6.8	4.9	3.7	2.8	3.5	3.5	3.6	6.9	6.6	4.9	7.3	6.8	6.5
U.S. state/local governments	2.3	1.9	2.8	3.1	3.6	2.6	4.5	4.2	6.7	5.0	6.2	5.3	2.5	2.1	3.2	3.3	3.9	2.9
Non-profit	3.9	3.4	3.8	6.7	6.5	6.4	6.8	7.1	6.7	6.5	6.4	6.8	7.1	6.7	4.1	3.9	4.9	4.1
Other or unknown	15.6	14.6	6.0	8.9	10.6	11.7	22.6	22.3	9.5	11.9	14.4	16.1	16.0	15.2	6.3	9.2	11.2	12.1
Total employed	100.0	100.0	100.0	100.0	100.0	100.0	100.0	100.0	100.0	100.0	100.0	100.0	100.0	100.0	100.0	100.0	100.0	100.0
Humanities																		
College/university	87.2	88.6	94.1	91.1	80.6	88.2	84.0	84.2	91.4	89.5	79.6	85.3	86.7	87.7	93.4	90.7	80.3	87.6
Business/industry	.8	.8	.8	.9	2.1	1.1	.4	.3	.4	.7	1.9	.9	.7	.7	.7	.9	2.0	1.0
U.S. Government	1.3	.8	.5	.9	1.4	1.0	.5	.5	.5	.7	.6	.6	1.2	.8	.5	.9	1.2	.9
U.S. state/local governments	.3	.3	.3	.5	.8	.4	.1	.4	.4	.1	.5	.3	.3	.4	.3	.4	.7	.4
Non-profit	1.7	1.5	1.3	1.4	2.6	1.7	1.7	1.8	.6	1.1	1.5	1.3	1.7	1.5	1.2	1.3	2.3	1.6
Other or unknown	8.7	8.0	3.1	5.2	12.6	7.6	13.3	12.8	6.8	7.8	15.8	11.6	9.4	8.9	3.9	5.9	13.6	8.5
Total employed	100.0	100.0	100.0	100.0	100.0	100.0	100.0	100.0	100.0	100.0	100.0	100.0	100.0	100.0	100.0	100.0	100.0	100.0
Professions																		
College/university	68.1	73.8	84.1	79.8	75.9	76.2	66.9	72.1	80.4	72.4	79.3	74.2	67.9	73.6	83.6	78.8	76.3	76.0
Business/industry	4.4	5.0	4.6	5.2	6.0	5.1	.7	1.5	1.2	2.7	1.5	1.5	4.0	4.6	4.2	4.9	5.4	4.6
U.S. Government	1.3	1.1	1.9	2.3	2.8	1.9	2.5	1.5	3.1	3.3	2.7	2.6	1.5	1.1	2.1	2.4	2.8	1.9
U.S. state/local governments	.5	.7	.7	1.1	1.1	.8	2.5	1.2	4.6	2.1	.9	2.1	.8	.8	1.2	1.2	1.1	1.0
Non-profit	11.3	7.4	4.6	7.6	9.6	8.1	6.5	5.0	5.4	8.6	7.1	6.6	10.7	7.2	4.7	7.8	9.3	7.9
Other or unknown	14.4	12.0	4.1	4.0	4.6	7.9	20.9	18.8	5.4	11.0	8.6	13.0	15.2	12.8	4.3	4.9	5.1	8.5
Total employed	100.0	100.0	100.0	100.0	100.0	100.0	100.0	100.0	100.0	100.0	100.0	100.0	100.0	100.0	100.0	100.0	100.0	100.0
Education																		
College/university	56.8	61.0	67.5	60.1	47.6	58.6	64.2	66.1	74.1	68.4	59.2	65.8	58.2	62.0	68.8	62.0	50.7	60.1
Business/industry	.8	.9	.9	.9	1.2	.9	.3	.6	.7	.6	1.2	.7	.7	.8	.8	.8	1.2	.9
U.S. Government	1.3	1.0	.9	1.4	1.8	1.3	.6	1.1	.8	1.1	1.5	1.1	1.2	1.0	.9	1.3	1.7	1.3
U.S. state/local governments	3.7	3.3	5.5	5.9	8.4	5.4	2.7	2.4	4.1	4.2	5.8	4.0	3.5	3.2	5.2	5.5	7.7	5.1
Non-profit	2.8	3.1	2.9	3.6	4.1	3.3	3.3	3.5	3.8	3.6	3.7	3.6	2.9	3.2	3.1	3.6	4.0	3.4
Other or unknown	34.6	30.6	22.3	28.0	36.8	30.5	28.9	26.3	16.5	22.2	28.7	24.8	33.5	29.8	21.1	26.7	34.7	29.2
Total employed	100.0	100.0	100.0	100.0	100.0	100.0	100.0	100.0	100.0	100.0	100.0	100.0	100.0	100.0	100.0	100.0	100.0	100.0

Table A7-1 Continued.

	Men						Women						Total					
Field of Doctorate	1960-1964	1965-1968	1969-1970	1971-1972	1973-1974	Total, 1960-1974	1960-1964	1965-1968	1969-1970	1971-1972	1973-1974	Total, 1960-1974	1960-1964	1965-1968	1969-1970	1971-1972	1973-1974	Total, 1960-1974
Non-Science Total																		
College/university	70.3	73.3	78.7	72.9	62.4	71.5	71.8	74.1	81.7	76.9	68.5	74.2	70.5	73.5	79.3	73.8	64.0	72.0
Business/industry	1.2	1.3	1.3	1.5	2.1	1.5	.4	.5	.6	.8	1.5	.8	1.1	1.2	1.2	1.3	1.9	1.3
U.S. Government	1.3	1.0	.9	1.4	1.8	1.3	.7	.9	.9	1.1	1.2	1.0	1.2	.9	.9	1.3	1.6	1.2
U.S. state/local governments	2.0	1.9	3.1	3.5	4.9	3.0	1.7	1.5	2.6	2.5	3.4	2.4	1.9	1.8	3.0	3.3	4.5	2.9
Non-profit	3.4	3.0	2.6	3.4	4.2	3.3	3.0	2.9	2.6	2.9	3.0	2.9	3.3	3.0	2.6	3.3	3.9	3.2
Other or unknown	21.9	19.6	13.4	17.4	24.6	19.4	22.5	20.1	11.8	15.9	22.4	18.7	22.0	19.7	13.1	17.1	24.0	19.3
Total employed	100.0	100.0	100.0	100.0	100.0	100.0	100.0	100.0	100.0	100.0	100.0	100.0	100.0	100.0	100.0	100.0	100.0	100.0
Grand total																		
College/university	55.5	58.7	65.3	63.9	55.8	59.7	65.7	68.3	77.6	74.1	66.5	70.2	56.6	59.8	67.0	65.6	58.0	61.2
Business/industry	15.8	15.1	16.1	11.7	13.9	14.6	2.2	2.1	1.9	1.9	3.1	2.3	14.3	13.5	14.1	10.1	11.7	12.8
U.S. Government	5.0	4.6	3.4	4.9	4.8	4.6	2.3	1.9	1.5	1.9	2.0	2.0	4.7	4.3	3.1	4.4	4.3	4.2
U.S. state/local governments	2.2	1.9	2.9	3.3	4.2	2.8	2.8	2.5	4.0	3.3	4.4	3.5	2.3	2.0	3.1	3.3	4.2	2.9
Non-profit	3.7	3.2	3.3	3.5	4.4	3.6	4.4	4.2	3.9	4.3	4.4	4.3	3.8	3.4	3.4	3.6	4.4	3.7
Other or unknown	17.8	16.5	9.0	12.7	16.9	14.8	22.5	21.0	11.0	14.5	19.6	17.8	18.3	17.0	9.3	13.0	17.4	15.2
Total employed	100.0	100.0	100.0	100.0	100.0	100.0	100.0	100.0	100.0	100.0	100.0	100.0	100.0	100.0	100.0	100.0	100.0	100.0

Source: National Research Council, *A Century of Doctorates* (Washington, D.C.: National Academy of Sciences, 1978), Table 32, pp. 82–83.

Table A7-2   STOCK OF COLLEGE TEACHERS
1970

Type	Total	Non-Black	Black	Percentage Non-Black	Percentage Black
Agriculture	5,157	5,070	87	98.3	1.7
Atmosphere, earth, marine, space science	4,782	4,782	0	100.0	0.0
Biology	20,398	19,920	478	97.7	2.3
Chemistry	15,382	15,092	290	98.1	1.9
Physics	14,212	14,066	146	99.0	1.0
Engineering	26,474	26,236	238	99.1	0.9
Mathematics	25,641	24,814	827	96.8	3.2
Health	28,178	26,966	1,212	95.7	4.3
Psychology	12,908	12,595	313	97.6	2.4
Business and Commerce	13,915	13,296	619	95.6	4.4
Economics	10,183	10,055	128	98.7	1.3
History	17,092	16,589	503	97.1	2.9
Sociology	6,918	6,573	345	95.0	5.0
Social Science	12,732	12,345	387	97.0	3.0
Art, Drama, and Music	30,654	29,599	1,055	96.6	3.4
Physical Education	17,023	16,375	648	96.2	3.8
Education	7,552	7,226	326	95.7	4.3
English	39,412	38,302	1,110	97.2	2.8
Foreign Language	21,256	20,910	346	98.4	1.6
Home Economics	4,285	4,010	275	93.6	6.4
Law	3,005	2,943	62	97.9	2.1
Theology	5,189	5,119	70	98.7	1.3
Trade, industrial and technical	3,433	3,122	311	90.9	9.1
Miscellaneous	19,393	19,109	284	98.5	1.5
Not specified	140,538	134,015	6,523	95.4	4.6
Total	496,412	479,830	16,582	96.7	3.3

Source: U.S. Bureau of the Census, Detailed Characteristics of the Population, 1970. Reproduced in The Case for Affirmative Action for Blacks in Higher Education, Fleming, Gill, and Swinton, ISEP, Washington, D.C. (1978), Table 7-2, p. 215.

Table A7-3   PROPORTION OF POPULATION HOLDING ADVANCED DEGREES

Cohort Birth Years	Census* Year	Gender	Population Age 25 and Up	Master's and Professional Degrees		Ph.D. Degrees Granted in the Decade		
				Number	Percentage	Corresponding Ph.D. Years	Number† (from DRF)	Per Million Population Age 25 and Up
1886-1895‡	1940	M	7,962,019	107,941	1.36	1916-1925	6,527	820
		F	7,550,052	46,224	0.61		1,189	157
		Total	15,512,071	154,165	0.99		7,716	497
1896-1905	1940	M	9,164,794	156,938	1.71	1926-1935	17,922	1,956
		F	9,168,426	83,720	0.91		3,114	340
		Total	18,333,220	227,308	1.24		21,037	1,147
1906-1915	1940	M	10,520,974	216,152	2.05§	1936-1945	23,553	2,239
		F	10,818,052	86,040	0.80§		3,974	367
		Total	21,339,026	302,216	1.42§		27,503	1,289
1916-1925	1960	M	11,757,900	590,594	5.02	1946-1955	55,542	4,724
		F	12,336,433	224,778	1.83		6,304	420
		Total	24,094,333	815,372	3.38		61,874	2,568
1926-1935	1970	M	11,273,090	890,602	7.90	1956-1965	101,442	8,999
		F	11,865,637	345,966	2.91		12,269	1,034
		Total	23,138,727	1,236,060	5.34		113,713	4,983
1936-1945	1970	M	12,162,643	926,285	7.61§	1966-1975	243,324	20,005
		F	12,676,202	400,401	3.16§	(1975	46,586	3,675
		Total	24,838,845	1,326,685	5.34§	estimated)	289,873	11,670

Source: National Research Council, *A Century of Doctorates,* Washington, D.C. (1978), Table 14, p. 46.

*The 1950 census provided no data on postcollege degrees. Where a later census provided larger figures, for either population or degree holders, the later and larger figure was used.

†Ph.D. data were from the DRF, supplemented by USOE data for 1916-1919 (sex breakout estimated) and an estimate for 1975, for which complete data were unavailable.

‡Data for birth cohorts prior to 1886 were deemed too inaccurate for use because of deaths by 1940, the earliest date for which postcollege degree data were available.

§The data for these years in the census indicated are probably underestimates by 50-75 percent for the graduate degrees other than the Ph.D. Differences of

Table A7-4   NUMBER OF Ph.D.-GRANTING INSTITUTIONS IN THE UNITED STATES 1920-74

Time Period

Field of Doctorate	1920–1924	1925–1929	1930–1934	1935–1939	1940–1944	1945–1949	1950–1954	1955–1959	1960–1964	1965–1969	1970–1974
Mathematics	22	33	43	45	47	49	71	74	91	127	159
Physics	28	37	46	55	55	54	74	84	114	150	167
Chemistry	43	47	66	76	74	84	100	112	143	171	194
Earth Sciences	24	24	37	38	39	38	50	59	74	96	121
Engineering	19	24	32	37	37	49	63	75	97	127	151
Life Sciences	42	57	65	70	74	81	99	122	144	178	224
Psychology	28	31	43	46	49	53	77	88	112	149	183
Social Sciences	30	45	51	54	58	63	79	92	104	128	166
Humanities and Professions	41	53	64	71	77	85	96	113	134	172	212
Education	34	44	53	58	60	67	86	99	116	138	173
Total	61	75	87	102	107	126	142	171	208	244	307

Source: National Research Council, *A Century of Doctorates*, Washington, D.C. (1978), Table 39, p. 95.

Table A7-5   MAJOR FIELD DISTRIBUTION OF DEGREES AWARDED TO
              BLACK STUDENTS
              1975-76

| | Baccalaureates | | Master's | | Doctorates | |
Major Field	All Students	Black Students	All Students	Black Students	All Students	Black Students
Total	100.0	100.0	100.0	100.0	100.0	100.0
Agriculture	2.1	0.4	1.1	0.4	2.7	1.5
Architecture	1.0	0.4	1.0	1.0	0.2	0.4
Biological Sciences	5.9	3.9	2.1	1.1	10.0	4.3
Business and Management	15.5	16.1	13.6	7.6	2.8	1.4
Education	16.9	24.0	41.4	61.1	23.0	55.2
Engineering	4.9	2.3	5.1	1.1	8.3	1.6
Health Professions	5.8	4.6	4.0	3.1	1.7	1.3
Mathematics	1.7	1.4	1.2	0.6	2.5	0.7
Physical Sciences	2.3	1.1	1.7	0.7	10.1	3.4
Psychology	5.4	5.4	2.5	2.0	7.6	5.4
Public Affairs	3.6	5.6	5.5	7.9	0.9	2.4
Social Sciences	13.7	18.6	5.1	4.3	12.2	9,6
All others	21.2	16.2	15.7	9.1	18.0	12.8

Source: Preliminary data from OCR/U.S. Department of Health, Education and Welfare. Published in National Advisory Committee on Black Education and Black Colleges and Universities, Higher Education Equity: *The Crisis of Appearance Versus Reality, First Annual Report 1977,* Washington, D.C. (1978), Chart 8, p. 15.

Table A7-6   DISTRIBUTION OF ESTIMATED GRADUATE ENROLLMENTS,
              DOCTORATES AWARDED, AND U.S. POPULATION (IN
              PERCENTAGES)

Racial/Ethnic Identity	Estimated Graduate Enrollments	Doctorates Awarded to Native Born U.S. Citizens, 1973-74	Distribution in U.S. Population, 1970
Total	100.0	100.0	100.0
White	90.8-94.6	94.5	83.1
Total minority	5.4-9.1	5.5	16.9
Black	3.3-5.2	3.5	11.1
American Indian	0.3-0.4	0.5	0.4
Oriental	0.8-0.2	0.6	0.9
Spanish-surnamed	1.0-0.4	0.9	4.6
Mexican American, Chicano, Spanish American	—	0.6	3.9
Puerto Rican	—	0.3	0.7

Source: National Board on Graduate Education, Minority Group Participation in Graduate Education (Washington, D.C.: National Board on Graduate Education, 1976), p. 45. Reproduced in Fleming, Gill, and Swinton, *The Case for Affirmative Action,* ISEP, Washington, D.C. (1978).

Table A7-7   MAJOR FIELD DISTRIBUTION OF PROFESSIONAL STUDENTS
IN THE UNITED STATES (IN PERCENTAGES)
1974

Major Field	Male		Female		Total	
	White	Black	White	Black	White	Black
Dentistry	10.4	10.8	3.2	8.6	9.1	10.0
Law	41.4	42.2	45.8	39.2	42.2	41.3
Medicine	26.0	32.9	24.6	31.9	25.7	32.6
Veterinary Medicine	2.8	0.1	3.4	0.3	3.0	0.2
Undecided	1.4	0.3	1.5	0.4	1.4	0.4
Other	18.0	13.7	21.6	19.6	13.6	15.5
Total (100% =)	(144,199)	(6,473)	(31,209)	(2,861)	(175,408)	(9,334)

Source: Gail Thomas, Equality of Representation of Race and Sex Group in Higher Education, Center for Social Organization of Schools, Baltimore, Maryland, Report No. 263 (October 1978), Table 3.

Note: At the graduate level professional refers to persons who have previously attained professional degrees in Nursing, Medicine, Law, Dentistry, etc., and are pursuing graduate degrees (i.e., Master's, Ph.D., LLD, etc.).

Table A7-8   FIRST-PROFESSIONAL EARNED DEGREES
Academic Years 1964–80

Academic Year Ending	Total	Male	Female
	Actual		
1965	28,755	27,748	1,007
1966	30,799	28,657	1,142
1967	32,472	31,178	1,294
1968	34,787	33,237	1,550
1969	36,018	34,499	1,519
1970	35,724	33,940	1,784
1971	37,946	35,544	2,402
1972	43,411	40,723	2,698
1973	50,018	46,489	3,529
1974	53,816	48,530	5,286
1975	55,916	48,956	6,960
1976	62,649	52,892	9,757
	Projected		
1977	61,800	50,250	11,550
1978	65,400	51,580	13,820
1979	66,600	51,380	15,210
1980	68,000	51,700	16,300
1981	69,700	52,480	17,240

Source: NCES, Department of Health, Education, and Welfare, The Condition of Education, 1978, Table 3.16, p. 138.

Table A7-9 FULL- AND PART-TIME ENROLLMENT IN INSTITUTIONS OF HIGHER EDUCATION BY SELECTED FIELDS OF STUDY, LEVEL OF ENROLLMENT, RACE AND ETHNICITY, AND NATURE OF CITIZENSHIP AND OTHER AREAS*
Fall 1976

Agriculture and Natural Resources	Black		Minority		White		Total
	Number	Percentage	Number	Percentage	Number	Percentage	Total
Undergraduate							
Full-time	2,292	1.89	6,915	5.71	112,370	92.86	121,010
Part-time	646	4.17	1,801	11.64	13,525	87.41	15,472
Total	2,938	2.15	8,716	6.38	125,895	92.24	136,482
Graduate							
Full-time	155	1.46	428	4.05	7,850	74.38	10,553
Part-time	96	1.93	293	5.91	3,956	79.80	4,957
Total	251	1.61	721	4.64	11,806	76.11	15,510
Professional							
Full-time	0	.00	2	8.69	16	69.56	23
Part-time	0	.00	0	.00	0	.00	0
Total	0	.00	2	8.69	16	69.56	23
U + G + P	3,189	2.09	9,439	6.20	137,723	90.59	152,021
Unclassified	37	.82	216	4.79	4,195	93.03	4,509
Total enrollment	3,226	2.06	9,655	6.16	141,918	90.66	156,530
Enrollment Figures Excluding Non-Resident/Alien Students							
U + G + P	3,189	2.16	8,408	5.63	137,723	92.23	147,162
Unclassified	37	.83	216	4.89	4,195	95.10	4,411
Total enrollment	3,226	2.12	8,919	5.88	141,918	93.63	153,731

Enrollment Figures Excluding Non-Resident/Alien and U.S. Trust Territory Students

	Black		Minority		White		Total
	Number	Percentage	Number	Percentage	Number	Percentage	
U + G + P	3,189	2.21	7,677	5.34	137,719	95.82	143,726
Unclassified	0	.00	5	100.00	0	.00	5
Total enrollment	3,189	2.21	7,682	5.34	137,719	95.81	143,731

Architecture and Environmental Design	Black		Minority		White		Total
	Number	Percentage	Number	Percentage	Number	Percentage	
Undergraduate							
Full-time	1,983	4.09	5,564	11.49	40,964	84.65	48,391
Part-time	568	5.68	1,586	15.59	8,399	82.56	10,172
Total	2,551	4.35	7,150	12.20	49,363	84.29	58,563
Graduate							
Full-time	397	5.03	786	9.96	6,307	79.99	7,884
Part-time	121	6.34	252	13.22	1,517	79.59	1,906
Total	518	5.29	1,038	10.6	7,824	79.9	9,790
Professional							
Full-time	1	4.00	2	8.00	23	92.00	25
Part-time	0	.00	0	.00	0	.00	0
Total	1	4.00	2	8.00	23	92.00	25
U + G + P	3,070	4.48	8,190	11.97	57,210	83.66	68,378
Unclassified	47	3.56	188	14.27	1,058	80.33	1,316
Total enrollment	3,117	4.47	8,378	12.02	58,268	83.60	69,694

Enrollment Figures Excluding Non-Resident/Alien Students

	Black		Minority		White		Total
U + G + P	3,070	4.68	8,190	12.50	57,210	87.35	65,492
Unclassified	47	3.84	188	15.37	1,058	86.50	1,223
Total enrollment	3,117	4.67	8,378	12.55	58,268	87.33	66,715

Table A7-9 Continued.

Architecture and Environmental Design	Black		Minority		White		Total
	Number	Percentage	Number	Percentage	Number	Percentage	
Enrollment Figures Excluding Non-Resident/Alien and U.S. Trust Territory Students							
U + G + P	3,070	4.81	7,311	11.47	57,210	89.76	63,734
Unclassified	47	3.96	169	14.26	1,058	89.28	1,185
Total enrollment	3,117	4.80	7,480	11.52	58,268	89.75	64,919

Biological Sciences	Black		Minority		White		Total
	Number	Percentage	Number	Percentage	Number	Percentage	
Undergraduate							
Full-time	16,929	7.24	32,826	14.04	196,731	84.18	233,696
Part-time	2,590	7.14	5,396	14.89	30,280	83.58	36,227
Total	19,519	7.23	38,222	14.16	227,011	84.10	269,923
Graduate							
Full-time	607	2.22	1,659	6.08	23,151	84.97	27,244
Part-time	518	3.34	1,279	8.25	13,431	86.64	15,502
Total	1,125	2.63	2,938	6.87	36,582	85.57	42,746
Professional							
Full-time	2	3.17	3	4.76	57	90.47	63
Part-time	0	.00	0	.00	5	100.00	5
Total	2	2.94	3	4.41	62	91.17	68
U + G + P	20,646	6.60	41,163	13.16	263,655	84.30	312,737

	Black		Minority		White		
Engineering	Number	Percentage	Number	Percentage	Number	Percentage	Total
Unclassified	453	5.42	976	11.68	7,206	86.25	8,354
Total enrollment	21,099	6.57	42,139	13.12	270,861	84.35	321,091

Enrollment Figures Excluding Non-Resident/Alien Students

	Black		Minority		White		
	Number	Percentage	Number	Percentage	Number	Percentage	Total
U + G + P	206,646	6.50	41,163	12.96	263,655	83.02	317,545
Unclassified	453	5.29	976	11.39	7,206	84.15	8,563
Total enrollment	21,099	6.46	42,139	12.92	270,851	83.05	326,108

Enrollment Figures Excluding Non-Resident/Alien and U.S. Trust Territory Students

	Black		Minority		White		
	Number	Percentage	Number	Percentage	Number	Percentage	Total
U + G + P	20,613	6.57	37,230	11.87	263,565	84.07	313,489
Unclassified	444	5.31	934	11.18	7,141	85.55	8,347
Total enrollment	21,057	6.54	38,164	11.85	270,706	84.11	321,836

	Black		Minority		White		
Engineering	Number	Percentage	Number	Percentage	Number	Percentage	Total
Undergraduate							
Full-time	15,677	5.06	35,830	11.57	251,617	81.30	309,457
Part-time	5,796	8.06	11,721	16.30	57,839	80.44	71,899
Total	21,473	5.63	47,551	12.46	309,456	81.14	381,356
Graduate							
Full-time	327	1.10	1,863	6.28	17,632	59.48	29,641
Part-time	497	1.75	2,424	8.58	22,595	79.98	28,248
Total	824	1.42	4,287	7.40	40,227	69.48	57,889
Professional							
Full-time	0	.00	1	1.19	78	92.85	84
Part-time	0	.00	0	.00	0	.00	0
Total	0	.00	0	.00	78	92.85	84

Table A7-9   Continued.

Engineering	Black		Minority		White		Total
	Number	Percentage	Number	Percentage	Number	Percentage	
U + G + P	22,297	5.07	51,839	11.79	349,761	79.61	439,329
Unclassified	461	3.72	1,508	12.17	10,139	81.83	12,389
Total enrollment	22,758	5.03	53,347	11.80	359,900	79.67	451,718

Enrollment Figures Excluding Non-Resident/Alien Students

	Black		Minority		White		Total
U + G + P	22,297	5.77	51,839	13.42	349,761	90.57	386,168
Unclassified	461	4.05	1,508	13.26	10,139	89.20	11,366
Total enrollment	22,758	5.72	53,347	13.41	359,900	90.53	397,534

Enrollment Figures Excluding Non-Resident/Alien and U.S. Trust Territory Students

	Black		Minority		White		Total
U + G + P	22,290	5.83	48,018	12.55	349,736	91.47	382,345
Unclassified	460	4.06	1,483	13.10	10,134	89.56	11,315
Total enrollment	22,750	5.77	49,501	12.57	359,870	91.42	393,630

Dentistry	Black		Minority		White		Total
	Number	Percentage	Number	Percentage	Number	Percentage	
Professional							
Full-time	797	3.95	1,983	9.85	17,893	88.88	20,131
Part-time	25	13.08	30	15.70	140	73.29	191
Total	822	4.04	2,013	9.90	18,033	88.73	20,322

	Black		Minority		White		Total
	Number	Percentage	Number	Percentage	Number	Percentage	
Unclassified	1	.58	11	6.43	152	88.88	171
Total enrollment	823	4.01	2,024	9.87	18,185	88.73	20,493

Enrollment Figures Excluding Non-Resident/Alien Students

	Black		Minority		White		Total
	Number	Percentage	Number	Percentage	Number	Percentage	
Professional	822	4.10	2,013	10.04	18,033	89.95	20,046
Unclassified	1	.61	11	6.74	152	93.25	163
Total enrollment	823	4.07	2,024	10.01	18,185	89.98	20,209

Enrollment Figures Excluding Non-Resident/Alien and U.S. Trust Territory Students

	Black		Minority		White		Total
	Number	Percentage	Number	Percentage	Number	Percentage	
Professional	822	3.98	1,793	8.63	18,032	87.33	20,647
Unclassified	1	.65	0	.00	152	99.35	153
Total enrollment	823	3.96	1,793	8.62	18,184	87.42	20,800

Medicine	*Black*		*Minority*		*White*		*Total*
	Number	*Percentage*	*Number*	*Percentage*	*Number*	*Percentage*	
Professional							
Full-time	3,431	5.93	6,724	11.63	50,330	87.10	57,778
Part-time	23	5.75	56	14.00	338	84.50	400
Total	3,454	5.93	6,780	11.65	50,668	87.09	58,178
Unclassified	10	2.39	17	4.07	378	90.64	417
Total enrollment	3,464	5.91	6,797	11.59	51,046	87.11	58,595

Enrollment Figures Excluding Non-Resident/Alien Students

	Black		Minority		White		Total
	Number	Percentage	Number	Percentage	Number	Percentage	
Professional	3,454	5.74	6,780	11.26	50,668	84.20	60,172
Unclassified	10	2.61	17	4.43	378	98.69	383
Total enrollment	3,464	5.72	6,797	11.22	51,046	84.29	60,555

Table A7-9   Continued.

Medicine	Black		Minority		White		Total
	Number	Percentage	Number	Percentage	Number	Percentage	
Enrollment Figures Excluding Non-Resident/Alien and U.S. Trust Territory Students							
Professional	3,454	5.78	6,277	10.52	50,661	84.91	59,662
Unclassified	10	2.61	17	4.43	378	98.69	383
Total enrollment	3,464	5.76	6,294	10.48	51,039	85.00	60,045

Veterinary Medicine	Black		Minority		White		Total
	Number	Percentage	Number	Percentage	Number	Percentage	
Professional							
Full-time	122	2.08	254	4.34	5,579	95.38	5,849
Part-time	3	1.08	4	1.44	270	97.47	277
Total	125	2.04	258	4.21	5,849	95.47	6,126
Unclassified	0	.00	0	.00	0	.00	0
Total enrollment	125	2.04	258	4.21	5,849	95.47	6,126
Enrollment Figures Excluding Non-Resident/Alien Students							
Professional	125	2.04	258	4.22	5,849	95.77	6,107
Unclassified	0	.00	0	.00	0	.00	0
Total enrollment	125	2.04	258	4.22	5,849	95.77	6,107
Enrollment Figures Excluding Non-Resident/Alien and U.S. Trust Territory Students							
Professional	125	2.04	258	4.22	5,849	95.77	6,107

	Black		Minority		White		
---	Number	Percentage	Number	Percentage	Number	Percentage	Total
Unclassified	0	.00	0	.00	0	.00	0
Total enrollment	125	2.04	258	4.22	5,849	95.77	6,107

Law	Number	Percentage	Number	Percentage	Number	Percentage	Total
Graduate							
Full-time	22	1.87	64	5.44	915	77.80	1,176
Part-time	36	1.55	97	4.20	2,119	91.77	2,309
Total	58	1.66	161	4.61	3,034	87.05	3,485
Professional							
Full-time	4,425	4.54	8,656	8.89	88,183	90.60	97,324
Part-time	947	4.90	1,816	9.39	17,411	90.10	19,323
Total	5,372	4.60	10,472	8.97	105,594	90.52	116,647
G + P	5,430	4.52	10,633	8.85	108,628	90.42	120,132
Unclassified	11	3.24	23	6.78	272	80.23	339
Total enrollment	5,441	4.51	10,656	8.84	108,900	90.39	120,471
Enrollment Figures Excluding Non-Resident/Alien Students							
G + P	5,430	4.38	10,633	8.58	108,628	87.73	123,820
Unclassified	11	4.19	23	8.77	272	92.20	295
Total enrollment	5,441	4.38	10,656	8.58	108,900	87.74	124,115
Enrollment Figures Excluding Non-Resident/Alien and U.S. Trust Territory Students							
G + P	5,430	4.38	9,743	7.86	108,628	87.74	123,001
Unclassified	11	4.19	23	8.77	272	92.20	295
Total enrollment	5,441	4.38	9,766	7.86	108,900	87.75	124,096

Table A7-9   Continued.

Physical Science	Black		Minority		White		
	Number	Percentage	Number	Percentage	Number	Percentage	Total
Undergraduate							
Full-time	4,916	4.71	9,548	9.15	91,626	87.81	104,335
Part-time	1,156	6.14	2,272	12.07	16,206	86.13	18,815
Total	6,072	4.93	11,820	9.59	107,832	87.56	123,150
Graduate							
Full-time	345	1.41	1,166	4.78	19,008	78.01	24,364
Part-time	287	2.68	758	7.08	8,959	83.76	10,695
Total	632	1.80	1,924	5.48	27,967	79.77	35,059
Professional							
Full-time	1	7.14	3	21.42	10	71.42	14
Part-time	0	.00	0	.00	1	50.00	2
Total	1	6.25	3	18.75	11	68.75	16
U + G + P	6,705	4.23	13,747	8.68	135,810	85.83	158,225
Unclassified	279	5.22	533	9.98	4,673	87.55	5,337
Total enrollment	6,984	4.26	14,280	8.73	140,483	85.88	163,562
Enrollment Figures Excluding Non-Resident/Alien Students							
U + G + P	6,705	4.54	13,747	9.31	135,810	92.01	147,594
Unclassified	279	5.21	533	9.95	4,673	87.28	5,354
Total enrollment	6,984	4.56	14,280	9.33	140,483	91.85	152,947

Enrollment Figures Excluding Non-Resident/Alien and U.S. Trust Territory Students

	Black		Minority		White		Total
	Number	Percentage	Number	Percentage	Number	Percentage	
U + G + P	6,701	4.56	13,059	8.88	135,799	92.43	146,906
Unclassified	279	5.22	520	9.73	4,673	87.49	5,341
Total enrollment	6,980	4.58	13,579	8.91	140,462	92.25	152,247

All Others	Black		Minority		White		Total
	Number	Percentage	Number	Percentage	Number	Percentage	
Undergraduate							
Full-time	473,397	10.98	789,569	18.13	3,507,157	80.56	4,353,185
Part-time	219,881	10.46	403,175	19.18	1,679,620	79.93	2,101,356
Total	698,278	10.82	1,192,744	18.48	5,186,777	79.93	6,454,541
Graduate							
Full-time	18,157	6.53	31,553	11.35	226,065	81.37	277,816
Part-time	37,694	7.61	57,560	11.62	427,589	86.33	495,246
Total	55,851	7.22	89,112	11.52	653,654	84.55	773,062
Professional							
Full-time	1,236	3.09	2,888	7.22	35,752	89.43	39,976
Part-time	128	3.54	199	5.50	3,346	92.63	3,612
Total	1,364	3.12	3,087	7.08	39,098	89.69	43,588
U + G + P	755,493	10.39	1,284,944	17.67	5,879,529	80.86	7,271,191
Unclassified	86,575	7.56	153,432	13.41	972,296	84.99	1,143,981
Total enrollment	842,068	10.00	1,438,376	17.09	6,851,825	81.42	8,415,172

Enrollment Figures Excluding Non-Resident/Alien Students

	Black		Minority		White		Total
U + G + P	755,233	9.66	1,284,944	16.44	5,879,529	75.25	7,812,988
Unclassified	86,575	7.25	1,534,432	12.84	972,296	81.42	1,194,050
Total enrollment	842,068	9.34	1,438,376	15.96	6,851,825	76.06	9,007,298

Table A7-9   Continued.

Enrollment Figures Excluding Non-Resident/Alien and U.S. Trust Territory Students

All Others	Black		Minority		White		Total
	Number	Percentage	Number	Percentage	Number	Percentage	
U + G + P	754,897	9.75	1,214,361	15.68	5,877,673	75.93	7,740,213
Unclassified	85,426	7.19	140,053	12.47	971,626	81.86	1,186,852
Total enrollment	840,323	9.41	1,362,414	15.26	6,849,299	76.72	8,927,065

Business and Management	Black		Minority		White		Total
	Number	Percentage	Number	Percentage	Number	Percentage	
Undergraduate							
Full-time	84,922	11.08	130,513	17.04	620,251	81.99	765,828
Part-time	30,562	9.44	55,626	17.19	264,508	81.77	323,467
Total	115,484	10.60	186,139	17.08	884,759	81.22	1,089,295
Graduate							
Full-time	2,048	4.00	4,046	7.90	39,998	78.18	51,161
Part-time	4,038	4.18	7,924	8.21	85,767	88.94	96,429
Total	6,086	4.12	11,970	8.11	125,765	85.21	147,590
Professional							
Full-time	14	7.52	17	9.13	150	80.64	186
Part-time	26	4.99	31	5.95	471	90.40	521
Total	40	5.65	48	6.78	621	87.83	707
U + G + P	121,610	9.82	198,157	16.01	1,011,145	81.70	1,237,592

	Black Number	Black Percentage	Minority Number	Minority Percentage	White Number	White Percentage	Total
Unclassified	3,740	6.41	7,480	12.82	49,948	85.63	58,326
Total enrollment	125,350	9.67	205,637	15.86	1,061,093	81.87	1,295,918

Enrollment Figures Excluding Non-Resident/Alien Students

	Black Number	Black Percentage	Minority Number	Minority Percentage	White Number	White Percentage	Total
U + G + P	121,610	10.06	198,157	15.21	1,011,145	77.62	1,209,286
Unclassified	3,740	6.51	7,480	13.02	49,948	86.97	57,428
Total enrollment	125,350	.98	205,637	16.23	1,061,093	83.76	1,266,714

Enrollment Figures Excluding Non-Resident/Alien and U.S. Trust Territory Students

	Black Number	Black Percentage	Minority Number	Minority Percentage	White Number	White Percentage	Total
U + G + P	121,511	9.43	184,037	14.29	1,010,962	78.48	1,288,220
Unclassified	3,723	6.14	7,099	11.70	49,825	82.15	60,647
Total enrollment	125,234	9.09	191,136	13.88	1,060,787	77.03	1,377,157

	Black		Minority		White		
Summary	Number	Percentage	Number	Percentage	Number	Percentage	Total
Undergraduate							
Full-time	605,116	10.19	1,010,765	17.02	4,820,716	81.21	5,936,902
Part-time	261,199	10.13	481,577	18.68	2,070,377	80.32	2,577,408
Total	866,315	10.17	1,492,342	17.52	6,891,093	80.94	8,513,310
Graduate							
Full-time	22,058	5.13	41,565	9.66	340,926	79.31	429,839
Part-time	43,287	6.60	70,587	10.77	565,933	86.36	655,292
Total	65,345	6.02	121,152	10.33	908,859	83.75	1,085,131
Professional							
Full-time	10,029	4.52	20,533	9.27	198,071	89.44	221,453
Part-time	1,152	4.73	2,136	8.77	21,988	90.34	24,337
Total	11,181	4.54	22,669	9.22	220,059	89.53	245,790

Table A7-9   Continued.

Summary	Black		Minority		White		Total
	Number	Percentage	Number	Percentage	Number	Percentage	
U + G + P	942,841	9.57	1,627,163	16.52	8,018,011	81.44	9,844,231
Unclassified	91,614	7.12	164,384	13.30	1,050,317	85.03	1,235,139
Total	1,034,455	9.33	1,791,547	16.17	9,068,328	81.84	11,079,370

Source: OCR, Department of Health, Education and Welfare, *Opening Fall Enrollment, 1976.*

Note: Percentages may not total 100% because of rounding.

*Other Areas: = American Samoa, Canal Zone, Guam, Puerto Rico, Trust Territories, and Virgin Islands.

Notes

Introduction

1. *Regents of University of California* v. *Bakke,* 98 S.Ct. 2733 (1978). Also see statement from Institute for the Study of Educational Policy (ISEP) on the *Bakke* case, November 1978.

Chapter 1

1. See Amicus Curiae brief of the National Association for Equal Opportunity in Higher Education, *Adams* v. *Califano,* 430 F. Supp. 118 (D.C.D.C. 1977).
2. See Samuel Bowles and Herbert Gintis, *Schooling in Capitalist America* (New York: Basic Books, 1976).
3. On concepts of policy as "distributive" and "redistributive," see Theodore Lowi, *The End of Liberalism* (New York: W. W. Norton, 1969).
4. Norman C. Thomas, *Education in National Politics* (New York: David McKay, 1965), p. 3.
5. Martin Carnoy, *Education as Cultural Imperialism* (New York: David McKay, 1974), p. 238.
6. Lawrence Gladieux and Thomas Wolanin, "Federal Politics," ed. David Breneman and Chester Finn, *Public Policy and Private Higher Education* (Washington, D.C.: Brookings Institution, 1978), p. 200.
7. Joel Spring, *The Sorting Machine: National Educational Policy Since 1945* (New York: David McKay, 1976), p. 259.
8. Ibid., p. 262. On the privatization of political authority (power) as an effect of interest group politics, see Grant McConnell, *Private Power and American Democracy* (New York: Alfred Knopf, 1967).
9. Marguerite Ross Barnett, "A Theoretical Perspective on American Racial Public Policy," Barnett and James A. Hefner, eds., *Public Policy for the Black Community* (New York: Alfred Publishing, 1976), p. 31.

10. N. Thomas, p. 8. (Emphasis added.)

11. Ellen Coughlin, "Tax Credits for Tuition: This Might be the Year," *The Chronicle of Higher Education*. XV, 20 (January 30, 1978), p. 5.

12. Gene Maeroff, "Carter Gives Congress His Plan for Wider Aid to College Students," *New York Times* (February 9, 1978), p. A16.

13. Coughlin, Ibid.

14. I have discussed "technology-centered ideology" more fully in Morris, *The Invisible Politics: Political Participation in Black and White America* (forthcoming). See also Lawrence H. Tribe, "Policy Science: Analysis or Ideology?" *Philosophy and Public Affairs*, 2 (Fall 1972), pp. 66–110.

15. National Urban League. *The State of Black America, 1978*, p. 49.

16. The Administration bill S991, presented in the Senate Committee on Governmental Affairs in February 1978, contains sixteen programs with a budget of $17.5 billion, the fifth largest of the twelve Cabinet-level departments, with a staff of over 23,000, "the eighth largest in the federal government." See Anne C. Roark, "Carter's Education Blueprint," *The Chronicle of Higher Education*, XVI, 9 (April 24, 1978), pp. 12–13.

17. Cited in David Breneman and Noel Epstein, "Uncle Sam's Growing Clout in the Classroom," *The Washington Post* (August 6, 1978), pp. D1 and D4.

18. Ibid.

19. Leo A. Munday, "College Access for Nontraditional Students," *Journal of Higher Education*, XLVII, 6 (December 1976), p. 682.

Chapter 2

1. At the end of *Current Population Reports*, issued by the U.S. Census, the statistical techniques used for "weighting" samples of blacks and other minority groups are discussed. This weighting technique is intended to compensate for the special difficulties involved in sampling studies of minorities. However, the technique is not fully effective, first, because the range of error remains large, and second, because subsequent Census data analyses generally give only limited consideration to this problem. Frank Brown and Madelon Stent discuss some of the sampling problems in *Minorities in U.S. Institutions of Higher Education* (New York: Praeger, 1977), pp. 9–10.

2. Carlos H. Arce, *Historical, Institutional and Contextual Determinants of Black College Enrollment in Predominantly White Colleges and Universities, 1946 to 1974*. Ph.D. Dissertation, The University of Michigan, 1976, p. 96.

3. On the importance of subjectivity in sociological methods, see Aaron Cicourel, *Method and Measurement in Sociology* (New York: The Free Press, 1964), pp. 19–25.

4. ISEP, *Equal Educational Opportunity: More Promise Than Progress* (1978), p. 28.

5. The standard error is described at the end of the *Census Population Reports*. It is defined in terms of the standard deviations for blacks in education by year. Special tables showing ranges of error are displayed.

6. Christopher Jencks, *et al.*, *Inequality: A Reassessment of the Effect of Family and Schooling in America* (New York: Harper & Row, 1972).

7. Ibid., p. 255.

8. Jencks, *et al., Inequality* . . . ., pp. 309–316.

9. Edward B. Fiske, "An Issue That Won't Go Away," *The New York Times Magazine* (March 27, 1977), p. 58. See also D. D. Dorfman, "The Cyril Burt Question: New Findings," *Science*, 201, 4362 (September 22, 1978), pp. 1177–1186.

Chapter 3

1. ISEP, *Equal Educational Opportunity for Blacks in U.S. Higher Education: An Assessment* (Washington, D.C.: Howard University Press, 1976). Written by Elizabeth Abramowitz. Research for this study was completed in 1975.

2. Ibid., p. 19.

3. Ibid., p. 34.

4. U.S. Bureau of the Census, *Current Population Reports*, Series P-20, No. 314, "Educational Attainment in the United States: March 1977 and 1976" (Washington, D.C.: U.S. Government Printing Office, 1977.)

5. U.S. Bureau of the Census, *Current Population Reports*, Series P-20, No. 307, "Population Profile of US: 1976" (Washington, D.C.: U. S. Government Printing Office, 1977).

6. U.S. Bureau of the Census, *Current Population Reports*, Series P-25, No. 721, "Estimates of the Population of the U.S., by Age, Sex, and Race: 1970 to 1977" (Washington, D.C.: U.S. Government Printing Office, 1978), p. 1.

7. National Center for Educational Statistics, *The Condition of Education 1977*, Part 1 (Washington, D.C.: U.S. Government Printing Office, 1977).

8. Adjusted figures for counting errors in census surveys are relatively higher for blacks. For example, the adjusted Census figures for 1977 for those 18–24 years old total 29,072,000; blacks constitute 3,912,000. The white population is overcounted and the black population is undercounted. As a consequence, the black percentage of the population goes up from 12.58 to 13.46.

9. ISEP, *Equal Educational Opportunity: An Assessment*, pp. 15–80.

10. *The Chronicle of Higher Education*, XVI, 7 (April 10, 1978), p. 2. Based on US Census Bureau data.

11. See, for example, Robert Crain and Rita Mahard, "School Racial Composition and Black College Attendance and Achievement Test Performance," *Sociology of Education*, Vol. 51 (April 1978), pp. 81–101.

12. See for example, Gail E. Thomas, "Race and Sex Effects on Access to College," Report No 229 (May 1977), Center for Social Organization of Schools, Johns Hopkins University, Baltimore, Maryland.

13. ISEP, *Equal Educational Opportunity: An Assessment*, p. 86.

14. Kenneth Clark's 1934 study has served as evidence that black children in segregated conditions develop a sense of inferiority. In an experiment he found that, given a choice, white and black girls both preferred white dolls to play with. The preferences of black girls were taken as evidence of low self-esteem based on color.

15. ISEP, *Equal Educational Opportunity: An Assessment*, pp. 86–87.

16. Ibid., p. 86.

17. Lorenzo Morris, "The Socialization of IQ: A Political History of Intelligence Testing in American Schools" (1977), p. 13.

18. Max Weber, "The Rationalization of Education and Training," ed., Sam Seiber and David Wilder, *The School in Society* (New York: The Free Press, 1973),

pp. 19–20. See also H. H. Gerth and C. W. Mill, editors, from *Max Weber: Essays in Sociology* (New York: Oxford University Press, 1946), pp. 240–43.

19. John A. Creager, *Selected Policies and Practices in Higher Education*, American Council on Education, 8, 4 (1973), Table 2. Cited in ISEP, *Equal Educational Opportunity: An Assessment*, pp. 308–9.

20. William Bowen, "Admissions and the Relevance of Race," American Council on Education, *Educational Record* (Fall 1977), p. 336.

21. Carnegie Council on Policy Studies in Higher Education. *Selective Admissions in Higher Education* (San Francisco: Jossey-Bass, 1970), pp. 9–10.

22. See Barry Castro, "Hostos: Report From a Ghetto College," *Harvard Educational Review*, 44, 2 (May 1974), p. 284.

23. Edward B. Fiske, "One of 3 at City University Needs Remedial Aid," *New York Times* (27 February 1977), p. B3.

24. Jerome Karabel and Alexander W. Astin, "Social Class, Academic Ability, and College Quality," *Social Forces* (March 1975), 381–398, in Gail Thomas, *et al., Access to Higher Education: How Important are Race, Sex, Social Class and Academic Credentials for College Access?*, Report No. 226 (Baltimore: Johns Hopkins University Center for Social Organization of Schools, April 1977).

25. David Lavin, Richard Alba and Richard Silberstein, "Ethnicity and Equality: The Fate of Ethnic Groups Under an Open Access Model of Higher Education" (June 1978), prepublication draft. Forthcoming in the *Harvard Educational Review*.

26. Ibid., p. 7.

27. W. E. Sedlacek, J. A. Lewis and S. C. Brooks, "Black and Other Minority Admissions to Large Universities: A Four Year National Survey of Policies and Outcomes." Paper presented at American College Personnel Association Convention, April 1973.

28. G. Thomas, "Access", Report No. 226, p. 3.

29. The standard deviation measures the normal distribution of scores around the mean. Two-thirds of all scores fall within the range of 1 SD around the mean, and one-third fall on either side of the mean in a normal distribution. See, for example, Hubert Blalock, *Social Statistics* (New York: McGraw-Hall, 1960), p. 81.

30. Ray Rist, "Student Social Class and Teacher Expectations: The Self-Fulfilling Prophecy in Ghetto Education," *Harvard Educational Review*, 40, 3 (August 1970).

31. Carnegie Council on Policy Studies in Higher Education. *Selective Admissions in Higher Education* (San Francisco: Jossey-Bass, 1977), pp. 125, 138–139.

32. William Boyd, "SATs and Minorities: The Dangers of Underprediction," *Change* (November 1977), p. 64.

33. Orville Brin, David Goslin, David Glass and Isadore Goldberg, *The Uses of Standardized Ability Tests in American Secondary Schools and Their Impact on Students, Teachers and Administrators*, Report No. 3, Russell Sage Foundation (New York, 1965).

34. Alexander Astin, "The Myth of Equal Access in Public Higher Education," Southern Educational Foundation (1975), p. 2.

35. "When Blacks Make It into the Middle Class," *U. S. News and World Report* (June 5, 1978), p. 5.

36. Scientific Manpower Commission, *Manpower Comments*, 12, 3, (1975), p. 17.

37. National Center For Education Statistics (NCES), "Opening Fall Enrollment in Colleges and Universities, 1977, Preliminary Estimates," *Bulletin* (December 1977).

38. National Direct Student Loans, which are by definition financially oriented, may be considered culturally based in that this program was motivated originally by a concern for the protection of national security, and geared to the encouragement of science and technology in higher education. However, the structure of the program aims directly only at supporting higher education, and redirects only indirectly, if at all, student academic interest and choice. In this sense, it is not explicitly cultural.

39. NCES, *The Condition of Education, 1978,* p. 201.

40. See Joseph Froomkin, "Middle Income Students and the Cost of Education," *Educational Record* (Summer 1978), pp. 254–267. According to Froomkin, "the likelihood of 18–24 year-olds continuing to live with their parents is inversely proportional to the income of the household. For example, two-thirds of the dependents 18–24 whose parents have incomes under $10,000 become independent, as contrasted to one in eight dependents in families with yearly incomes of more than $25,000," (p. 263).

41. Lois D. Rice, prepared Testimony before Subcommittee on Postsecondary Education Committee on Education and Labor, U. S. House of Representatives (February 23, 1978), pp. 5–6 (See Appendix, Table A-4).

42. Joseph Froomkin, prepared Testimony before Committee on Ways and Means, U.S. House of Representatives, "Middle Income Tax Relief" (February 17, 1978). *The Survey of Income and Education* (SIE) is a special survey of the U.S. Census Bureau, completed in 1978. It is perhaps the most extensive survey of its kind.

43. National Advisory Committee on Black Higher Education and Black Colleges and Universities, "Access: Increasing the Participation of Black Americans in Higher Education," Committee Staff Draft (June 1978), p. 7.

44. Robert L. Crain and Rita E. Mahard, "The Influence of High School Racial Composition on Black College Attendance and Achievement Test Performance," Rand Corporation (1978). Prepared for the National Center for Education Statistics.

45. These are the same factors which are associated with academic performance. See David Lavin, "Sociological Determinants of Academic Performance," eds. Sam Sieber and David Wilder, *The School in Society* (New York: The Free Press, 1973), pp. 78–98.

46. The conclusion is supported by juxtaposing the data displayed in Figures 3A-1 and 3A-2, in the Appendix.

47. For 1976, the Census Bureau reports that 10.7 percent of all American students in higher education are black. Excluding non-American students from our data raised the black percentage to 9.6; however, a difference remains. For reasons discussed in chapter 2, we rely on the OCR data for 1976 from which our 9.3 percent enrollment figure is derived.

48. We do not suspect deliberate or conscious misrepresentation. Rather, typical overestimates result from the inclusion of a few African students in a very small student population of American blacks.

49. Enrollment by race from HEGIS is not presently available, except in preliminary form.

50. U.S. Bureau of the Census, *Current Population Reports,* Series P-20, No. 307, "Population Profile of the United States: 1976" (Washington, D.C.: U. S. Government Printing Office, 1977), Table 26.

51. Alan Pifer, "Black Progress: Achievement, Failure, and an Uncertain Future," Reprinted from *1977 Annual Report*, Carnegie Corporation (New York, 1977), p. 7.

52. Marcus Alexis, "Black and White Wealth," eds. Marguerite Barnett and J. Hefner, *Public Policy for the Black Community* (New York: Alfred Publishing, 1976), Table 6.2, p. 198. Based on Henry Terrell, "Wealth Accumulation of Black and White Families," *Journal of Finance* (May 1971).

53. J. Froomkin, "Middle Income Students . . . .", p. 258.

Chapter 4

1. Pierre Bourdieu and Claude Passeron, *La Réproduction: éléments pour une théorie du système d'enseignement* (Paris: Les Editions de Minuit, 1970), pp. 199–250.

2. Edward Gross and Paul Grambsch, *Changes in Universities Organization, 1964–1971*, Carnegie Commission on Higher Education (New York: McGraw Hill, 1974), p. 3.

3. From Donald Matthew, cited in Ira Katznelson *Black Men, White Cities: Race, Politics, and Migration in the United States, 1900–30 and Britain, 1948–68* (New York: Oxford University Press, 1973), p. 9.

4. Everett Ladd and Seymour Lipset, *The Divided Academy* (New York: W. W. Norton, 1975), pp. 13–14.

5. "Responses to Increased Black Student Enrollment," *Journal of Higher Education*, 49, 3 (1978), p. 213.

6. James Mingle, "Faculty and Departmental Responses to Increased Black Student Enrollment," *Journal of Higher Education*, 49, 3 (1978), p. 213.

7. W. E. B. DuBois edited *The Crisis* in the 1930s, a journal of the National Association for the Advancement of Colored People.

8. George Spears, "The Part-time Student: Higher Education's Major Client," *NUEA Spectator*, 24 (June 1976), pp. 39–40. Cited in Margaret Sanders Eddy, "Part-Time Students", ERIC/Higher Education, *Research Currents* (June 1978), p. 6.

9. On socialization in education, see, for example, Frederick Wirt and Michael Kirst, *Political and Social Foundation of Education* (Berkeley: McCutchan Publishing, 1975). See also Bernard C. Posen & Alan P. Bates, "The Structure of Socialization in Graduate School," ed., Ronald Pavalbo, *Sociology of Education*, 2nd ed., E. E. Peacock Publishers (1976), pp. 154–167.

10. Samuel Bowles, *Schooling in Capitalist America*, (New York: Basic Books, 1976).

11. Lyle and Magdaline Shannon, *Minority Migrants in the Urban Community* (Beverly Hills: Sage Publications, 1973), pp. 177–78.

12. Carnegie Council on Policy Studies in Higher Education, *Selective Admissions in Higher Education* (Washington, D.C.: Jossey-Bass, 1977), p. 53.

13. Albert H. Berrian, "Supportive Services," Institute for Services to Education, 1977. Unpublished paper. See also K. Patricia Cross, "The Elusive Goal of Educational Equality" in John F. Hughes and Olive Mills, eds., *Formulating Policy in Postsecondary Education* (Washington, D.C.: American Council on Education, 1975), pp. 191–201. She describes such programming as a melting-pot approach to equalizing educational outcomes.

14. Alexander A. Astin, "The Myth of Equal Access in Public Higher Education." A paper from the Southern Education Foundation (July 1975), pp. 8–14. Mean per student subsidy is calculated as educational and general expenditures plus financial aid minus tuition.

15. Ibid., p. 9.

16. Gail Thomas, "Equality of Representation of Race and Sex Group in Higher Education," Center for the Social Organization of Schools, Johns Hopkins University (October 1978), p. 1.

17. Warren Brown, "The Racial Wall on Campus: After the Turmoil, A Separate Peace.", *The Washington Post*, "Outlook" (November 13, 1977).

18. U.S. Bureau of the Census, *School Enrollment*, p. 20, No. 319.

19. Margot Sanders Eddy, "Part-time Students," *Research Currents, ERIC*, American Association for Higher Education (June 1978).

20. Gail Thomas. "Equality . . . " See also, A. J. Jaffe, W. Adams and G. Meyers, *Negro Higher Education in the 1960s* (New York: F. A. Preager, 1968).

21. NCES, *The Condition of Education, 1978*, Chart 3.3, p. 113.

22. Kenneth A. Feldman and Theodore M. Newcomb, *The Impact of College on Students* (San Francisco: Jossey-Bass Publishers, 1976).

23. William M. Jackson, Testimony on the National Science Foundation Fiscal Year 1977 Budget. U.S. House of Representatives Appropriations Committee on Independent Agencies, April 7, 1976.

24. W. M. Jackson, Testimony on the National Science Foundation Budget. U.S. Senate Subcommittee on Health and Scientific Research, March 3, 1976.

25. W. M. Jackson, Testimony on the National Science Foundation Budget Authorization, Fiscal Year 1978. U.S. Senate Subcommittee on Health and Scientific Research, March 3, 1977.

26. *Chronicle of Higher Education*, XV, 18 (January 16, 1978), p. 9. Edited from report based on Everett C. Ladd and Seymour M. Lipset, "1977 Survey of 4,400 Faculty Members at 161 Colleges and Universities."

27. James Mingle, "Faculty and Departmental Responses" (1978), pp. 211–213.

Chapter 5

1. ISEP, *Equal Educational Opportunity: . . . An Assessment*, p. 66.

2. ISEP, *Equal Educational Opportunity: More Promise . . .* , p. 90.

3. ISEP, *Equal Educational Opportunity: An Assessment*, p. 68.

4. ISEP, *Equal Educational Opportunity: More Promise . . .* , p. 96.

5. Alexander Astin, *College Dropouts: A National Profile*, Table 3. Cited in ISEP, *Equal Educational Opportunity: An Assessment* (1976), p. 67.

6. ISEP, *Equal Educational Opportunity: An Assessment*, (1976), p. 73.

7. Published in the National Advisory Committee on Black Higher Education and Black Colleges and Universities. *First Annual Report: Higher Education Equity* (June 1978).

8. Scientific Manpower Commission, *Professional Women and Minorities: A Manpower Resource*. Prepared by Betty M. Vetter and Eleanor L. Baber (Washington, D.C.: Scientific Manpower Commission, 1975).

9. National Academy of Science, Manpower Commission Reports . . .

10. The fact that blacks do not attend professional schools at the same rate as whites may be a limiting condition for the rate of M.A. degree acquisition.

11. The 8.7 percent figure is probably not too high to use as a measure of black retention and distribution. However, as discussed in chapter 2, the Census Bureau estimates of black enrollment are probably too high, by about 0.5 percent.

12. ISEP, *Equal Educational Opportunity: An Assessment* (1976), p. 83.

13. Andrew Kolstad. "Attrition From Colleges: The Class of 1972 Two and One-half Years After High School Graduation," (Washington, D.C.: H.E.W., 1977), p. 7.

14. Ibid., Table 2.

15. Astin, *Preventing Students From Dropping-Out* (San Francisco: Jossey-Bass, 1975), pp. 148–49.

16. See annotated bibliography.

17. See, for example, Paul Fiddler and Eunice Ponder, "A Comparative Study of the University of South Carolina Student Survival Rates by Race, 1973-76," *Research Notes* (January 1977).

18. Joseph L. Martin, "The College Environment: A Longitudinal Study of Black and White Students at Predominantly Black Colleges." Institute for Services to Education (1973).

Chapter 6

1. Joseph A. Califano, Secretary of the U.S. Department of Health, Education and Welfare, speech delivered at the 83rd Annual Convention and Scientific Assembly of the National Medical Association, Washington, D.C., August 1, 1978.

2. The case developed through a series of desegregation suits initiated by the NAACP Legal Defense Fund in 1972 against then Secretary of HEW, Elliot Richardson, with the aim of compelling ten southern states to desegregate white institutions of higher education. The sequence of cases is: *Adams* v. *Richardson*, 351 F. Supp 636 (D.C.D.C. 1972, amended 1973; *Adams* v. *Richardson*, 356 F. Supp 92 (D.C.D.C. 1973); *Adams* v. *Richardson* 480 F. 2d 1159 (C.A.D.C. 1973); *Adams* v. *Califano*, 430 F. Supp 118 (D.C.D.C. 1977). See also *amicus curiae* of the National Association for Equal Opportunity in Higher Education (NAFEO).

3. J. Califano, Speech before the National Medical Association (1978).

4. ISEP, *Equal Educational Opportunity: More Promise Than Progress*, p. 117.

5. Institute for Services to Education, *Profile of Enrollments in the Historically Black Colleges*. Cited in *Higher Education and National Affairs*, XXVII, 21, p. 6.

6. Ibid.

7. ISEP, *Equal Educational Opportunity: More Promise Than Progress*, p. 116.

8. Robert L. Crain and Rita E. Mahard, "School Racial Composition and Black College Attendance and Achievement Test Performance," *Sociology of Education*, Vol. 51 (April 1978), pp. 81–101.

9. National Advisory Committee on Black Higher Education and Black Colleges and Universities, *First Annual Report: Higher Education Equity* (1978), p. 22.

10. Crain and Mahard, *Sociology of Education* (April 1978), p. 98.

11. American College Testing Program, "Some Characteristics of the Historically Black Colleges." Paper presented to National Advisory Committee on Black Higher Education and Black Colleges and Universities (Washington, D. C., 1978), p. 11.

12. One TBI, Howard University, has had a unique financial relationship with the federal government for the last fifty years: Howard is a "line item" in the federal budget. Its location in Washington, D. C., as well as its historic mission to educate "freedmen and Indians," explain, in part its special status.

13. Henry A. Bullock, *A History of Negro Education in the South* (Cambridge, Massachusetts: Harvard University Press, 1967). See chapter 4: "Decisions at Capon Springs," pp. 89–116.

Chapter 7

1. The National Research Council, *A Century of Doctorates* (Washington, D. C.: National Academy of Sciences, 1978), pp. 82–83.

2. John Fleming, Gerald Gill and David Swinton, *The Case for Affirmative Action for Blacks in Higher Education*, Institute for the Study of Educational Policy (Washington, D.C.: Howard University Press, 1978), p. 215. Data drawn from the U.S. Census. See Appendix Table A7-2.

3. Ibid., p. 246.

4. National Science Foundation, *Projections of Science and Engineering Doctorate Supply and Utilization, 1980 and 1985* (Washington, D. C.: U. S. Government Printing Office, 1975), p. 24.

5. National Research Council, *A Century of Doctorates*, p. 37. These estimates assume, for example, that the father of a 1969-71 Ph.D. recipient was born between 1906 and 1915.

6. E. F. Rosinski, "Social Class of Medical Students: A Look at an Untapped Pool of Possible Medical School Applicants," *JAMA* 193 (1965), pp. 95–98.

7. Rashi Fein and Gerald Weber, *Financing Medical Education* (New York: McGraw-Hill, 1971), p. 102.

8. Leonard Baird, *Careers and Curricula* (Princeton: Educational Testing Service, 1974), pp. 135–149.

9. There is some slight variation in figures on the proportion of blacks awarded Ph.D. degrees in 1976. The figure we rely on is 3.6, which is based on our analysis of OCR data. The percentages of blacks reported, however, range from 3.4 to 4.0. This degree of variation is a logical product of variations in the definition and identification of subpopulations.

10. J. Fleming, G. Gill and D. Swinton, *The Case for Affirmative Action for Blacks in Higher Education*, p. 42.

11. Racial proportions in Podiatry, like those in Business and Management enrollment, may be rather deceptive because the total numbers of students are so small.

12. *Regents of the University of California* v. *Allan Bakke* (1978), p. 76–811.

13. Ibid., p. 76–811.

14. Boyd Sleeth and Robert Mishell, "Black Underrepresentation in United States Medical Schools," *New England Journal of Medicine*, 297 (November 1977), p. 1147.

15. Janet M. Cuca, *et al.*, *The Medical School Admission Process: A Review of the Literature, 1955–76* (Washington, D.C.: Association of American Medical Colleges, 1976).

16. See, for example, Evans, Jones, Worthman and Jackson, "Traditional Criteria as Predictors of Minority Student Success in Medical School, *Journal of Medical Education*, 50, 10, pp. 934–939. R. W. Ingersoll and G. O. Graves, "Predictability of Success in the First Year of Medical School," *Journal of Medical Education*, Vol. 40 (1965), pp. 351–363.

Bibliography

Books and Monographs

American Bar Association. *Law Schools and Bar Admissions Requirements.* Chicago: American Bar Association, 1977.

Astin, Alexander W. *College Dropouts: A National Profile.* ACE Research Report, Washington, D.C.: American Council on Education, 1972.

————. ·*Preventing Students from Dropping Out.* San Francisco: Jossey-Bass, 1975.

Astin, A. W.; King, M. R.; Light, J. M.; and Richardson, Gerald. *The American Freshman: National Norms for Fall 1974.* Los Angeles: Graduate School of Education/UCLA, 1974.

Astin, Alexander; King, Margo; and Richardson, Gerald. *The American Freshman: National Norms for Fall 1976.* Los Angeles: CIRP/UCLA, 1977.

Atelsek, Frank, and Gomberg, Irene. *Estimated Number of Student Aid Recipients 1976–77.* HEPR, No. 36. Washington, D.C.: American Council on Education, September 1977.

Baird, Leonard. *Careers and Curricula: A Report on the Activities and Views of Graduates a Year After Leaving College.* Princeton: Educational Testing Service, 1974.

Bourdieu, Pierre and Passeron, Claude. *La Réproduction: éléments pour une théorie du système d'enseîgnement.* Paris: Les Èditions de Minuit, 1970.

Bowles, Samuel, and Gintis, Herbert. *Schooling in Capitalist America.* New York: Basic Books, 1976.

Brin, Orville; Goslin, David; Glass, David; and Goldberg, Isadore. *The Uses of*

Standardized Ability Tests in American Secondary Schools and Their Impact on Students, Teachers, and Administrators. Report No. 3. New York: Russell Sage Foundation, 1965.

Brown, Frank, and Stent, Madelon D. *Minorities in U.S. Institutions of Higher Education.* New York: Praeger, 1977.

Bullock, Henry A. *A History of Negro Education in the South.* Cambridge, Massachusetts: Harvard University Press, 1967.

Carnegie Council on Policy Studies in Higher Education. *Selective Admissions in Higher Education.* San Francisco: Jossey-Bass, 1970.

_____. *Selective Admissions in Higher Education.* Washington, D.C.: Jossey-Bass, 1977.

Carnoy, Martin. *Education as Cultural Imperialism.* New York: David McKay, 1974.

Cicourel, Aaron. *Method and Measurement in Sociology.* New York: Free Press, 1964.

Creager, John A. *Selected Policies and Practices in Higher Education.* Vol. 8, No. 4. Washington, D.C.: American Council on Education, 1973.

Cuca, Janet M.; Sakakeeny, Linda A.; and Johnson, Davis G. *The Medical School Admissions Process: A Review of the Literature, 1955–76.* Washington, D.C.: Association of American Medical Colleges, 1976.

Educational Testing Service. *1977 Review of Legal Education.* Princeton: Educational Testing Service, 1977.

Educational Testing Service. *1976 Review of Legal Education.* Princeton: Educational Testing Service, 1976.

Engineering Manpower Commission. *Trends in Engineering Degrees Earned by Women and Minority Members.* New York: Engineers Joint Council, January 1976.

Fein, Rashi, and Weber, Gerald I. *Financing Medical Education.* New York: McGraw-Hill, 1971.

Feldman, Kenneth A., and Newcomb, Theodore M. *The Impact of College on Students.* San Francisco: Jossey-Bass, 1976.

Fleming, John; Gill, Gerald R.; and Swinton, David H. *The Case for Affirmative Action for Blacks in Higher Education.* Washington, D.C.: Howard University Press, 1978.

Freeman, Richard B. *Black Elite: The New Market for Highly Educated Black Americans.* New York: McGraw-Hill, 1976.

Gerth, H. H., and Mill, C. W., eds. *Max Weber: Essays in Sociology.* New York: Oxford University Press, 1946.

BIBLIOGRAPHY

Gilford, Dorothy M., and Snyder, Joan. *Women and Minority Ph.D.'s in the 1970s: A Data Book.* Washington, D.C.: National Academy of Sciences, 1977.

Gross, Edward, and Grambsch, Paul. *Changes in University Organization, 1964–1971.* New York: McGraw-Hill, 1974.

Institute for the Study of Educational Policy. *Equal Educational Opportunity for Blacks in U.S. Higher Education: An Assessment.* Washington, D.C.: Howard University Press, 1976.

_____. *Equal Educational Opportunity: More Promise Than Progress.* Washington, D.C.: Howard University Press, 1978.

Jaffe, A. J.: Adams, W.; and Meyers, G. *Negro Higher Education in the 1960s.* New York: F. A. Praeger, 1968.

Jencks, Christopher, *et al. Inequality: A Reassessment of the Effect of Family and Schooling in America.* New York: Harper & Row, 1972.

Katznelson, Ira. *Black Men, White Cities: Race, Politics, and Migration in the United States, 1900–30 and Britain, 1948–68.* New York: Oxford University Press, 1973.

Ladd, Everett Carl, and Lipset, Seymour. *The Divided Academy.* New York: W. W. Norton, 1975.

Leslie, Larry. *Higher Education Opportunity: A Decade of Progress.* ERIC/AAHE Research Report No. 3. Washington, D.C.: American Association for Higher Education, 1977.

Lowi, Theodore. *The End of Liberalism.* New York: W. W. Norton, 1969.

McConnell, Grant. *Private Power and American Democracy.* New York: Alfred Knopf, 1967.

Martin, Joseph L. *The College Environment: A Longitudinal Study of Black and White Students at Predominantly Black Colleges.* Washington, D.C.: Institute for Services to Education, 1977.

Morris, Lorenzo, and Henry, Charles. *The Chit'lin Controversy: Race and Public Policy in America.* Washington, D.C.: University Press of America, 1978.

National Board on Graduate Education. *Minority Group Participation in Graduate Education.* Washington, D.C.: National Board on Graduate Education, 1976.

National Research Council. *A Century of Doctorates.* Washington, D.C.: National Academy of Sciences, 1978.

National Urban League. *The State of Black America 1978.* New York: National Urban League, Inc., 1978.

Scientific Manpower Commission. *Professional Women and Minorities: A Manpower Resource.* Prepared by Betty M. Vetter and Eleanor L. Baber. Washington, D.C.: Scientific Manpower Commission, 1975.

Shannon, Lyle, and Shannon, Magdaline. *Minority Migrants in the Urban Community*. Beverly Hills: Sage Publications, 1973.

Spring, Joel. *The Sorting Machine: National Educational Policy Since 1945*. New York: David McKay, 1976.

Thomas, Gail E. *Equality of Representation of Race and Sex Group in Higher Education*. Baltimore: Johns Hopkins University Center for Social Organization of Schools, June 1978.

_____. *Race and Sex Effects on Access to College*. Report No. 229, Baltimore: Johns Hopkins University Center for Social Organization of Schools, May 1977.

Thomas, Norman C. *Education in National Politics*. New York: David McKay, 1965.

Wirt, Frederick, and Kirst, Michael. *Political and Social Foundation of Education*. Berkeley: McCutchan Publishing Co., 1975.

Articles

Alexis, Marcus. "Black and White Wealth." In *Public Policy for the Black Community*, edited by Marguerite Ross Barnett and James A. Hefner. New York: Alfred Publishing Co., 1976.

Barnett, Marguerite Ross. "A Theoretical Perspective on American Racial Public Policy." In *Public Policy for the Black Community*, edited by Marguerite Ross Barnett and James A. Hefner. New York: Alfred Publishing Co., 1976.

Bowen, William. "Admissions and the Relevance of Race." *Educational Record* (Fall 1977): 336.

Boyd, William. "SAT's and Minorities: The Dangers of Underprediction." *Change* (November 1977): 64.

Breneman, David, and Epstein, Noel. "Uncle Sam's Growing Clout in the Classroom." *Washington Post*, 6 August 1978, pp. D1 and D4.

Brown, Warren. "The Racial Wall on Campus: After the Turmoil, A Separate Peace." *Washington Post* (Outlook Section), (November 13, 1977).

Castro, Barry. "Hostos: Report From a Ghetto College." *Harvard Educational Review* 44(May 1974): 284.

Coughlin, Ellen. "Tax Credits for Tuition: This Might Be The Year." *Chronicle of Higher Education* (January 30, 1977), p. 5.

Crain, Robert L., and Mahard, Rita E. "School Racial Composition and Black College Attendance and Achievement Test Performance." *Sociology of Education* 51(April 1978): 81–101.

Cross, K. Patricia. "The Elusive Goal of Educational Equality." In *Formulating*

Policy in Postsecondary Education, edited by John F. Hughes and Olive Mills. Washington, D.C.: American Council on Education, 1975.

Dorfman, D. D. "The Cyril Burt Question: New Findings." *Science,* (September 22, 1978): pp. 1177–1186.

Eddy, Margot Sanders. "Part-Time Students." AAHE/ERIC Higher Education, *Research Currents.* Washington, D.C.: American Association for Higher Education, June 1978.

Evans; Jones; Worthman; and Jackson. "Traditional Criteria as Predictors of Minority Student Success in Medical School." *Journal of Medical Education* 50: 934–39.

Dubé, W. F. "Datagram: Medical Student Enrollment 1972-73 Through 1976-77." *Journal of Medical Education* 52(February 1977): 164–66.

Fiddler, Paul, and Ponder, Eunice. "A Comparative Study of the University of South Carolina Student Survival Rates by Race, 1973–76." *Research Notes.* No. 33-77, Academic Planning Office, University of South Carolina, January 1977.

Fiske, Edward B. "An Issue That Won't Go Away." *New York Times Magazine,* 27 March 1977, p. 58.

———. "One of 3 at City U. Needs Remedial Aid." *New York Times,* 27 February 1973, p. B3.

Froomkin, Joseph. "Middle Income Students and the Cost of Education." *Educational Record* (Summer 1978): 254–67.

Gladieux, Lawrence, and Wolanin, Thomas. "Federal Politics." In *Public Policy and Private Higher Education,* edited by David Breneman and Chester E. Finn. Washington, D.C.: Brookings Institution, 1978.

Gordon, Travis L. "Datagram: Applicants for 1976-77 First-Year Medical School Class." *Journal of Medical Education* 52(September 1977): 780–82.

Gordon, Travis L., and Johnson, Davis G. "Study of U.S. Medical School Applicants, 1975-76." *Journal of Medical Education* 52(September 1977): 707–30.

Ingersoll, R. W., and Graves, G. O. "Predictability of Success in the First Year of Medical School." *Journal of Medical Education* 40(1965): 351–63.

Institute for Services to Education. "Profile of Enrollments in the Historically Black Colleges." *Higher Education and National Affairs* 27:6.

Institute for Services to Education. "Preliminary Fall 1976 Enrollment in Historically Black Colleges." *Research Profile* 5(February 1977): 1.

Johnson, Davis, and Sedlacek, William. "Retention by Sex and Race of 1968-72 U.S. Medical School Entrants." *Journal of Medical Education* 50(1975): 925–33.

Karabel, Jerome, and Astin, Alexander W. "Social Class, Academic Ability, and College "Quality." *Social Forces* 53(March 1975): 381–98. In Gail Thomas, *et al.*

Access to Higher Education: How Important are Race, Sex, Social Class and Academic Credentials for College Access? Report No. 226, Baltimore: Johns Hopkins University Center for Social Organization of Schools, April 1977.

Ladd, Everett C., and Lipset, Seymour Martin. "Professors Found to be Liberal But Not Radical: The Ladd-Lipset Survey." *Chronicle of Higher Education*, 16 January 1978, p. 9.

Lavin, David. "Sociological Determinants of Academic Performance." In *The School in Society*, edited by Sam Seiber and David Wilder. New York: Free Press, 1973.

Lavin, David; Alba, Richard; and Silberstein, Richard. "Ethnicity and Equality: The Fate of Ethnic Groups Under An Open Access Model of Higher Education." Pre-publication draft, forthcoming in the *Harvard Educational Review*.

Maeroff, Gene. "Carter Gives Congress His Plan For Wider Aid to College Students." *New York Times*, 9 February 1978, p. A-16.

Magarrell, Jack. "More People Over 25 Are Going to College." *Chronicle of Higher Education*, 10 April 1978, p. 2.

Mingle, James. "Faculty and Departmental Responses to Increased Black Student Enrollment." *Journal of Higher Education* 49(1978): 206, 211–13.

Munday, Leo A. "College Access for Non-Traditional Students." *Journal of Higher Education* 47(December 1976): 682.

Pifer, Alan. "Black Progress: Achievement, Failure, and an Uncertain Future." In Carnegie Corporation, *1977 Annual Report*. New York: Carnegie Corporation, 1977.

Posen, Bernard C., and Bates, Alan P. "The Structure of Socialization in Graduate School." In *Sociology of Education: A Book of Readings*, 2nd ed., edited by Ronald Pavalko. Itasca, Ill.: F. E. Peacock Publishers, 1976.

"Responses to Increased Black Student Enrollment." *Journal of Higher Education* 49(1978): 218.

Rist, Ray. "Student Social Class and Teacher Expectations: The Self-Fulfilling Prophecy in Ghetto Education." *Harvard Educational Review* 40(August 1970): 10.

Roark, Anne C. "Carter's Education Blueprint." *Chronicle of Higher Education*, 24 April 1978, pp. 12–13.

———. "Federal Student Aid and How It Grew." *Chronicle of Higher Education*, 11 October 1977, p. 5.

Rosinski, E. F. "Social Class of Medical Students: A Look at an Untapped Pool of Possible Medical School Applicants." *Journal of the American Medical Association* 193(1965): 95–98.

Sleeth, Boyd, and Mishell, Robert. "Black Underrepresentation in United States Medical Schools." *New England Journal of Medicine* 297(November 1977): 1148.

Spears, George. "The Part-Time Student: Higher Education's Major Client." *NUEA Spectator* 24(June 1976): 39–40.

Terrell, Henry S. "Wealth Accumulation of Black and White Families: The Empirical Evidence." *Journal of Finance* 26(May 1971): 364.

Thomas, Gail E.; Alexander, Karl; and Eckland, Bruce K. "Access to Higher Education: How Important are Race, Sex, Social Class, and Academic Credentials for College Access?" Report No. 226, Baltimore: Johns Hopkins University Center for Social Organization of Schools, April 1977.

Tribe, Lawrence H. "Policy Science: Analysis or Ideology?" *Philosophy and Public Affairs* 2(Fall 1972): 66–110.

Weber, Max. "The Rationalization of Education and Training." In *The School in Society*, edited by Sam Seiber and David Wilder. New York: Free Press, 1973.

"When Blacks Make It Into The Middle Class." *U.S. News and World Report*, 5 June 1978, p. 5.

Public Documents

DeFunis v. *Odegaard.* 416 U.S. 312 (1974).

Federal Interagency Committee on Education. "Federal Agencies and Black Colleges." *FICE Reports*, Vol. 4, No. 2, December 1977.

Halstead, D. Kent. *Statewide Planning in Higher Education.* Washington, D.C.: U.S. Office of Education, 1974.

Mantovani, Richard E.; Gordon, Travis L.; and Johnson, Davis G. *Medical Student Indebtedness and Career Plans, 1974–1975: Health Manpower References.* Prepared by the Association of American Medical Colleges. Washington, D.C.: U.S. Department of Health, Education, and Welfare, Public Health Service, Health Resources Administration, Bureau of Health Manpower, 1976.

National Science Foundation. *Projections of Science and Engineering Doctorate Supply and Utilization, 1980 and 1985.* Washington, D.C.: Government Printing Office, 1975.

Regents of the University of California v. *Allan Bakke*, 98 S. Ct. 2733 (1978).

U.S. Bureau of the Census. *Current Population Reports.* Series P-20, No. 314. "Educational Attainment in the United States: March 1977 and 1976." Washington, D.C.: Government Printing Office, 1977.

_____. *Current Population Reports.* Series P-25, No. 721. "Estimates of the Population of the U.S. by Age, Sex, and Race: 1970–1977." Washington, D.C.: Government Printing Office, 1978.

_____. *Current Population Reports.* Series P-60, No. 116. "Money, Income, and Poverty Status of Families and Persons in the United States: 1977." Advanced Report. Washington, D.C.: Government Printing Office, 1978.

_____. *Current Population Reports.* Series P-20, No. 307. "Population Profile of U.S.: 1976." Washington, D.C.: Government Printing Office, 1977.

_____. *Current Population Reports.* Series P-20, No. 319. "School Enrollment— Social and Economic Characteristics of Students: October 1976." Washington, D.C.: Government Printing Office, 1978.

_____. *Vital Statistics of the United States.* Vol. 1. Washington, D.C.: Government, Printing Office, 1977.

U.S. Department of Health, Education, and Welfare, Advisory Council on Developing Institutions. *Strengthening Developing Institutions: Title III of the Higher Education Act of 1965.* Annual Report, Washington, D.C.: U.S. Office of Education, March 1977 and March 1978.

_____. National Advisory Committee on Black Higher Education and Black Colleges and Universities. *First Annual Report—Higher Education Equity: The Crisis of Appearance Versus Reality.* Washington, D.C.: U.S. Office of Education, June 1978.

_____. National Center for Education Statistics. *The Condition of Education.* 1977, Vol. 3, Part 1. Washington, D.C.: Government Printing Office, 1977.

_____. National Center for Education Statistics. *The Condition of Education.* 1978 edition Washington, D.C.: Government Printing Office, 1978.

_____. National Center for Education Statistics. "Opening Fall Enrollment, Final." *Bulletin,* August 1977.

_____. National Center for Education Statistics. "Opening Fall Enrollment in Colleges and Universities, Preliminary Estimates." *Bulletin,* December 1977.

_____. Kolstad, Andrew. "Attrition From College: The Class of 1972 Two and One-Half Years After High School Graduation." *National Longitudinal Study of the High School Class of 1972.* Washington, D.C.: National Center for Education Statistics, 1977.

Unpublished Material

American Bar Association. *Memorandum QS 7677-9* (1977).

American College Testing Program. "Some Characteristics of the Historically Black College." Paper presented to the National Advisory Committee on Black Higher Education and Black Colleges and Universities, Washington, D.C., 1978.

Arce, Carlos H. "Historical, Institutional, and Contextual Determinants of Black College Enrollment in Predominantly White Colleges and Universities, 1946 to 1974." Ph.D. dissertation, University of Michigan, 1976.

Astin, Alexander. "The Myth of Equal Access in Public Higher Education." A paper from the Southern Education Foundation, July 1975.

Berrian, Albert H. "Supportive Services." Institute for Services to Education, 1977.

Califano, Joseph A. Secretary of the U.S. Department of Health, Education, and Welfare. Speech delivered at the 83rd Annual Convention and Scientific Assembly of the National Medical Association, Washington, D.C., August 1, 1978.

Froomkin, Joseph. "Middle Income Tax Relief." Prepared testimony before Committee on Ways and Means, U.S. House of Representatives, February 17, 1978.

Jackson, William M. Testimony on the National Science Foundation FY 1977 Budget. U.S. House of Representatives, Appropriations Committee on Independent Agencies, April 7, 1976.

_____. Testimony on the National Science Foundation Budget. U.S. Senate Subcommittee on Health and Scientific Research, March 3, 1976.

_____. Testimony on the National Science Foundation Budget Authorization, FY 1978. U.S. Senate Subcommittee on Health and Scientific Research, March 3, 1977.

Morris, Lorenzo. "The Invisible Politics: Political Participation in Black and White America." (Forthcoming).

Morris, Lorenzo. "The Socialization of IQ: A Political History of Intelligence Testing in American Schools."

Rice, Lois. Prepared testimony before the Subcommittee on Postsecondary Education, Committee on Education and Labor, U.S. House of Representatives, February 23, 1978, pp. 5-6.

Sedlacek, W. E.; Lewis, J. A.; and Brooks, S. C. "Black and Other Minority Admissions to Large Universities: A Four Year National Survey of Policies and Outcomes." Paper presented at the American College Personnel Association Convention, April 1973.

Selected Annotated Bibliography on Black Student Attrition Publications Since 1970*

Anderson, Ernest and Freeman, Hrabowski. "Graduate School Success of Black Students From White Colleges and Black Colleges." *Journal of Higher Education* 48(1977): 294.

Study compares the scholastic performance of 300 black graduate students who graduated from traditionally black institutions and traditionally white colleges. Results show that there are no significant differences between the two counterparts on graduate school GPA, retention rate, or graduation rate. It is concluded that there are no advantages or disadvantages in receiving an undergraduate degree from either a black or white collegiate institution.

Asbaugh, J.; Levin, C.; and Zaccaria, L. "Persistence and the Disadvantaged College Student." *Journal of Educational Research* 67(October 1973): 64–66.

"Study examines the influence of several intellective (e.g., high school rank, scholastic aptitude tests) and nonintellective variables (e.g., achievement motivation) on the persistence of college students from educationally disadvantaged environments who participated in a special advisement program. Academic aptitude appears to account for the success of persisting women whereas the greater use of counseling resources distinguishes the persisting men, thus reinforcing the effectiveness of this form of personalized support for disadvantaged students. Neither achievement motivation nor high school achievement seem to be associated with persistence in the sample."

Astin, Alexander W. *Financial Aid and Student Persistence.* Los Angeles: Higher Education Research Institute, 1976.

* Prepared with the assistance of Schuyler Webb and Steven R. Jones.

"In general, any form of aid appears to be most effective if it is not combined with other forms. This is particularly true of work-study programs which tend to lose their beneficial impact when combined with grants or loans. This loss is especially marked among low-income students. The only combination associated with greater persistence is work-study and major (rather than minor) loan support."

_____. *Preventing Students From Dropping Out.* San Francisco: Jossey-Bass, 1975.

Astin provides information about student characteristics (at the time of college matriculation) which predict dropping out—academic ability, family background, study habits, future aspirations—and develops estimates of "drop out proneness." He shows how attrition is related to such institutional characteristics as cost, religious affiliation, location, selectivity, the "fit" between the student and the college, and he analyzes policies regarding financial aid, employment, and residential arrangements and their relationships to the predictability of attrition.

Burbach, Harold J. and Thompson, Myron A., III. "Alienation Among College Freshman: A Comparison of Puerto Rican, Black, and White Students." *Journal of College Student Personnel* 12(July 1971): 248–52.

". . . purpose is to compare black, white, and Puerto Rican entering freshmen on alienation and three of its components: powerlessness, normlessness, and social isolation." Black group attained highest mean score on each of the three components' in subscale and in the total scale, whereas the Puerto Rican group, except for a slightly higher mean score on powerlessness than the white group, obtained the lowest mean score on each scale, possibly because they are affluent surbanites with stable family backgrounds, which is not representative of the urban Puerto Rican population. "Sensitivity to these issues is observable in increased specialized services, financial assistance, academic programs, and vigorous campaigns to recruit professional staff from minority groups."

_____. "Note on Alienation, Race, and College Attrition." *Psychological Reports* 33(1973): 273–74.

Purpose of this followup study is to compare persisters and nonpersisters by race (Puerto Ricans, blacks, and whites) on alienation and three of its components: powerlessness, normlessness, and social isolation. Although the students from the two minority groups had a significantly higher attrition rate than their white counterparts, the overall results show that alienation and its three components did not differentiate between persisters and nonpersisters by race.

Chickering, Arthur W. *Commuting Versus Resident Students.* San Francisco: Jossey-Bass, 1974.

"Residents engage more fully with the academic program and associated intellectual activities. They have more frequent and wider ranging contact with faculty members and fellow students. They more frequently participate in extracurricular activities and assume positions of leadership... attend cultural events and discuss political, religious, and social issues."

Copeland, Large Lee. *An Exploration of the Causes of Black Attrition at Predominantly White Institutions of Higher Education.* (Ph.D. Dissertation, University of Michigan)

Primary intent of this study is to explore the causes of black attrition at predominantly white institutions of higher education. Findings indicate that dropouts go to college for nonspecific reasons significantly more than persisters do, and there are no sex or financial aid differences between persisters and nonpersisters. Too much or too little parental expectation is seen to cause attrition. It is found that most black students have had bad experiences at white colleges such that discrimination is found to cause most black attrition at white colleges.

Council, Kathryn A. *Graduation and Attrition of Black Students at North Carolina State University.* Division of Student Affairs, North Carolina State University.

The purpose of this survey is to examine the relationship between grades, SAT scores, high school rank and retention/attrition. Results indicate that the first year GPA is the best predictor of persistence.

Dalton, Starrett; Anastasiow, Mary; and Brigman, S. Leellen. "The Relationship of Underachievement and College Attrition." *Journal of College Student Personnel* 18(November 1977): 501.

Collegiate dropouts from the fall 1974 Freshman Class at Indiana University, Bloomington, were divided into two categories: those with a satisfactory GPA (nonacademic dropouts) and those who were forced to withdraw due to a low GPA (academic dropouts). Principal purpose is to determine whether underachievement is characteristic of all dropouts or only those who are forced to withdraw due to academic failure. Contrary to much research findings, results indicate that nonacademic dropouts are not characterized by underachievement.

Davis, Billy Hampton. "The Community Junior College Experience as Perceived by Students Who Have Withdrawn." (Doctoral Dissertation).

Study deals with pressing issues confronting junior colleges by investigating the students' perceptions of their college experience, whereby 141 withdrawees who enrolled in fall 1967 as full-time, first-time freshmen at three Florida junior colleges were interviewed. Withdrawees chose junior colleges because of finances, convenience, and because they presented less of a threat than four-year colleges. Black withdrawees entering with a higher level of confidence than whites leave with less positive perceptions. Major reasons for withdrawal are: finances, irrelevancy of college education, discouragement with meeting academic standards, marriage, and family problems.

Davis, Joe L. and Caldwell, Steve. "An Intercampus Comparison of Commuter and Residential Student Attitudes." *Journal of College Student Personnel* 18(1977): 286–90.

This study compares student attitudes at a residential campus (Michigan State University) with those at a commuter campus (University of Nebraska, Omaha). Commuter students identify more with the academic community than do residential students and feel that their environment is intellectually stimulating and their studies relevant to society. Commuter students feel that the faculty is responsive to their needs and to them as individuals, indicate more support from the staff than do residential students, and feel better prepared for their future jobs.

Di Cesare, A.; Sedlacek, W.; and Brooks, G. "Nonintellectual Correlates of Black Student Attrition." *Journal of College Student Personnel* 13(July 1972): 310–24.

"Study attempts to determine whether or not demographic and attitudinal differences exist between returning and nonreturning black students at the University of Maryland (1969–70). Black returnees are more self-confident, have higher expectations, feel more strongly that the university should influence social conditions, while at the same time they observe more racism at the university, and are more likely to live on campus and use campus facilities than nonreturning black students."

Fiddler, Paul and Ponder, Eunice. "A Comparative Study of USC Student Survival Rates by Race, 1973–76." *Research Notes* 33–77 (Academic Planning Office, University of South Carolina, Columbia).

Study conducted at the University of South Carolina comparing the survival rates of full-time black and white students entering as freshmen during the fall semesters of 1973, 1974, and 1975. Results show that black students returned for their second year at a significantly higher rate than did white students, and the margin of difference between black and white survival rates actually increased the longer the students were enrolled.

Gibbs, Jewelle Taylor. "Patterns of Adaptation Among Black Students at a Predominantly White University: Selected Case Studies." *American Journal of Orthopsychiatry* 44(October 1974): 728

"Recent studies of black students in white colleges indicate that many perceive the university as a hostile environment. Case studies of black students at Stanford University who obtained counseling at the college mental health clinic from 1969–70 are analyzed to illustrate four modes of adaptation—withdrawal, separation, assimilation, and affirmation. Withdrawal is the far more prevalent mode of adaptation. Knowledge of the patterns of response of minority students is of value to counselors in anticipating problems as they develop. The need for adequate counseling, remedial, and tutoring services to enhance the adaptation of those identified as high risk students is indicated."

Jones, J. Charles; Harris, Lynn; and Hauck, William E. "Differences in Perceived Sources of Academic Difficulties: Black Students in Predominantly Black and Predominantly White Colleges." *Journal of Negro Education* 44(Fall 1975): 519–29.

"The purpose of this study is to determine whether black students attending predominantly white colleges attribute their academic difficulties to different sources and see themselves as having a different set of problems than their black counterparts in predominantly black colleges. In general, inadequate social life and communication problems with instructors are the most serious problems for females, while males cited financial problems and poor study habits at black colleges. At predominantly white colleges, both males and females cite inadequate social life as their most serious distraction contributing to academic difficulties."

Kolstad, Andrew. *Attrition From Colleges: The Class of 1972 Two and One-Half Years After High School Graduation.* Washington, D.C.: Department of Health, Education, and Welfare, 1977.

"This report examines attrition from two-year and four-year colleges and universities based on the National Center for Education Statistics' National Longitudinal Study of the High School Class of 1972. Results indicate that two-year institutions have a higher attrition rate than four-year institutions, and private colleges with higher than average SAT scores have lower attrition. The majority of students who leave college do so for nonacademic reasons. Socioeconomic status (SES) is associated with withdrawal such that in both types of institutions, low SES students withdrew at least 15 percent more often than high SES students, and black and Hispanic students withdrew more frequently than white students."

Landis, Raymond B. "Improving the Retention of Minority Engineering Students." *Engineering Education* 66(April 1976): 737–39.

Article maintains that the components of a viable retention program for minorities in Engineering include: close academic advisement; a particular emphasis on orientation and adjustment to the environment of the institution; a concerted motivational program; the development of a positive, success-oriented environment; a study skills-building program; a comprehensive and accessible tutoring program; close monitoring of student progress; a personal counseling component; a mechanism for social interaction and development; and career development.

McDew, Carolyn and Cobb, Jewell Plummer (eds.). *The Morning After—A Retrospective View of a Select Number of Colleges and Universities With Increased Black Student Enrollment in the Past Five Years.* Report of a Conference at the University of Connecticut, Storrs, April 30, 1973.

"A group of six New England colleges which had experienced a marked increase in their black student population from 1967-73, convened a conference to retrospectively look at the nature of higher education's response to this black influx. The percentage of attrition is low for black students when compared to the national norm; supportive prefreshman and on-going academic programs geared especially to help minority students have been very successful. The best counseling is done by black adults because of the trust factor, yet there is a paucity of black role models on these campuses."

Martin, Joseph L. *The College Environment: A Longitudinal Study of Black and White Students at Predominantly Black Colleges.* Washington, D.C.: Institute for Services to Education, 1973.

Purpose is to assess the perceptions of black and white students attending predominantly black colleges. Expectations of students at black colleges are higher than their perceptions of the college environment, and the college environment is perceived as being more supportive of black students than white students. Black students perceive college environment as having a greater instrumental value than white students attending black colleges. White students tend to experience a greater decline in expectations than black students, correspondingly black students attending white college have similar attitudinal changes after exposure to the white college environment.

Menning, Arnold J., *et al.* "Attrition." *College and University* 50(Summer 1975): 753-56.

According to Menning, certain demographic factors have an influence on retention rates. Larger public institutions in an urban setting typically have the highest attrition rates, and high school class rank is the most significant predictor of college success. Residence hall students and those in institutions with viable student activities programs have lower attrition rates. According to Cochran, a co-author, three main problem areas primarily account for attrition: administrative bureaucracy; a single-sanction reward system; and failure to integrate students into the university environment. Advising and counseling programs, academic and minority programs, as well as financial aid programs and those utilizing the process of peer aid exemplify successful retention programs.

Mingle, James. "Faculty and Departmental Response to Increased Black Student Enrollment." *Journal of Higher Education* 49(1978).

Mingle finds that white faculty members consciously interact less with black students than with other students. "When the faculty believes that black students should meet the same standards as whites, this tends to be translated into an unwillingness to alter traditional teaching styles or support institutional changes. Resistance and indifference to black students' needs are often built into the institutional structure. Those faculty members who felt that there was necessity for 'particularizing' the educational process in terms of students served were those who supported black students."

Morrison, James L. and Ferrante, Reynolds. "Why the Disadvantaged Dropout: The Administrator's View." *College Student Journal* 7(April 1973): 54–56.

"The chief administrative officers of two-year institutions are asked to identify the three most important conditions/factors on a 10-item questionnaire which are the prominent causes of dropping out among college students identified as "academically disadvantaged and coming from a minority social group." The four most prominent factors in descending order of percentages are: finances (48 percent); emotional stability (39 percent); motivation (37 percent); and academic abilities (34 percent). The fifth area of inadequacy is "institutional finances." A large number of respondents indicated that there was a lack of institutional support of such students. It is concluded that "if public two-year colleges are to adequately perform their role in providing educational opportunity for those who've been traditionally denied it, greater effort in terms of energy, financial resources, and support and training of an adequate administrative staff is essential."

Moton Consortium on Admissions and Financial Aid. *Some Highlights of the Astin Study of Dropouts and Implications for the Black Colleges.*

This Moton paper highlights some of the major aspects of the Astin study on dropouts, draws implications that have special significance to black colleges, and suggests areas for further research that would be of importance to decision making at black colleges. Findings indicate that the most salient factors affecting attrition are: financial aid, residence and campus environment, employment, and the characteristics of the college.

Pandey, R. E. "A Comparative Study of Dropouts at an Integrated University: The 16 Personality Factor Test." *Journal of Negro Education* 42(Fall 1973): 447–51.

A test designed to measure a number of individual personality traits was administered to 468 black and white freshmen entering Lincoln University, Jefferson City, Missouri, for the purpose of trying to establish a relationship between these traits and the students' academic status (good standing, dropout, probationary). Results indicate that dropouts are more "assertive, stubborn, and independent" than students retained, who are found to be more "humble and submissive."

Pascarella, Ernest T. and Terenzini, Patrick. "Patterns of Student-Faculty Informal Interaction Beyond the Classroom and Voluntary Freshman Attrition." *Journal of Higher Education* 48(1977): 540–551.

"In a test of Tinto's theoretical model of attrition, this study examines the pattern of relationships between different types of student-faculty interaction beyond the classroom and college persistence during the freshman year. Briefly, Tinto's model of attrition states, with other things being equal, the higher the levels of academic and social integration, the less likely the student is to voluntarily leave the institution, with one factor being the student's nonclassroom interaction with the faculty. After controlling for student sex, academic aptitude, and personality factors, freshmen persisters are found to have a significantly higher frequency of interactions with the faculty than are voluntary leavers, thus supporting Tinto's model." Student-faculty interactions focusing on discussions of intellectual or course-related concerns impacted positively on persistence.

Pedrini, B. T. and Pedrini, D. T. "Multivariate Prediction of Attrition/Persistence for Disadvantaged and Control Collegians." *College Student Journal* 11(Fall 1977): 239–42.

The persistence among 150 students at the University of Nebraska, Omaha is most closely related to freshman GPA. Grades are the best predictor of attrition. Without grades, persistence could not be predicted using race, sex, employment, financial aid, or socioeconomic status.

Pedrini, D. T. and Pedrini, B. T. "Assessment and Prediction of Grade Point and/or Attrition/Persistence for Disadvantaged and Regular College Freshmen." *College Student Journal* 10(Fall 1976): 260–64.

The authors evaluate factors used in predicting GPA and attrition/persistence of disadvantaged and regular college freshmen at the University of Nebraska, Omaha. Assessors and predictors included race, sex, ACT composite scores, special instruction program, and financial aid. Special instruction with financial aid program students tend to raise grades, and students with financial aid tend to earn higher grades and persist more than students without financial aid. Students with higher ACT scores tend to persist; those with lower ACT scores tended to drop out. Study concludes that it is advantageous to use a combination of assessors and predictors.

Peng, Samuel S. and Fetters, William B. *College Student Withdrawal: A Motivational Problem.* Paper presented at the Annual Meeting of the American Educational Research Association, 1977.

This paper draws on the National Longitudinal Survey of the High School Class of 1972. Results indicate that "women students are more likely to withdraw than men only in two-year colleges; whites are more likely to withdraw than blacks when other variables are controlled; high school program, college grades, and educational aspirations account for most variance of withdrawal behavior; and financial aid does not have a significant effect on college persistence." Data indicate that withdrawal is more a motivational than a socioeconomic problem.

Pennsylvania State Department of Education, Bureau of Curriculum Development and Evaluation. *Academically Disadvantaged Minority Group Students in Public Two-Year Colleges* (October 1971).

It is observed that characteristics common to disadvantaged students at two-year institutions are: minority background; underrepresentation in higher education; little economic support; and marginal, traditional academic qualifications.

Study implies that administrators of two-year colleges need to be more sensitive to the needs of these students. The administrators view the major causes of disadvantaged student attrition as: inadequate motivation, student finances, emotional stability, and academic ability.

Pfeifer, C. Michael, Jr. "Relationship Between Scholastic Aptitude, Perception of University Climate, and College Success for Black and White Students." *Journal of Applied Psychology* 61(1976): 341–47.

Analysis of the relationship of both university climate (student's perceptions) and tests of academic ability with two criterion measures: (a) grade point average (GPA) and (b) student's educational expectations. GPA significantly correlated with estimated probability of receiving a degree in both racial groups. Negative perceptions of university tend to be related to low grades and estimated low probability of receiving a degree for whites and to high grades and an estimated high probability of receiving a degree for black students, possibly because blacks' negative perceptions made them work harder to earn good grades. Blacks having high SAT's perceived university as being racist because they didn't receive any special consideration (counseling, tutoring, etc.) which low SAT students received, and thus had to compete on same grounds as white students.

Pulliams, Preston. "Black Students Feel Left Out." *Community College Review* 5(1977): 11–15.

"Although community colleges offer education to black students, many black students have trouble persisting because of low self-concepts and a lack of proper orientation," according to study. "Black peer counselors could be helpful, and more black staff should be hired who could serve as 'models of survival' to encourage black students. Raising the sensitivity of community college staff to the needs of black students would be useful as well as one-to-one tutoring sessions to assist these students."

Sedlacek, W. E. "Issues in Predicting Black Student Success in Higher Education." *Journal of Negro Education* 43(Fall 1974): 512–16.

Examined problems using predictors of student success (high school grades, ACT & SAT scores, first semester GPA). Because of racism and prejudice at white institutions, blacks often require a longer period of time to adjust to higher education as indicated by the increase in sophomore grades over freshman grades. High school grades are not good predictors for black males, whereas second year grades are more relevant in predicting attrition for blacks.

Selby, James E. "Relationships Existing Among Race, Student Financial Aid, and Persistence in College." *Journal of College Student Personnel* 14(January 1973): 38–40.

Purpose is to ascertain what relationships exist among race, the amount of financial aid awarded to students, and persistence in college. Findings "suggest that no significant relationships exist between persistence and the amount of financial aid received for any racial subgroup or the total group of students," although black females were the only group of students who received financial aid and did not persist. "The contention that black students do not persist as well as white students is not supported by this study. When the two groups are carefully matched, especially on SES and scholastic ability, they persist through freshman year on almost an equal basis." Limitations of this study are that only thirty students from each race were included in the study, and persistence is measured for only one school year.

Shaffer, Phyllis E. "Academic Progress of Disadvantaged Minority Students: A Two-Year Study." *Journal of College Student Personnel* 14(January 1973): 41–46.

"In the summer of 1968, eighty-nine disadvantaged minority high school graduates were selected to attend a special preparatory program before entering San Fernando Valley State College as freshmen in the fall semester. This study, based on the 1968 program, attempts (a) to assess the college progress of the minority students after two years and (b) to determine relationship between college achievement and the results from high school achievement measures, standardized test scores, and "credit" in summer preparatory program. Factors contributing most toward successful collegiate achievement for these disadvantaged students are: "orientation toward and motivation for academic pursuits, an acceptance of their educational goals and their professors, positive attitudes and techniques for studying, and scholastic aptitude, particularly verbal ability. Satisfactory completion of summer program contributed to students' subsequent academic success in the first two years of college."

Smith, Noel T., *et al.* "Student Retention Studies." *College and University* 51(Summer 1976): 652–54.

"When parents have high expectations for their children's education, there is a positive influence on the retention rates." Students having lower dropout rates receive more parental advice, praise, and interest. First semester GPA is most significant predictor of attrition and is more important than high school grades or rank. Higher proportion of men graduate from college than women, and entering freshmen not planning to pursue graduate or professional degrees are more likely to dropout. "Students with solid academic ability, but moderately low commitment (degree expectation), tend to withdraw and later transfer to another school. Students' positive association with their peer group in informal associations, activities, increases persistence, and freshmen living in residence halls drop out less frequently during the semester than students who commute or live off campus."

Spurlock, Langley A. "Still Struggling: Minorities and White Colleges in the Mid-Seventies." *Educational Record* 57(1977): 186–93.

"Spurlock poses policy questions that focus on today's problems which minorities face in realizing equal educational opportunity. Policy questions for undergraduate retention relate to two influences—remedial programs and psychosocial supports. In retaining minority students, author contends that more than academic support is needed because of faculty's and administrators' insensitivity to the cultural backgrounds of minority students which is often cited as a major cause for withdrawal."

Stanfiel, J. D. "Socioeconomic Status as Related to Aptitude, Attrition, and Achievement of College Students." *Sociology of Education* 46(Fall 1973): 480–88.

"Black college students from three socioeconomic levels were compared in the following variables: SAT scores (V,M); attrition two years after matriculation; GPA at the end of the first college semester and after two years; correlation between SAT-V and first semester GAP within each SES group. SAT-V predicts GAP for lower SES students as well as for the higher SES students. Attrition and SES are inversely related. Economics and other factors work in favor of higher SES students in terms of remaining in college. High attrition rate in lower SES student group reflects serious obstacles confronting less advantaged students seeking higher education."

Tinto, Vincent. "Dropout From Higher Education: A Theoretical Synthesis of Recent Research." *Review of Educational Research* 45(Winter 1975): 89–125.

Author seeks to formulate a theoretical model that explains the processes of interaction between the individual and the institution that lead some students to drop out from institutions of higher education, and that also distinguishes between those processes that result in varying forms of dropout behavior. Essay draws on Durkheim's Theory of Suicide according to which suicide is more likely to occur when individuals are insufficiently integrated into the fabric of society. With respect to the collegiate environment," insufficient interactions with others in the college and insufficient congruency with the prevailing value patterns of the college collectivity will lead to low commitment to that social system and will increase the probability that individuals will decide to leave the college."

Individual characteristics (social status, high school background, community of residence, and individual attributes such as sex, ability, race, and ethnicity) in conjunction with the student's educational expectations (individual's educational goal commitment and institutional commitment) are the cornerstones of this model, which argues that it is the individual's integration into the academic and social systems of the college that more directly relates to his continuance in that college. Institutional type, status, and quality also impact on persistence.

Tsai, Yung-mei and Perry, Floyd, Jr. *Factors Affecting Academic Performance and Persistence Among the Mexican-American, the Black and the Anglo Students in a Southwestern University.* Paper presented at the Annual Meeting of the Southwestern Sociological Association, San Antonio, Texas.

An examination of factors affecting college students' GPA and persistence and a comparison of these factors among black, Mexican, and Anglo students. High school background including high school GPA and SAT scores dominate the predictability of collegiate GPA, whereas college GPA does not enhance the students' persistence, but seems to hinder it.

Washington, K. R. "Special Minority Programs: "Dupe or New Deal?" *Journal of Afro-American Issues* 5(Winter 1977): 60–65.

"High attrition rates among black students attending predominantly white colleges suggest that special programs designed for minority students serve the "revolving door" or "phase out" function such that some large universities admit almost all secondary school students who apply, while at the same time, flunking out a high percentage, especially those who came with poor preparation. It is argued that institutions of higher education need to take responsibility for minority students beyond the initial recruitment step, and there is a need for these institutions to reexamine the special minority programs on their respective campuses to improve the retention of minority students. The factors of a successful program would include: institutional commitment; strong program leadership; support services; financial aid; and student commitment."

Webster, D. W., *et al. A Comparison of Problems Perceived by Minority and White University Students.* Research Report No. 14–77, Counseling Center, University of Maryland.

At the University of Maryland, a stratified random sample of 200 juniors and seniors anonymously completed a 51-item check list. For black students, the principle problems are racism and discrimination. Other problems which black students cite are alienation, financial aid, residence-related problems, and study skills.

Wright, Erik Olin. "A Study of Student Leaves of Absence." *Journal of Higher Education* 44(March 1973): 235–47.

"Survey conducted among 135 randomly selected Harvard undergraduates who had returned from voluntary leaves of absence and 250 randomly selected undergraduates who never left college. The two variables that prove to be most strongly associated with leaving college are 'psychological stress' and 'social integration.' Students withdraw from college because they experience high levels of stress—both stress stemming from inner conflicts and stress generated by the college environment—and because they lack sufficient ties to the college community to counteract the push from stress."

Index